Solid Answers

DR. JAMES DOBSON

Solid

ANSWERS

America's foremost family
counselor responds to tough questions
facing today's families

Tyndale House Publishers, Inc.
WHEATON, ILLINOIS

Visit Tyndale's exciting Web site at www.tyndale.com

Library of Congress Cataloging-in-Publication Data

Dobson, James C., date
   Solid answers : America's foremost family counselor responds to tough questions facing today's families / James Dobson.
     p. cm.
   Includes bibliographical references.
   ISBN 0-8423-0623-4 (hardcover : alk. paper)
   1. Child rearing—Religious aspects—Christianity—Miscellanea. 2. Child rearing— United States—Miscellanea. 3. Family—Religious aspects—Christianity— Miscellanea. 4. Family— Religious life—United States—Miscellanea. 5. Family—United States— Miscellanea. I. Title.
HQ769.3.D623 1997
649'.1—dc21   97-23017

Printed in the United States of America

03 02 01 00 99 98 97
9   8   7   6   5   4   3   2   1

Table of Contents

Appreciation Page vii

Introduction ix

1 Understanding the Nature of Children 1

2 Raising the Preschool Child 17

3 Disciplining the Preschool Child 27

4 Children's Health and Well-Being 47

5 Attention Deficit Disorder in Children and Adults 65

6 Effective Parenting Today 75

7 Disciplining the Elementary School Child 101

8 To Spank or Not to Spank 137

9 What's a Mother to Do? 149

10 Education: Public, Private, and Home Schooling 159

11 Sex Education: Where, When, and How 191

12 Spiritual Life of the Family 209

13 The Tougher Spiritual Questions 231

14 Sibling Rivalry 251

15 Help for Single Parents and Stepparents 259

16 Living with a Teenager 269

17 The Delicate Art of Letting Go 321

93813

18 Advice to Young Adults 327

19 Building Self-Confidence in Children and Teens 369

20 Making Marriage Work 391

21 Money Matters 429

22 Families under Fire 437

23 The Great Marriage Killers 479

24 The Sanctity of Life 497

25 Other Issues Facing the Family 509

26 Principles and Concepts Drawn from Dr. Dobson's Books and
    Statements through the Years 539

Endnotes 551

Index 561

Index of Scripture References 575

Appreciation Page

Because of the breadth of family-related topics addressed in this book, a considerable amount of support was needed for research, computer technology, aesthetic design, and administrative assistance. Fortunately, I was blessed to have the assistance of a highly professional and dedicated team throughout this project. These gifted people worked tirelessly to help me review current literature, to identify the common questions submitted through the years to Focus on the Family, and to validate my own responses in consultation with specialists in medicine, education, psychology, and other fields. Without the diligence of all these individuals, this book would not yet be off the presses.

Great appreciation is hereby expressed to Craig Osten, Steve Johnson, Karen Bethany, Kevin Triguero, Athena MacMillan, Jim Ware, Jeff Stoddard, Ken Janzen, John Perrodin, Kurt Bruner, Diane Passno, and Tricia Jones. Though you can't see their fingerprints on the pages of this book, I assure you that they are there.

This book is dedicated to these very special friends and colleagues.

Introduction

A few years ago, I strolled into a store that featured the latest electronic gadgets and games. There on display was an advanced computerized chess set and a little sign that invited customers to play the game. I took the bait. This remarkable device had a mechanical arm that actually reached out and grabbed its pieces, moving them to the selected positions. That was impressive enough. What bothered me, however, was its smug attitude. The machine was designed to taunt mere mortals like me. On the end of its mechanical arm were two handlike devices that clapped wildly when the computer made a tricky move. It led me into a deadly trap and then sat there applauding itself. I can't tell you how intimidating it was to be mocked by a machine that knew (and then told the other customers) that I wasn't so hot.

It's bad enough to be eclipsed by the gifted people with whom we live and work. It's worse when a little plastic box can make us feel like nerds. But in a sense, my encounter with the computer is symbolic of the confusing world in which we live. Advancing technology and changing times stress our ability to cope and understand. Everything seems more complicated now than in the old days when life was slow and predictable. New challenges and troubling ethical questions spring up faster than we can resolve them. And all the old rules are under assault as revolutionary change flows through our lives.

A recent public-opinion poll revealed this confusion about what is valid and certain. The answer is "not much." Fully 72 percent of Americans have concluded that absolute truth doesn't even exist.[*] For them, nothing transcends time and eternity. Nothing can be counted on in all circumstances and situations. Everything is relative and existential—subject to individual interpretation and guesswork.

This uncertainty has affected many of today's families, too. Millions of moms and dads are guided by no underlying philosophy of child

---

[*]George Barna, *Virtual America* (Ventura, Calif.: Gospel Light, 1994), 83.

rearing, and hence, they are hazy about how they should be relating to their sons and daughters. It hasn't always been that way, of course. Our ancestors knew what they believed and why they believed it. Most of them held common convictions about truth and falsehood, right and wrong, good and bad. They knew what was proper and improper in every situation. And they systematically taught those beliefs to their offspring.

When a child was born during or before the 1900s, the new mother was tended by many friends and relatives, who hovered around her to offer their advice and help. These aunts, grandmothers, and neighbors hadn't read many books on child rearing, but they didn't need them. They were guided by a certain traditional wisdom that gave them confidence in handling babies and children. They had answers, whether right or wrong, for every question, and they were willing to share what they knew with those they loved. So a new mother was undergirded by older women who had many years' experience in caring for babies and children.

That loving support system has all but disappeared in recent decades. Many women live in a mobile society in which neighbors are often strangers. Their own mothers, aunts, and sisters have moved far away to Detroit or Dallas or Portland—and they might not be trusted even if they were available to help. This isolation has shaken the confidence of new mothers who are aware that there is too much they don't know about kids.

Dr. Benjamin Spock, the author of *Baby and Child Care*, observed this insecurity in hospital maternity wards. He wrote, "I can remember mothers who cried on the morning they were to take their baby home. 'I won't know what to do,' they wailed."*

This anxiety has brought parents rushing to the "experts" for information and advice. They turn to pediatricians, psychologists, psychiatrists, and educators for answers to their questions about the complexities of parenthood. Consequently, increasing numbers of children in Western nations since the 1920s have been reared accord-

*Dr. Benjamin Spock, "How Not to Bring Up a Bratty Child," *Redbook* (February 1974): 31.

ing to this professional consultation. In fact, no country on earth has embraced the teachings of child psychology and the offerings of family specialists more than has the United States.

It is now appropriate that we ask, "What has been the effect of this professional influence?" One would expect that the mental health of our children would exceed that of individuals raised in nations not having this technical assistance. Such has not been the case. Juvenile delinquency, drug abuse, alcoholism, unwanted pregnancies, mental illness, and suicide are rampant among the young and continue their steady rise. In many ways, we have made a mess of parenthood! Of course, I would not blame all these woes on the bad advice of the "experts," but I believe they played a role in creating the problem. Why? Because in general, behavioral scientists have disregarded the Judeo-Christian ethic and the timeless wisdom that it offers.

Instead, the twentieth century spawned a generation of professionals who ignored the parental attitudes and practices of more than two thousand years, substituting their own wobbly legged insights of the moment. Each authority, writing from his own limited experience and reflecting his own unique biases, has sold us his guesses and suppositions as though they represented Truth itself.

These false teachings have included the notions that loving discipline is damaging, religious instruction is hazardous, defiance is a valuable ventilator of anger, authority is dangerous, chaos produces creativity, and on and on it goes. In more recent years, this humanistic perspective has become even more extreme and anti-Christian, from homosexual propaganda taught to children to safe-sex indoctrination of today's teenagers.

This is where moral relativism leads—this is the ultimate product of a human endeavor that accepts no standards, honors no cultural values, acknowledges no absolutes, and serves no god except the human mind. King Solomon wrote about such foolish efforts in Proverbs 14:12: "There is a way which seemeth right unto a man, but the end thereof are the ways of death" (KJV).

Now admittedly, the book you are reading also contains many

suggestions and perspectives that I have not attempted to prove. How do my writings differ from the unsupported recommendations of those whom I have criticized? And where do I get the temerity to title this book *Solid Answers*, which may sound like the ultimate arrogance from an author? There is a single answer to both questions. The advice I've offered is more than a reflection of my own guesses and suppositions about this and that. Nestled behind and below most of these responses is a guiding philosophy that has been drawn from two reliable and time-honored sources.

The first comes from the wisdom of the ages. I have drawn heavily from the traditional approach to marriage and parenthood that was born of two thousand years' experience. It has been handed down generation to generation as the centuries unfolded. Surely something of value was learned by all those men and women who have gone before. We should consider how they did things and what they believed before we abandon their secure moorings.

The second foundation for this book emanates from the Judeo-Christian system of values. There are numerous principles woven into the Holy Scriptures that apply to everyday family life. They were inspired by the Creator Himself, who is the originator of the institutions of marriage and parenthood. Whether or not it is obvious, those concepts have provided the basis for many of the "solid answers" I have provided. And within that scriptural foundation lies the confidence of which I spoke.

The eternal plan for the family, as I understand it, begins with a lifelong commitment between a man and a woman, undergirded by absolute loyalty and fidelity to one another. The husband then devotes himself to the best interests of his wife, providing for her needs and protecting her to the point of death if necessary. The wife honors her husband, devotes herself to him, and respects his leadership in the family. If they are blessed with children, those children are recognized to have inestimable worth and dignity—not for what they produce or accomplish, but for who they are as God's own handiwork. They are taught while very young to yield to the authority of their parents.

Boundaries of behavior are established in advance and then enforced with reasonable firmness. They learn honesty, integrity, humility, self-control, personal responsibility, sexual purity, concern for others, the work ethic, and the fundamentals of their faith. They are never subjected to humiliation, rejection, sexual exploitation, or abuse of any kind. Instead, they enjoy unconditional love and are raised "in the fear and admonition of the Lord."

I hope you'll find this advice and counsel to be helpful. I invite you to write to me with your additional questions or your own points of view. My staff and I will consider those additional ideas in future revisions of this book and in later publications.

Let me leave you with this thought: When you and I have reached the end of our brief journey on this earth, *nothing* will matter more to us than the quality of our families and the depth of our relationship with God. "Meaning" in this human experience is drawn essentially from these two sources. If that is true, then should we not live by those priorities every day that remains to us? It is my prayer that the advice in this book will be helpful in building both a warm and satisfying family and a personal relationship with Jesus Christ.

James C. Dobson, Ph.D.
Focus on the Family
Colorado Springs, CO 80995

1

Understanding the Nature
of Children

QUESTION 1

**I took a class in child development, and the professor empha-
sized the influence of culture in shaping the human personality. He said, "All behavior is caused by what we experience."
What does that mean, and do you agree with it?**

It means that children are merely responders to environmental influences occurring in a lifetime and that if all those experiential factors
were known, every behavior (and misbehavior) would be explained.
Do I agree with this view? Not for a minute. It is a mechanistic,
deterministic theory that makes robots out of human beings. If it were
valid, we would never be capable of independent action, free choice,
or discernment of right and wrong. This is an unbiblical theory that
strikes at the heart of the God-man relationship. We are morally
accountable because the Creator put within us the ability to think, to
choose, to judge, and even the freedom to do evil. We are capable of
rational thought that is greatly influenced, but not "caused," by what
we experience. There are other influences that come from within—including those related to the temperament with which we arrive in the
delivery room. Human behavior is far more complicated than believed
in the past, yet some learned people still think we are the sum total of
our experiences.

The psychologist who spoke at your school was expressing a historic tenet of his (and my) profession. I just happen to disagree with it emphatically.

*Q*UESTION 2

Talk more about the inborn temperament in babies. What do we know about their little personalities before they have interacted with the world at all?

Philosophers Locke and Rousseau told us in the seventeenth and eighteenth centuries that babies came into the world as *tabula rasas,* or "blank slates," upon which society and the environment wrote the fundamentals of personality.[1] But they were also wrong. Every newborn is unique from every other baby, even from the first moments outside the womb. Except for identical twins, triplets, etc., no two are alike in biochemistry or genetics.

How foolish of philosophers and behavioral scientists to have thought otherwise. If God makes every grain of sand unique and every snowflake like no other, how simplistic to have believed He mass-produces little human robots. That is nonsense. We are, after all, made in His image.

Just ask the real experts—the mothers who understand their babies better than anyone. They'll tell you that each of their infants had a different "feel"—a different personality—from the first moment they were held. If these mothers are eventually blessed with six or eight or even twenty children, they will continue to say emphatically that every one of them was unique and distinct from the others when only one hour old. They are right—and their perceptions are being confirmed by scientific inquiry.

*Q*UESTION 3

What does research tell us about the personalities of newborns?

One of the most ambitious studies yet conducted took a period of three decades to complete. That investigation is known in professional literature as the New York Longitudinal Study. The findings from this investigation, led by psychiatrists Stella Chess and Alexander Thomas, were reported in their excellent book for parents entitled *Know Your Child.*

Chess and Thomas found that babies not only differ significantly from one another at the moment of birth, but those differences tend to be rather persistent throughout childhood. Even more interestingly, they observed three broad categories, or patterns of temperaments, into which the majority of children can be classified. First they referred to "the difficult child," who is characterized by negative reactions to people, intense mood swings, irregular sleep patterns and feeding schedules, frequent periods of crying, and violent tantrums when frustrated.

Does that sound familiar? I described those individuals many years ago as "strong-willed" children.

The second pattern is called "the easy child," who manifests a positive approach to people, quiet adaptability to new situations, regular sleep patterns and feeding schedules, and a willingness to accept the rules of the game. The authors concluded, "Such a youngster is usually a joy to his or her parents, pediatrician and teachers."[2] Amen.

My term for the easy child is "compliant."

The third category was given the title "slow-to-warm-up" or "shy." These youngsters respond negatively to new situations, and they adapt slowly. However, they are less intense than difficult children, and they tend to have regular sleeping and feeding schedules. When they are upset or frustrated, they typically withdraw from the situation and react mildly, rather than explode with anger and rebellion.

Not every child fits into one of these categories, of course, but approximately 65 percent do. Drs. Chess and Thomas also emphasized that babies are fully human at birth, being able immediately to relate to their parents and learn from their environments. I doubt if that news will come as a surprise to most mothers, who never believed in the "blank slate" theory, anyway.

It should not be difficult to understand why these findings from longitudinal research have been exciting to me. They confirm my own clinical observations, not only about the wonderful complexity of human beings, but also about the categories of temperament identified by Drs. Chess and Thomas.

QUESTION 4

Tell me why some kids with every advantage and opportunity seem to turn out bad, while others raised in terrible homes become pillars in the community. I know one young man who grew up in squalid circumstances, yet he is such a fine person today. How did his parents manage to raise such a responsible son when they didn't even seem to care?

That illustrates just the point I have been trying to make. Neither heredity nor environment will account for all human behavior. There is something else there—something from within—that also operates to make us who we are. Some behavior is caused, and some plainly isn't.

Several years ago, for example, I had dinner with two parents who had unofficially "adopted" a thirteen-year-old boy. This youngster followed their son home one afternoon and asked if he could spend the night. As it turned out, he stayed with them for almost a week without so much as a phone call coming from his mother. It was later learned that she works sixteen hours a day and has no interest in her son. Her alcoholic husband divorced her several years ago and left town without a trace. The boy had been abused, unloved, and ignored through much of his life.

Given this background, what kind of kid do you think he is today— a druggie? a foul-mouthed delinquent? a lazy, insolent bum? No. He is polite to adults; he is a hard worker; he makes good grades in school and enjoys helping around the house. This boy is like a lost puppy who desperately wants a good home. He begged the family to adopt him officially so he could have a real father and a loving mother. His own mom couldn't care less.

How could this teenager be so well disciplined and polished despite his lack of training? I don't know. It is simply within him. He reminds me of my wonderful friend David Hernandez. David and his parents came to America illegally from Mexico more than fifty years ago and nearly starved to death before they found work. They eventually survived by helping to harvest the potato crop throughout the state of California. During this era, David lived under trees or in the open fields. His father made a stove out of an oil drum half-filled with dirt. The open campfire was the centerpiece of their home.

David never had a roof over his head until his parents finally moved into an abandoned chicken coop. His mother covered the boarded walls with cheap wallpaper, and David thought they were living in luxury. Then one day, the city of San Jose condemned the area, and David's "house" was torn down. He couldn't understand why the community would destroy so fine a place.

Given this beginning, how can we explain the man that David Hernandez became? He graduated near the top of his class in high school and was granted a scholarship to college. Again, he earned high marks and four years later entered Loma Linda University School of Medicine. Once more, he scored in the top 10 percent of his class and continued in a residency in obstetrics and gynecology. Eventually, he served as a professor of OB-GYN at both Loma Linda University and the University of Southern California medical schools. Then, at the peak of his career, his life began to unravel.

I'll never forget the day Dr. Hernandez called me on the telephone. He had just been released from the hospital following a battery of laboratory tests. The diagnosis? Sclerosing cholangitis, a liver disorder that was invariably fatal at that time. We lost this fine husband, father, and friend six years later at the age of forty-three. I loved him like a brother, and I still miss him today.

Again, I ask, how could such discipline and genius come from these infertile circumstances? Who would have thought that this deprived Mexican boy sitting out there in the dirt would someday become one of the most loved and respected surgeons of his era? Where did the motivation originate? From what bubbling spring did his ambition and thirst for knowledge flow? He had no books, took no educational trips, knew no scholars. Yet he reached for the sky. Why did it happen to David Hernandez and not the youngster with every advantage and opportunity?

Why have so many children of prominent and loving parents grown up in ideal circumstances only to reject it all for the streets of Atlanta, San Francisco, or New York? Good answers are simply not available. It apparently comes down to this: God chooses to use individuals in unique ways. Beyond that mysterious relationship, we must simply conclude that some kids seem born to make it and others are determined to fail. Someone reminded me recently that the same boiling water that softens the carrot also hardens the egg. Likewise, some individuals react positively to certain circumstances and others negatively. We don't know why.

Two things are clear to me from this understanding. First, parents have been far too quick to take the credit or blame for the way their children turn out. Those with bright young superstars stick out their chests and say, "Look what we accomplished." Those with twisted and irresponsible kids wonder, "Where did we go wrong?" Well, neither is entirely accurate. No one would deny that parents play an important role in the development and training of their children. But they are only part of the formula from which a young adult is assembled.

Second, behavioral scientists have been far too simplistic in their explanation of human behavior. We are more than the aggregate of our experiences. We are more than the quality of our nutrition. We are more than our genetic heritage. We are more than our biochemistry. And certainly, we are more than our parents' influence. God has created us as unique individuals, capable of independent and rational thought that is not attributable to any source. That is what makes the task of parenting so challenging and rewarding. Just when you think you have your kids figured out, you had better brace yourself! Something new is coming your way.

QUESTION 5

Does Scripture confirm that babies have temperaments or personalities before birth?

Yes, in several references we learn that God knows and relates to unborn children as individuals. He said to the prophet Jeremiah, "Before I formed you in the womb I knew you, and before you were born I consecrated you; I appointed you a prophet to the nations" (Jeremiah 1:5, RSV). The apostle Paul said he was also chosen before birth (see Ephesians 1:4). And in a remarkable account, we are told of the prenatal development of the twins Jacob and Esau. As predicted before their births, one turned out to be rebellious and tough while the other was something of a mama's boy. They were fighting before they were born and continued in conflict through much of their lives (see Genesis 25:22-27). Then later, in one of the most mysterious and disturbing statements in the Bible, the Lord said, "Jacob have I loved, but Esau have I hated" (Romans 9:13, KJV). Apparently, God discerned a rebellious nature in Esau before he was born and knew that he would not be receptive to the divine Spirit.

These references tell us that unborn children are unique individuals with whom God is already acquainted. These examples also confirm for me, at least, the wickedness of abortion, which destroys those embryonic little personalities.

QUESTION 6

I have two children who are as different as night and day. In fact, they conform perfectly to your description of the "strong-willed" and "compliant" children. One is a spitfire, and the other is a sweetheart. I am very interested in knowing more about what this means for them long-term. Beyond everyday issues of discipline and relating within a family, what can you tell me about these kids?

You'll be interested to know that more than thirty-five thousand parents participated in a study I conducted to answer those specific questions. It is described in detail in my book *Parenting Isn't for Cowards,* but let me boil down eleven of the most important findings. Remember that these conclusions represent common traits and characteristics that may or may not apply to your two children. These descriptions represent what typically happens with very strong-willed children (SWC) and very compliant children (CC) as the years unfold.

Conclusion 1: In the human family, there are nearly three times as many SWCs as CCs. Nearly every family with multiple children has at least one SWC.

Conclusion 2: Male SWCs outnumber females by about 5 percent, and female CCs outnumber males by about 6 percent. Thus, there is a

7

slight tendency for males to have tougher temperaments and for females to be more compliant, but it can be, and often is, reversed.

Conclusion 3: The birth order has nothing to do with being strong-willed or compliant. These elements of temperament are basically inherited and can occur in the eldest or in the baby.

Conclusion 4: Most parents know they have an SWC very early. One-third can tell it at birth. Two-thirds know by the first birthday, and 92 percent are certain by the third birthday. Parents of compliant children know it even earlier.

Conclusion 5: The temperaments of children tend to reflect those of their parents. Although there are many exceptions, two strong-willed parents are more likely to produce tough-minded kids and vice versa.

Conclusion 6: What can parents expect from SWCs in the teen years? The answer? A battle! Fully 74 percent of SWCs rebel significantly during adolescence.

Conclusion 7: Incredibly, only 3 percent of CCs experience severe rebellion in adolescence, and just 14 percent even go into mild rebellion. They start out life with a smile on their face and keep it there into young adulthood.

Conclusion 8: The best news for parents of SWCs is the rapid decrease in their rebellion in young adulthood. It drops almost immediately in the early twenties and then trails off even more from there. Some are still angry into their twenties and early thirties, but the fire is gone for the majority. They peacefully rejoin the human community.

Conclusion 9: The CC is much more likely to be a good student than the SWC. Nearly three times as many SWCs made Ds and Fs during the last two years of high school as did CCs. Approximately 80 percent of CCs were A and B students.

Conclusion 10: The CC is considerably better adjusted socially than the SWC. It would appear that the youngster who is inclined to challenge the authority of his parents is also more likely to behave offensively with his peers.

Conclusion 11: The CC typically enjoys much higher self-esteem than the SWC. It is difficult to overestimate the importance of this finding. Only 19 percent of compliant teenagers either disliked themselves (17 percent) or felt extreme self-hatred (2 percent). Of the very strong-willed teenagers, however, 35 percent disliked themselves, and 8 percent experienced extreme self-hatred.

Those were the primary findings from our study. It yielded a picture of the compliant child as being someone more at peace with himself or herself, as well as with parents, teachers, and peers.

The strong-willed child, by contrast, seems compelled from within to fuss, fight, test, question, resist, and challenge. Why is he or she like that? It is difficult to say, except to affirm that they are more unsettled in every aspect of their lives. We do know that lower self-esteem is related to the excessive peer dependency, academic difficulties, social problems, and even rebellion we have seen. Acceptance of one's intrinsic worth is the core of the personality. When it is unsteady, everything else is affected.

Q UESTION 7

What are the long-range implications of raising a strong-willed child? What can we expect as the years go by?

Well, I can give you a few encouraging conclusions from our study. The tendency of strong-willed children is to return to parental values when they reach adulthood. Parents told us that 85 percent of their grown SWCs (twenty-four years of age and older) came back to what they had been taught—entirely or at least "somewhat." That is good news. Only 15 percent were so headstrong that they rejected their family's core values in their midtwenties. In those exceptional cases, I'll wager that other problems and sources of pain were involved.

What this means, first of all, is that these tough-minded kids will argue and fight and complain throughout their years at home, but the majority will turn around when they reach young adulthood and do what their parents most desired. That should be reassuring. Furthermore, if we could have evaluated these individuals at thirty-five instead of twenty-four years of age, we would have seen that even fewer were still in rebellion against parental values.

Second, raising a strong-willed child (or a houseful of them) can be a lonely job for parents. You can begin to feel like yours is the only family that has gone through these struggles. Don't believe it. In another study of three thousand parents, we found that 85 percent of families had at least one strong-willed child. *This is parenthood. This is human nature.*

Third, I urge you as parents of strong-willed children not to feel "cheated" or depressed by the assignment of raising such individuals. You are not an exception or the butt of some cruel cosmic joke. All human beings, including the very compliant child, arrive with a generous assortment of flaws. Yes, it is more difficult to raise an independent little fellow or gal, but you can do it! You can, through prayer and supplication before the Lord, bring him or her to that period of harmony in early adulthood that makes the effort worthwhile. I also believe that you can increase the odds of transmitting your values to these individuals by following some time-honored principles found in Scripture. So hang in there! Nothing of value in life comes easy anyway, except the free gift of salvation from Jesus Christ.

Hold tightly to Solomon's encouraging words, "Train up a child in the way he should go: and when he is old, he will not depart from it" (Proverbs 22:6, KJV).

QUESTION 8

OK, I understand the strong-willed child better than I did. But tell me how to get our son through these tough years. He is tough as nails. What specific suggestions do you have for us?

Here is a summary of some approaches or ideas that I think are important:

1. You should not blame yourself for the temperament with which your child was born. He (or she) is simply a tough kid to handle, and your task is to rise to the challenge.
2. He is in greater danger because of his inclination to test the limits

and scale the walls. Your utmost diligence and wisdom will be required to deal with him.

3. If you fail to understand his lust for power and independence, you can exhaust your resources and bog down in guilt. It will benefit no one.

4. For parents who have just begun, take charge of your babies. Hold tightly to the reins of authority in the early days, and build an attitude of respect during your brief window of opportunity. You will need every ounce of "awe" you can get during the years to come. Once you have established your right to lead, begin to let go systematically, year by year.

5. Don't panic, even during the storms of adolescence. Better times are ahead.

6. Don't let your son get too far from you emotionally. Stay in touch. Don't write him off, even when every impulse is to do just that. He needs you now more than ever before.

7. Give him time to find himself, even if he appears not to be searching.

8. Most important, I urge you to hold your children before the Lord in fervent prayer throughout their years at home. I am convinced that there is no other source of confidence and wisdom in parenting. There is not enough knowledge in the books, mine or anyone else's, to counteract the evil that surrounds our kids today. Teenagers are confronted by drugs, alcohol, sex, and foul language wherever they turn. And, of course, the peer pressure on them is enormous. We must bathe them in prayer every day of their lives. The God who made your children will hear your petitions. He has promised to do so. After all, He loves them more than you do.

And a concluding word: Remember that anyone can raise the easy kid. Guiding an SWC through the rebellious years takes a pro with a lot of love to give. I'll bet you're up to the task!

UESTION **9**

What are the special needs of a compliant kid—one that goes along to get along? Does he have any special needs?

That's a great question, and the answer is yes. When one child is a stick of dynamite and the other is an all-star sweetheart, the cooperative, gentle individual can easily be taken for granted. If there's an unpleasant job to be done, he may be expected to do it because Mom and Dad just don't have the energy to fight with the tiger. When it is necessary for one child to sacrifice or do without, there's a tendency to pick the one who won't complain as loudly. Under these circumstances, the compliant boy or girl comes out on the short end of the stick.

The consequences of such inequity should be obvious. The responsible child often becomes angry over time. He has a sense of powerlessness and resentment that simmers below the surface. He's like the older brother in the parable of the Prodigal Son told by Jesus. He didn't rebel against his father. He stayed behind and ran the farm while his irresponsible brother squandered his money on fun and games. Who could blame him for resenting little bro? His response is typical of the compliant, hardworking sibling.

I strongly recommend that parents seek to balance the scales in dealing with the compliant child. Make sure he gets his fair share of parental attention. Help him find ways to cope with his overbearing sibling. And, within reason, give him the right to make his own decisions.

There's nothing simple about raising kids, is there? Even the "easiest" of them needs our very best effort.

QUESTION 10

How can you say that precious little newborns come into the world inherently evil? I agree with the experts who say that babies are born good and they only learn to do wrong later.

Please understand that the issue here is not with the purity or innocence of babies. No one would question their preciousness as creations of God. The point of disagreement concerns the tendencies and inclinations they have inherited. People who believe in "innate goodness" would have us believe that human beings are naturally unselfish, honest, respectful, kind to others, self-controlled, obedient to authority, etc. Children, as you indicated, then subsequently learn to do wrong when they are exposed to a corrupt and misguided society.

Bad *experiences* are responsible for bad behavior. To raise healthy kids, then, it is the task of parents to provide a loving environment and then stay out of the way. Natural goodness will flow from within.

This is the humanistic perspective on childish nature. Millions of people believe it to be true. Most psychologists have also accepted and taught this notion throughout the twentieth century. There is only one thing wrong with the concept. It is entirely inaccurate.

QUESTION 11

How can you be so sure about the nature of children? What evidence do you have to support the belief that their tendency is to do wrong?

We'll start with what the "Owner's Manual" has to say about human nature. Only the Creator of children can tell us how He made them, and He has done that in Scripture. It teaches that we are born in sin, having inherited a disobedient nature from Adam. King David said, "In sin did my mother *conceive* me" (Psalm 51:5, KJV, italics added), meaning that this tendency to do wrong was transmitted genetically. Paul tells us it has infected every person who ever lived. "For *all* have sinned, and come short of the glory of God" (Romans 3:23, KJV, italics added). Therefore, with or without bad associations, children are naturally inclined toward rebellion, selfishness, dishonesty, aggression, exploitation, and greed. They don't have to be taught these behaviors. They are natural expressions of their humanness.

Although this perspective is viewed with disdain by the secular world today, the evidence to support it is overwhelming. How else do we explain the pugnacious and perverse nature of every society on earth? Bloody warfare has been the centerpiece of world history for more than five thousand years. People of every race and creed around the globe have tried to rape, plunder, burn, blast, and kill each other century after century. Peace has been but a momentary pause when they stopped to reload! Plato said more than 2,350 years ago, "Only dead men have seen an end to war."[3] He was right, and it will continue that way until the Prince of Peace comes.

Not only have nations warred against each other since the beginning of time, we also find a depressing incidence of murder, drug abuse, child molestation, prostitution, adultery, homosexuality, and dishonesty among individuals. How would we account for this pervasive evil in a world of people who are naturally inclined toward good? Have they really drifted into these antisocial and immoral behaviors despite their inborn tendencies? If so, surely *one* society in all the world would have been able to preserve the goodness with which children are born. Where is it? Does such a place exist? No, although admittedly some societies are more moral than others. Still, none reflect the harmony that might be expected from the natural-goodness theorists. Why not? Because their basic premise is wrong.

QUESTION 12

What, then, does this biblical understanding mean for parents? Are they to consider their babies guilty before they have done anything wrong?

Of course not. Children are not responsible for their sins until they reach an age of accountability—and that time frame is known only to God. On the other hand, parents should not be surprised when rebellious or mischievous behavior occurs. It *will* happen, probably by the eighteenth month or before. Anyone who has watched a toddler throw a temper tantrum when she doesn't get her way must be hard pressed to explain how that expression of "innate goodness" got so mixed up! Did her mother or father model the tantrum for her, falling on the floor, slobbering, kicking, crying, and screaming? I would hope not. Either way, the kid needs no demonstration. Rebellion comes naturally to his and her entire generation—although in some individuals it is more pronounced than in others.

For this reason, parents can and must train, mold, correct, guide, punish, reward, instruct, warn, teach, and love their kids during the formative years. Their purpose is to shape that inner nature and keep it from tyrannizing the entire family. Ultimately, however, only Jesus Christ can cleanse it and make it "wholly acceptable" to the Master. This is what the Bible teaches about people, and this is what I firmly believe.

Q UESTION 13

Why can't parents get children to obey just by explaining what they want them to do? Why is it so often necessary to punish or raise our voices to get them to cooperate? Why can't they just accept a few reasonable rules and avoid all that conflict? It just doesn't add up to me.

After working with children for years, I'm convinced that their challenging behavior is motivated in part by the desire for power that lies deep within the human spirit. From a very early age, they just don't want anyone telling them what to do. They are also great admirers of strength and courage. Maybe this is why mythical characters like Superman, Robin Hood, and Wonder Woman have been so prominent in the folklore of children. Perhaps it is also why kids brag that "My dad can beat up your dad!" (One child said in reply, "That's nothing; my mom can beat up my dad, too!")

It is a fact that most boys, and some girls, care about the issue of "who's toughest." Whenever a youngster moves into a new neighborhood or a new school district, he often has to fight, either verbally or physically, to establish himself on the hierarchy of strength. There is usually a "top dog" in a group of children, who bosses everyone else around. There is also a little defeated pup at the bottom of the heap, who takes the brunt of everyone's abuse. And each child between those extremes usually knows where he or she ranks in relation to the others.

I believe this admiration for power also makes children want to know how tough their leaders are. They will occasionally disobey adults for the precise purpose of testing their determination and courage. Thus, whether you are a parent or grandparent or Boy Scout leader or bus driver or Brownie leader or schoolteacher, I can guarantee that sooner or later, one of the children under your authority will clench his little fist and challenge your leadership. He will convey this message by his disobedient manner: "I don't think you are tough enough to make me do what you say." The way you handle that confrontation is being watched closely by every child in the group.

15

Your reaction will determine how soon another occurs and with what intensity it is driven.

QUESTION 14

My wife and I have two very strong-willed kids who are hard to handle. They seem to need to test us, and they're the happiest and most contented when we are the toughest on them. Why do they insist on making us growl at them and even punish them more than we'd like to?

It is curious, isn't it, that some children seem to enjoy fighting with their parents. It's a function of the pugnacious temperament with which they are born. Many kids just like to run things and seem to enjoy picking fights.

There is another factor that is related to a child's sense of security. Let me illustrate it this way. Imagine you're driving a car over the Royal Gorge Bridge in Colorado, which is suspended hundreds of feet above the canyon floor. As a first-time traveler, you're pretty tense as you drive across. It is a scary experience. I knew one little fellow who was so awed by the view over the side of the bridge that he said, "Wow, Daddy! If you fell off of here, it'd kill you constantly!"

Now suppose there were no guardrails on the side of the bridge. Where would you steer the car? Right down the middle of the road. Even though you don't plan to hit those protective railings along the side, you just feel more secure knowing that they're there.

It's the same way with children. There is security in defined limits. They need to know precisely what the rules are and who's available to enforce them. Whenever a strong-willed child senses that the boundaries may have moved, or that his or her parents may have lost their nerve, he or she will often precipitate a fight just to test the limits again. They may not admit that they want you to be the boss, but they breathe easier when you prove that you are.

2
Raising the Preschool Child

QUESTION 15

I have a very fussy eight-month-old baby, who cries whenever I put her down. My pediatrician says she is healthy and that she cries just because she wants me to hold her all the time. I do give her a lot of attention, but I simply can't keep her on my lap all day long. How can I make her less fussy?

The crying of infants is an important form of communication. Through their tears we learn of their hunger, fatigue, discomfort, or diaper disaster. Thus, it is important to listen to those calls for help and interpret them accordingly. On the other hand, your pediatrician is right. It is possible to create a fussy, demanding baby by rushing to pick her up every time she utters a whimper or a sigh. Infants are fully capable of learning to manipulate their parents through a process called reinforcement, whereby any behavior that produces a pleasant result will tend to recur. Thus, a healthy baby can keep her mother hopping around her nursery twelve hours a day (or night) by simply forcing air past her sandpaper larynx. To avoid this consequence, it is important to strike a balance between giving your baby the attention she needs and establishing her as a tiny dictator. Don't be afraid to let her cry for a reasonable period of time (which is thought to be healthy for the lungs), although it is necessary to listen to the tone of her voice for the difference between random discontent and genuine distress. Most mothers learn to recognize this distinction very quickly.

When my daughter was one year of age, I used to stand out of sight at the doorway of her nursery for four or five minutes, awaiting a momentary lull in the crying before going to pick her up. By so doing, I reinforced the pauses rather than the tears. You might try the same approach.

QUESTION 16

We have a one-year-old daughter, and we want to raise her right. I've heard that parents can increase the mental abilities of their children if they stimulate them properly during the early years. Is this accurate, and if so, how can I accomplish this with my baby?

Research has shown that parents can, indeed, increase the intellectual capability of their children. This conclusion was first reached through the renowned Harvard University Preschool Project. A team of researchers led by Dr. Burton White studied young children aged eight to eighteen months over a ten-year period, hoping to discover which experiences in the early years of life contribute to the development of healthy, intelligent human beings. The results of this important study are summarized below.

a. It is increasingly clear that the origins of human competence are to be found in a critical period of development between eight and eighteen months of age. The child's experiences during these brief months do more to influence future intellectual competence than any time before or after.

b. The single most important environmental factor in the life of the child is his or her mother. "She is on the hook," said Dr. White, and exercises more influence on her child's experiences than any other person or circumstance.

c. The amount of live language directed to a child (not to be confused with television, radio, or overheard conversations) is vital to his or her development of fundamental linguistic, intellectual, and social skills. The researchers concluded, "Providing a rich social life for a twelve- to fifteen-month-old child is the best thing you can do to guarantee a good mind."

d. Those children who were given free access to living areas of their homes progressed much faster than those whose movements were restricted.

e. The nuclear family is the most important educational delivery system. If we are going to produce capable, healthy children, it will be by strengthening family units and by improving the interactions that occur within them.

f. The best parents were those who excelled at three key functions:

  1. They were superb designers and organizers of their children's environments.

  2. They permitted their children to interrupt them for brief, thirty-second episodes, during which personal consultation, comfort, information, and enthusiasm were exchanged.

  3. They were firm disciplinarians while simultaneously showing great affection for their children.[4]

Occasionally, information comes along that needs to be filed away for future reference. These findings from the Harvard University Preschool Project are that significant. You will not want to forget those six findings. I believe they hold the keys to raising healthy children.

*Q*UESTION 17

Can the findings from Dr. White's study be applied by parents whose children are placed in child-care centers?

Of course. It is just more difficult and challenging when an employee substitutes for a mother and father during the prime-time hours of the day.

*Q*UESTION 18

At age twenty-one, I became pregnant and had a baby girl. The father and I never married. My daughter is almost three years old now, and I know she will soon be asking questions

about her daddy. How should I explain this situation to her, and when should that explanation be given?

Eventually, you will want to tell your daughter the whole story about her father and describe your relationship with him, but now is not the time to do that. She must be mature and emotionally ready to deal with those details. On the other hand, you don't want to treat the subject as a dark secret that haunts the two of you. Neither do you want to be untruthful and tell yarns that will later have to be admitted.

At this early stage, I'd suggest that you respond confidently and lovingly to the inevitable questions about "Daddy." When the appropriate occasions surface, begin giving her vague explanations that are based in truth but are short of the whole story. You may wish to say something like this, "Your daddy went away before you were born. He didn't want to live with me. I'm not sure why. Maybe he had some problems that made it hard to be a husband. I don't know. I'm sure if he had ever met you, he'd have loved you very much. But he left before you were born. Do you know what I think? I think we should start praying that the Lord will send us another man to be my husband and your daddy. Would you like that?"

I recognize that there are potential problems with a reply of this nature and that it may not be entirely appropriate for every case. It simply attempts to lay the foundation for the more in-depth discussions to follow. Just as important, it likely will defuse the situation early on while conveying a sense of affirmation, security, and mutual reliance upon the Lord. And once you've achieved that, take a deep breath and let it rest for a while! If you're at peace, your daughter will be, too—and there will be ample time to add detail to the picture as God directs.

QUESTION 19

I get very upset because my two-year-old boy will not sit still and be quiet in church. He knows he's not supposed to be noisy, but he hits his toys on the pew and sometimes talks out loud. Should I reprimand him for being disruptive?

With all respect, your question reveals a rather poor understanding of the nature of toddlers. Most two-year-olds, those who are normally active, can no more fold their hands in church and listen to a sermon intended for adults than they could swim the Atlantic Ocean. They squirm and churn and burn because they must. You just can't hold a toddler down. All their waking hours are spent in activity, and that's normal for this stage of development. So I do not recommend that your child be punished for this behavior. I think he should be left in the church nursery, where he can shake the foundations without disturbing the worship service. If there is no nursery, I suggest, if it is possible from a financial point of view, that he be left at home with a sitter until he is at least three years of age.

QUESTION 20

My five-year-old is developing a problem with lying, and I don't know how to handle it. What can I do to get him to tell the truth?

Lying is a problem with which every parent must deal. All children distort the truth from time to time, and some become inveterate liars. Responding appropriately is a task that requires an understanding of child development and the characteristics of a particular individual. I'll offer some general advice that will have to be modified to fit specific cases.

First, understand that a young child may or may not fully comprehend the difference between lies and the truth. There is a very thin line between fantasy and reality in the mind of a preschool boy or girl. So before you react in a heavy-handed manner, be sure you know what he understands and what his intent is.

For those children who are clearly lying to avoid unpleasant consequences or to gain an advantage of some sort, parents need to use that circumstance as a "teachable moment." The greatest emphasis should be given to telling the truth in all situations. It is a virtue that should be taught—not just when a lie has occurred, but at other times as well. In your personal devotions with the children, turn to Proverbs 6:16-19 and read that insightful passage together. It says, "There are six things

21

the Lord hates, seven that are detestable to him: haughty eyes, a lying tongue, hands that shed innocent blood, a heart that devises wicked schemes, feet that are quick to rush into evil, a false witness who pours out lies and a man who stirs up dissension among brothers."

These are insightful verses around which to structure devotional periods with children. Explain who Solomon was, why his teachings are so important to us, and why the Scripture is our friend. It is like a flashlight on a dark night, guiding our footsteps and keeping us on the right path. It will even protect us while we are asleep, if we will bind it on our heart forever. Memorize the passage in Proverbs together so it can be referred to in other contexts. Use it as a springboard to discussions of virtues and behavior that will please God. Each verse can be applied to everyday situations so that a child can begin to feel accountable for what he does and says.

Returning to the specific issue of lying, point out to the child that in a list of seven things the Lord hates most, two of them deal with dishonesty. Telling the truth is something God cares about, and therefore it should matter to us. This will explain why you are going to insist that your son or daughter learn to tell the truth even when it hurts to do so. Your goal is to lay a foundation that will help you underscore a commitment to honesty in the future.

The next time your child tells a blatant lie, you can return to this discussion and to the Scripture on which it was based. At some point, when you feel the maturity level of the youngster makes it appropriate, you should begin to insist that the truth be told and to impose mild punishment if it isn't. Gradually, over a period of years, you should be able to teach the virtue of truthfulness to your sons and daughters.

Of course, you can undermine everything you're trying to establish by your own dishonesty in front of your kids. Believe me, they will note it and behave likewise. If Daddy can twist the truth, he'll have little authority in preventing them from doing the same.

QUESTION 21

I'm concerned about the violent content of some children's cartoon shows and the toys and other products connected

with them. My husband thinks they're harmless. What's your point of view?

I share your misgivings. There's a trend toward a brand of violence in some of today's cartoons and toys that I see as a dangerous departure from the more traditional combat-type games in which boys have always engaged. For one thing, the characters tend to be adults involved in adult activities, some of which are highly questionable. I don't feel that they are appropriate role models for impressionable young children. In addition, there's an occult or New Age flavor to many of these programs and products. The settings are mythical or futuristic, and the action often revolves around superstition, sorcery, and magic. For these reasons they concern me for spiritual as well as psychological reasons.

The electronic media has incredible power to "sell" these dubious heroes and their exploits to our children. Studies have measured actual physiological changes that occur when kids are watching a violent television program or movie: the pulse rate quickens, the eyes dilate, the hands sweat, the mouth goes dry, and breathing accelerates. It should be obvious that this kind of "entertainment" has a dramatic emotional impact—especially if it's repeated often enough. And the toys that are marketed as "spin-offs" from such programs only serve to reinforce or extend those negative effects. What's more, there's no balancing positive, healthy, or educational component to these products.

That's why our organization, Focus on the Family, and others have made major investments in high-quality videos and other materials for children. We must provide alternatives for families that want their kids to have wholesome entertainment but are determined to protect them from the popular culture. We will continue to do what we can to meet that need.

*Q*UESTION 22

Do you think a child should be required to say "thank you" and "please" around the house?

I sure do. Requiring these phrases is one method of reminding the child that his is not a "gimme-gimme" world. Even though his mother is cooking for him and buying for him and giving to him, he must assume a few attitudinal responsibilities in return. Appreciation must be taught, and this instructional process begins with fundamental politeness at home.

QUESTION 23

I have a friend whose children drive me crazy when I'm around them. They are the most undisciplined brats I've ever seen. We can't even talk when they are around. I would love to help my friend with a few disciplinary tips. How can I do this without offending her?

When you want to point out a flaw or shortcoming in someone else's behavior or character, you do it the way porcupines make love: very, very carefully. Otherwise, you're likely to lose a friend.

Pointing out parenting mistakes in others is even riskier. You're liable to get your ears pinned back for trying it—even when your motives are honorable and you have a child's interest at heart. That's why I never offer unsolicited advice about other people's children, no matter how badly I think it is needed.

If you insist on telling the other mother what she doesn't want to hear, let me suggest that you first invest some time and effort in your friend. When a relationship of confidence has been carefully constructed, you'll have then earned the right to offer her some gentle advice.

There are no shortcuts to this process.

24

QUESTION 24

My children love to do things for themselves, but they make such messes that it's easier for me to do things for them. I just don't have the patience to see them fumble with stuff. Do you think I'm wrong to step in and do things for them?

I think you *are* wrong, even though I understand how you feel. I heard a story about a mother who was sick in bed with the flu. Her darling daughter wanted so much to be a good nurse. She fluffed the pillows and brought a magazine to read. And then she even showed up with a surprise cup of tea.

"Why, you're such a sweetheart," the mother said as she drank the tea. "I didn't know you even knew how to make tea."

"Oh, yes," the little girl replied. "I learned by watching you. I put the tea leaves in the pan, and then I put in the water, and I boiled it, and then I strained it into a cup. But I couldn't find a strainer, so I used the flyswatter instead."

"You what?" the mother screamed.

And the little girl said, "Oh, don't worry, Mom, I didn't use the new flyswatter. I used the old one."

Well, when kids try their hardest and they get it all wrong in spite of themselves, what's a parent to do? What mothers and fathers often do is prevent their children from carrying any responsibility that could result in a mess or a mistake. It's just easier to do everything for them than to clean up afterward. But I urge parents not to fall into that trap.

Your child needs her mistakes. That's how she learns. So go along with the game every now and then . . . even if the tea you drink tastes a little strange.

3

Disciplining the Preschool Child

*Q*UESTION **25**

You have been very critical of behavioral scientists and other writers who recommend a more permissive approach to child rearing. Explain why this concerns you. Why is it ever wrong to be kind and merciful to a boy or girl?

The issue is not one of kindness and mercy. It is one of loving authority and leadership at home, which is in the child's best interest. The majority of books and seminars since 1950 on child raising have effectively stripped parents of the ability to deal with willful defiance when it occurs. First, they haven't admitted that such behavior happens, and second, they have given parents no tools with which to confront it. This bad advice has led to a type of paralysis in dealing with kids. In the absence of "permission" to step in and lead, parents were left with only their anger and frustration in response to defiant behavior.

Let me give an example from a parenting text entitled *Your Child from Two to Five*, published during the permissive 1950s. In it was a bit of characteristic advice from that era, paraphrased from the writings of a Dr. Luther Woodward as follows:

> What do you do when your preschooler calls you a "big stinker" or threatens to flush you down the toilet? Do you scold—punish—or

sensibly take it in your stride? Dr. Woodward recommends a positive policy of understanding as the best and fastest way to help a
child outgrow this verbal violence. When parents fully realize that
all little tots feel angry and destructive at times, they are better able
to minimize these outbursts. Once the preschooler gets rid of his
hostility, the desire to destroy is gone and instinctive feelings of
love and affection have a chance to sprout and grow. Once the child
is six or seven, parents can rightly let the child know that he is
expected to be outgrowing sassing his parents.[5]

Having recommended that passive approach, with which I disagree
strongly, Dr. Woodward then told parents to brace themselves for
unjust criticism. He wrote, "But this policy [of letting children engage
in defiance] takes a broad perspective and a lot of composure, especially when friends and relatives voice disapproval and warn that you
are bringing up a brat."[6]

In this case, your friends and relatives will be right: You *will* be
bringing up a bratty kid—and maybe a houseful of them! Dr. Woodward's recommendation encourages parents to stand passively
through the formative years when respect for authority can so easily
be taught. His philosophy is based on the simplistic notion that
children will develop sweet and loving attitudes if adults will permit
and encourage their temper tantrums during childhood. According to
the optimistic Dr. Woodward, the tot who has been calling his mother
a "big stinker" for six or seven years can be expected to transform,
like a butterfly emerging from a cocoon, into a sweet and loving
seven-year-old. That outcome is most improbable. Dr. Woodward's
"policy of understanding" (which means "policy of permissiveness")
leads directly to adolescent rebellion in strong-willed children.

28

QUESTION 26

**You said Dr. Woodward's philosophy of child rearing was
rather typical of the advice given to parents a generation ago.
Apart from the specific example you cited, how do your views**

differ? What is the basic distinction between your perspective and those of more permissive advice-givers?

I never met the man, but I would think from his writings that Woodward and I perceive human nature very differently. He apparently believed in the "innate goodness" of children, which means they will turn out fine if adults will simply leave them alone. Most of Woodward's contemporaries believed just that. It is my conviction, by contrast, that boys and girls learn (and become) what they are *taught.* Thus, it is our task as parents to "civilize" them—to introduce them to manners and morals and proper behavior. If it is desirable for children to be kind, appreciative, and pleasant, those qualities should be instilled in them—not simply hoped for. If we want to see honesty, truthfulness, and unselfishness in our offspring, then these characteristics should be the conscious objectives of our early instructional process. If it is important to produce respectful, responsible young citizens, then we should teach them first to respect us as their parents. In short, heredity does not equip a child with proper attitudes; we must build the foundations of character ourselves. If that assumption is doubted, take a good look at adults whose parents did not do their homework—those who were raised on the streets with very little parental instruction. A large percentage of them have prison records today.

*Q*UESTION 27

If you had to choose between a very authoritarian style of parenting versus one that is permissive and lax, which would you prefer? Which is healthier for kids?

Both extremes leave their characteristic scars on children, and I would be hard pressed to say which is more damaging. At the oppressive end of the continuum, a child suffers the humiliation of total domination. The atmosphere is icy and rigid, and he lives in constant fear. He is unable to make his own decisions, and his personality is squelched beneath the hobnailed boot of parental authority. Lasting characteristics of dependency, deep abiding anger, and serious adolescent rebellion often result from this domination.

But the opposite extreme is also damaging to kids. In the absence of adult leadership the child is her own master from her earliest babyhood. She thinks the world revolves around her heady empire, and she often has utter contempt and disrespect for those closest to her. Anarchy and chaos reign in her home. Her mother is often the most frazzled and frustrated woman on her block. It would be worth the hardship and embarrassment she endures if her passivity produced healthy, secure children. It typically does not.

The healthiest approach to child rearing is found in the safety of the middle ground between disciplinary extremes. I attempted to illustrate that reasonable parenting style on the cover of my first book, *Dare to Discipline*, which included this little diagram:

Children tend to thrive best in an environment where these two ingredients, love and control, are present in balanced proportions. When the scale tips in either direction, problems usually begin to develop at home.

Unfortunately, parenting styles in a culture tend to sweep back and forth like a pendulum from one extreme to the other.

QUESTION 28

I like your idea of balancing love with discipline, but I'm not sure I can do it. My parents were extremely rigid with us, and I'm determined not to make that mistake with my kids. But I don't want to be a pushover, either. Can you give me some help in finding the middle ground between extremes?

Maybe it would clarify the overall goal of your discipline to state it in the negative. It is not to produce perfect kids. Even if you implement a flawless system of discipline at home, which no one in history has done, your children will still be children. At times they will be silly, lazy, selfish, and, yes, disrespectful. Such is the nature of the human species. We as adults have the same weaknesses. Furthermore, when it comes to kids, that's how it should be. Boys and girls are like clocks;

you have to let them run. My point is that the purpose of parental discipline is not to produce obedient little robots who can sit with their hands folded in the parlor thinking patriotic and noble thoughts! Even if we could pull that off, it wouldn't be wise to try.

The objective, as I see it, is to take the raw material with which our babies arrive on this earth, and then gradually mold them into mature, responsible, and God-fearing adults. It is a twenty-year process that will bring progress, setbacks, successes, and failures. When the child turns thirteen, you'll swear for a time that he's missed everything you thought you had taught—manners, kindness, grace, and style. But then maturity begins to take over, and the little green shoots from former plantings start to emerge. It is one of the richest experiences in living to watch that blossoming at the latter end of childhood.

QUESTION 29

You place great emphasis on instilling respect during the developmental years. Why is that so important? Do you just want adults to feel powerful and in control of these little people?

Certainly not. Respect is important for several very specific reasons. First, the child's relationship with his parents provides the basis for his attitude toward every other form of authority he will encounter. It becomes the cornerstone for his later outlook on school officials, law-enforcement officers, future employers, and the people with whom he will eventually live and work. Teachers, for example, can tell very quickly when a boy or girl has been allowed to be defiant at home—because those attitudes are brought straight into the class-room. Again, relationships at home are the first and most important social encounters a youngster will have, and the problems experienced there often carry over into adult life.

Second, if you want your child to accept your values when she reaches her teen years, then you must be worthy of her respect during her younger days. When a child can successfully defy your authority during his first fifteen years, laughing in your face and stubbornly flouting your leadership, he develops a natural contempt for everything you stand for. *Stupid old Mom and Dad!* he thinks. *I've got them wound around my little finger. Sure they love me, but I really think they're afraid of me.* A child may not utter these words, but he feels them each time he wins the confrontation with his mom or dad.

Third, and related to the second, respect is critical to the transmission of faith from one generation to the next. The child who disdains his mother and father is less likely to emulate them on the things that matter most. Why? Because young children typically identify their parents—and especially their fathers—with God. Therefore, if Mom and Dad are not worthy of respect, then neither are their morals, their country, or even their most deeply held convictions.

Q UESTION 30

At what age should discipline begin?

There should be no physical punishment for a child younger than fifteen to eighteen months old, regardless of the circumstance. An infant is incapable of comprehending his or her "offense" or associating it with the resulting consequences. Some parents do not agree and find themselves "swatting" a baby for wiggling while being diapered or for crying in the midnight hours. This is a terrible mistake. Other parents will shake a child violently when they are frustrated or irritated by incessant crying. Let me warn those mothers and fathers of the dangers of that punishing response. Shaking an infant can cause serious neurological damage, which can occur as the brain is slammed against the skull. Do not risk *any* kind of injury with a baby!

Especially during the first year, a youngster needs to be held, loved, and calmed by a soothing human voice. He should be fed when hungry and kept clean and dry and warm. The foundation for emotional and physical health is laid during this twelve-month period, which should be characterized by security, affection, and warmth.

32

Q UESTION 31

If punishment is never recommended for an infant, what form of discipline *is* appropriate at that age?

The answer is loving leadership. Parents should have the courage to do what is right for their babies, even if they protest vigorously. Dr. Bill Slonecker, a Nashville pediatrician and a good friend, has stressed the importance of parents taking charge right from the day of birth. Too often he has seen mothers in his private practice who were afraid of their infants. They would call his office and frantically huff, "My six-month-old baby is crying and seems very hot." The doctor would ask if the child had a fever, to which Mom would reply, "I don't know. He won't let me take his temperature." These mothers had already yielded their authority to their infants. Some would never regain it.

Good parenting and loving leadership go hand in hand. And it should begin on "Day One."

QUESTION 32

I believe one of the primary tasks for parents is to prepare children for the independence and responsibility of adulthood. I have an infant son, and I certainly want to teach him to be self-disciplined and responsible as the years unfold. But I don't know where to start. How can I instill these characteristics in my son, and how early should I begin?

Well, that *is* what good parenting is all about. Let me describe the task in developmental terms. A little child at birth is, of course, completely helpless. That little guy lying in his crib can do nothing for himself: He doesn't roll over or hold his bottle. He can't say please or thank you, and he doesn't apologize for getting you up six times in one night. He doesn't even have to appreciate your efforts. In other words, a child begins his life in a state of complete and total dependency, and you are in his servitude.

About twenty years later, however, some dramatic changes should have occurred in that individual. He should have developed the skills and self-discipline necessary for successful adult living. He is expected to spend his money wisely, hold a job, be loyal to one spouse (if he's married), support the needs of his family, obey the laws of the land, and be a good citizen. In other words, during the short course of childhood, an individual should progress systematically from dependency to independency—from irresponsibility to responsibility.

The question is, how does little John or Nancy or Paul get from Position A to Position B? How does that magical transformation from babyhood to maturity take place? Some parents seem to believe that it all will coalesce toward the latter end of adolescence, about fifteen minutes before the individual leaves home. I reject that notion categorically. The best preparation for adulthood comes from training in responsibility during the childhood years. This is not to say that the child should be required to work like an adult. It does mean that he can be encouraged to progress in an orderly timetable of events, carrying the level of responsibility that is appropriate for his age. Shortly after birth, for example, the mother begins transferring responsibilities from her shoulders to those of her infant. Little by little he learns to sleep through the night, hold his own bottle, and reach for what he wants. Later he is potty trained, and he learns to walk and talk. As each new skill is mastered, his mother "frees" herself that much more from his servitude.

Each year the child should make more of his own decisions as the responsibilities of living shift from his parents' shoulders to his own. A seven-year-old, for example, is usually capable of selecting his own clothing for the day (within reason). He should be keeping his room straight and making his bed each morning. A nine- or ten-year-old may be enjoying more freedom, such as choosing from approved television programs. I am not suggesting that we abdicate parental leadership during these years; rather, I believe we should give conscious thought to the reasonable, orderly transfer of freedom and responsibility so that we are preparing the child each year for that moment of full independence that must come.

Returning to your question about your infant son, let me cite two insightful phrases coined by Marguerite and Willard Beecher that will guide the instructional process I have described. They are (1) the parent needs to gain his or her freedom from the child, so that the child can obtain his or her freedom from the parent; and (2) a parent should do nothing for a child that the child can profit from doing for himself or herself.[7] If you apply those two recommendations, you'll get that boy or girl ready to be a responsible man or woman.

*Q*UESTION 33

Please describe the best approach to the discipline of a one-year-old child.

Many children will begin to gently test the authority of their parents as they approach their first birthday. The confrontations will be minor and infrequent at first, yet the beginnings of future struggles can be seen. My own daughter, for example, challenged her mother for the first time when she was nine months old. My wife was waxing the kitchen floor when Danae crawled to the edge of the linoleum. Shirley said, "No, Danae," gesturing to the child not to enter the kitchen. Since our daughter began talking very early, she clearly understood the meaning of the word *no*. Nevertheless, she crawled straight onto the sticky wax. Shirley picked her up and set her down in the doorway while saying no even more strongly as she put her down. Seven times this process was repeated until Danae finally yielded and crawled away in tears. As far as we can recall, that was the first direct confrontation of wills between my daughter and my wife. Many more were to follow.

How does a parent discipline a one-year-old? Very carefully and gently! A child at this age is easy to distract and divert. Rather than jerking a wristwatch from his or her hands, show him or her a brightly colored alternative—and then be prepared to catch the watch when it falls. When unavoidable confrontations do occur, as with Danae on the waxy floor, win them by firm persistence but not by punishment. Have the courage to lead the child without being harsh or mean or gruff.

Compared to the months that are to follow, the period around one year of age is usually a tranquil, smooth-functioning time in a child's life.

*Q*UESTION 34

Dear Dr. Dobson:

The reason I'm writing is this: The Lord has blessed us so much I should be full of joy. But I have been depressed for months now. I don't know whether to turn to a pastor, a doctor, a psychologist, a nutritionist, or a chiropractor!

Last year the Lord gave us a beautiful baby boy who is now fourteen months of age. He is just wonderful. He is cute, and he is smart, and he is strong. We just can't help but love him. But he has been very demanding. The thing that made it hardest for me was last month Jena was taking some college classes two nights a week, and I took care of Rolf. He cried and sobbed the whole time and eventually cried himself to sleep. Then I would either hold him because he would awaken and continue crying, or if I did get to put him down, I wouldn't make any noise because I was afraid I would wake him up.

I am used to being able to pay bills, work on the budget, read and file mail, answer letters, type papers, etc., in the evening. But all this must be postponed to a time when Jena is here.

That's why it has been such a depressing time for me. I just can't handle all that crying. It was even worse when Jena was breast-feeding Rolf. That woke me up too, and I got very tired and had a great deal of trouble getting up in the morning to go to work. I was sick a lot at that time.

I love our baby a lot and wouldn't trade him for anything in the world, but I don't understand why I'm so depressed. Sure, Jena gets tired too because we can't seem to get Rolf to go down for the night before eleven or twelve midnight, and he wakes up twice every night.

Another thing that has been a constant struggle is leaving Rolf in the nursery at church. He isn't content to be away from us very long, so the workers end up having to track Jena down almost every week. We hardly ever get to be together for the worship service. And this has been going on for several months!

We have all the things we would ever dream of at our age—our own neat little house in a good neighborhood, a good job that I enjoy, and not least of all, our life in Christ.

I have no reason to be depressed and to be so tired all the time. I come home from work so exhausted that I'm in no frame of mind to take Rolf out of his mother's hair so she can fix dinner. He hangs on her all the time. I just don't know how

she stands it. She must have a higher tolerance for frustration than I do.

If you have any insights as to what we should do, please let me know. Thanks, and God bless you!

Chuck

It might be difficult for parents of "easy babies" to believe that a fourteen-month-old child could take charge of two mature adults, but your description of Rolf has a familiar ring to it. What is occurring is an interaction between his touchy temperament and what he has learned about how to get his way. There's nothing sinister in how Rolf is behaving. The problem, in fact, is not primarily his—it is yours. In your well-intentioned zeal to make him happy and maintain a little peace and quiet in the house, you've allowed yourselves to be tyrannized by tears. It is simply not necessary for you to hold your child every moment or to be unable to leave him in the care of others. Nor should you have to tiptoe around the house to avoid disturbing his sleep. By quickly satisfying Rolf's noisy demands, you are actually reinforcing his crying and teaching him how to make you dance. It's time to pull the plug on that game.

To change the pattern, you have to be convinced first that Rolf's crying will not hurt him. As long as you're sure he doesn't have a fever and he isn't wet or in some kind of discomfort, no long-term damage will be done by a tearful session. Having made that point, I recommend that this evening you and Jena feed and diaper Rolf. Play with him and hold him close. Then when bedtime comes, place him in his crib, pat him on the back two or three times, and quietly walk away. He'll scream bloody murder, of course, but you *must not* pick him up. Even if he cries for an hour or two, you need to get across the idea that he's down for the night.

Screaming is not only unpleasant for parents to hear—it is also very hard work for the screamer. As he becomes convinced that his protest is not going to bring those big, loving people to his bed, the behavior will gradually disappear. Stay with the program for as long as necessary to change the pattern. Be sure you're giving Rolf plenty of love and attention before leaving him on each occasion. He'll get the message in time.

This probably won't be the last struggle you'll have with little Rolfie. If he is a bona fide strong-willed child, as I suspect, you and Jena can anticipate a few hundred thousand more clashes on other battlefields in the years to come. The great satisfaction in parenting, however, is to take a challenging child like Rolf and turn him into a self-disciplined, well-adjusted, and productive adult about twenty years later. You can do it!

By the way, let nothing I have said imply that you or other parents should allow *newborns* to "cry it out." During the first few months of life, crying is the only way the baby can alert parents that something is wrong. It is only later when they learn to "use" this technique that we must not let it succeed.

QUESTION 35

I have a two-year-old boy who is as cute as a bug's ear, and I love him dearly, but he nearly drives me crazy. He throws the most violent temper tantrums and gets into everything. Why is he like this, and are other toddlers so difficult?

Your description of your toddler comes right out of the child-development textbooks. That time of life begins with a bang (like the crash of a lamp or a porcelain vase) at about eighteen months of age and runs hot and heavy until about the third birthday. A toddler is the most hard-nosed opponent of law and order, and he honestly believes that the universe circles around him. In his cute little way, he is curious and charming and funny and lovable and exciting and selfish and demanding and rebellious and destructive. Comedian Bill Cosby, father of five, had some personal experience with toddlers. He is quoted as saying, "Give me two hundred active two-year-olds and I could conquer the world."

Children between fifteen and thirty-six months of age do not want to be restricted or inhibited in any manner, nor are they inclined to conceal their opinions. Bedtime becomes an exhausting, dreaded ordeal each night. They want to play with everything in reach, particularly fragile and expensive ornaments. They prefer using their pants rather than the potty and insist on eating with their hands. And most of what goes in their mouth is not food. When they break loose in a store, they run as fast as their little legs will carry them. They pick up the kitty by its ears and then scream bloody murder when scratched. They want Mommy within three feet of them all day, preferably in the role of their full-time playmate. Truly, the toddler is a tiger—but a precious one.

I hope you won't get too distressed by the frustrations of the toddler years. It is a very brief period of development that will be over before you know it. With all its challenges, it is also a delightful time when your little boy is at his cutest. Approach him with a smile and a hug. But don't fail to establish yourself as the boss during this period. All the years to come will be influenced by the relationship you build during this eighteen-month window.

*Q*UESTION **36**

Our twenty-four-month-old son is not yet toilet trained, although my mother-in-law feels he should be under control now. Should we spank him for using his pants instead of the potty?

No. Suggest that your mother-in-law cool down a bit. It is entirely possible that your child can't control himself at this age. The last thing you want to do is punish a child of any age for an offense that he can't comprehend. If I had to err on this matter, it would be in the direction of being too late rather than too early. Furthermore, the best approach to potty training is with rewards and encouragement rather than with punishment. Give him a sucker (or sugarless candy) for performing his duty. When you've proved that he can comply, then you can hold him responsible in the future.

*Q*UESTION **37**

If it is natural for a toddler to break all the rules, should he be disciplined for routine misbehavior?

As I've said, toddlers get into trouble most frequently because of their natural desire to touch, bite, taste, smell, and break everything within their grasp. These are normal and healthy reactions that should not be inhibited. When, then, should they be subjected to mild discipline? When they openly defy their parents' very clear commands! When he runs the other way when called, purposely slams his milk glass on the floor, dashes into the street when being told to stop, screams and throws a tantrum at bedtime, or hits his friends. These behavior patterns should be discouraged. Even in these situations, however, severe punishment is unwarranted. A firm rap on the fingers or a few minutes sitting on a chair will usually convey the same message as convincingly. Spankings should be reserved for a child's moments of greatest antagonism, usually occurring after the second, third, or fourth birthdays.

Without watering down anything I have written about discipline, it should also be understood that I am a firm believer in the judicious use of grace (and humor) in parent-child relationships. In a world in which children are often pushed to grow up too fast, their spirits can dry out like prunes beneath the constant gaze of critical eyes. It is refreshing to see parents temper their harshness with a measure of "unmerited favor." Likewise, there's nothing that buoys every member of a family quite like laughter and a lighthearted spirit in the home.

QUESTION 38

My three-year-old can be counted on to behave like a brat whenever we are in the mall or in a restaurant. He seems to know I will not punish him there in front of other people. How should I handle this tactic?

Let me answer you with an illustration from nature. They tell me that a raccoon can usually kill a dog if he gets him in a lake or river. He will simply pull the hound underwater until he drowns. Most other predatory animals prefer to do battle on the turf of their own choosing. So do children. If they're going to pick a fight with Mom or Dad, they'd rather stage it in a public place, such as a supermarket or in the church foyer. They are smart enough to know that they are "safer" in front of other people. They will grab candy or speak in disrespectful ways that would never be attempted at home. Again, the most successful military generals are those who surprise the enemy in a terrain advantageous to their troops. Public facilities represent the high ground for a rambunctious preschooler.

You may be one of the parents who has fallen into the trap of creating "sanctuaries" in which the old rules aren't enforced. It is a certainty that your strong-willed son or daughter will notice those safe zones and behave offensively and disrespectfully when there. There is something within the tougher child that almost forces him to "test the limits" in situations where the resolve of adults is in question. Therefore, I recommend that you lay out the ground rules before you enter those public arenas, making it clear that the same rules will apply. Then if he misbehaves, simply take him back to the car or around the corner and do what you would have done at home. His public behavior will improve dramatically.

Question 39

I need more help understanding how to interpret childish behavior. My problem is that I don't know how to react when my son, Chris, annoys me. I'm sure there are many minor infractions that a parent should just ignore or overlook. At other times, immediate discipline is necessary. But I'm not sure I'll react in the right way on the spur of the moment.

Obviously, the first thing you have to do is determine Chris's intent, his feelings, and his thoughts. Is there evidence that Chris is challenging your authority? The more blatant his defiance, the more critical it is to respond with decisiveness. But if he has simply behaved immaturely, or perhaps he's forgotten or made a mistake, you will want to be much more tolerant. It is a very important distinction. In the first instance, the child knows he was wrong and is waiting to see what his parent will do about it; in the second, he has simply blundered into a situation he didn't plan.

Let me be specific. Suppose Chris is acting silly in the living room and falls into a table, breaking some expensive china cups and other trinkets. Or maybe he loses his books on the way home from school. These are acts of childish irresponsibility and should be handled as such. Perhaps you will want to ignore what he did, or maybe you'll

41

require him to work to pay for whatever he lost—depending on his age and level of maturity. However, these accidents and miscalculations do not represent direct challenges to authority. Since they aren't motivated by haughty defiance, they shouldn't result in serious reprimands or punishment.

On the other hand, when a child screams obscenities at his mother or stamps his foot and tells her to shut up, something very different is going on. He has moved into the realm of willful defiance. As the words imply, it is a deliberate act of disobedience that occurs when the child knows what his parents want but he clenches his fists, digs in his heels, and prepares for battle. It is a refusal to accept parental leadership, such as running when called, or disobeying and then perhaps lying about it. When this kind of nose-to-nose confrontation occurs between generations, parental leadership is on the line. It is not time for quiet discussions about the virtues of obedience. It is not the occasion for bribes or bargaining or promises. Nor is it wise to wait until Dad comes home from work to handle the misbehavior.

You have drawn a line in the dirt, and Chris has tossed his cute little toe across it. Who is going to win? Who has the most courage? Who is in charge here? Those are the questions he is asking, and it is vital that you answer them for him. If you equivocate at that moment, he will precipitate other battles designed to ask them again and again. That's just the way a strong-willed child thinks. It is the ultimate paradox of childhood that youngsters want to be led but insist that their parents earn the right to lead them.

In summary, when misbehavior occurs, your obligation is to look first at the issue of intent, and second, at the issue of respect. From your interpretation of these two attitudes, you should know instantly how to respond.

42

*Q*UESTION 40

Are you suggesting that I punish Mark for every little thing he does wrong? I would be on his back every minute of the day.

I am *not* suggesting that you be oppressive in dealing with everyday behavior. The issues that should get your attention are those that deal with respect for you as Mark's mother. When he is defiant, sassy, and disobedient, you should confidently and firmly step in and lead. This disobedient behavior is distinctly different, however, from that which is natural and necessary for learning and development. Let me explain.

Toddlers most often get in trouble for simply exploring and investigating their world. That is a great mistake. Preschoolers learn by poking their fingers into things that adults think they should leave alone. But this busy exploration is extremely important to intellectual stimulation. Whereas you and I will look at a crystal trinket and obtain whatever information we seek from that visual inspection, a toddler will expose that pretty object to all of her senses. She will pick it up, taste it, smell it, wave it in the air, pound it on the wall, throw it across the room, and listen to the pretty sound that it makes when shattering. By that process she learns a bit about gravity, rough versus smooth surfaces, the brittle nature of glass, and some startling things about Mother's anger.

I am not suggesting that your child be allowed to destroy your home and all of its contents. Neither is it right to expect her to keep her hands to herself. Parents should remove those items that are fragile or dangerous, and then strew the child's path with fascinating objects of all types. Permit her to explore everything possible, and do not ever punish her for touching something that she did not know was off-limits, regardless of its value. With respect to dangerous items, such as electric plugs and stoves, as well as a few untouchable objects, such as the knobs on the television set, it is possible and necessary to teach and enforce the command "Don't touch!" If the child refuses to obey even after you have made your expectations clear, a mild slap on the hands while saying no will usually discourage repeat episodes.

I would, however, recommend patience and tolerance for all those other everyday episodes that involve neither defiance nor safety.

QUESTION 41

My baby is only a year old, and she is a joy to my husband and me. But your description of toddlerhood is kind of scary. It's just around the corner. Are the "terrible twos" really so terrible?

I think the toddler years are delightful. It is a period of dynamic blossoming and unfolding. New words are being learned daily, and the cute verbal expressions of that age will be remembered for half a century. It is a time of excitement over fairy stories and Santa Claus and furry puppy dogs. And most important, it is a precious time of love and warmth that will scurry by all too quickly and will never return.

Admittedly, the toddler years can also be quite challenging to a busy mother. Not the least of her frustrations is the negativism of that period of development. It has been said that all human beings can be classified into two broad categories: Those who would vote yes to the various propositions of life, and those who would be inclined to vote no. I can tell you with confidence that each toddler around the world would definitely cast a negative vote! If there is one word that characterizes the period between fifteen and twenty-four months of age, it is *no!* No, he doesn't want to eat his cereal. No, he doesn't want to play with his dump truck. No, he doesn't want to take his bath. And you can be sure, no, he doesn't want to go to bed anytime at all. It is easy to see why this period of life has been called "the first adolescence," because of the negatives, conflict, and independence of the age.

Perhaps the most irritating aspect of the "terrible twos" is the tendency of kids to spill things, destroy things, eat horrible things, fall off things, flush things, kill things, and get into things. They also have a knack for doing embarrassing things, like sneezing on a nearby man at a lunch counter. During these toddler years, any unexplained silence of more than thirty seconds can throw an adult into a sudden state of panic. What mother has not had the shock of opening the bedroom door to find Tony Tornado covered with lipstick from the top of his pink head to the carpet on which he stands? On the wall is his own artistic creation with a red handprint in the center, and throughout the room is the aroma of Chanel No. 5, with which he has anointed his baby brother. Wouldn't it be interesting to hold a national convention sometime, bringing together all the mothers who have experienced that exact trauma?

Yes, toddlerhood is challenging, but it is also a wonderful time of life. It will last but a brief moment in time. There are millions of older parents today with grown children, who would give all they possess to relive those bubbly days with their toddlers. Enjoy these years to the full.

Q UESTION 42

What would you say to my husband and me? We are doing far too much disciplining of our kids. Is there another way to encourage them to cooperate?

The best way to get children to do what you want is to spend time with them before disciplinary problems occur, having fun together and enjoying mutual laughter and joy. When those moments of love and closeness happen, kids are not as tempted to challenge and test the limits. Many confrontations can be avoided by building friendships with kids and thereby making them want to cooperate at home. It sure beats anger as a motivator of little ones!

Q UESTION 43

My children are still young, and they are doing fine now, but I worry a lot about the adolescent years that lie ahead. I've seen other parents go through some pretty terrible things when their teenagers began to rebel. How can I help my sons avoid that turmoil ten years from now?

The apprehension that you describe is well founded, and many parents feel something similar today. The most important suggestion I can make is for you to redouble your efforts to build good relationships with your kids while they are young. That is the key to surviving the adolescent years. If they emerge from childhood with doubts about whether you really love and care for them, anything is possible during the turbulent teens. Boundaries, restrictions, and threats will be no match for adolescent anger, frustration, and resentment. As author Josh McDowell said, "Rules without relationship lead to rebellion."[8] He is right. That's why parents can't afford to get preoccupied with business and other pursuits that interfere with the task of raising children. Kids are young for such a brief period. During that window of opportunity, they must be given priority.

Once you've done what you can to lay the proper foundation, I urge you to approach your parenting duties with confidence. Anxiety about the future is risky in itself. It can make parents tentative and insecure in dealing with their youngsters. They don't dare cross them or deny their wishes for fear of being hated in the teen years. Teenagers pick up those vibes intuitively, which often generates disrespect in return. Don't make that mistake. God has placed you in a position of authority over your young children. Lead them with confidence—and then stay on your knees for help from above.

4

Children's Health
and Well-Being

QUESTION 44

I have great fear that my baby will die when I put her in her crib. What is known now about sudden infant death syndrome (SIDS)? Have researchers figured out what causes these tragic cases where seemingly healthy babies die while sleeping?

Sudden infant death syndrome is still a major concern, killing about six thousand babies each year in the United States alone. We do know more, however, about the circumstances that are often associated with this terrible event. A study was conducted by the U.S. Consumer Product Safety Commission with the collaboration of researchers at the University of Maryland and the Washington University School of Medicine in St. Louis, Missouri. The results were presented at a meeting of the Society for Pediatric Research in 1996. The epidemiologist who directed the investigation, Dr. N. J. Scheers, said, "We have not found a cause of SIDS, but our results show that specific items of bedding used in the U.S., such as comforters and pillows, were associated with an increased risk for death to prone-sleeping infants whose faces became covered, compared to infants on their sides or backs without soft bedding under them."

It was concluded that babies placed on their stomachs in soft bedding are more likely to rebreathe their own carbon dioxide that is trapped in the blankets and pillows around them. In about 30 percent of the 206 SIDS deaths in the research project, babies were found with bedding pressed against their noses and mouths. Most of them were under four months old and could not extricate themselves.[9]

The advice now being offered by doctors is that parents place their infants on their backs, not on their stomachs, and that a minimum amount of loose bedding be kept in the crib. Following this advice won't eliminate all cases of SIDS, but it could save thousands of lives every year.

Q UESTION 45

My wife and I are above average in height, being six-feet-three-inches and five-feet-nine-inches tall. We both had rather tall parents, too. Nevertheless, our daughter is very tiny. She is nine years old and is only at the third percentile for height. What could be causing this, and what do you think we should do?

There are many factors that influence a child's growth, including a deficiency of growth hormones, heredity, nutrition, and the status of the boy or girl's general health. There is only one way to know what is causing your daughter's failure to grow, and that is to take her to an endocrinologist or other physician who specializes in these problems. The right doctor can identify her condition and even predict with accuracy how tall she will eventually become. In some cases, growth hormones may be administered, although I'll leave it to your physician to make that recommendation. Since your girl is nine years old, you have no time to lose. Get her to the right medical authority quickly.

Let me ask, by the way, is your daughter an anxious child?

Q UESTION 46

Yes, as a matter of fact, she is. Lannie is the most insecure of all our children. Why do you ask?

Because some recent studies have shown that persistently anxious girls tend to be shorter than their peers. This was the finding of Dr. Daniel Pine and others at Columbia University College of Physicians, New

York. They found that the most insecure girls tended to be about two inches shorter as adults and were twice as likely to be under five-feet-two-inches tall than girls who were less anxious. Two specific disorders in the formative years were most predictive of less height in adults: (1) separation anxiety—seen in girls who don't have the confidence to spend the night at a friend's house or go away to summer camp; and (2) overanxiousness—not just being uneasy about a threat or problem, but a generalized worry about many things over years of time.

One study showed that anxious girls had high blood levels of the stress hormone cortisol, which can stunt growth. Interestingly, anxious boys in the investigation were not found to have higher cortisol levels, and they did not tend to be shorter than their peers. This suggests that girls may respond to stress biologically differently than boys. For whatever reasons, anxiety is linked to lesser growth in females alone.

Once again, you need to have your daughter examined and evaluated medically. There may be a more obvious and treatable reason for her growth deficiency.[10]

QUESTION 47

Should a parent try to force a child to eat?

No. In fact, the dinner table is one potential battlefield where a parent can easily get ambushed. You can't win there! A strong-willed child is like a good military general who constantly seeks an advantageous place to take on the enemy. He need look no farther than the dinner table. Of all the common points of conflict between generations—bedtime, hair, clothes, schoolwork, etc.—the advantages in a food fight are all in the child's favor! Three times a day, a very tiny youngster can simply refuse to open his mouth. No amount of coercing can make him eat what he doesn't want to eat.

I remember one three-year-old who was determined not to eat his green peas, despite the insistence of his father that the squishy little vegetables were going down. It was a classic confrontation between the irresistible force and an immovable object. Neither would yield. After an hour of haranguing, threatening, cajoling, and sweating, the father had not achieved his goal. The tearful toddler sat with a forkload of peas pointed ominously at his sealed lips.

Finally, through sheer intimidation, the dad managed to get one bite of peas in place. But the lad wouldn't swallow them. I don't know everything that went on afterward, but the mother told me they had no choice but to put the child to bed with the peas still in his mouth. They were amazed at the strength of his will.

The next morning, the mother found a little pile of mushy peas where they had been expelled at the foot of the bed! Score one for Junior, none for Dad. Tell me in what other arena a thirty-pound child could whip a grown man!

Not every toddler is this tough, of course. But many of them will gladly do battle over food. It is their ideal power game. Talk to any experienced parent or grandparent and they will tell you this is true. The sad thing is that these conflicts are unnecessary. Children will eat as much as they need if you keep them from indulging in the wrong stuff. They will not starve. I promise!

The way to deal with a poor eater is to set good food before him. If he claims to not be hungry, wrap the plate, put it in the refrigerator, and send him cheerfully on his way. He'll be back in a few hours. God has put a funny little feeling in his tummy that says, "Gimme food!" When this occurs, do not put sweets, snacks, or confectionery food in front of him. Simply retrieve the earlier meal, warm it up, and serve it again. If he protests, send him out to play again. Even if twelve hours or more go by, continue this procedure until food—all food—begins to look and smell wonderful. From that time forward, the battle over the dinner table should be history.

QUESTION **48**

What causes a child to wet the bed? Our five-year-old soaks his sheets nearly every night, which drives me crazy.

There are about seven million kids in the United States who wet the bed nightly.[11] They are a misunderstood lot. Many of their parents believe that their bed-wetting is deliberate and that it can be eliminated by punishment. Others think these kids are just too lazy to go to the bathroom. These are wrong and unfortunate notions.

Bed-wetting is often caused by medical factors, such as a small bladder, physical immaturity, or other physical conditions. That's why you should begin by consulting a pediatrician or a urologist when bed-wetting starts. About 50 percent of the kids can be helped or cured by medication.

For other boys and girls, the problem is emotional in origin. Any change in the psychological environment of the home may produce midnight moisture. During summer camps conducted for young children, the directors routinely put plastic mattress covers on the beds of all the little visitors. The anxiety associated with being away from home apparently creates a high probability of bed-wetting during the first few nights, and it is particularly risky to be sleeping on the lower level of bunk beds!

There is a third factor that I feel is a frequent cause of enuresis. During children's toddler years, they wet the bed simply because they are too immature to maintain nighttime bladder control. Some parents, in an effort to head off another episode, begin getting these kids up at night to go to the potty. The youngster is still sound asleep, but he or she is told to "go tinkle," or whatever. After this conditioning has been established, the child who needs to urinate at night dreams of being told to "go." Particularly when jostled or disturbed at night, the child can believe he or she is being ushered to the bathroom. I would recommend that parents of older bed wetters stop getting them up at night, even if the behavior continues for a while.

QUESTION 49

I get so mad at my kid for wetting the bed. Every morning I have to strip and wash his bedding and pajamas. I told him last week that I would spank him if it happened again. Do you think that will help?

Most certainly not! Unless your child's bed-wetting is an act of defiance occurring after he is awake, which I doubt, his enuresis is an *involuntary* act for which he is not responsible. Punishment under those circumstances is dangerous and unfair. Your son is humiliated by waking up wet anyway, and the older he gets, the more foolish he will feel about it.

The bed wetter needs reassurance and patience from parents, and they should be there for him or her. They would be wise to try to conceal the embarrassing problem from those who would laugh at him. Even good-natured humor within the family, associated with bed-wetting, is often very painful.

QUESTION 50

Aside from medical help, what suggestions do you have for dealing with enuresis?

There are other remedies that sometimes work, such as electronic devices that ring a bell and awaken the child when the urine completes an electrical circuit. This conditions a child to associate the feeling of needing to urinate with the bell that awakens him. I have seen some dramatic success stories where "hard-core" bed wetters were cured within a few weeks using such a device. Trying it certainly can't hurt.

Until the problem is solved, I hope you can keep your frustrations at a minimum. A smile sometimes helps. I received a letter from a mother who wrote down her three-year-old son's bedtime prayer. He said, "Now I lay me down to sleep. I close my eyes; I wet the bed."

QUESTION 51

My seven-year-old son has just recently begun demonstrating some rather cruel behavior toward animals. We've caught him doing some pretty awful things to neighborhood dogs and cats. Of course we punished him, but I wonder if there is anything to be more concerned about here?

Cruelty to animals is often a symptom of serious psychological dysfunction to be evaluated by a professional. Children who do such things are not typically just going through a phase. It should be seen as a warning sign of possible emotional problems that could be rather persistent. It also appears to be associated with sexual abuse in childhood. I don't want to alarm you or overstate the case, but adults committed to a life of violent crime were often cruel to animals in their childhood. This fact was verified in a recent study by the American Humane Association.[12] I suggest that you take your son to a psychologist or other behavioral specialist who can evaluate his mental health. And by all means, do not tolerate unkindness to animals.

QUESTION 52

My daughter is five years old, and she has been having some very scary nightmares lately. She wakes up screaming in the middle of the night, but she can't tell us what frightened her. The next morning, she doesn't seem to recall the dream, but something is obviously troubling her. My wife and I are worried that she may be developing psychological problems that are being expressed in these terrible dreams. Is that possible?

I think your daughter is all right. She is probably having a "night terror" rather than a nightmare. Let me describe the difference between the two. Nightmares occur primarily in what is known as "stage-three" sleep and are often remembered if the dreamer awakens. They are sometimes linked to emotional distress during waking hours and may play a role in "working through" those disturbing experiences. A person can often talk about a nightmare and recount its scary story.

Night terrors, by contrast, usually occur in "stage-four" sleep, which is even deeper and further from consciousness. In this physiological state, the body mechanisms are reduced to a minimum to sustain life. Breathing, heart rate, metabolism, and every other function go into super-slow motion. Some children experience strange dreams during this phase, which cause them to sit up and scream in terror. However, when adults come to the child's rescue, they find that the child is unresponsive. The eyes are open, but the boy or girl is obviously not awake. And the next morning, there is no memory of what was so deeply disturbing.

This appears to be what you are describing with reference to your daughter. You'll be encouraged to know that there seems to be no connection between night terrors and psychological stress. It is not predictive of any known health problems or emotional disruption. Nor do we know what causes them.

The good news is that your little girl is apparently fine. The bad news is that you may have to deal for a time with her midnight terrors that drag you from your own stage-four sleep.

QUESTION 53

Is there any way to prevent the child from having night terrors? It is happening in our house nearly every night, and it is really hard on my husband and me.

Yes, you can usually prevent your child from going into stage-four sleep by giving him or her a minor amount of medication. I wouldn't suggest that you do that unless the night terrors are regular and disruptive to adult sleep patterns. You should talk to your physician about this matter if that is the case.

QUESTION 54

Did either of your children experience night terrors?

No, but our daughter once had a very unusual nightmare. When she was four years old, she woke up screaming at about midnight. When I came to her bed, she told me excitedly that the wall was about to collapse on her.

"It's falling! It's falling, Daddy! The wall is falling!" she screamed.

She was obviously very frightened by the dream. I took her hand and said, "Danae, feel that wall. It has been there a long time. It isn't going to fall. You are OK. Now go back to sleep."

As she settled down in the covers, I went back to bed and was quickly asleep again. But six hours later, a powerful earthquake rattled the city of Los Angeles and shook my wife and me right out of bed. I rushed to Danae's room to bundle her up and get her out of the way of that wall, which was jumping and shaking like crazy.

Did our four-year-old have some kind of forewarning of the earthquake in the midnight hours? I don't know, but I'll tell you this: I made up my mind that day to believe her the next time she told me the wall was going to fall.

Q UESTION 55

How do you feel about the dangers of marijuana use? I've heard that it isn't addictive and therefore isn't harmful; I've also heard that it is very dangerous. What are the facts?

Let me quote Harold Voth, M.D., senior psychiatrist for the Menninger Foundation in Topeka, Kansas, and associate chief of psychiatry for education at Topeka Veterans Administration Medical Center, Topeka, Kansas. These are the facts he provided, which speak for themselves:

> Ninety percent of those using hard drugs such as heroin started with marijuana.
>
> Five marijuana cigarettes have the same cancer-causing capacity as 112 conventional cigarettes.
>
> Marijuana stays in the body, lodged in the fat cells, for three to five weeks. Mental and physical performance is negatively affected during this entire period of time.
>
> A person smoking marijuana on a regular basis suffers from a cumulative buildup and storage of THC, a toxic chemical, in the fat cells of the body, particularly in the brain. It takes three to five months to effectively detoxify a regular user.
>
> The part of the brain that allows a person to focus, concentrate, create, learn, and conceptualize at an advanced level is still growing during the teenage years. Continuous use of marijuana over a period of time will retard the normal growth of these brain cells.
>
> A study at Columbia University revealed that female marijuana smokers suffer a sharp increase in cells that damage DNA (the chemical that carries the genetic code). It was also found that the female reproductive eggs are especially vulnerable to damage by marijuana.
>
> A second Columbia University study found that a control group

smoking a single marijuana cigarette every other day for a year had a white-blood-cell count that was 39 percent lower than normal, thus damaging the immune system and making the user far more susceptible to infection and sickness.

One marijuana cigarette causes a 41 percent decrease in driving skills. Two cigarettes cause a 63 percent decrease.[13]

Given these facts, it is unconscionable that people who should know better continue to advocate the legalization of marijuana.

QUESTION 56

I just found out that I'm pregnant. When the doctor told me, he warned me not to drink anything with alcohol in it until the child is born. I'm used to having a few beers after work, and I like a cocktail several times a week. Is it really necessary for me to give up all alcohol until my baby arrives?

I urge you to heed the advice of your physician. That precious baby inside of you could be severely damaged if you continue to drink in the next few months. Your child could have what is known as "fetal alcohol syndrome," which can cause heart anomalies, central nervous system dysfunction, head and facial abnormalities, and lifelong behavior problems. Fetal alcohol syndrome is also thought to be the leading cause of mental retardation.[14] It is a terrible thing to inflict on a child.

Babies can be harmed by alcohol in the blood of the mother at any time throughout gestation, but they are especially vulnerable during the first trimester. That's why you should not drink during the remaining seven months of your pregnancy, but by all means, don't swallow a drop of alcohol right now.

You may remember the Old Testament story of Samson, who terrorized his enemies, the Philistines. Before he was born, his mother was told by an angel that her child was destined for greatness and that she must not weaken him by imbibing strong drink while she was pregnant. Medical science has now verified the wisdom of that advice.

That's why a similar warning to pregnant women is posted by law wherever liquor, beer, or wine is sold.

For you and for all pregnant women and those who anticipate becoming pregnant—don't take chances with your babies' future. There is no level of alcohol that is known to be safe. Abstain for the entire nine months. You and your baby will be glad you did.

QUESTION **57**

Clarify the terms *anorexia* and *bulimia* for me, and indicate what causes these eating problems.

The anorexic individual is one who starves himself or herself (it's usually a woman) by refusing to eat enough to sustain his or her body's minimal requirements. Before long, a woman with a normal weight of 130 pounds may have starved herself down to 80 pounds. And though she may actually be starving to death, she may still perceive herself to be overweight.

A person with bulimia follows the opposite pattern. She gorges uncontrollably and then purges herself by vomiting or by using harsh laxatives. Like the anorexic, she can do serious damage to her health if not diagnosed and treated.

It's generally believed that both anorexia and bulimia represent an intense desire for control of one's life. The typical anorexic patient is a female in late adolescence or early adulthood. She is usually a compliant individual who was always a "good little girl." She withheld her anger and her frustration at being powerless throughout the developmental years. Then one day, her need for control began being manifested as a serious eating disorder. There, at least, was one area where she could be the boss. Such individuals also perceive fatness to be hated and ridiculed by their peer groups, which strikes terror into their hearts.

I would strongly recommend that parents of adolescent girls keep a very close eye on their daughters' weight and behavior after thirteen years of age. Seeking proper treatment for an eating disorder can mean the difference between life and death.

QUESTION 58

Our school psychologist said she thinks our son is suffering from childhood depression. My goodness! The kid is only nine years old. Is it reasonable that this could be his problem?

We used to believe that depression was exclusively an adult problem, but that understanding is changing. Now we're seeing signs of serious despondency in children as young as five years old.

Symptoms of depression in an elementary school child may include general lethargy, a lack of interest in things that used to excite him or her, sleep disturbances, chewed fingernails, loss of appetite, and violent emotional outbursts. Other common reactions are stomach complaints and low tolerance for frustration of any kind.

If depression is a problem for your child, it is only symptomatic of something else that is bothering him or her. Help him or her verbalize feelings. Try to anticipate the explanation for sadness, and lead the youngster into conversations that provide an opportunity to ventilate. Make yourself available to listen, without judging or belittling the feelings expressed. Simply being understood is soothing for children and adults alike.

If the symptoms are severe or if they last more than two weeks, I urge you to take the advice of the school psychologist or seek professional help for your son. Prolonged depression can be destructive for human beings of any age and is especially dangerous to children.

QUESTION 59

Do childhood traumas inevitably twist and warp a person in the adult years?

No. It is well known that difficult childhoods leave some people wounded and disadvantaged, but for others, they fuel great achievement and success. The difference appears to be a function of individual temperaments and resourcefulness.

In a classic study called "Cradles of Eminence," Victor and Mildred Goertzel investigated the home backgrounds of three hundred highly successful people. The researchers sought to identify the early experiences that may have contributed to remarkable achievement. All of the subjects were well known for their accomplishments; they included Einstein, Freud, Churchill, and many others.

The backgrounds of these people proved very interesting. Three-fourths of them came from troubled childhoods, enduring poverty, broken homes, or parental abuse. One-fourth had physical handicaps. Most of those who became writers and playwrights had watched their own parents embroiled in psychological dramas of one sort or another. The researchers concluded that the need to compensate for disadvantages was a major factor in the drive toward personal achievement.[15]

One of the best illustrations of this phenomenon is seen in the life of Eleanor Roosevelt, a former First Lady. Being orphaned at ten, she underwent a childhood of utter anguish. She was very homely and never felt she really belonged to anybody. According to Victor Wilson, Newhouse News Service, "She was a rather humorless introvert, a young woman unbelievably shy, unable to overcome her personal insecurity and with a conviction of her own inadequacy." The world knows, however, that Mrs. Roosevelt rose above her emotional shackles. As Wilson said, ". . . From some inner wellspring, Mrs. Roosevelt summoned a tough, unyielding courage, tempered by remarkable self-control and self-discipline. . . ." That "inner wellspring" has another appropriate name: compensation!

Obviously, one's attitude toward a handicap determines its impact on one's life. It has become popular to blame adverse circumstances for irresponsible behavior (e.g., poverty causes crime, broken homes produce juvenile delinquents, a sick society imposes drug addiction on its youth). There is some truth in this assumption, since people in those difficult circumstances are more likely to behave in destructive ways. But they are not forced to do so. To say that adverse conditions *cause* irresponsible behavior is to remove all responsibility from the shoulders of the individual. The excuse is hollow. We must each decide what we will do with inner doubt and outer hardship.

The application to an individual family should be obvious. If a child has gone through a traumatic experience or is physically disadvantaged, his or her parents need not give up hope. They should identify his or her strengths and natural abilities, which can be used to overcome the hurdle. The problem that seems so formidable today may become the inspiration for greatness tomorrow.

QUESTION 60

I have been teaching school for thirty years, and I am noticing a significant change in the health of my children. More of them are overweight, and they just don't get enough exercise. I wonder if my observation is accurate, and if so, what is causing it.

You are absolutely correct. A recent medical study conducted at Columbia Children's Hospital in Ohio has confirmed that today's children are heavier and have significantly higher cholesterol and triglyceride levels than kids did even fifteen years ago. One of the researchers, Dr. Hugh Allens, said, "Unless these trends change, 30 million of the 80 million children alive today in the United States will eventually die of heart disease."

Dr. Allens said, "Kids need to turn off the TV, get off the couch, and stop the nincompooping of America."[16] The problem is that high-fat junk food has replaced good nutrition. And even when healthy foods are consumed, kids are not exercising the calories off. Between television, car pools, computer games, and just hanging out at the pizza parlor, kids just don't run and jump like they used to.

So Mom and Dad should find activities to do together with kids that are active. Things like walking and bicycling and playing catch or hiking. They can also get their children involved in community or school sports programs ranging from softball to soccer.

Children are busy forming habits for a lifetime, so eating right and exercising every day will contribute to greater health in the future.

60

QUESTION 61

Should I be concerned about my two-and-a-half-year-old son's tendency to stammer and repeat words? If he has a real stuttering problem, I don't want to wait too long before doing something about it.

It is too early to be concerned about speech impediments in your boy. Here is the recommendation of DuPont Hospital for Children, located in Wilmington, Delaware, which deals specifically with speech therapy for children:

> The first signs of stuttering may appear after the second birthday or when a child is beginning to put words together to form sentences. To parents it may be upsetting, but it is considered a normal stage in speech development. Showing patience with the child and adopting a cautious, accepting, and informed attitude are best during the preschool years. A child may be disfluent for a few weeks or several months, with symptoms disappearing and perhaps appearing again. Most children in whom stuttering begins before the age of five will lose the disfluency, usually within twelve months of onset. Children sharpen their communication skills as they become school age (six or seven years old). By then, normal disfluency drops to very low levels.[17]

The bottom line is that the experts say you should wait until your little boy is six or seven before taking action. If he's still stuttering, then he should be seen at a clinic for a complete speech evaluation.

QUESTION 62

You have recommended for many years that parents take their preteens away from home for what you called a "Preparing for Adolescence" weekend, during which they talk about the physical and emotional changes about to occur. I'm interested in your comment that kids want this information before they

become teenagers, but they won't want to talk about it after
puberty. Do their attitudes really change that much overnight?

As a matter of fact, they do. A study of 1,023 children between ten and
thirteen showed that the number who felt uncomfortable talking to
their parents about sexuality nearly doubled after puberty occurred.
Prior to that, they were very open to instruction and guidance at home.
Ninety-three percent of those aged ten to twelve felt loved by their
parents "all the time," said Dr. Alvin Poussaint, a psychiatrist at
Harvard University. He said, "I think parents may be surprised that
children of this age are saying, 'We want to be close to you. We need
you and we're still afraid. We need the sense of safety and security that
you supply.'"[18]

The study showed, however, that attitudes changed dramatically
when the children reached the eighth grade. Those who had been open
to advice the year before were suddenly unwilling to talk to their
parents. The window of accessibility had closed.

The moral to the story? Invest a little time in the months before
puberty to get your children ready for the stresses of adolescence. The
effort will pay big dividends.

QUESTION 63

**Our family physician wants to examine my thirteen-year-old
son without my being in the room. That's OK with me, but I
expect him to tell me what my boy says and what his medical
condition is. That's where we disagree. He says he must keep
their conversation confidential. Am I right to expect to be
informed and involved?**

Teenagers are typically sensitive and modest about their bodies—especially when their parents are around—so I can understand the need
for privacy during a physical exam. The larger issue here, however, is
the physician's accountability to you as the mother, and at this point,
I agree entirely with the position you have taken. Other parents have
expressed similar concerns to me.

I'm reminded of a mother who told me that she took her fourteen-year-old daughter to their pediatrician for a routine physical exam. The mother was aware that her daughter was beginning to develop physically and might be sensitive to her being in the examining room with her. She offered to remain in the waiting room, but the girl objected.

"I don't want to go in there by myself," she said. "Please come with me." After arguing with her daughter for a moment, the mother agreed to accompany her to the examining room.

When the exam was over, the doctor turned to the mother and criticized her for intruding. He said in front of the girl, "You know, you really had no business being in the examining room. It is time I related directly to your daughter. You should not even be aware of the care that I give her or the medication I prescribe. Nor should you know the things that are said between us. My care of your daughter should now be a private matter between her and me."

The girl had been going through a period of rebellion, and the mother felt her authority was weakened by the doctor's comments. It was as though he were saying, "Your day of supervision of your daughter has now passed. She should now make her own decisions." Fortunately, that mother was unwilling to do as she was told and promptly found a new doctor. Good for her!

I have discussed this conversation with several pediatricians, and they have each agreed with the doctor in this case. They emphasized the importance of a youngster having someone to talk with in private. Perhaps. But I object to the autonomy demanded by the physician. Fourteen-year-old boys and girls are not grown, and their parents are still the best people to care for them and oversee their development. It is appropriate for a physician to have some private moments with a young patient, but he or she should never forget to whom accountability is owed.

Furthermore, if greater authority is to be granted to the doctor, the parent had better find out just what he or she believes about contraceptives for minors, premarital sex, spiritual matters, and the like. Be careful whom you choose to trust with the body and the soul of your child. The pace of living is so frantic today that we have become dangerously willing to accept surrogate parenting from a variety of professionals who meander through our lives. Educators, youth ministers, athletic coaches, music instructors, psychologists, counselors, and physicians are there to assist parents in raising their kids—but never to replace them.

QUESTION 64

My family and I have been in France for four years, but I'm told I still have a strong accent. My nine-year-old daughter, however, speaks perfect French. How come children can learn a language so much easier than adults?

It is true that children can learn to speak perfect Russian, Chinese, Spanish, or any other language used around the world, yet fifteen or twenty years later, most of them will have a much harder time trying to make those same sounds. Researchers now know why this is true. It's explained by a process known as "phoneme contraction." The larynx of a young child assumes a shape necessary to make any sounds that he or she is learning to use at that time. It then solidifies, or hardens, in those positions, making it impossible or very difficult to make other sounds later in life. In other words, there's a window of opportunity when anything is possible linguistically, but it closes very quickly.

Keep working on your French, even though you'll probably never get rid of your accent.

5

Attention Deficit Disorder in Children and Adults

QUESTION 65

I hear so much about children who have ADD. Can you describe this problem for me and tell me how I might recognize it in my son?

The term *ADD* stands for attention deficit disorder, which is an inherited neurological syndrome that affects approximately 5 percent of children in the United States. It refers to individuals who are easily distracted, have a low tolerance for boredom or frustration, and tend to be impulsive and flighty. Some of them are also hyperactive, and hence, they are said to have ADHD (attention deficit/hyperactivity disorder.)

Children with ADD have a pattern of behavior that sets them up for failure in school and conflict with their parents. They have difficulty finishing tasks, remembering details, focusing on a book or assignment, or even remaining seated for more than a few minutes. Some appear to be driven from within as they race wildly from one thing to another. They are often very bright and creative, yet they're seen as lazy, disruptive, and terribly disorganized. ADD children often suffer from low self-esteem because they have been berated as goof-offs and anarchists who refuse to follow the rules. They sometimes have few friends because they can drive everyone crazy—even those their own age.

As for how you can recognize such a child in your home, it is unwise for a parent to attempt to do so. There are many other problems, both psychological and physical, that can cause similar symptoms. Disorders of the thyroid, for example, can make a child hyperactive or sluggish; depression and anxiety can cause the distractibility associated with ADD. Therefore, you must have assistance from a physician, a child developmentalist, or a psychologist who can confirm the diagnosis.

If you see in your child the symptoms I've described, I urge you to have him or her seen professionally. Again, you should *not* try to diagnose your child! The sooner you can get that youngster in to see a person who specializes in this disorder, the better.

QUESTION 66

I understand that I can't diagnose my own son, but it would be helpful if you would list the kinds of behavior to look for in a child who may have ADD. You've described the condition in general terms, but what are the specific characteristics of someone who has this disorder?

Hallowell and Ratey, authors of an excellent text entitled *Driven to Distraction*, list twenty symptoms that are often evident in a person with ADD or ADHD. They are:

Suggested Diagnostic Criteria for Attention Deficit Disorder

1. A sense of underachievement, of not meeting one's goals (regardless of how much one has accomplished)
2. Difficulty getting organized
3. Chronic procrastination or trouble getting started
4. Many projects going simultaneously; trouble with follow-through
5. Tendency to say what comes to mind without necessarily considering the timing or appropriateness of the remark
6. An ongoing search for high stimulation
7. A tendency to be easily bored

8. Easy distractibility, trouble focusing attention, tendency to tune out or drift away in the middle of a page or a conversation, often coupled with an ability to focus at times
9. Often creative, intuitive, highly intelligent
10. Trouble going through established channels, following proper procedure
11. Impatient; low tolerance for frustration
12. Impulsive, either verbally or in action, as in impulsive spending of money, changing plans, enacting new schemes or career plans, and the like
13. Tendency to worry needlessly, endlessly; tendency to scan the horizon looking for something to worry about alternating with inattention to or disregard for actual dangers
14. Sense of impending doom, insecurity, alternating with high risk-taking
15. Depression, especially when disengaged from a project
16. Restlessness
17. Tendency toward addictive behavior
18. Chronic problems with self-esteem
19. Inaccurate self-observation
20. Family history of ADD, manic-depressive illness, depression, substance abuse, or other disorders of impulse control or mood[19]

Q UESTION 67

My daughter has some of the symptoms you described, but she is a very quiet child. Are some ADD kids withdrawn and sedate?

Yes. ADD is not always associated with hyperactivity, especially in girls. Some of them are "dreamy" and detached. Regrettably, they are sometimes called "airheads" or "space cadets." Such a child can sit looking at a book for forty-five minutes without reading a word. One teacher told me about a girl in her class who would lose every article of clothing that wasn't hooked to her body. Nearly every day, the teacher would send this child back to the playground to retrieve her sweater or coat, only to have her return fifteen minutes later without it. She had forgotten what she went after. A boy or girl with that kind of distractibility would find it extremely difficult, if not impossible, to get home night after night with books and assignments written down, and then to complete the work and turn it in the next morning.

Frankly, the "faraway" child worries me more than the one who is excessively active. She may be seen as a good little girl who just isn't very bright, while the troublemaker is more likely to get the help he needs. He's too irritating to ignore.

Those who are and are not hyperactive have one characteristic in common. It is distractibility. Even though they flit from one thing to another, the name attention deficit disorder is not quite on target. It's better than the old term ("minimal brain damage"), but there is also misinformation in the current designation. The problem is not that these children have a short attention span. At times, they can become lost in something that greatly interests them to the point that they aren't aware of anything going on around them. Instead, they have an insatiable need for mental stimulation during every waking moment. The moment they become bored with what they are doing, they dash off in search of the next exciting possibility.

One father told me about his four-year-old son with ADD. He said, "If you let that kid get bored, you deserve what he's going to do to you." That applies to millions of children.

Q UESTION 68

What causes attention deficit disorder?

It is believed to be inherited. Russell Barkley of the University of Massachusetts Medical Center estimates that 40 percent of ADHD kids have a parent with similar symptoms, and 35 percent have an affected sibling. If one identical twin is affected, the chances are between 80 and 92 percent that his or her sibling will be also. ADD is two to three times as likely to be diagnosed in boys as girls.[20]

The cause of ADD is unknown, but it is probably associated with subtle differences in brain structure, its neural pathways, its chemistry, its blood supply, or its electrical system. As of this writing, some interesting hypotheses are emerging, although definitive conclusions can't yet be drawn.

QUESTION 69

I've heard that ADD is controversial and that it may not even exist. You obviously disagree.

Yes, I disagree, although the disorder has become faddish and tends to be overdiagnosed. But when a child actually has this problem, I assure you that his or her parents and teachers don't have to be convinced.

QUESTION 70

Does ADD go away as children grow up?

We used to believe the problem was eliminated with the onset of puberty. That's what I was taught in graduate school. Now it is known that ADD is a lifelong condition, usually influencing behavior from the cradle to the grave. Some ADD adults learn to be less disorganized and impulsive as they get older. They channel their energy into sports activities or professions in which they function very well. Others have trouble settling on a career or holding a job. Follow-through remains a problem as they flit from one task to another. They are particularly unsuited for desk jobs, accounting positions, or other assignments that demand attention to detail, long hours of sitting, and the ability to juggle many balls at once.

Another consequence of ADD in adolescence and adulthood is the thirst for high-risk activity. Even as children, they are accident-prone, and their parents get well acquainted with the local emergency room. As they get older, rock climbing, bungee jumping, car racing, motorcycle riding, white-water rafting, and related activities are among their favorite activities. Adults with ADD are sometimes called "adrenaline junkies" because they are hooked on the "high" produced by the adrenaline rush associated with dangerous behavior. Others are more susceptible to drug use, alcoholism, and other addictive behaviors. Approximately 40 percent will have been arrested by eighteen years of age.[21]

Some of those who have ADD are at higher risk for marital conflict, too. It can be very irritating to a compulsive, highly ordered husband or wife to be married to a "messie"—someone whose life is chaotic and one who forgets to pay the bills, fix the car, or keep records for income-tax reports. Such a couple usually need professional counseling to help them learn to work together and capitalize on each other's strengths.

QUESTION 71

You've given us a pretty bleak picture. Is there anything good you can tell those of us who are raising an ADHD child?

There are some advantages to having attention deficit disorder. In a sense, even the word *disorder* is misleading because the syndrome has many positive features. As *Time* reported, "[ADD adults] see themselves as creative; their impulsiveness can be viewed as spontaneity; hyperactivity gives them enormous energy and drive; even their distractibility has the virtue of making them alert to changes in the environment. Kids with ADHD are wild, funny, effervescent. They have lots of life."[22]

Let's not forget, also, that ADD can be treated successfully in many cases.

QUESTION 72

What kind of treatment is available?

Treatment involves a range of factors, beginning with education. The adult with ADD is often greatly relieved to learn that he or she has an identifiable, treatable condition. Dr. Robert Reid from the University of Nebraska calls it the "label of forgiveness." He said, "The kid's problems are not his parents' fault, not the teacher's fault, not the kid's fault."[23] That is good news to the person who has been told all his life that he's dumb, stupid, lazy, obnoxious, and disruptive.

The first step in rebuilding the self-concept of an adult, then, is to get an understanding of the forces operating within. My advice to that individual and to his or her family is to read, read, read! One helpful book for laymen is *Driven to Distraction,* by Edward Hallowell, M.D., and John Ratey, M.D. An excellent set of cassette tapes by these authors is also available. Another well-written book by a Christian psychologist is entitled *The Hyperactive Child,* by Grant Martin, Ph.D.[24]

The second step is to teach the ADD person, especially the adult, to minimize his or her distractibility and impulsivity. They can learn to use "to-do lists," daily calendars, schedules, and written plans. "It ain't easy," as they say, but it can be done.

The third step is to secure the assistance of what Hallowell and Ratey call "a coach." A knowledgeable friend is needed to stand nearby with a whistle—offering encouragement, pointing out mistakes, teaching, and modifying behavior. If a wise instructor can teach a novice to play tennis or golf, a caring coach can help a person with ADD learn to behave in more successful ways.

In regard to children, a knowledgeable professional is needed to advise and encourage parents who are often bewildered and frustrated by behavior they neither control nor understand.

Finally, there are the considerable benefits to the use of prescription drugs for both children and adults. Approximately 70 percent of ADD patients benefit from appropriate medication.[25] Surprisingly, certain *stimulants* are often effective in helping ADD children—including those who are hyperactive. No one knows exactly how they work, but they probably affect the electrochemical processes in frontal lobes of the brain that regulate behavior. The most commonly prescribed drug is Ritalin, although some patients do better on Dexedrine or Cylert. In some instances, these substances have a remarkably positive effect.[26]

Q UESTION 73

Do you worry about Ritalin and other drugs being over-prescribed? Should I be reluctant to give them to my ten-year-old?

Yes. Prescription drugs have been used as a cure-all for various forms of misbehavior. That is unfortunate. We should never medicate kids just because their parents have failed to discipline them properly or because someone prefers to have them sedated. Every medication has undesirable side effects and should be administered only after careful evaluation and study. Ritalin, for example, can reduce the appetite and cause insomnia in some patients. It is, nevertheless, considered remarkably safe.

If your child has been evaluated and diagnosed with ADD by a professional who is experienced in treating this problem, you should not hesitate to accept a prescription for an appropriate medication. Some dramatic behavioral changes can occur when the proper substance is identified for a particular child. A boy or girl who sits and stares off into the distance or one who frantically climbs the walls is desperately in need of help. To give that individual a focused mind and internal control is a blessing. Medication often works just that way.

QUESTION 74

We have a five-year-old son who has been diagnosed with ADD. He is really difficult to handle, and I have no idea how to manage him. I know he has a neurological problem; I don't feel right about making him obey like we do our other children. It is a big problem for us. What do you suggest?

I understand your dilemma, but I urge you to discipline your son. Every youngster needs the security of defined limits, and the ADD or ADHD boy or girl is no exception. Such a child should be held responsible for his or her behavior, although the approach may be a little different. For example, most children can be required to sit on a chair for disciplinary reasons, whereas some very hyperactive children would not be able to remain there. Similarly, corporal punishment is sometimes ineffective with a highly excitable little bundle of electricity. As with every aspect of parenthood, disciplinary measures for the ADD child must be suited to his or her unique characteristics and needs.

72

Question 75

How, then, is such a child to be managed?

Let me share a list of eighteen suggestions that were provided in a book by Dr. Domeena Renshaw entitled *The Hyperactive Child.* Though her book is now out of print, Dr. Renshaw's advice on this problem is still valid.

1. Be consistent in rules and discipline.
2. Keep your own voice quiet and slow. Anger is normal. Anger can be controlled. Anger does not mean you do not love a child.
3. Try hard to keep your emotions cool by bracing for expected turmoil. Recognize and respond to any positive behavior, however small. If you search for good things, you will find a few.
4. Avoid a ceaselessly negative approach: "Stop"—"Don't"—"No."
5. Separate behavior which you may not like, from the child's person, which you like, e.g., "I like you. I don't like your tracking mud through the house."
6. Have a very clear routine for this child. Construct a timetable for waking, eating, play, TV, study, chores, and bedtime. Follow it flexibly when he disrupts it. Slowly your structure will reassure him until he develops his own.
7. Demonstrate new or difficult tasks, using action accompanied by short, clear, quiet explanations. Repeat the demonstration until learned. This uses audiovisual-sensory perceptions to reinforce the learning. The memory traces of a hyperactive child take longer to form. Be patient and repeat.
8. Designate a separate room or a part of a room that is his own special area. Avoid brilliant colors or complex patterns in decor. Simplicity, solid colors, minimal clutter, and a worktable facing a blank wall away from distractions assist concentration. A hyperactive child cannot filter out overstimulation himself yet.
9. Do one thing at a time: Give him one toy from a closed box; clear the table of everything else when coloring; turn off the radio/TV

when he is doing homework. Multiple stimuli prevent his concentration from focusing on his primary task.

10. Give him responsibility, which is essential for growth. The task should be within his capacity, although the assignment may need much supervision. Acceptance and recognition of his efforts (even when imperfect) should not be forgotten.

11. Read his preexplosive warning signals. Quietly intervene to avoid explosions by distracting him or discussing the conflict calmly. Removal from the battle zone to the sanctuary of his room for a few minutes is useful.

12. Restrict playmates to one or at most two at one time, because he is so excitable. Your home is more suitable, so you can provide structure and supervision. Explain your rules to the playmate and briefly tell the other parent your reasons.

13. Do not pity, tease, be frightened by, or overindulge this child. He has a special condition of the nervous system that is manageable.

14. Know the name and dose of his medication. Give it regularly. Watch and remember the effects to report back to your physician.

15. Openly discuss with your physician any fears you have about the use of medications.

16. Lock up all medications to avoid accidental misuse.

17. Always supervise the taking of medication, even if it is routine over a long period of years. Responsibility remains with the parents! One day's supply at a time can be put in a regular place and checked routinely as he becomes older and more self-reliant.

18. Share your successful "helps" with his teacher. The outlined ways to help your hyperactive child are as important to him as diet and insulin are to a diabetic child.[27]

6

Effective Parenting Today

QUESTION 76

What has been your greatest challenge as a father? What did you learn from it?

Raising healthy, well-educated, self-disciplined children who love God and their fellow human beings is, I believe, the most challenging responsibility in living. Not even rocket science can approach it for complexity and unpredictability. And of course, the job is even more difficult today when the culture undermines and contradicts everything Christian parents are trying to accomplish at home. Fortunately, we are not asked to do everything perfectly as moms and dads. Our kids usually manage to survive our mistakes and failures and turn out better than we have any right to boast about.

I certainly made my share of mistakes as a father. Like millions of other men of my era, I often had a tough time balancing the pressure of my profession with the needs of my family. Not that I ever became an "absentee father," but I did struggle at times to be as accessible as I should have been. As it happened, my first book, *Dare to Discipline*, was published the same week that our second child, Ryan, arrived. A baby always turns a house upside down, but the reaction to my book added to the turmoil. I was a full-time professor at a medical school, and yet I was inundated by thousands of letters and requests of every sort. There was no mechanism to handle this sudden notoriety. I remember flying to New York one Thursday night, doing seventeen television shows and press interviews in three days, and returning to work on Monday morning. It was nothing short of overwhelming.

My father, who always served as a beacon in dark times, saw what was happening to me and wrote a letter that was to change my life. First he congratulated me on my success, but then he warned that all the success in the world would not compensate if I failed at home. He reminded me that the spiritual welfare of our children was my most important responsibility and that the only way to build their faith was to model it personally and then to stay on my knees in prayer. That couldn't be done if I invested every resource in my profession. I have never forgotten that profound advice.

It eventually led to my resignation from the university and to the development of a ministry that permitted me to stay at home. I quit accepting speaking requests, started a radio program that required no travel, and refused to do "book tours" or accept other lengthy responsibilities that would take me away from my family. As I look back on that era today, I am so grateful that I chose to preserve my relationship with my children. The closeness that we enjoy today can be traced to that decision to make time for them when they needed me most. I could easily have made the greatest mistake of my life at that time.

I'm sure many fathers will read this response and find themselves today where I was back then. If you are one of them, I urge you to give priority to your family. Those kids around your feet will be grown and gone before you know it. Don't let the opportunity of these days slip away from you. No professional accomplishment or success is worth that cost. When you stand where I am today, the relationship with those you love will outweigh every other good thing in your life.

76

Q UESTION 77

I worry so much about my children and wonder if I'm raising them wisely. Every few days my husband and I encounter a problem we don't know how to handle. Is it common for parents to feel this way?

Yes, it has never been easy to raise healthy and productive children. After all, babies come into the world with no instructions, and you pretty much have to assemble them on your own. They are also maddeningly complex, and there are no guaranteed formulas that work in every instance. And finally, the techniques that succeed magnificently with one child can fail bewilderingly with another.

This difficulty in raising children is a recurring theme in the letters we receive at Focus on the Family. We have heard it so often, in fact, that we decided to conduct a poll to ascertain the common frustrations of parenting. The answers received from more than a thousand mothers and fathers were very revealing. Some responded with humor, especially those who were raising toddlers. They told the most delightful stories about sticky telephones, wet toilet seats, and knotted shoestrings. Their experiences reminded me of the days when Shirley and I were chasing ambitious preschoolers.

Tell me why it is that a toddler never throws up in the bathroom? Never! To do so would violate some great unwritten law of the universe. It is even more difficult to understand why he or she will gag violently at the sight of a perfectly wonderful breakfast of oatmeal, eggs, bacon, and orange juice—and then go play in the toilet. I have no idea what makes a kid do that. I only know that it drives a mother crazy!

Unfortunately, the majority of those who responded to our questionnaire did not share funny stories about cute kids. Many of them were experiencing considerable frustration in their parenting responsibilities. Rather than being critical of their children, however, most said they were troubled by their *own* inadequacies as mothers and fathers!

Their answers, including these actual responses, revealed the self-doubt that is prevalent among parents today:

- "I don't know how to cope with my children's problems"
- "I'm not able to make the kids feel secure and loved"
- "I've lost confidence in my ability to parent"
- "I've failed my children"
- "I'm not the example I should be"
- "Seeing my own bad habits and character traits in my children"
- "My inability to relate to my children"

- "The guilt I feel when it seems that I have failed my daughters"
- "My inability to cope"
- "Knowing it's too late to go back and do it right"
- "I'm overwhelmed by the responsibility of it all"

Isn't it incredible to observe just how tentative we have become about this task of raising children? Parenting is hardly a new technology. Since Adam and Eve graced the Garden, perhaps 15 billion people have lived on this earth, yet we've become increasingly nervous about bringing up the baby. It is a sign of the times.

Q UESTION 78

Why do you think parents are so quick to criticize themselves? What is the source of the self-doubt you mentioned?

It is a cultural phenomenon. Mothers, especially, have been blamed for everything that can conceivably go wrong with children. Even when their love and commitment are incalculable, the experts accuse them of making grievous errors in toilet training, disciplining, feeding, medicating, and educating their youngsters. They are either over-possessive or undernurturing. Their approach is either harsh or permissive. One psychiatrist even wrote an entire book on the dangers of religious training, blaming parents for scaring kids with talk of the next world. Thus, no matter how diligently Mom approaches her parenting responsibilities, she is likely to be accused of twisting and warping her children.

Perhaps this explains why women are more critical of themselves than men. Eighty percent of the respondents to our poll were women, and their most frequent comment was "I'm a failure as a mother!" What nonsense! Women have been taught to think of themselves in this way, and it is time to set the record straight.

The task of procreation was never intended to be so burdensome. Of course it is demanding. And children are challenging, to be sure. But the guilt and self-doubt that often encumber the parenting responsibility are not part of the divine plan. Throughout the Scriptures, the raising of children is presented as a wonderful blessing from God—a welcome, joyful experience. And today, it remains one of the greatest privileges in living to bring a baby into the world to love and care for. What a wonderful opportunity it is to teach these little ones to revere God with all their hearts and to serve others throughout their lives. There is no higher calling than that!

QUESTION 79

I don't believe my parents went through this kind of anxiety when my sisters and I were young. We were all relatively happy, and none of us rebelled. Am I right in assuming that a good family life was easier to achieve in those days?

I'm sure your memory is generally correct despite the exceptions we can all recall. The majority of parents in earlier years spent less energy worrying about their children. They had other things on their minds. I remember talking to my dad about this subject a few years before his death. Our children were young at the time, and I, like you, was feeling the heavy responsibility of raising them properly.

I turned to my father and asked, "Do you remember worrying about me when I was a kid? Did you think about all the things that could go wrong as I came through the adolescent years? How did you feel about these pressures associated with being a father?"

Dad was rather embarrassed by my question. He smiled sheepishly and said, "Honestly, Bo," (his pet name for me) "I never really gave that a thought."

How do we explain his lack of concern? Was it because he didn't love me or because he was an uninvolved parent? No. He prayed for me until the day he died. And as I have said on many occasions, he was a wonderful father to me. Instead, his answer reflected the time in which I grew up. People worried about the depression that was just ending, and the war with Germany and Japan, and later the cold war with Russia. They did not invest much effort in hand-wringing over their children . . . at least not until some kind of problem developed. Trouble was not anticipated.

And why not? Because there were fewer land mines for kids in that era. I attended high school during the "Happy Days" of the 1950s, and

I never saw or even heard of anyone taking an illegal drug. It happened, I suppose, but it was certainly no threat to me. Some students liked to get drunk, but alcohol was not a big deal in my social environment. Others played around with sex, but the girls who did were considered "loose" and were not respected. Virginity was still in style for males and females. Occasionally a girl came up pregnant, but she was packed off in a hurry, and I never knew where she went. As for homosexuals and lesbians, I heard there were a few around, but I didn't know them personally. There were certainly no posters on our bulletin boards advertising Gay Pride Month or Condom Week. Most of my friends respected their parents, went to church on Sundays, studied hard enough to get by, and lived fairly clean lives. There were exceptions, of course, but this was the norm.

Today's kids, by contrast, are walking through the valley of the shadow! Drugs, sex, alcohol, rebellion, and deviant lifestyles are everywhere. Those dangers have never been as evident as they are now, and the worst may be yet to come.

QUESTION 80

What does behavioral research tell us about the best way to raise children? Have scientific studies spelled out what works and what doesn't, especially regarding how to discipline properly?

My answer may sound like heresy coming from a man who spent ten years of his life as a professor of pediatrics, responsible for medical and behavioral research, but I don't believe the scientific community is capable of determining the best parenting techniques. There have been some worthwhile studies, to be sure, but the subject of discipline almost defies definitive investigation.

Why? Because the only way to study this topic scientifically would be to place newborns randomly in "permissive" vs. "disciplined" families and then keep them under close observation for ten or fifteen years. Since it is impossible to do that, researchers have tried to tease out information where they could find it. But family relationships are so multidimensional and complicated that they almost defy rigorous scrutiny. Indeed, most of the studies reported in the literature are scientifically useless. For example, Dr. David Larson, psychiatrist and formerly a researcher at the National Institutes of Health, reviewed 132 articles in professional journals that purported to investigate the long-term consequences of corporal punishment. He found most of them flawed in design. Ninety percent of the studies failed to distinguish between good homes where spanking was administered by loving parents, and those bordering on (or actually inflicting) child abuse. This distinction is critical for obvious reasons. Dr. Larson concluded that the findings were invalidated by this failure to consider the overall health of family relationships.[28]

To repeat, the consequences of various approaches to parental discipline appear to be beyond the reach of social research. It is simply not possible to study this complex subject scientifically without warping families to set up the research design. Even if such studies were conducted, the researchers would be studying contrived families—not typical parent-child relationships.

Q UESTION **81**

My wife and I are keenly aware of how difficult it is to be good parents, and at times, we feel very inadequate to do the job. How does a mom or dad know what's best for a child from day to day?

The most dedicated parents go through times when they fear they aren't responding properly to their children. They wonder if they're overreacting or underreacting, being too strict or too lenient. They suspect that they're making major mistakes that will haunt them later on. Fortunately, parents don't have to do everything right. We all make thousands of little mistakes—and a few big ones—that we wish we could reverse. But somehow, most kids roll with these blunders and come out just fine anyway.

Let me give you what I consider to be the key to good parenting. It is to learn how to get behind the eyes of your child, seeing what he sees and feeling what he feels. When you know his frame of mind, your response becomes obvious. For example, when he's lonely, he needs your company. When he's defiant, he needs your help in controlling impulses. When he's afraid, he needs the security of your embrace. When he's happy, he needs to share his laughter and joy with those he loves. Raising healthy children, then, is not so much a science as it is a highly developed art, and most of us have the natural intuitive faculties to learn it.

Take the time to observe those kids who live in your house. If you tune in closely to what they say and do, the feelings behind those behaviors will soon become apparent. Then your reaction to what you've seen will lead to more confident parenthood.

QUESTION 82

My husband's parents are wonderful people, and we love them very much. They have always refrained from interfering in our family; that is, until our daughter was born. Now they're arguing with us about how we're raising her and are undermining the things we're trying to teach. We want to base Amy's upbringing on biblical principles, but not being Christians, my in-laws don't really understand this. How can we deal with this situation without offending them?

It is time to have a loving but candid conversation with your in-laws about how your child will be raised. I would suggest that you take them to dinner some evening, during which this topic will be addressed. When the moment is right, tell them of your concerns. Make it clear that you love them and want them to enjoy their granddaughter. But the responsibility for how she is being managed must rest entirely with you and your husband. Remind them that they had their day—when the decisions about child rearing were theirs alone. Spell out the issues that mean the most to you, including your desire to raise your daughter according to Christian principles. Try to help them understand your reasons, but recognize that their worldview might make it impossible for them to agree. If that is the case, they'll need to honor your wishes anyway.

It is likely that sparks will fly during this conversation. If so, try to remain calm and stand your ground. If the worst occurs and the dinner ends in an emotional walkout, I suggest that you give your in-laws

82

some space while they're cooling off. When you do come back together, let love and respect continue to be your guides—but don't back off on the issue at hand. You have the right to do what you're doing. Your in-laws are the ones who are out of line. But remember that Amy needs her grandparents, and your goal should be to harmonize your relationship. In most cases, that will occur in time.

Q UESTION 83

Should schoolchildren be required to wear clothes that they dislike?

Generally not. Children are very concerned about the threat of being laughed at by their friends and will sometimes go to great lengths to avoid that danger. Conformity is fueled by the fear of ridicule. Teens, particularly, seem to feel, *The group can't laugh at me if I am identical to them.* From this perspective, it's unwise to make a child endure unnecessary social humiliation. Children should be allowed to select their own clothes, within certain limits of budget and good taste.

Q UESTION 84

Do you think children between five and ten should be allowed to listen to rock music on the radio, TV, or CDs?

Not if it can be avoided. Today's contemporary music is an expression of an increasingly unsavory adolescent culture. The lyrics often deal with drug use, sex, and violence. This is just what you don't want your seven-year-old thinking about. Instead, his or her entertainment should consist of adventure books, children's productions, Bible stories and other Christian literature, and family activities—camping, fishing, sporting events, games, etc.

    On the other hand, it is unwise to appear dictatorial and oppressive in such matters. I would suggest that you keep your preteen so involved with wholesome activities that he does not need to dream of the days to come.

Question 85

It seems to me that children are far too familiar—too informal—with adults today. When I was a kid, we always addressed grown-ups as "Mr." or "Mrs.," or if they were in the family, we called them "Uncle" or "Aunt" or "Grandpa" or "Grandma." We would never have referred to an adult as Sam or Alice. But today's parents don't teach that courtesy to their children. Some of them introduce other adults to four-year-olds by their first names. Am I the only one who is concerned about this? What can I do to counteract this trend with my own son and daughter?

I've been bothered by that same observation. It's a by-product of a cultural shift within society itself. We are less respectful of one another today in many ways. Fifty years ago, for example, men didn't curse around women, and cultured women didn't curse at all. How that has changed! Both men and women used to address each other with formal titles (Mr., Mrs., Miss, etc.) unless they had become very close friends. Now, a waitress whom you've never met approaches your table and says, "Hi, I'm Stephanie, and I'm going to be serving you today."

I don't suppose today's informality is harmful, although I agree that children should be taught to speak to their elders with a certain deference. I still like to hear them respond with "Yes, ma'am" and "No, sir," instead of "yeah," "yep," and "nope." When their manners are respectful, their entire demeanor is on a higher plane.

As for how you can instill these and other courtesies in your child, you simply make up your mind to do it. You might explain that there are many things your family does differently than others: For example, "We don't use bad language, we don't attend certain kinds of movies, and we don't (fill in the blank). Why? Because we've set a higher standard for ourselves. This is what makes us unique as a family, and we believe it is what God would have us do. Someday you will understand that, too."

84

Q UESTION 86

We are not able financially to take long car trips or get into expensive hobbies, like skiing. Could you suggest some simple traditions that will appeal to small children?

You don't have to spend huge amounts of money to have a meaningful family life. Children love the most simple, repetitive kinds of activities. They want to be read the same stories hundreds of times and to hear the same jokes long after they've heard the punch lines. These interactions with parents are often more fun than expensive toys or special events.

A friend of mine once asked his grown children what they remembered most fondly from their childhoods. Was it the vacations they took together or the trips to Disney World or the zoo? No, they told him. It was when he would get on the floor and wrestle with the four of them. They would gang-tackle the "old man" and laugh until their sides hurt. That's the way children think. The most meaningful activities within families are often those that focus on that which is spontaneous and personal.

This is why you can't buy your way out of parenting responsibilities, though many have tried. Busy and exhausted mothers and fathers, especially those who are affluent, sometimes attempt to "pay off" their deprived kids with toys, cars, and expensive experiences. It rarely works. What boys and girls want most is time spent with their parents—building things in the garage or singing in the car or hiking to an old fishing pond.

I would also recommend reserving at least one night a week for reading out loud with the family. That can be difficult to accomplish with children of varying ages. If your sons and daughters are clustered in age, I think it's a great activity. You can read *Tom Sawyer, Little House on the Prairie, Stuart Little,* and other books that have been so popular down through the years. The idea is to read together as a family.

In short, many families have forgotten how to have fun in everyday experiences. The things they do together can become hallmarks of their years together. No toy to be played with alone can ever compete with the enjoyment of such moments. And they will be remembered for a lifetime.

QUESTION 87

We have an adopted girl who came to us when she was four years old. She is very difficult to handle and does pretty much what she pleases. For us to make her obey would be very unpleasant for her, and frankly, we don't feel we have the right to do that. She has been through a lot in her short life. Besides, we're not her real parents. Do you think she'll be OK if we just give her a lot of love and attention?

I'm afraid you have a formula for serious problems with this girl later on. The danger is in seeing yourselves as substitute or stand-in parents who don't have the right to lead her. That is a mistake. Since you have legally adopted this child, you *are* her "real" parents, and your failure to see it that way may be setting up the defiant behavior you mentioned. It is a common error made by parents of older adopted children. They pity their youngsters too much to confront them. They feel that life has already been too hard on them, and they must not make things worse by discipline and occasional punishment. As a result, they are tentative and permissive with a child who is crying out for leadership.

Transplanted children have the same needs for guidance and discipline as those remaining with their biological parents. One of the surest ways to make them feel insecure is to treat them as though they are different, unusual, or brittle. If the parents view such a child as an unfortunate waif to be shielded, he will tend to see himself that way too.

Parents of sick and disabled children often make this same mistake. They find discipline harder to implement because of the tenderness they feel for that child. Thus, a boy or girl with a heart condition or some terminal illness can become a little terror, simply because the usual behavioral boundaries are not established and defended. It must be remembered that the need to be led and governed is almost universal in childhood, and it isn't lessened by other problems and difficulties in life. In some cases, the desire for boundaries is actually increased by other troubles, for it is through loving control that parents build security and a sense of personal worth in a child.

Returning to the question, I advise you to love that little girl like crazy—and hold her to the same standards of behavior that you would your own flesh and blood. Remember, you *are* her parents!

QUESTION 88

Are adopted children more likely to be rebellious than children raised by biological parents? If so, are there any steps I can take to prevent or ease the conflict? My husband and I are thinking about adopting a toddler, and the question has me worried.

Every child is different, and adopted kids are no exception. They come in all sorts of packages. Some boys and girls who were abused or unloved prior to the adoption will react to those painful experiences in some way . . . usually negatively. Others, even those who were not mistreated, will struggle with identity problems and wonder why their "real" mothers and fathers didn't want them. They may be driven to find their biological parents during or after adolescence to learn more about their heritage and family of origin. I must emphasize, however, that many adopted kids do not go through any of these personal crises. They take root where they are replanted and never give a thought to the questions that trouble some of their peers. As with so many other behavioral issues, the critical factors are the particular temperament of the child and how he or she is handled by the parents.

I hope you won't be reluctant to adopt that child because some special problems might—but probably won't—develop. *Every* child has his or her own particular challenges. *Every* child can be difficult to raise. *Every* child requires all the creative energy and talent a parent can muster. But *every* child is also worth the effort, and there is no higher calling than to do that job excellently.

Let me add one more thought. I knew a man and woman who had waited for years to adopt a baby. When a female infant was finally made available to them, they were anxious to know if she was healthy and of good heritage. They asked if her biological parents had used drugs, how tall they were, whether or not they had attended college, etc. Then, the father told me later, he realized what he and his wife were doing. They were approaching the adoption of this baby much like they would have bought a used car. They were "kicking tires" and "testing the engine." But then they thought, *What in the world are we doing? That little girl is a human being with an eternal soul. We have been given the opportunity to mold and shape her as a child of God, and here we are demanding that she be a high-quality product.* They repented of their inappropriate attitudes and embraced that child in love.

Adopted children, like all children, are a blessing from God, and we are privileged indeed to be granted the honor of raising one of His precious kids.

QUESTION 89

How would you go about telling a child he or she is adopted, and when should that disclosure occur?

First, begin talking to your toddlers about their adoption before they can understand the meaning of the words. That way there will never be a moment when disclosure is necessary. To learn of adoption from a neighbor or other family member can be an awful shock to an individual. Don't risk the devastation of a later discovery by failing to take the sting out of the issue in babyhood.

Second, celebrate two birthdays with equal gusto each year: the anniversary of her birth, and the anniversary of the day she became your daughter. That is a handy mechanism by which the fact of adoption can be introduced. It also provides a way to equalize the status of siblings. Biological children have a psychological advantage that they sometimes lord over their adopted brother or sister. That one-upmanship is neutralized somewhat when the adopted child gets a second birthday.

Third, present the adoptive event as a tremendous blessing (as implied above) that brought great excitement to the household. Tell about praying for a child and waiting patiently for God's answer. Then describe how the news came that the Lord had answered those prayers and how the whole family thanked Him for His gift of love. Let your child know your delight when you first saw him lying in a crib, and how cute he looked in his blue blanket, etc. Tell him that his adoption was one of the happiest days of your life, and how you raced to the telephone to call all your friends and family members to share the fantastic news. (Again, I'm assuming that these details are true.)

Tell him the story of Moses' adoption by Pharaoh's daughter, and how God chose him for a great work with the children of Israel. Look for similar situations that convey respect and dignity to the adoptee. You see, the child's interpretation of the adoptive event is almost totally dependent on the manner in which it is conveyed during the early years. Most certainly, one does not want to approach the subject sadly, admitting reluctantly that a dark and troublesome secret must now be confessed.

Fourth, when the foundation has been laid and the issue defused, then forget it. Don't constantly remind the child of his uniqueness to the point of foolishness. Mention the matter when it is appropriate, but don't reveal anxiety or tension by constantly throwing adoption in the child's face. Youngsters are amazingly perceptive at reading these thinly disguised attitudes.

I believe it is possible, by following these commonsense suggestions, to raise an adopted child without psychological trauma or personal insult.

QUESTION 90

What should you tell an adopted child about his or her biological parents in "closed" adoption situations? How do you answer his tough questions about why he wasn't wanted, etc.?

I'll give you an answer written by Dr. Milton Levine in a vintage parenting book entitled *Your Child from Two to Five*, then I'll comment on his recommendation. Dr. Levine was Associate Professor of Pediatrics, New York Hospital, at the time. He listed three possible ways to tell an adopted child about his origin, as follows:

1. Tell the child his biological parents are dead.
2. State plainly that the biological parents were unable to care for their baby themselves.
3. Tell the child nothing is known about the biological parents but that he was secured from an agency dedicated to finding good homes for babies.

Dr. Levine preferred the first approach because "the child who is told that his biological parents are dead is free to love the mother and father he lives with. He won't be tormented by a haunting obligation to search for his biological parents when he's grown."

He continued, "Since the possibility of losing one's parents is one of childhood's greatest fears, it is true that the youngster who is told that his biological parents are dead may feel that all parents, including his second set, are pretty impermanent. Nevertheless, I feel that in the long run the child will find it easier to adjust to death than to abandonment. To tell a youngster that his parents gave him up because they were unable to take care of him is to present him with a complete rejection. He cannot comprehend the circumstances which might lead to such an act. But an unwholesome view of himself as an unwanted object, not worth fighting to keep, might be established."[29]

I disagree with Dr. Levine at this point. I am unwilling to lie to my child about anything and would not tell him that his natural parents were dead if that were not true. Sooner or later, he will learn that he has been misled, which could undermine our relationship and bring the entire adoption story under suspicion.

Instead, I would be inclined to tell the child that very little is known about his biological parents. Several inoffensive and vague possibilities could be offered to him, such as, "We can only guess at the reasons the man and woman could not raise you. They may have been extremely poor and were unable to give you the care you needed, or maybe the woman was sick, or she may not have had a home. We just don't know. But there is one thing we *do* know. She must have loved you very, very much—enough to give you life and to make sure you were raised in a loving home where you would be taken care of. We're so thankful that the Lord led her to let us raise you."

QUESTION 91

Are there times when good, loving parents don't like their own kids very much?

Yes, just as there are times in a good marriage when husbands and wives don't like each other for a while. What you should do in both situations is hang tough. Look for ways to make the relationship better, but never give up your commitment to one another. That is especially true during the teen years, when the person we see will be very different in a few years. Wait patiently for him or her to grow up. You'll be glad you did.

QUESTION 92

Don't you think most of the differences between the sexes result from cultural conditioning? If we would raise boys and girls the same way, these differences would disappear.

I couldn't disagree more. God created two sexes, not one. He built genetic characteristics in males and females that no amount of training in childhood will eliminate. Let me quote Christina Hoff Sommers, author of *Who Stole Feminism?* She wrote:

> The feminist fight against the facts of life is unceasing. Last year, Hasbro Toys tested a doll house they were considering marketing to both boys and girls. The Hasbro researchers found that girls and boys did not interact with the doll house in the same way. The girls dressed the dolls and played house; the boys catapulted the baby carriage from the roof. Sharon Hartley, a Hasbro general manager, explained what in prior times would have been considered obvious: "Boys and girls have different play patterns."
>
> Despite the overwhelming evidence that males' and females' brains are wired differently, feminists still cling to the mistaken belief that cultural influences are all that separate them. They are wrong. Nevertheless, Gloria Steinem still believes "We badly need to raise our boys more like girls."[30]

There used to be an old proverb that proclaimed "Boys will be boys." Guess what? It's true. And girls will be girls. That's the way they're made.

QUESTION 93

Is there a way I as a father can influence my daughter's attitude toward boys? If she chooses to marry, she will need to understand men and know how to relate to them. Is that something I should be thinking about?

You bet it is. Long before a girl finds her first real boyfriend or falls in love, her attitude toward men has been shaped quietly by her father. Why? Because the father-daughter relationship sets the stage for all future romantic involvements.

If a young woman's father rejects her, she'll spend her life trying to find a man who can meet the needs he never fulfilled in her heart. If he's warm and nurturing, she'll look for a lover to equal him. If he thinks she's beautiful and feminine, she'll be inclined to see herself that way. But if he rejects her as unattractive and uninteresting, she's likely to carry self-image problems into her adult years.

It's also true that a woman's relationship with her husband is significantly influenced by the way she perceived her father's authority. If he was overbearing or capricious during her earlier years, she may precipitate power struggles with her husband throughout married life. But if Dad blended love and discipline in a way that conveyed strength, she may be more comfortable with a give-and-take marriage characterized by mutual respect.

So much of what goes into marriage starts with the bride's father. That's why it behooves those of us with daughters to give our best effort to raising them properly. You are right to be thinking about that vital relationship.

92

QUESTION 94

When do children begin to develop a sexual nature? Does this occur suddenly during puberty?

No, it occurs long before puberty. Perhaps the most important concept suggested by Freud was his observation that children are not asexual. He stated that sexual gratification begins in the cradle and is first associated with feeding.[31] Behavior during childhood is influenced considerably by sexual curiosity and interest, although the happy hormones do not take full charge until early adolescence. Thus, it is not uncommon for a four-year-old to be interested in nudity and the sexual apparatus of the opposite sex.

The elementary school years are an important time in the forming of sexual attitudes. Parents should be careful not to express shock and disgust over this kind of curiosity, even though they have to disapprove of exploratory behavior. It is believed that many sexual problems begin as a result of inappropriate training during early childhood.

*Q*UESTION 95

My four-year-old has recently "discovered" his penis and seems rather preoccupied with it. Do you think it's unusual or sinful for him to fondle himself so much?

The answer to both of your questions is an emphatic no! Unintentional (or even intentional) self-arousal in young children, specifically boys, is neither unusual nor sinful. Your little guy is simply showing that he is "properly wired." There are no long-term consequences to this kind of innocent childish behavior, and it will soon resolve itself.

The only significance to early fondling activity is in how you as a parent deal with it. I've received letters from mothers who say they have spanked their preschoolers for touching themselves. Some have described great concerns about this behavior, seeing it as evidence of an immoral nature that had to be crushed. That is a very dangerous posture to take. I suggest that you not make a big deal over it.

*Q*UESTION 96

That's easy for you to say. My four-year-old daughter doesn't just fondle herself at home, where we ignore it. She rubs

herself whenever we are in public, such as at church or at a restaurant. How should I deal with that?

You should respond as a teacher, not a disciplinarian. Take your daughter aside and talk about your concern. Explain that there are some things that we don't do in public—not because they are wrong, but because they are impolite. Just as you wouldn't urinate in front of other people, you should not be touching yourself when others can see you. If she continues to fondle herself, other people will think she is strange and some may laugh at her—something you're sure she wouldn't like. Your purpose in speaking this way is to sensitize her to the social implications involved in what she's doing. Show yourself to be firm and confident, not shocked or embarrassed.

The key to your approach is the avoidance of any suggestion that her body is dirty or "wrong" or evil. Such an implication might raise a whole host of other problems for your child that could carry over into adolescence and even adulthood.

QUESTION 97

I am concerned about the impact of television in our home. How can we control it without resorting to dictatorial rules and regulations?

It seems that we have three objectives as parents: First, we want to monitor the quality of the programs our children watch. Second, we want to regulate the quantity of television they see. Even good programs may have an undesirable influence on the rest of children's activities if they spend too much time watching them. Third, we should include the entire family in establishing a TV policy.

I read about a system recently that is very effective in accomplishing all three of these purposes. First, it was suggested that parents sit down with the children and agree upon a list of approved programs that are appropriate for each age level. Then type that list (or at least write it clearly) and enclose it in clear plastic so it can be referred to throughout the week.

Second, either purchase or make a roll of tickets. Issue each child ten tickets per week, and let him or her use them to "buy" the privilege of watching the programs on the approved list. When the tickets are gone, television viewing is over for that week. This teaches a child to be discriminating about what is watched. A maximum of ten hours of viewing per week might be an appropriate place to start, compared with the national average of forty to fifty hours per week. That's far too much, especially for an elementary school child.

This system can be modified to fit individual home situations or circumstances. If there's a special program that all the children want to see, such as a feature broadcast or a holiday program during Christmas and Thanksgiving, you can issue more tickets. You might also give extra tickets as rewards for achievement or some other laudable behavior.

The real test will occur when parents reveal whether or not they have the courage to put themselves on that limited system, too. We often need the same regulations in our viewing habits!

Q UESTION 98

I am very irritated by all the sex and violence on television night after night. The movies are bad enough, but now the sitcoms are just as bad. Is there any way we can influence the networks to be more responsible in their programming?

We have more power to influence television programming than we think. I'm told that every letter received is estimated to represent forty thousand viewers who didn't take time to write. It's important to know, however, where those letters should be sent. In earlier days, I wrote directors, producers, and other executives at the television networks. My complaints either received rude replies or were largely ignored. I've since learned it's more beneficial to write the sponsors—the people who pay the bills. They have better reason to care what I think.

Witness the success of Fort Worth dentist Dr. Richard Neill, who became upset with the kind of filthy programming aired regularly on the *Phil Donahue* show during hours when children could have been watching. He began writing the commercial sponsors and informing them of what their money was supporting. One after another, more than one hundred of these advertisers began dropping the show. By 1996, the Donahue program was no longer viable, and it went off the air. Almost single-handedly, Dr. Neill took on a media giant—an icon—and put an end to the junk he was producing.[32] This kind of effort can and should be duplicated all over the country. It is the only way we will clean up the tube.

Advertisers are very responsive to the opinions of viewers because they are spending millions of dollars to promote their products. We can bring pressure on them by letting them know how we feel—positively and negatively. And indeed, we must do this.

Q UESTION 99

The children who play with my kids in the neighborhood are familiar with terrible programs on television and cable. I can't believe that their parents let them watch such violent and sexualized stuff. What is the long-term consequence of this programming on children?

It is sad and very difficult to understand why so many parents fail to supervise what their kids watch. To those who let them watch anything they wish, I would pose this proposition: Suppose a complete stranger came to your door and said, "You look tired. Why don't you let me take care of your children for a day or two?" I doubt if many of you would say, "Great idea. Come on in."[33]

That's a story Peggy Charren, president of Action for Children's Television, likes to tell. Her point is well taken. When we sit our children in front of the television set, we're giving control over them to complete strangers; and more and more, that's a risky thing to do. An increasing number of studies have found that violence on television frequently leads to later aggressive behavior by children and teenagers.

One of the most conclusive studies was conducted by Dr. Leonard D. Aaron. He examined a group of children at age eight and then again at nineteen and finally at thirty. Children in the United States, Australia, Finland, Israel, and Poland were studied. The outcome was the same; the more frequently the participants watched violent television at age eight, the more likely they were to be convicted of crimes by age thirty, and the more aggressive was their behavior when drinking.[34]

It's time for parents to control the amount and the content of television that their children are watching. The consequences of not doing so can be catastrophic.

QUESTION 100

What is your opinion of Nintendo and other kinds of video games? They've been claiming a big portion of our son's time over the past few months, and I'm getting uneasy about it.

Depending on the particular games in question, you may have a valid cause for concern. Dr. Vince Hammond, head of the National Coalition on Television Violence, has described the potentially harmful nature of video games, especially those with violent themes.[35] Some observers have come to the conclusion that these games can become obsessive and encourage aggressive behavior. There's even evidence to suggest that children between the ages of eight and ten are 80 percent more likely to fight with one another after playing with them.[36]

I'd advise you to put clear limits on the amount of time your son will be allowed to spend with video games or the Internet so that he won't become obsessed with them. Insist that he avoid the violent ones altogether. With realistic guidelines I think it's possible to keep this kind of activity under control rather than let it control your son and your family.

QUESTION 101

What's the appeal of all this human suffering and violence on television and in movies? Why do people want more of it?

I'm sure it has something to do with our desire for excitement and our need to escape from the boring existence many people experience. But I have to admit I don't fully understand it. It is difficult to comprehend why people enjoy watching such bloody events. A number of years ago, the number one television program of the entire year, watched by more people than all the sporting events or any other single program in the course of the twelve-month period, was *Helter-Skelter*, the story of the Charles Manson family.[37] One incident in that TV special was the murder of a woman, eight-months pregnant, who was brutally stabbed in the abdomen. Why would anyone want to see such brutality? The popularity of that program and others like it speaks dramatically about the depravity of the American people and our lust for violence.

QUESTION 102

What do you think it will do to us to continue watching extreme violence night after night?

Walter Lippman once wrote that a saturation of this kind of sensationalism can actually destroy a people and a culture. I agree with him completely. We've already come to the point where decent people are afraid to go outdoors at night. We live in terror. No one is safe, not even old people who have so little that criminals really want. Television *does* have the power to destroy us as a nation. I fear it may already have damaged us beyond repair.

QUESTION 103

I have a friend who guards her kids as if they were in mortal danger. I feel like I should let my daughters spread their wings a little, even though they're only nine and eleven years of age. Who do you think is right?

Two decades ago I would have suggested that you give them space, because overprotection of children creates some characteristic problems. Today, however, I have to agree with your friend. The environment in which children are being raised has changed dramatically in recent years. Unspeakable dangers that were almost unheard of a generation ago haunt our schools and streets. Yesterday's families didn't worry much about drive-by shootings, illegal drugs, sexual molesters, and kidnappers. When I was a kid in the early 1950s, my folks were more concerned about a disease called polio than all sources of violence combined. As a ten-year-old, I moved freely around my hometown. If I was a half hour late coming home for dinner, the Dobson household was not seized by panic. But now we worry about our kids playing in the front yard. Indeed, little Polly Klaas was abducted in 1993 from her bedroom, where she was surrounded by friends, and then was brutally murdered for the perverse pleasure of her killer. When that horrible news broke, a collective shudder was felt by every loving parent in the nation. Three years later, beautiful little six-year-old JonBenet Ramsey was sexually assaulted and beaten to death in the basement of her own home on Christmas night, 1996. Between these two tragedies and in the years since, tens of thousands of other children were murdered and abducted. During my term of service on the Attorney General's Board on Missing and Exploited Children, I was dismayed by what I saw happening to innocent boys and girls.

There was a time when the culture interceded on behalf of kids to protect them from anything harmful or immoral. Movies were censored, music was monitored, and young couples were chaperoned. But this generation is exposed to every kind of evil and violence. Some boys and girls live in a combat zone. Indeed, a child in the United States is fifteen times more likely to be killed by gunfire than one growing up in Northern Ireland! More American children are shot per year than are police officers![38] Parents in some inner-city neighborhoods make their kids sleep in bathtubs to protect them from stray bullets crashing through the walls. Some mothers keep short leashes on their little ones when walking through malls to protect them from potential molesters. Instruction is given to wide-eyed preschoolers on how to scream when approached by a stranger and how to report unwelcome touches. Many children spend their after-school hours behind bolted doors and barred windows. That is the way it is in most Western nations today, and especially in the United States.

How can you as a parent protect your precious children? By watching them every moment! Never leave them in the care of those whom you don't know personally and aren't sure you can trust. *Do not let teenage boys baby-sit your girls.* I know that is a controversial recommendation, but I've seen too many tragic cases of abuse result-ing from masculine adolescence and the sexual curiosity that is typical of that age. Walk your kids to and from school or the school bus. Pick them up on time. Watch for any unusual behavior that may signal sexual abuse or molestation from neighbors or child-care work-ers. Protect them at every turn.

Does that sound unnecessarily cautious? Just remember this: The average pedophile abuses 150 children in the course of a lifetime.[39] Each sexual exploitation lasts for seven years, typically, before the truth comes to light.[40] Boys and girls are often too intimidated to call for help. Don't give a child abuser a shot at your kids.

As for your own anxieties, I suggest that you take them to the Lord in prayer. He loves your girls even more than you do, and I believe He will help you take care of them. Hold their names before Him every day in prayer. Commit to intercede not only for their physical safety but also for their spiritual welfare. Then when you've done everything you can to be a good parent, put your children in God's hands and let Him help you carry the burden.

7

Disciplining the Elementary School Child

QUESTION 104

Philosophically, I recognize the need to take charge of my kids, but I need more specifics. Give me a step-by-step approach to discipline that will help me do the job correctly.

All right, let me outline six broad guidelines that I think you'll be able to apply. These principles represent the essence of my philosophy of discipline.

First: Define the boundaries before they are enforced. The most important step in any disciplinary procedure is to establish reasonable expectations and boundaries in advance. The child should know what is and what is not acceptable behavior before he is held responsible for those rules. This precondition will eliminate the sense of injustice that a youngster feels when he is slapped or punished for his accidents, mistakes, and blunders. If you haven't defined it—don't enforce it!

Second: When defiantly challenged, respond with confident decisiveness. Once a child understands what is expected, she should then be held accountable for behaving accordingly. That sounds easy, but as we have seen, most children will assault the authority of their elders and challenge their right to lead. In a moment of rebellion, a little child will consider her parents' instructions and defiantly choose to disobey. Like a military general before a battle, she will calculate the potential risk, marshal her forces, and attack the enemy with guns blazing. When that nose-to-nose confrontation occurs between generations, it is extremely important for the adult to win decisively and confidently. The child has made it clear that she's looking for a fight, and her parents would be wise not to disappoint her! Nothing is more destructive to parental leadership than for a mother or father to disintegrate during that struggle. When parents consistently lose those battles, resorting to tears and screaming and other evidence of frustration, some dramatic changes take place in the way they are seen by their children. Instead of being secure and confident leaders, they become spineless jellyfish who are unworthy of respect or allegiance.

Third: Distinguish between willful defiance and childish irresponsibility. A child should not be punished for behavior that is not willfully defiant. When he forgets to feed the dog or make his bed or take out the trash—when he leaves your tennis racket outside in the rain or loses his bicycle—remember that these behaviors are typical of childhood. It is the mechanism by which an immature mind is protected from adult anxieties and pressures. Be gentle as you teach him to do better. If he fails to respond to your patient instruction, it then becomes appropriate to administer some well-deserved consequences (he may have to work to pay for the item he abused or be deprived of its use, etc.). Just remember that childish irresponsibility is very different from willful defiance and should be handled more patiently.

Fourth: Reassure and teach as soon as the confrontation is over. After a time of conflict during which the parent has demonstrated his or her right to lead (particularly if it resulted in tears for the child), the youngster between two and seven (or older) may want to be loved and reassured. By all means, open your arms and let her come! Hold her close and tell her of your love. Rock her gently and let her know, again, why she was punished and how she can avoid the trouble next time. This moment of communication builds love, fidelity, and family unity. And for the Christian family, it is extremely important to pray with the child at that time, admitting to God that we have all sinned and no one is perfect. Divine forgiveness is a marvelous experience even for a very young child.

Fifth: Avoid impossible demands. Be absolutely sure that your child is capable of delivering what you require. Never punish him for wetting the bed involuntarily or for not becoming potty trained by one year of age or for doing poorly in school when he is incapable of academic success. These impossible demands put the child in an unresolvable conflict: There is no way out. That condition brings inevitable damage to human emotional apparatus.

Sixth: Let love be your guide! A relationship that is characterized by genuine love and affection is likely to be a healthy one, even though some parental mistakes and errors are inevitable.

QUESTION 105

I want to manage and lead my strong-willed child properly, but I'm afraid I'll break his spirit and damage him in some way. How can I deal with his misbehavior without hurting his self-concept?

I sense that you do not have a clear understanding of the difference between breaking the spirit and shaping the will of a child. The human spirit, as I have defined it, relates to the self-esteem or the personal worth that a child feels. As such, it is exceedingly fragile at all ages and must be handled with care. You as a parent correctly assume that you can damage your child's spirit quite easily—by ridicule, disrespect, threats to withdraw love, and by verbal rejection. Anything that depreciates his self-worth can be costly to his spirit.

However, while the spirit is brittle and must be treated gently, the will is made of steel. It is one of the few intellectual components that arrives full strength at the moment of birth. In a past issue of *Psychology Today*, this heading described the research findings from a study of infancy: "A baby knows who he is before he has language to tell us so. He reaches deliberately for control of his environment, especially his parents."[41] This scientific disclosure would be no surprise to the parents of a strong-willed infant. They have walked the floor with him in the wee small hours, listening to this tiny dictator as he made his wants and wishes abundantly clear.

Later, some defiant toddlers can become so angry that they are capable of holding their breath until they lose consciousness. Anyone who has ever witnessed this full measure of willful defiance has been shocked by its power. One headstrong three-year-old recently refused to obey a direct command from her mother, saying, "You're just my mommy, you know!" Another mere mommy wrote me that she found herself in a similar confrontation with her three-year-old son over something that she wanted him to eat. He was so enraged by her insistence that he refused to eat or drink anything for two full days. He became weak and lethargic but steadfastly held his ground. The mother was worried and guilt-ridden, as might be expected. Finally, in desperation, the father looked the child in the eyes and convinced him that he was going to receive a well-deserved spanking if he didn't eat his dinner. With that maneuver, the contest was over. The toddler surrendered. He began to consume everything he could get his hands on and virtually emptied the refrigerator.

Now tell me, please, why have so few child-development authorities recognized this willful defiance? Why have they written so little about it? My guess is that the acknowledgment of childish imperfection would not fit neatly with the humanistic notion that little people are infused with sunshine and goodness and merely learn the meaning of selfishness and disobedience. To those who hold that rosy view I can only say, "Take another look!"

Returning to your question, your objective as a parent is to shape the will of your child while leaving his spirit intact.

QUESTION 106

How early in life is a child capable of making a stand like that?

Depending on the temperament of the individual, defiant behavior can be displayed by very young children. A father once told me of taking his three-year-old daughter to a basketball game. The child was, of course, interested in everything in the gym except the athletic contest. The father permitted her to roam freely and climb on the bleachers, but he set up definite limits regarding how far she could stray. He took her by the hand and walked with her to a stripe painted on the gym floor.

"You can play all around the building, Janie, but don't go past this line," he instructed her.

Dad had no sooner returned to his seat than the toddler scurried in the direction of the forbidden territory. She stopped at the border for a moment, then flashed a grin over her shoulder to her father and deliberately placed one foot over the line as if to say, "Whacha gonna do about it?" Virtually every parent the world over has been asked the same question at one time or another. That's the way some kids are made.

QUESTION 107

Are we all rather like that little girl, or is the inclination toward disobedience something people grow out of when they get older?

The entire human race is afflicted with the same rebellious nature, although it takes different forms when we get older. Think about it. The behavior of that child in the gym is not so different from the disobedience of the first family, Adam and Eve. The Creator had told them they could eat anything in the Garden of Eden except the forbidden fruit (i.e., "do not go past this line"). Yet they foolishly disobeyed God and thereby introduced a character flaw into the human race. Perhaps our willful behavior is the essence of original sin, which has infected our species. It certainly explains why I place such stress on the proper response to disobedience during childhood. Rebellion is dangerous, whether it responds to parental leadership or to the authority of God Himself.

QUESTION 108

My little boy always wants to know just how far I will let him go. Once he has tested me and found I'm serious about what I say, he'll usually cooperate at that point. What is going on in his mind?

Your child, like most other kids, has a great need to know where behavioral boundaries are and who has the courage to enforce them. Let me illustrate how that works.

Years ago, during the early days of the progressive-education movement, an enthusiastic theorist decided to take down the chain-link fence that surrounded the nursery-school yard. He thought the children would feel more freedom of movement without that visible barrier surrounding them. When the fence was removed, however, the boys and girls huddled near the center of the play yard. Not only did they not wander away, they didn't even venture to the edge of the grounds. Clearly, there is a security for all of us in defined boundaries. That's why a child will push a parent to the point of exasperation at times. She's testing the resolve of the mother or father and exploring the limits of her world.

Do you want further evidence of this motivation? Consider the relationships within a family where the dad is a firm but loving disciplinarian, the mother is indecisive and weak, and the child is a strong-willed spitfire. Notice how the mother is pushed, challenged, sassed, disobeyed, and insulted—but the father can bring order with a word or two. What is going on here? The child simply understands and accepts Dad's strength. The limits are clear. There is no reason to test him again. But Mom has established no rules, and she is fair game for a fight—every day, if necessary.

The very fact that your child accepts the boundaries you have set tells you that he or she respects you. That youngster will still test the outer limits occasionally to see if the "fence" is still there.

QUESTION 109

I think you are right about the motivation of a strong-willed child. My five-year-old is one of those rambunctious kids who gives us fits. There are times when I think he's trying to take over the entire family. I've never really understood him before, but I guess he just doesn't want anyone telling him what to do.

That is precisely how he feels. It is surprising how commonly this basic impulse of children is overlooked. Indeed, I think the really tough kids understand the struggle for control even better than their parents, who are bogged down with adult responsibilities and worries. Children devote their primary effort to the power game while we grown-ups play only when we must. Sometime you might ask a group of children about the adults who lead them. They will instantly tell you, with one voice, which grown-ups are skilled in handling them and which aren't. Every schoolchild can name the teachers who are in control and those who are intimidated by kids.

One father overheard his five-year-old daughter, Laura, say to her little sister, who was doing something wrong, "Mmmm, I'm going to tell Mommy on you. No! I'll tell Daddy. He's worse!" Laura had evaluated the authority of her two parents and concluded that one was more effective than the other.

This same child was observed by her father to have become especially disobedient and defiant. She was irritating other family members and looking for ways to avoid minding her parents. Her dad decided not to confront her directly but to punish her consistently for every offense until she settled down. Thus, for three or four days, he let Laura get away with nothing. She was spanked, stood in the corner, and sent to her bedroom. Near the end of the fourth day, she was sitting on the bed with her father and younger sister. Without provocation, Laura pulled the hair of the toddler, who was looking at a book. Her dad promptly thumped her on the head with his large hand. Laura did not cry but sat in silence for a moment or two and then said, "Harrumph! All my tricks are not working!"

This is the conclusion you want your strong-willed son to draw: "It's too risky to take on Mom or Dad, so let's get with the program."

Q UESTION 110

Are children *really* that calculating about their misbehavior? If so, I've not understood them at all.

Some are; some aren't. We're talking here about the child who is driven to be his own boss—to take orders from no one. That kid can be very deliberate about his purposes. I had a friend when I was a child who best typified this calculating spirit. Earl was like a military general who had deciphered the enemy code, permitting him to outmaneuver his opponents at every turn. He seemed to know every move his parents were going to make. I once spent the night with him, and after we were tucked into our own twin beds, he gave me an astounding description of his father's temper.

Earl said, "When my dad gets very angry, he uses some really bad words that will amaze you." He gave me three or four startling examples of things his dad would say.

I replied, "I don't believe it!"

Mr. Walker was a very tall, reserved man who seemed to have it all together. I just couldn't conceive of his saying the words Earl had quoted.

"Want me to prove it to you?" said Earl mischievously. "All we have to do is keep on laughing and talking instead of going to sleep. My dad will come and tell us to be quiet over and over, and he'll get madder and madder every time he has to settle us down. Then you'll hear his cuss words. Just wait and see."

I was a bit dubious about this plan, but I did want to see the dignified Mr. Walker at his profane best. So Earl and I kept his poor father running back and forth like a yo-yo for over an hour. And as predicted, he became more intense and angry each time he returned to our bedroom. I was getting very nervous and would have called off the project, but Earl had been through it all before. He kept telling me, "It won't be long now."

Finally, about midnight, it happened. Mr. Walker ran out of patience. He came thundering down the hall toward our room, shaking the entire house as his feet pounded the floor. He burst through the bedroom door and leaped on Earl's bed, flailing at the boy who was safely buried beneath three or four layers of blankets. Then from his lips came a stream of words that had seldom reached my tender ears. I was shocked, but Earl was delighted.

Even while his father was whacking the covers with his hand and screaming his profanity, Earl shouted to me from beneath the blankets, "Did ya hear 'em? Huh? Didn't I tell ya? I told ya he would say it!" It's a wonder that Mr. Walker didn't kill his son that night!

I lay awake in the dark thinking about what had happened and made up my mind never to let a child manipulate me like that when I grew up. Don't you see how important disciplinary techniques are to a boy's or girl's respect for parents? When a forty-five-pound bundle of trouble can deliberately reduce his or her powerful mother or father to a trembling, snarling mass of frustrations, something changes in their relationship. Something precious is lost. The child develops an attitude of contempt that is certain to erupt during the stormy adolescent years to come. I sincerely wish every adult understood that simple characteristic of human nature.

*Q*UESTION 111

I understand your emphasis on a child's being taught to respect the authority of his or her parents. But doesn't that coin have two sides? Don't parents have an equal responsibility to show respect for their children?

They certainly do! The self-concept of a child is extremely fragile, and it must be handled with great care. A youngster should live in complete safety at home, never belittled or embarrassed deliberately, never punished in front of friends, never ridiculed in a way that is hurtful. His strong feelings and requests, even if foolish, should be considered and responded to politely. He should feel that his parents "really do care about me." My point is that respect is *the* critical ingredient in all human relationships, and just as parents should insist on receiving it from their children, they are obligated to model it in return.

*Q*UESTION 112

Sometimes my husband and I disagree on our discipline and argue in front of our children about what is best. Do you think this is damaging?

Yes, I do. You and your husband should present a united front, especially when children are watching. If you disagree on an issue, it can be discussed later in private. Unless the two of you can come to a consensus, your children will begin to perceive that standards of right and wrong are arbitrary. They will also make an "end run" around the tougher parent to get the answers they want. There are even more serious consequences for boys and girls when parents are radically different in their approach.

Here's the point of danger: Some of the most hostile, aggressive teenagers I've seen have come from family constellations where the parents have leaned in opposite directions in their discipline. Suppose the father is unloving and disinterested in the welfare of his kids. His approach is harsh and physical. He comes home tired and may knock them around if they get in his way. The mother is permissive by nature. She worries every day about the lack of love in the father-child relationship. Eventually she sets out to compensate for it. When Dad sends their son to bed without his dinner, Mom slips him milk and cookies. When he says no to a particular request, she finds a way to say yes. She lets the kids get away with murder because it is not in her spirit to confront them.

What happens under these circumstances is that the authority figures in the family contradict and cancel out each other. Consequently, the child is caught in the middle and often grows up hating both. It doesn't always work that way, but the probability for trouble is high. The middle ground between extremes of love and control must be sought if we are to produce healthy, responsible children.

Q UESTION 113

Isn't it our goal to produce children with self-discipline and self-reliance? If so, how does your approach to *external* discipline imposed by parents get translated into *internal* control?

There are many authorities who suggest that parents take a passive approach to their children for the reason implied by your question: They want their kids to discipline themselves. But since young people lack the maturity to generate that self-control, they stumble through childhood without experiencing either internal *or* external discipline. Thus, they enter adult life having never completed an unpleasant assignment or accepted an order that they disliked or yielded to the leadership of their elders. Can we expect such a person to exercise self-discipline in young adulthood? I think not. That individual doesn't even know the meaning of the word.

My belief is that parents should introduce their children to discipline and self-control by any reasonable means available, including the use of external influences, when they are young. By being required to behave responsibly, he gains valuable experience in controlling his own impulses and resources. Then as he grows into the teen years, responsibility is transferred year by year from the shoulders of the parent directly to the child. He is no longer required to do what he has learned during earlier years in hopes that he will want to function on his own initiative. To illustrate, a child should be required to keep his room relatively neat when he is young. Then somewhere during the midteens, his own self-discipline should take over and provide the motivation to continue the task. If it does not, the parent should close the door and let him live in a dump, if that is his choice.

In short, self-discipline does not come automatically to those who have never experienced it. Self-control must be learned, and it must be taught.

Q UESTION 114

You have described the nature of willfully defiant behavior and how parents should handle it. But does all unpleasant behavior result from rebellion and disobedience?

No. Defiance can be very different in origin from the "challenging" response I've been describing. A child's negativism may be caused by frustration, disappointment, fatigue, illness, or rejection and therefore must be interpreted as a warning signal to be heeded. Perhaps the toughest task in parenthood is to recognize the difference between these behavioral messages. A child's resistant behavior always contains a message to his parents, which they must decode before responding.

For example, a disobedient youngster may be saying, "I feel unloved now that I'm stuck with that screaming baby brother. Mom used to care for me; now nobody wants me. I hate everybody." When this kind of message underlies the defiance, the parents should move quickly to pacify its cause. The art of good parenthood, then, revolves around the interpretation of behavior.

Question 115

My six-year-old has suddenly become sassy and disrespectful in her manner at home. She told me to "buzz off" when I asked her to take out the trash, and she calls me names when she gets angry. I feel it is important to permit this emotional outlet, so I haven't tried to suppress it. Do you agree?

I'm afraid I don't. Your daughter is aware of her sudden defiance, and she's waiting to see how far you will let her go. If you don't discourage disrespectful behavior now, you can expect some wild experiences during the adolescent years to come.

With regard to your concern about emotional ventilation, you are right in saying your daughter needs to express her anger. She should be free to say anything to you provided it is said in a respectful manner. It is acceptable to say, "I think you love my brother more than me," or "You weren't fair with me, Mommy." There is a thin line between what is acceptable and unacceptable behavior at this point. The child's expression of strong frustration, even resentment and anger, should be encouraged if it exists. You certainly don't want her to bottle it inside. On the other hand, you should not permit your daughter to resort to name-calling and open rebellion. "Mom, you hurt my feelings in front of my friends" is an acceptable statement. "You stupid idiot, why didn't you shut up when my friends were here?!" is obviously unacceptable.

If approached rationally, as described in the first statement, it would be wise for the mother to sit down and try to understand the child's viewpoint. She should be big enough to apologize to the child if she was wrong. If she feels she was right, however, she should calmly explain why she reacted as she did and tell the child how he or she can avoid a collision next time. It is possible to ventilate feelings without sacrificing parental respect, and the child should be taught how to do it. This communicative tool will be very useful later in life, especially in a possible future marriage.

QUESTION 116

What is the most common error made by parents in disciplining their children?

I would have to say it is the inappropriate use of anger in attempting to manage boys and girls. It is one of the most ineffective methods of attempting to influence human beings (of all ages). Unfortunately, most adults rely primarily on their own emotional response to secure the cooperation of children. One teacher said on a national television program, "I like being a professional educator, but I hate the daily task of teaching. My children are so unruly that I have to stay mad at them all the time just to control the classroom." How utterly frustrating to be required to be mean and angry to do a job year after year. Yet many teachers (and parents) know of no other way to manage children. Believe me, it is exhausting and it doesn't work!

Consider your own motivational system and your own response to the anger of others. Suppose you are driving your automobile home from work this evening and you exceed the speed limit by forty miles per hour. Standing on the street corner is a lone police officer who has not been given the means to arrest you. He has no squad car or motorcycle; he wears no badge, carries no gun, and can write no tickets. All he is commissioned to do is stand on the curb and scream insults as you speed past. Would you slow down just because he turns red in the face and shakes his fist in protest? Of course not! You might wave to him as you streak by. But his anger would achieve little except to make him appear comical and foolish.

On the other hand, nothing influences the way you drive quite like seeing a black-and-white vehicle in hot pursuit with nineteen red and blue lights flashing in the rearview mirror. When you pull your car over to the curb, a dignified, courteous officer approaches the window. He is six-foot-nine, has a voice like the Lone Ranger, and carries a gun on his right hip.

"Sir," he says firmly but politely, "our radar unit indicates that you were traveling sixty-five miles per hour in a twenty-five-miles-per-hour zone. May I see your driver's license, please?" He opens his leather-bound book of citations and leans toward you. He has revealed no hostility and offers no criticism, yet you immediately go to pieces. You fumble nervously to locate the license with that ugly picture on it. Why are your hands moist and your mouth dry? Why is your heart thumping in your throat? Because the course of action that John Law is about to take is notoriously unpleasant. It is that *action* that dramatically affects your future driving habits. Alas, children think and respond in much the same way you do.

Disciplinary *action* influences behavior; anger does not. When it comes to boys and girls, in fact, I am convinced that adult anger incites a malignant kind of disrespect in their minds. They perceive that our frustration is caused by our inability to control the situation. We represent justice to them, yet we're on the verge of tears as we flail the air with our hands and shout empty threats and warnings. Let me ask: Would you respect a superior court judge who behaved that way in administering legal justice? Certainly not. This is why the judicial system is carefully designed to appear objective, rational, and dignified.

I am not recommending that parents and teachers conceal their legitimate emotions from their children. I am not suggesting that we be like bland and unresponsive robots who hold everything inside. There are times when our kids become insulting or disobedient and our irritation is entirely appropriate. In fact, it *should* be revealed, or else we appear artificial and insincere. My point is merely that anger often becomes a tool used for the purpose of influencing behavior. It is ineffective and can be damaging to the relationship between generations. Instead, try taking action that your children will care about. Then administer it with cool.

114

*Q*UESTION 117

I see now that I've been doing many things wrong with my children. Can I undo the harm?

I doubt if it is too late to do things right, although your ability to influence your children lessens with the passage of time. Fortunately we are permitted to make many mistakes with our kids. They are resilient, and they usually survive most of our errors in judgment. It's a good thing they do, because none of us can be a perfect parent. Besides, it's not the occasional mistakes that hurt a child—it is the consistent influence of destructive conditions throughout childhood that does the damage.

QUESTION 118

What place should fear occupy in a child's attitude toward his mother or father?

There is a narrow difference between acceptable, healthy respect and destructive fear. A child should have a general apprehension about the consequences of defying his or her parent. But he or she should not lie awake at night worrying about parental harshness or threats of punishment. Perhaps a crude example will illustrate the difference between these aspects of fear. A busy highway can be a dangerous place to take a walk. In fact, it would be suicidal to stroll down the fast lane of a freeway at 6:00 P.M. on any Friday. I would not be so foolish as to get my exercise in that manner because I have a healthy fear of fast-moving automobiles. However, as long as I don't behave stupidly, I have no cause for alarm. I am not threatened by this source of danger because it only reacts to my willful defiance. Without stretching the analogy too far, I want my child to view me with the same healthy regard. As long as she does not choose to challenge me, openly and willfully, she lives in total safety. She need not duck and flinch when I suddenly scratch my eyebrow. She should have no fear that I will ridicule her or treat her unkindly. She can enjoy complete security and safety—until she defies me. Then she'll have to face the consequences. This concept of fear, which is better labeled "awe" or "respect," is modeled after God's relationship with man. "Fear of God is the beginning of wisdom," we are taught. He is a God of justice, and at the same time, a God of infinite love and mercy. These attributes are complementary and should be represented in our homes.

QUESTION 119

I find I'm more likely to say no to my children than to say yes, even when I don't feel strongly about the permission they are seeking. I wonder why I automatically respond so negatively.

It is easy to fall into the habit of saying no to our kids.

"No, you can't go outside."

"No, you can't have a cookie."

"No, you can't use the telephone."

"No, you can't spend the night with a friend."

We could have answered affirmatively to all of these requests, but we chose almost automatically to respond in the negative. Why? Because we didn't take time to stop and think about the consequences; because the activity could cause us more work or strain; because there could be danger in the request; because our children ask for a thousand favors a day and we find it convenient to refuse them all.

While every child needs to be acquainted with denial of some of his or her more extravagant wishes, there is also a need for parents to consider each request on its own merit. There are so many necessary nos in life that we should say yes whenever we can.

QUESTION 120

The children in our neighborhood are bratty with one another and disrespectful with adults. This upsets me, but I don't know what to do about it. I don't have a right to discipline the children of my neighbors, so they get away with murder. How can I deal with this?

Parents in a neighborhood need to learn to talk to each other about their kids—although that is difficult to do! There is no quicker way to anger one mother than for another woman to criticize her precious cub. It is a delicate subject, indeed. That's why the typical neighborhood is like yours, providing little feedback to parents in regard to the behavior of their children. The kids know there are no lines of communication between adults, and they take advantage of the barrier. What each block needs is a mother who has the courage to say to her neighbors, "I want to be told what my child does when she is beyond her own yard. If she is a brat with other children, I would like to know it. If she is disrespectful with adults, please mention it to me. I will not consider it tattling, and I won't resent your coming to me. I hope I can share my insights regarding your children, too. None of our kids is perfect, and we'll know better how to teach them if we can talk openly to each other as adults."

Until this openness exists between parents living nearby, the children will create and live by their own rules in the neighborhood.

QUESTION 121

My husband and I are divorced, so I have to handle all the discipline of the children myself. How does this change the recommendations you've made about discipline in the home?

Not at all. The principles of good discipline remain the same, regardless of the family setting. The procedures do become somewhat harder for one parent to implement since they have no one to support them when the children become testy. Single mothers and fathers have to play both roles, which is not easily done. Nevertheless, children do not make allowances for difficult circumstances. Parents must earn their respect, or they will not receive it.

QUESTION 122

My little girl, Tara, is sometimes sugar sweet, and other times she is unbearably irritating. How can I get her out of a bad mood when she has not really done anything to deserve punishment?

I would suggest that you take her in your arms and talk to her in this manner: "I don't know whether you've noticed it or not, Tara, but you have two 'personalities.' A personality is a way of acting and talking and behaving. One of your personalities is sweet and loving. No one could possibly be more lovable and happy when this personality is in control. It likes to work and looks for ways to make the rest of the family happy. But all you have to do is press a little red button, *ding*, and out comes another personality. It is cranky and noisy and silly. It wants to fight with your brother and disobey your mom. It gets up grouchy in the morning and complains all day.

"Now, Tara, I know that you can press the button for the neat personality or you can call up the unpleasant one. Sometimes you need help to make you want to press the right button. That's where I come in. If you keep on pressing the wrong button, like you have been today, then I'm going to make you uncomfortable one way or the other. I'm tired of the cranky character, and I want to see the grinny one. Can we make a deal?"

When discipline becomes a game, as in a conversation such as this, then you've achieved your purpose without conflict and animosity.

QUESTION 123

Our six-year-old is extremely negative and disagreeable. He makes the entire family miserable, and our attempts to discipline him have been ineffective. He just happens to have a sour disposition. How should we deal with him?

The objective with such a child is to define the needed changes and then reinforce those improvements when they occur. Unfortunately, attitudes are abstractions that a six-year-old may not fully understand, and you need a system that will clarify the "target" in his or her mind. To help accomplish this, I have developed an Attitude Chart (see illustration), which translates these subtle mannerisms into concrete mathematical terms. Please note: The system that follows would not be appropriate for the child who merely has a bad day, or one whose unpleasantness is associated with illness, fatigue, or environmental circumstances. Rather, it is a remedial tool to help change persistently negative and disrespectful attitudes by making the child conscious of his problem.

The Attitude Chart should be prepared and then reproduced, since

---

MY ATTITUDE CHART ———————

DATE

	EXCELLENT 1	GOOD 2	OKAY 3	BAD 4	TERRIBLE 5
My Attitude toward Mother					
My Attitude toward Dad					
My Attitude toward Sister					
My Attitude toward Friends					
My Attitude toward Work					
My Attitude at Bedtime					

TOTAL POINTS ——————————

CONSEQUENCES

6–9 POINTS   The family will do something fun together

10–18 POINTS   Nothing happens, good or bad

19–20 POINTS   I have to stay in my room for one hour

21–22 POINTS   I get one swat with paddle

23+ POINTS   I get two swats with paddle

---

a separate sheet will be needed every day. Place an X in the appropriate square for each category, and then add the total points earned by bedtime. Although this nightly evaluation process has the appearance of being objective to a child, it is obvious that the parent can influence the outcome by considering it in advance (it's called cheating). Mom or Dad may want Junior to receive eighteen points on the first night, barely missing the punishment but realizing he must stretch the following day. I must emphasize, however, that the system will fail miserably if a naughty child does not receive the punishment he deserves, or if he hustles to improve but does not obtain the family fun he was promised. This approach is nothing more than a method of applying reward and punishment to attitudes in a way that children can understand and remember.

For the child who does not fully comprehend the concept of numbers, it might be helpful to plot the daily totals on a cumulative graph, such as the one provided below.

I don't expect everyone to appreciate this system or to apply it at home. In fact, parents of compliant, happy children will be puzzled as to why it would ever be needed. However, the mothers and fathers of sullen, ill-tempered children will comprehend more quickly. Take it or leave it, as the situation warrants.

Q UESTION 124

I understand reward and punishment with young children work better if they are applied very quickly. Delayed consequences don't have the same impact. If that's true, why don't you think God rewards and punishes us more quickly? Some people seem to get away with bad behavior for years, and the ultimate reward for those who live a Christian life will come only after death. Surely the Lord knows about the importance of immediate reinforcement.

He certainly does. He created the characteristics we only observe and try to understand. So why does He not reinforce the behavior He desires more quickly? I don't know, although the principle of immediate response is acknowledged in Scripture: Solomon, one of the wisest men to ever live, wrote: "When the sentence for a crime is not quickly carried out, the hearts of the people are filled with schemes to do wrong. Although a wicked man commits a hundred crimes and still lives a long time, I know that it will go better with God-fearing men, who are reverent before God" (Ecclesiastes 8:11-12).

The thirty-seventh psalm also dealt with the issue of evil people seeming to prosper despite their wrongdoing. Although they appear to be succeeding, the psalmist assured us that justice will eventually prevail. It is written, "Do not fret when men succeed in their ways, when they carry out their wicked schemes" (37:7). "A little while, and

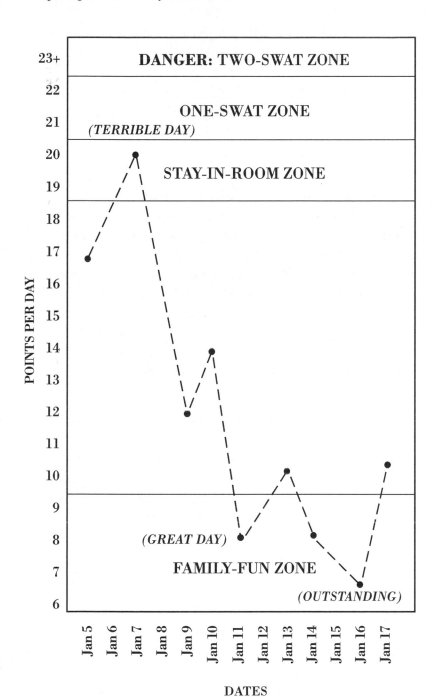

the wicked will be no more; though you look for them, they will not be found. But the meek will inherit the land and enjoy great peace" (37:10-11). Whether the consequences of evil arrive on time or not, the warnings and promises in Scripture are more reliable than anything else in the universe. He will have the last word!

QUESTION 125

I could use some advice about a minor problem we're having. Tim, my six-year-old son, loves to use silly names whenever he speaks to my husband and me. This past week it's been "You big hot dog." Nearly every time he sees me now he says, "Hi, Hot Dog." Before that it was "Dummy," then "Moose" (after he studied *M* for *moose* in school). I know it's silly and it's not a huge problem, but it gets so annoying after such a long time. He's been doing this for a year now. How can we get him to talk to us with more respect, calling us Mom or Dad instead of Hot Dog and Moose?

Ordinarily, it would not be a big deal for a child to use a playful name for his parent. But that isn't what appears to be happening with Tim. It sounds more like a classic power game to me. And contrary to what you said, it is not so insignificant. Your son is continuing to do something that he knows is irritating to you and your husband, yet you are unable to stop him. That is the issue. He has been using humor as a tactic of defiance for a full year.

It is time for you to sit down and have a quiet little talk with young Timothy. Tell him that he is being disrespectful and that the next time he calls either you or his father a name of any kind, he will be punished. You must then be prepared to deliver on the promise, because he will continue to challenge you until it ceases to be fun. That's the way he is made. If that response never comes, his insults will probably become more pronounced. Appeasement for a strong-willed child is an invitation to warfare. This is the time to deal with it.

Q UESTION 126

How can I acquaint my twelve-year-old with the need for responsible behavior throughout his life? He is desperately in need of this understanding.

One important objective during the preadolescent period is to teach the child that actions have inevitable consequences. One of the most serious casualties in a permissive society is the failure to connect those two factors, behavior and consequences. A three-year-old child screams insults at his mother, but Mom stands blinking her eyes in confusion. A first grader defies his teacher, but the school makes allowances for his age and takes no action. A ten-year-old is caught stealing candy in a store but is released to the recognizance of her parents. A fifteen-year-old sneaks the keys to the family car, but her father pays the fine when she is arrested. A seventeen-year-old drives his Chevy like a maniac, and his parents pay for the repairs when he wraps it around a telephone pole. All through childhood, loving parents seem determined to intervene between behavior and consequences, breaking the connection and preventing the valuable learning that could and should have occurred.

Thus, it is possible for a young man or woman to enter adult life not really knowing that life bites—that every move we make directly affects our future—and that irresponsible behavior eventually produces sorrow and pain. Such a person secures his first job and arrives late for work three times during the first week. Later, when he is fired in a flurry of hot words, he becomes bitter and frustrated. It was the first time in his life that Mom and Dad couldn't come running to rescue him from the unpleasant consequences. (Unfortunately, many American parents still try to bail out the grown children even when they are in their twenties and live away from home.) What is the result? This overprotection produces emotional cripples who often develop lasting characteristics of dependency and a kind of perpetual adolescence.

How does one connect behavior with consequences? By being willing to let the child experience a reasonable amount of pain or inconvenience when he behaves irresponsibly. When Jack misses the school bus through his own dawdling, let him walk a mile or two and enter school in midmorning (unless safety factors prevent this). If Janie carelessly loses her lunch money, let her skip a meal. Obviously, it is possible to carry this principle too far, being harsh and inflexible with an immature child. But the best approach is to expect boys and girls to carry the responsibility that is appropriate for their age and occasionally to taste the bitter fruit that irresponsibility bears. In so doing, behavior is wedded to consequences, just like in real life.

QUESTION 127

I have a horrible time getting my ten-year-old daughter ready to catch the school bus each morning. She will get up when I insist, but she dawdles and plays as soon as I leave the room. I have to goad and push and warn her every few minutes or else she will be late. So I get more and more angry and usually end up screaming insults at her. I know this is not the best way to handle the situation, but I declare, she makes me want to clobber her. Is there a way I can get her moving without a fight every day?

In a sense, you are perpetuating your daughter's folly by assuming the responsibility for getting her ready each morning. A ten-year-old should definitely be able to handle that task on her own initiative, but your anger is not likely to bring it about. We had a very similar problem with our own daughter when she was ten. Perhaps the solution we worked out will be helpful to you.

Danae's morning time problem related primarily to her compulsivity about her room. She would not leave for school each day unless her bed was made perfectly and every trinket was in its proper place. This was not something we taught her; she has always been very meticulous about her possessions. Danae could easily finish these tasks on time if she was motivated to do so, but she was never in a particular hurry. Therefore, my wife began to fall into the same habit you described, warning, threatening, punishing, and ultimately becoming angry as the clock moved toward the deadline.

Shirley and I discussed the problem and agreed that there had to be a better method of getting through the morning. I subsequently created a system that we called "Checkpoints." It worked like this: Danae was instructed to be out of bed and standing upright before six-thirty each morning. It was her responsibility to set her own clock radio and get herself out of bed. If she succeeded in getting up on time (even one minute later was considered a missed item), she immediately went to the kitchen, where a chart was taped to the refrigerator door. She then circled *yes* or *no*, with regard to the first checkpoint for that date. It couldn't have been more simple. She either did or did not get up by six-thirty.

The second checkpoint occurred forty minutes later, at seven-ten. By that time, she was required to have her room straightened to her own satisfaction, be dressed and have her teeth brushed, hair combed, etc., and be ready to begin practicing the piano. Forty minutes was ample time for these tasks, which could actually be done in ten or fifteen minutes if she wanted to hurry. Thus, the only way she could miss the second checkpoint was to ignore it deliberately.

Now, what meaning did the checkpoints have? Did failure to meet them bring anger and wrath and gnashing of teeth? Of course not. The consequences were straightforward and fair. If Danae missed one checkpoint, she was required to go to bed thirty minutes earlier than usual that evening. If she missed two, she hit the "lily whites" an hour before her assigned hour. She was permitted to read during that time in bed, but she could not watch television or talk on the telephone.

This little game took all the morning pressure off Shirley and placed it on our daughter's shoulders, where it belonged. There were occasions when my wife got up just in time to fix breakfast, only to find Danae sitting soberly at the piano, clothed and in her right mind.

This system of discipline can serve as a model for parents who have similar behavioral problems with their children. It was not oppressive; in fact, Danae seemed to enjoy having a target to shoot at. The limits of acceptable performance were defined beyond question. The responsibility was clearly placed on the child. And it required no adult anger or foot stamping.

Adaptations of this concept are available to resolve other problems in your home, too. The only limit lies in the creativity and imagination that you bring to the situation.

125

QUESTION 128

I am uncomfortable using rewards to influence my kids. It seems too much like bribery to me. I'd like to hear your views on the subject.

Many parents feel as you do, and in response I say, don't use them if you are philosophically opposed to the concept. It is unfortunate, however, that one of our most effective teaching tools is often rejected because of what I would consider to be a misunderstanding of terms. Our entire society is established on a system of rewards, yet we don't want to apply them where they are needed most: with young children. As adults, we go to work each day and receive a paycheck every other Friday. Getting out of bed each morning and meeting the requirements of a job are thereby rewarded. Medals are given to brave soldiers, plaques are awarded to successful businesspeople, and watches are presented to retiring employees. Rewards make responsible effort worthwhile.

The main reason for the overwhelming success of capitalism is that hard work and personal discipline are rewarded materially. The great weakness of socialism is the absence of reinforcement; why should a person struggle to achieve if there is nothing special to be gained? This system is a destroyer of motivation, yet some parents seem to feel it is the only way to approach children. They expect little Marvin to carry responsibility simply because it is noble for him to do so. They want him to work and learn and sweat for the sheer joy of personal accomplishment. He isn't going to buy it!

Consider the alternative approach to the "bribery" I've recommended. How are you going to get your five-year-old son to behave more responsibly? The most frequently used substitutes are nagging, complaining, begging, screaming, threatening, and punishing. The mother who objects to the use of rewards may also go to bed each evening with a headache, vowing to have no more children. She doesn't like anything resembling a bribe, yet later she will give money to her child when some opportunity comes along. Since her youngster never earns his own cash, he doesn't learn how to save it or spend it wisely or pay tithe on it. The toys she buys him are purchased with her money, and he values them less. But most important, he is not learning self-discipline and personal responsibility that are possible through the careful reinforcement of that behavior.

Yes, I do believe the judicious use of rewards can be very helpful to parents. But—they're not for everyone.

QUESTION 129

Isn't a mother manipulating the child by using rewards and punishment to get him to do what she wants?

No more than a factory supervisor manipulates his employees by docking their pay if they arrive late. No more than a policeman manipulates a speeding driver by giving him a traffic ticket. No more than an insurance company manipulates that same driver by increasing his premium. No more than the IRS manipulates a taxpayer who files his return one day late by charging a penalty for his tardiness. The word *manipulation* implies a sinister or selfish motive of the one in charge. I don't agree.

QUESTION 130

When would you *not* recommend the use of rewards?

Rewards should never be used as a payoff to a child for not disobeying. That becomes a bribe—a substitute for authority. For example, Mom is having trouble controlling her three-year-old in a supermarket. "Come here, Pamela," she says, but the youngster screams, "No!" and runs the other way. Then in exasperation Mom offers Pam a sucker if she'll come quickly. Rather than rewarding obedience, Mom has actually reinforced the child's defiance.

Another misuse of rewards is to pay a child for doing the routine jobs that are his responsibility as a member of the family. Taking out the trash and making his bed might be included in those regular duties. But when he is asked to spend half his Saturday cleaning the garage or weeding the garden, it seems very appropriate to make it worth his time.

QUESTION 131

I worry about putting undue emphasis on materialism with my kids. Do rewards have to be in the form of money or toys?

Certainly not. A word of praise is a great enticement to some children. An interesting snack can also get their attention, although that has its downside. When my daughter was three years of age, I began to teach her some prereading skills, including how to recognize the letters of the alphabet. By planning the training sessions to occur after dinner each evening, bits of chocolate candy provided the chief source of motivation. (I was less concerned about the effects of excess sugar consumption in those days than I am now.) Late one afternoon I was sitting on the floor drilling her on several new letters when a tremendous crash shook the neighborhood. The whole family rushed outside to see what had happened. A teenager had overturned his car on our quiet residential street. He was not badly hurt, but his automobile was a mess. We sprayed the smoldering car with water and called the police. It was not until the excitement passed that we realized our daughter had not followed us out of the house. I returned to the den where I found her elbow-deep in the large bag of candy I had left behind. She must have put a half-pound of chocolate in her mouth, and most of the remainder was distributed around her chin, nose, and forehead. When she saw me coming, she managed to jam another handful into her chipmunk cheeks. From this experience, I learned one of the limitations of using material, or at least edible, rewards.

Anything the child wants can be used as a reinforcer, from praise to pizza to playtime.

QUESTION 132

My four-year-old daughter, Karen, is a whiner. She rarely speaks in a normal voice anymore. How can I break her of this habit?

There is a process called "extinction" that is very useful in situations like this. Here is how it works: Any behavior that has been learned by reinforcement (i.e., by rewards) can be unlearned by withholding those rewards. It sounds complex, but the technique is simple and very applicable to Karen's problem.

Why do you think she whines instead of speaking in a normal voice? Because you have rewarded that sound by letting it get your attention! As long as Karen is speaking in her usual voice you are too busy to listen to her. Like most toddlers, she probably babbles all day long, so you have often tuned out most of her verbiage. But when she speaks in a grating, irritating, obnoxious tone, you turn to see what is wrong. Therefore, Karen's whining brings results; her normal voice does not, and she becomes a whiner.

In order to break the habit of whining, you must simply reverse the process. You should begin by saying, "I can't hear you because you're whining, Karen. I have funny ears; they just can't hear whining." After this message has been passed along for a day or two, you should show no indication of having heard a moan-tone. You should then offer immediate attention to anything she says in a normal voice. If this control of reward is applied properly, I guarantee it to achieve the desired results. Most human learning is based on this principle, and the consequences are certain and definite. Of course, Grandma and Uncle Albert may continue to reinforce the behavior you are trying to eliminate, and they can keep it alive.

QUESTION 133

I have to fight with my nine-year-old daughter to get her to do *anything* she doesn't want to do. It's so unpleasant that I've about decided not to take her on. Why should I try to force her to work and help around the house? What's the downside of my just going with the flow and letting her off the hook?

It is typical for nine-year-olds not to want to work, of course, but they still need to become acquainted with it. If you permit a pattern of irresponsibility to prevail in your child's formative years, she may fall behind her developmental timetable leading toward the full responsibilities of adult living. As a ten-year-old, she won't be able to do anything unpleasant since she has never been required to stay with a task until it is completed. She won't know how to give to anyone else because she's only thought of herself. She'll find it hard to make decisions or control her own impulses. A few years from now, she will steamroll into adolescence and then adulthood completely unprepared for the freedom and obligations she will find there. Your daughter will have had precious little training for those pressing responsibilities of maturity.

Obviously, I've painted a worst-case scenario with regard to your daughter. You still have plenty of opportunity to help her avoid it. I just hope your desire for harmony doesn't lead you to do what will be harmful to her in later years.

Q UESTION 134

You have said that your philosophy of discipline (and of family advice in general) was drawn from the Scriptures. On what specific verses do you base your views?

Since God is the Creator of children, He must certainly know how our kids ought to be raised and how our families should function. Indeed, He does! We find in His Word a very consistent and easily understood prescription for parents who want to do things His way. Let me quote a few verses that illustrate this divine wisdom. Note three concepts within them that I have emphasized: (1) The authority of parents is endorsed; (2) discipline is in the best interest of children; (3) discipline must not be harsh and destructive to the child's spirit. Here they are:

> *He [the father] must manage his own family well and see that his children obey him with proper respect. (If anyone does not know how to manage his own family, how can he take care of God's church?)*
> **1 TIMOTHY 3:4-5**

> *Children, obey your parents in the Lord, for this is right. "Honor your father and mother"—which is the first commandment with a*

promise—"that it may go well with you and that you may enjoy long life on the earth."
EPHESIANS 6:1-3

Fathers, do not exasperate your children; instead, bring them up in the training and instruction of the Lord.
EPHESIANS 6:4

Children, obey your parents in everything, for this pleases the Lord. Fathers, do not embitter your children, or they will become discouraged.
COLOSSIANS 3:20-21

"My son, do not make light of the Lord's discipline, and do not lose heart when he rebukes you, because the Lord disciplines those he loves, and he punishes everyone he accepts as a son." Endure hardship as discipline; God is treating you as sons. For what son is not disciplined by his father? If you are not disciplined (and everyone undergoes discipline), then you are illegitimate children and not true sons. Moreover, we have all had human fathers who disciplined us and we respected them for it. [Note the linkage between discipline and respect.] How much more should we submit to the Father of our spirits and live! Our fathers disciplined us for a little while as they thought best; but God disciplines us for our good, that we may share in his holiness. No discipline seems pleasant at the time, but painful. Later on, however, it produces a harvest of righteousness and peace for those who have been trained by it.
HEBREWS 12:5-11

Correct thy son, and he shall give thee rest; yea, he shall give delight unto thy soul.
PROVERBS 29:17, KJV

These Scriptures and related verses contain more wisdom than all the child-development textbooks ever written. They came from the heart of One who flung the stars in space and created Adam from a handful of dust. He makes no mistakes! To summarize the primary theme from all the related biblical passages, it is for parents to shape the will without breaking the spirit. That's the formula. That's the prescription.

QUESTION 135

What do you think of the phrase "Children should be seen and not heard"?

That statement reveals a profound ignorance of children and their needs. I can't imagine how any loving adult could raise a vulnerable little boy or girl by that philosophy.

QUESTION 136

I really believe in giving children the freedom to do wrong as long as there isn't any danger involved. For example, I let my kids curse and use swear words and don't see any harm in it. Do you agree?

No. I would hope that parents wouldn't use that kind of language and certainly don't believe they should permit their kids to do so. It is disrespectful, crude, and unnecessary to talk like that.

QUESTION 137

Why is it that children are often the most obnoxious and irritating on vacations and at other times when parents specifically try to please them? On those special days, you'd think the kids would say to themselves, *Wow! Mom and Dad are doing something really nice for us, taking us on this great vacation. We're going to give them a break and be really good kids today.* Isn't that reasonable?

Sure it's reasonable, but children just don't think that way. In fact, many boys and girls misbehave even more at these times. Why is this? One reason, I think, is because children often feel compelled to reexamine the boundaries whenever they think they may have moved. In other words, whenever the normal routine changes, the tougher kids often push the limits to see if the old rules still apply.

QUESTION 138

So how can parents preserve their own peace of mind and maintain harmony during car trips and family holidays?

Sometimes it helps to redefine the boundaries at the beginning of your time together. Let the children know exactly what you're doing and what's expected of them. If they still misbehave, respond with good, loving discipline right from the start.

No parent wants to be an ogre on vacation, but it helps to show a little firmness at the outset that can make the rest of the time together fun for the entire family.

QUESTION 139

Would you go so far as to apologize to a child if you felt you had been in the wrong?

I certainly would—and indeed, I have. A number of years ago I was burdened with pressing responsibilities that fatigued me and made me irritable. One particular evening I was especially grouchy and short-tempered with my ten-year-old daughter. I knew I was not being fair but was simply too tired to correct my manner. Through the course of the evening, I blamed Danae for things that were not her fault and upset her needlessly several times. After going to bed, I felt bad about the way I had behaved, and I decided to apologize the next morning. After a good night of sleep and a tasty breakfast, I felt much more optimistic about life. I approached my daughter before she left for school and said, "Danae, I'm sure you know that daddies are not perfect human beings. We get tired and irritable just like other people, and there are times when we are not proud of the way we behave. I know I wasn't fair with you last night. I was terribly grouchy, and I want you to forgive me."

Danae put her arms around me and shocked me down to my toes. She said, "I knew you were going to have to apologize, Daddy, and it's OK; I forgive you."

Can there be any doubt that children are often more aware of the struggles between generations than are their busy, harassed parents?

QUESTION 140

My children are still in elementary school, and I want to avoid adolescent rebellion in the future if I can. What can you tell me to help me get ready for this scary time?

I can understand why you look toward the adolescent years with some apprehension. This is a tough time to raise kids. Many youngsters sail right through that period with no unusual stresses and problems, but others get caught in a pattern of rebellion that disrupts families and scares their moms and dads to death. I've spent several decades trying to understand that phenomenon and how to prevent it. The encouraging thing is that the most rebellious teens usually grow up to be responsible and stable adults who can't remember why they were so angry in earlier days.

I once devoted a radio program to a panel of formerly rebellious teens that included three successful ministers, Rev. Raul Ries, Pastor Mike MacIntosh, and Rev. Franklin Graham, son of Dr. Billy and Ruth Graham. Each of them had been a difficult adolescent who gave his parents fits. With the exception of Raul, who had been abused at home, the other two couldn't recall what motivated their misbehavior or why they didn't just go along and get along.[42] That is often the way with adolescence. It's like a tornado that drops unexpectedly out of a dark sky, tyrannizes a family, shakes up the community, and then blows on by. Then the sun comes out and spreads its warmth again.

Even though the teen years can be challenging, they're also filled with excitement and growth. Rather than fearing that experience, therefore, I think you ought to anticipate it as a dynamic time when your kids transition from childhood to full-fledged adulthood.

Q UESTION 141

One more time, could you summarize your philosophy of child rearing in a single paragraph? What's the bottom line?

Let me emphasize my approach by stating its opposite. I am not recommending that your home be harsh and oppressive. I am not suggesting that you give your children a spanking every morning with their ham and eggs or that you make your boys sit in the living room with their hands folded and their legs crossed. I am not proposing that you try to make adults out of your kids so you can impress your adult friends with your parental skill, or that you punish your children whimsically, swinging and screaming when they didn't know they were wrong. I am not suggesting that you insulate your dignity and authority by being cold and unapproachable. These parental tactics do not produce healthy, responsible children. By contrast, I am recommending a simple principle: When you are defiantly challenged, win decisively. When the child asks, "Who's in charge?" tell him. When he mutters, "Who loves me?" take him in your arms and surround him with affection. Treat him with respect and dignity, and expect the same in return. Then begin to enjoy the sweet benefits of competent parenthood.

Q UESTION 142

My wife and I have a strong-willed child who is incredibly difficult to handle. I honestly believe we are doing our job about as well as any parents would do under the circumstances, yet she still breaks the rules and challenges our authority. I guess I need some encouragement. First, tell me if an especially strong-willed kid can be made to smile and give and work and cooperate. If so, how is that accomplished? And second, what is my daughter's future? I see trouble ahead but don't know if that gloomy forecast is justified.

There is no question about it, an especially willful child such as yours can be difficult to manage even when her parents handle her with great skill and dedication. It may take several years to bring her to a point of relative obedience and cooperation within the family unit, but it will happen. While this training program is in progress, it is important not to panic. Don't try to complete the transformation overnight. Treat your child with sincere love and dignity, but require her to follow your leadership. Choose carefully the matters that are worthy of confrontation; then accept her challenge on those issues and win decisively. Reward every positive, cooperative gesture she makes by offering your attention, affection, and verbal praise. Then take two aspirin and call me in the morning.

8

To Spank or Not to Spank

QUESTION 143

I have never spanked my three-year-old because I am afraid it will teach her to hit others and be a violent person. Do you think I am wrong?

You have asked an important question that reflects a common misunderstanding about child management. First, let me emphasize that it *is* possible—even easy—to create a violent and aggressive child who has observed this behavior at home. If he is routinely beaten by hostile, volatile parents or if he witnesses physical violence between angry adults or if he feels unloved and unappreciated within his family, that child will not fail to notice how the game is played. Thus, corporal punishment that is not administered according to very carefully thought-out guidelines is a risky thing. Being a parent carries no right to slap and intimidate a child because you had a bad day or are in a lousy mood. It is this kind of unjust discipline that causes some well-meaning authorities to reject corporal punishment as a method of discipline.

Just because a technique is used wrongly, however, is no reason to reject it altogether. Many children desperately need this resolution to their disobedience. In those situations when the child, aged two to ten, fully understands what he is being asked to do but refuses to yield to adult leadership, an appropriate spanking is the shortest and most effective route to an attitude adjustment. When he lowers his head, clenches his fists, and makes it clear he is going for broke, justice must speak swiftly and eloquently. Not only does this response not create aggression in children, it helps them control their impulses and live in harmony with various forms of benevolent authority throughout life. Many people disagree, of course. I can only tell you that there is not a single well-designed scientific study that confirms the hypothesis that spanking by a loving parent breeds violence in children.

QUESTION 144

It just seems barbaric to cause pain to a defenseless child. Tell me why you think it is healthy to spank him or her.

Corporal punishment, when used lovingly and properly, is beneficial to a child because it is in harmony with nature itself. Consider the purpose of minor pain in a child's life and how he learns from it. Suppose two-year-old Peter pulls on a tablecloth and with it comes a vase of roses that cracks him between the eyes. From this pain, he learns that it is dangerous to pull on the tablecloth unless he knows what sits on it. When he touches a hot stove, he quickly learns that heat must be respected. If he lives to be a hundred years old, he will never again reach out and touch the red-hot coils of a stove. The same lesson is learned when he pulls the doggy's tail and promptly gets a neat row of teeth marks across the back of his hand, or when he climbs out of his high chair when Mom isn't looking and discovers all about gravity.

During the childhood years, he typically accumulates minor bumps, bruises, scratches, and burns, each one teaching him about life's boundaries. Do these experiences make him a violent person? No! The pain associated with these events teaches him to avoid making the same mistakes again. God created this mechanism as a valuable vehicle for instruction.

When a parent administers a reasonable spanking in response to willful disobedience, a similar nonverbal message is being given to the child. He must understand that there are not only dangers in the physical world to be avoided. He should also be wary of dangers in his social world, such as defiance, sassiness, selfishness, temper tantrums, behavior that puts his life in danger, that which hurts others, etc. The minor pain associated with this deliberate misbehavior tends to inhibit it, just as discomfort works to shape behavior in the physical world. Neither conveys hatred. Neither results in rejection. Neither makes the child more violent.

In fact, children who have experienced corporal punishment from loving parents do not have trouble understanding its meaning. I recall my good friends Art and Ginger Shingler, who had four beautiful children whom I loved. One of them went through a testy period where he was just "asking for it." The conflict came to a head in a restaurant, when the boy continued doing everything he could to be bratty. Finally, Art took him to the parking lot for an overdue spanking. A woman passerby observed the event and became irate. She chided the father for "abusing" his son and said she intended to call the police. With that, the child stopped crying and said to his father, "What's wrong with that woman, Dad?" *He* understood the discipline even if his rescuer did not. A boy or girl who knows that love abounds at home will not resent a well-deserved spanking. One who is unloved or ignored will hate any form of discipline!

Q UESTION 145

As an advocate of spankings as a disciplinary tool, don't you worry about the possibility that you might be contributing to the incidence of child abuse in this country?

Yes, I do worry about that. One of my frustrations in teaching parents has been the difficulty in achieving a balance between permissiveness and oppression. The tendency is to drift toward one extreme or another. Let it never be said that I favor harshness of any kind with children. It can wound the spirit and inflict permanent scars on the psyche.

No subject distresses me more than the phenomenon of child abuse, which is so prevalent in North America today. There are millions of families out there in which crimes against children are being committed day after day. It is hard to believe just how cruel some mothers and fathers can be to defenseless, wide-eyed kids who don't understand why they are hated. I remember the terrible father who regularly wrapped his small son's head in the sheet that the boy had wet the night before. Then he crammed the tot upside down into the toilet bowl for punishment. I also think of the disturbed mother who cut out her child's eyes with a razor blade. That little girl will be blind throughout her life, knowing that her own mother deprived her of sight!

Unthinkable acts like these are occurring every day in cities and towns around us. In fact, it is highly probable that a youngster living within a mile or two of your house is experiencing abuse in one manner or another. Brian G. Fraser, attorney for the National Center for Prevention and Treatment of Child Abuse and Neglect, has written: "Child abuse . . . once thought to be primarily a problem of the poor and downtrodden . . . occurs in every segment of society and may be the country's leading cause of death in children."[43]

Let me say with the strongest emphasis that aggressive, hard-nosed, "Mommy Dearest" kinds of discipline are destructive to kids and must not be tolerated. Given the scope of the tragedy we are facing, the last thing I want to do is to provide a rationalization and justification for it. I don't believe in harsh discipline, even when it is well intentioned. Children must be given room to breathe and grow and love. But there are also harmful circumstances at the permissive end of the spectrum, and many parents fall into one trap in an earnest attempt to avoid the other.

QUESTION 146

Are all forms of child abuse illegal?

Not in any practical sense. Within certain limits it is not illegal to ignore a child or raise him or her without love. Nor is it against the law to ridicule and humiliate a boy or girl. Those forms of rejection may be more harmful even than some forms of physical abuse, but they are tougher to prove and are usually not prosecutable.

QUESTION 147

You have described two extremes that are both harmful to kids, being too permissive and being too harsh. Which is the most common error in Western cultures today?

Permissiveness is still more common and has been since the 1950s. But harshness and severity still occur frequently as well. These dual dangers are equally harmful to children and were described by Marguerite and Willard Beecher in their book *Parents on the Run.* This is how they saw the two extremes:

> The adult-centered home of yesteryear made parents the masters and children their slaves. The child-centered home of today has made parents the slaves and children the masters. There is no true cooperation in any master-slave relationship, and therefore no democracy. Neither the restrictive-authoritative technique of rearing children nor the newer "anything goes" technique develop the genius within the individual, because neither trains him to be self-reliant.[44]

The way to raise healthy children is to find the safety of the middle ground between disciplinary extremes.

QUESTION 148

What advice would you give parents who recognize a tendency within themselves to abuse their kids? Maybe they're afraid they'll get carried away when spanking a disobedient child. Do you think they should avoid corporal punishment as a form of discipline?

That's exactly what I think. Anyone who has ever abused a child—or has ever felt himself or herself losing control during a spanking—should not expose the child to that tragedy. Anyone who has a violent temper that at times becomes unmanageable should not use that approach. Anyone who secretly enjoys the administration of corporal punishment should not be the one to implement it. And grandparents probably should not spank their grandkids unless the parents have given them permission to do so.

QUESTION 149

Do you think you should spank a child for every act of disobedience or defiance?

No. Corporal punishment should be a rather infrequent occurrence. There is an appropriate time for a child to sit on a chair to think about his misbehavior, or he might be deprived of a privilege or sent to his room for a "time-out" or made to work when he had planned to play. In other words, you should vary your response to misbehavior, always hoping to stay one step ahead of the child. Your goal is to react continually in the way that benefits the child and is in accordance with his "crime." In this regard, there is no substitute for wisdom and tact in the parenting role.

QUESTION 150

On what part of the body would you administer a spanking?

It should be confined to the buttocks area, where permanent damage is very unlikely. I don't believe in slapping a child on the face or in jerking him around by the arms. A common form of injury seen in the emergency room at Children's Hospital when I was on the attending staff involved children with shoulder separations. Parents had pulled tiny arms angrily and dislocated the shoulder or elbow. If you spank a child only on the behind, you will be less likely to inflict any physical injury on him.

QUESTION 151

After I spank my child, she usually wants to hug me and make up. I don't feel good about that because I need to show her my displeasure at what she's done. That's why I continue to be cool to her for a few hours. Do you think that is right?

No, I think it is very important after punishment to embrace the child in love. That is the time to assure her that it was the misbehavior that brought your disapproval, rather than your dislike for her personally. It is also the best time to talk about why she got in trouble and how she can avoid your displeasure in the future. It is the "teachable moment," when the object of your discipline can be explained. Such a conversation is difficult or impossible to achieve when a rebellious, stiff-necked little child is clenching her fist and taking you on. But after a confrontation has occurred—especially if it involved tears— the child usually wants to hug you and get reassurance that you really care for her.

Many parents, like you, say they feel awkward showing affection after punishment because they've been upset with the child. I think that is wrong. It's best to open your arms and let that youngster come.

QUESTION **152**

How long do you think a child should be allowed to cry after being punished or spanked? Is there a limit?

Yes, I believe there should be a limit. As long as the tears represent a genuine release of emotion, they should be permitted to fall. But crying quickly changes from inner sobbing to an expression of protest aimed at punishing the enemy. Real crying usually lasts two minutes or less but may continue for five. After that point, the child is merely complaining, and the change can be recognized in the tone and intensity of his voice. I would require him to stop the protest crying, usually by offering him a little more of whatever caused the original tears. In younger children, crying can easily be stopped by getting them interested in something else.

QUESTION **153**

There is some controversy over whether a parent should spank with his or her hand or with some other object, such as a belt or paddle. What do you recommend?

I recommend a neutral object of some type. To those who disagree on this point, I'd encourage them to do what seems right. It is not a critical issue to me. The reason I suggest a switch or paddle is because the hand should be seen as an object of love—to hold, hug, pat, and caress. However, if you're used to suddenly disciplining with the hand, your child may not know when she's about to be swatted and can develop a pattern of flinching when you make an unexpected move. This is not a problem if you take the time to use a neutral object.

My mother always used a small switch, which could not do any permanent damage. But it stung enough to send a very clear message. One day when I had pushed her to the limit, she actually sent me to the backyard to cut my own instrument of punishment. I brought back a tiny little twig about seven inches long. She could not have generated anything more than a tickle with it. She never sent me on that fool's errand again.

As I conceded above, some people (particularly those who are opposed to spanking in the first place) believe that the use of a neutral object in discipline is tantamount to child abuse. I understand their concern, especially in cases when a parent believes "might makes right" or loses her temper and harms the child. That is why adults must always maintain a balance between love and control, regardless of the method by which they administer disciplinary action.

QUESTION 154

Is there an age when you begin to spank?

There is no excuse for spanking babies or children younger than fifteen to eighteen months of age. Even shaking an infant can cause brain damage and death at that delicate age! But midway through the second year (eighteen months), boys and girls become capable of knowing what you're telling them to do or not do. They can then very gently be held responsible for how they behave. Suppose a child is reaching for an electric socket or something that will hurt him. You say, "No!" but he just looks at you and continues reaching toward it. You can see the mischievous smile on his face as he thinks, *I'm going to do it anyway!* I'd encourage you to speak firmly so that he knows

144

he is pushing past the limits. If he persists, slap his fingers just enough to sting. A small amount of pain goes a long way at that age and begins to introduce children to realities of the physical world and the importance of listening to what you say.

Through the next eighteen months, you gradually establish yourself as the benevolent boss who means what you say and says what you mean. Contrary to what you have read in popular literature, this firm but loving approach to child rearing will *not* harm a toddler or make him violent. To the contrary, it is most likely to produce a healthy, confident child.

QUESTION 155

I have spanked my children for their disobedience, and it didn't seem to help. Does this approach fail with some children?

Children are so tremendously variable that it is sometimes hard to believe that they are all members of the same human family. Some kids can be crushed with nothing more than a stern look; others seem to require strong and even painful disciplinary measures to make a vivid impression. This difference usually results from the degree to which a child needs adult approval and acceptance. The primary parental task is to see things as the child perceives them, thereby tailoring the discipline to his or her unique needs. Accordingly, a boy or girl should never be so likely to be punished as when he or she knows it is deserved.

In a direct answer to your question, disciplinary measures usually fail because of fundamental errors in their application. It is possible for twice the amount of punishment to yield half the results. I have made a study of situations in which parents have told me that their children disregard the threat of punishment and continue to misbehave. There are four basic reasons for this lack of success:

1. The most common error is whimsical discipline. When the rules change every day and when punishment for misbehavior is capricious and inconsistent, the effort to change behavior is under-

mined. There is no inevitable consequence to be anticipated. This entices children to see if they can beat the system. In society at large, it also encourages criminal behavior among those who believe they will not face the bar of justice.

2. Sometimes a child is more strong-willed than his parent—and they both know it. He just might be tough enough to realize that a confrontation with his mom or dad is really a struggle of wills. If he can withstand the pressure and not buckle during a major battle, he can eliminate that form of punishment as a tool in the parent's repertoire. Does he think through this process on a conscious level? Usually not, but he understands it intuitively. He realizes that a spanking *must not* be allowed to succeed. Thus, he stiffens his little neck and guts it out. He may even refuse to cry and may say, "That didn't hurt." The parent concludes in exasperation, "Spanking doesn't work for my child."

3. The spanking may be too gentle. If it doesn't hurt, it doesn't motivate a child to avoid the consequence next time. A slap with the hand on the bottom of a multidiapered thirty-month-old is not a deterrent to anything. Be sure the child gets the message—while being careful not to go too far.

4. For a few children, spankings are simply not effective. The child who has attention deficit/hyperactivity disorder (ADHD), for example, may be even more wild and unmanageable after corporal punishment. Also, the child who has been abused may identify loving discipline with the hatred of the past. Finally, the very sensitive child might need a different approach. Let me emphasize once more that children are unique. The only way to raise them correctly is to understand each boy or girl as an individual and design parenting techniques to fit the needs and characteristics of that particular child.

QUESTION 156

Do you think corporal punishment will eventually be outlawed?

I don't doubt that an effort will be made to end it. The tragedy of child abuse has made it difficult for people to understand the difference between viciousness to kids and constructive, positive forms of punishment. Also, there are many "children's rights advocates" in the Western world who will not rest until they have obtained the legal right to tell parents how to raise their children. That has already happened in Sweden, where corporal punishment and other forms of discipline are prohibited by law.[45] Canadian courts are flirting with the same decision.[46] The American media has worked to convince the public that all spanking is tantamount to child abuse, and therefore, should be outlawed. If that occurs, it will be a sad day for families . . . and especially for children!

9

What's a Mother to Do?

QUESTION **157**

My husband and I just moved to Arizona from Pennsylvania, and I haven't established a network of friends yet. My family is back east, and I have no one but my husband to talk to about problems the kids are having. He is very busy, so all the "homework" is left to me. How can I deal with the feelings of loneliness and isolation as a mother?

It is vital that you build relationships with other women that can help satisfy the needs for friendship and emotional support. Failure to do that places too great a strain on the marital relationship, which can lead to serious interpersonal problems. I'm not saying that your husband has no responsibility to help you get through this period of loneliness, but unless he is a very unusual man, he will not be able to "carry" you emotionally while earning a living and handling the other responsibilities of living. Therefore, I recommend that you seek out women's groups that are designed to meet the needs you described. Many churches offer Bible study groups and classes called Mothers of Preschoolers (MOPS), which is an outstanding program that puts women in touch with one another. Other possibilities are out there, such as Mom's Day Out, Mothers on the Move, etc. For mothers of school-age children, there is a Christian ministry called Moms in

149

Touch, designed to bring women together to pray for their local school, its teachers, principal, school board, etc. It "bonds" them together in a common cause. What I'm saying is that you are not alone, even in a new city. There are other women out there who need you as much as you need them. You can find each other with a little effort. It is dangerous under the circumstances you described to sit and wait for the world to come to your front door.

QUESTION 158

What do you think of placing children in child-care centers so mothers can work?

Safe, clean, loving child-care facilities are a necessity in today's culture. They are especially needed by the millions of mothers who are forced to work for financial reasons. They are particularly vital to the many single parents who are the sole breadwinners in their families. Thus, we need not question the wisdom of providing well-supervised centers for children whose mothers and fathers require assistance in raising them. That debate is over.

What can be argued is whether children fare better in a child-care facility or at home with a full-time mom. Personally (and others will disagree), I don't believe any arrangement for children can compete with an intact family where the mother raises her kids and the father is also very involved in their lives. There are at least four reasons that is true.

First, children thrive and learn better when they enjoy one-on-one relationships with adults rather than as members of a group. Second, you can't pay an employee in a child-care center enough to care for children like their own mothers will do. Children are a mother's passion, and it shows. Third, research verifies that kids at home are healthier than those who are regularly exposed to diseases, coughs, and sneezes from other boys and girls.[47] Fourth, a bonding is more likely to occur between parents and children when the developmental milestones are experienced firsthand. Families should be there when the first step is taken and the first word is spoken and when fears and anxieties arise. Certainly, others can substitute for Mom in those special moments, but something precious is lost if a surrogate witnesses them.

In short, I recognize the need for healthy child-care facilities in situations that demand them, but group living is not in the best interests of kids.

QUESTION 159

If parents have to use child-care support, what kind of help do you think is best?

State-run facilities rank at the bottom of my list because Christian teaching is not permissible in public facilities. Children are not led in prayer before meals, and no reference can be made to Jesus as our friend and Lord. I also worry more about the possibility of child molestation in state centers, even though it is rare. For these and other reasons, I prefer church-run programs that are clean and safe. Even better, if available, is placement of children with relatives, such as grandparents or aunts, or supervision provided by other mothers. Children need to develop relationships with those who care for them. They should be left with adults they know and love, if possible, rather than being forced to relate to different employees from day to day in public facilities.

QUESTION 160

I'm a full-time mother with three children in the preschool years. I love them like crazy, but I am exhausted from just trying to keep up with them. I also feel emotionally isolated by being here in the house every day of the week. What do you suggest for mothers like me?

I talk to many women like you who feel that they're on the edge of burnout. They feel like they will explode if they have to do one more load of laundry or tie one more shoe. In today's mobile, highly energized society, young mothers are much more isolated than in years past. Many of them hardly know the women next door, and their sisters and mothers may live a thousand miles away. That's why it is so important for those with small children to stay in touch with the outside world. Though it may seem safer and less taxing to remain cloistered within the four walls of a home, it is a mistake to do so. Loneliness does bad things to the mind. Furthermore, there are many ways to network with other women today, including church activities, Bible study groups, and supportive programs such as Moms in Touch and Mothers of Preschoolers.

Husbands of stay-at-home mothers need to recognize the importance of their support, too. It is a wise man who plans a romantic date at least once a week and offers to take care of the children so Mom can get a much-needed break.

Burnout isn't inevitable in a busy household. It can be avoided in families that recognize its symptoms and take steps to head it off.

Q UESTION 161

You've talked about being a full-time mother versus having a full-time career. Give us your view of a woman handling both responsibilities simultaneously. Is it doable, and is it smart?

Some women are able to maintain a busy career and a bustling family at the same time, and they do it beautifully. I admire them for their discipline and dedication. It has been my observation, however, that this dual responsibility is a formula for exhaustion and frustration for many others. It can be a never-ending struggle for survival. Why? Because there is only so much energy within the human body, and when it is invested in one place it is not available for use in another. Consider what it is like to be a mother of young children who must rise early in the morning, get her kids dressed, fed, and situated for the day, then drive to work, labor from nine to five, go by the grocery store and pick up some stuff for dinner, retrieve the kids at the child-care center, and then drive home. She is dog tired by that point and needs to put her feet up for a few minutes. But she can't rest. The kids are hungry, and they've been waiting to see her all day.

"Read me a story, Mom," says the most needy.

This beleaguered woman then begins another four to six hours of very demanding "mothering" that will extend into the evening. She must fix dinner, wash the dishes, bathe the baby, help with homework, and give each child some "quality time." Then comes the task of getting the tribe in bed, saying prayers, and bringing six glasses of water to giggling kids who want to stall. I get tired just thinking of a schedule like this.

You might ask the married woman, "Where is your husband and father in all this exertion? Why isn't he carrying his share of the homework?" Well, he may be working a fifteen-hour day at his own job. Getting started in a business or a profession often demands that kind of commitment. Or he may simply choose not to help his wife. That is a common complaint among working mothers.

"Not fair," you say.

I agree, but that's the way the system often works.

The most difficult aspect of this lifestyle is the constancy of the load. Most of us could maintain such a schedule for a week or two, but the working mother must do it month after month for years on end. On weekends there's housecleaning to do and clothes to be ironed and pants to be mended. And this is the pace she maintains when things are going right. She has no reserve of time or energy when a member of the family gets sick or the car breaks down or marital problems develop. A little push in any direction and she could go over the edge.

Admittedly, I have painted a more stressful scenario than most families have to endure. But not by much. Overcommitted and frazzled families are commonplace in our culture. Husbands and wives have no time for each other. Life is nothing but work, work, work. They are continually frustrated, irritable, and harried. They don't take walks, read the Scriptures together, or do anything that is fun. Their sex life suffers because exhausted people don't even make love meaningfully. They begin to drift apart and eventually find themselves with "irreconcilable differences." It is a tragic pattern I have been observing for the past twenty-five years.

The issue, then, is not whether a woman should choose a career and be a mother, too. Of course she has that right, and it is nobody's business but hers and her husband's. I would simply plead that you not allow your family to get sucked into that black hole of exhaustion. However you choose to divide the responsibilities of working and

family management, reserve some time and energy for yourselves—
and for each other. Your children deserve the best that you can give
them, too.

QUESTION 162

**What would you and your wife do if the resources permitted
her to stay at home after the kids were in school?**

I don't have to speculate about the answer to that question. Shirley and
I *did* have that option (although we sold and "ate" a Volkswagen
initially to make it possible), and she stayed at home as a full-time
mom. Neither she nor I have ever regretted that decision. Now that our
kids are grown, we would not trade the time we invested in them for
anything on earth. Looking back today, we feel it was *especially*
important for Shirley to be at home during our kids' teen years.

QUESTION 163

**We need a little more income to make it in my family, but I
have preschool children and don't want to seek employment
outside the home. Is there an alternative for me to pursue?**

You might want to consider building a home-based business that can be
done while taking care of your children and keeping your sanity. Among
the possibilities are catering, desktop publishing, pet grooming, sewing,
consulting, transcribing legal documents, or even mail-order sales.
Choosing which business is right for you is the first of three practical
steps suggested by Donna Partow. She's the author of a book called
Homemade Business. You can start your own enterprise by taking a
personal-skills-and-interest inventory to identify your particular abilities and what you might like doing the best. The second step is to do your
homework. Begin by asking your librarian to help you research your
chosen field. Look up books, magazines, and newspaper articles. Talk
to other people who have done what you'd like to do. Join an industry
organization and a network. Subscribe to industry publications.

According to Mrs. Partow, the third step is to marshal as much support as you can. Get your children, your spouse, and your friends on your side. Setting up a small business can be stressful, and you'll need as much encouragement as you can get.[48]

If you've been torn between family and finances, having a home-based business may turn out to be the best of both worlds.

QUESTION 164

What answer do you have for those who say being a mother of small children and a homemaker is boring and monotonous?

Some women see the responsibility that way—but we should recognize that most other occupations are boring, too. How exciting is the work of a waiter who serves food to customers every day—or a medical pathologist who examines microscopic slides and bacterial cultures from morning to night—or a dentist who spends his lifetime drilling and filling, drilling and filling—or an attorney who reads dusty books in a secluded library—or an author who writes page after page after page? Few of us enjoy heart-thumping excitement each moment of our professional lives. Even the high-profile jobs have their boring dimensions.

On a trip to Washington, D.C., a few years ago, my hotel room was located next to the room of a famous cellist who was in the city to give a classical concert that evening. I could hear him through the walls as he practiced hour after hour. He did not play beautiful symphonic renditions; he repeated scales and runs and exercises, over and over and over. This practice began early in the morning (believe me!) and continued until the time of his concert. As he strolled on stage that evening, I'm sure many individuals in the audience thought to themselves, *What a glamorous life!* Some glamour! I happen to know that he had spent the entire day in his lonely hotel room in the company of his cello. Musical instruments, as you know, are terrible conversationalists.

No, I doubt if the job of a homemaker and mother is much more boring than most other jobs, particularly if the woman refuses to be isolated from adult contact. But as far as the importance of the assignment is concerned, no job can compete with the responsibility of shaping and molding a human being in the morning of his or her life.

QUESTION 165

My child is afraid of the dark. How can I lessen this fear?

I consulted with another mother who was also worried about her three-year-old daughter's fear of the dark. Maybe her story will be helpful to you. Despite the use of a night-light and leaving the bedroom door open, Marla was afraid to stay in her room alone. She insisted that her mother sit with her until she went to sleep each evening, which became very time-consuming and inconvenient. If Marla happened to awaken in the night, she would call for help. It was apparent that the child was not bluffing; she was genuinely frightened.

Fears such as this are not innate characteristics in the child; they have been learned. Parents must be very careful in expressing their own fears because their youngsters are inclined to adopt those same anxieties. For that matter, good-natured teasing can also produce problems for a child. If a youngster walks into a dark room and is pounced upon from behind the door, he has learned something from the joke: The dark is not always empty! In Marla's case, it is unclear where she learned to fear the dark, but I believe her mother inadvertently magnified the problem. In her concern for Marla, she conveyed her anxiety, and the child began to think that her fears must be justified: *Even Mother is worried about it.* The fright became so great that Marla could not walk through a dimly lit room without an escort. It was at this point that the child was referred to me.

I suggested that the mother use a process known as "extinction" to change Marla's pattern of fear. She needed to help her see that there was nothing to be afraid of. (It is usually unfruitful to try to talk a child out of fears, but it helps to show that you are confident and unthreatened in response to them.) The mother bought a package of stars and created a chart that showed how a new CD player could be earned. Then she placed her chair just outside Marla's bedroom door. Marla was offered a star if she could spend a short time (ten seconds) in her bedroom with the light on and the door open.

This first step was not very threatening, and Marla enjoyed the game. It was repeated several times; then she was asked to walk a few feet into a slightly darkened room with the door still open while Mother (clearly visible in the hall) counted to ten. She knew she could come out immediately if she wished. Mother talked confidently and quietly. The length of time in the dark was gradually lengthened, and instead of producing fear, it produced stars and eventually a CD player—a source of pleasure for a small child. Courage was being reinforced; fear was being extinguished. The cycle of fright was thereby broken, being replaced by a more healthy attitude.

Extinction may be useful in helping your own child overcome her fear of the dark. In summary, the best method of changing a learned behavior is to withhold its reinforcement while rewarding its replacement.

10
Education: Public, Private, and Home Schooling

QUESTION 166

I majored in education at a state university, and I was taught that children will provide their own motivation to learn if we give them an opportunity to do so. My professors favored a "student-led" classroom instead of one that depends on strong leadership from the teacher. The children will then want to learn rather than being forced to learn. Do you see it that way?

I certainly agree that we should try to motivate kids to work and study and learn. They'll enjoy the process more and retain the information longer if their motivation comes from within. So I think your professors are right in saying that we should capitalize on students' natural interest whenever we can. But it is naive to believe that any educational program can generate that kind of interest in every subject and sustain it for a majority of students day in and day out. That is not going to happen. Kids need to learn some things that may be boring to them, such as math or grammar, whether they choose to or not.

A former superintendent of public instruction in the state of California reacted to the notion that children have a natural interest in everything adults think they should know. He said, "To say that children have an innate love of learning is as muddleheaded as to say that children have an innate love of baseball. Some do. Some don't. Left to themselves, a large percentage of the small fry will go fishing, pick a fight, tease the girls, or watch Superman on the boob tube. Even as you and I."[49]

This educator was right. Many students will not invest one more ounce of effort in their studies than is required, and that fact has frustrated teachers for hundreds of years. Our schools, therefore, must have enough structure and discipline to require certain behavior from children whether or not they have a natural interest in the subject being taught.

QUESTION 167

Then you must favor a very structured, teacher-led program, where student behavior is rather tightly controlled. Why?

One of the purposes of education is to prepare a young person for later life. To survive as an adult in this society, one needs to know how to work, how to get there on time, how to get along with others, how to stay with a task until it's completed, and, yes, how to submit to authority. In short, it takes a good measure of self-discipline and control to cope with the demands of modern living. Maybe one of the greatest gifts a loving teacher can contribute to an immature child, therefore, is to help her learn to sit when she feels like running, to raise her hand when she feels like talking, to be polite to her neighbor, to stand in line without smacking the kid in front, and to do English when she feels like doing soccer. I would also like to see our schools readopt reasonable dress codes, eliminating suggestive clothing, T-shirts with profanity or those promoting heavy-metal bands, etc. Guidelines concerning good grooming and cleanliness should also be enforced.

I know! I know! These notions are so alien to us now that we can hardly imagine such a thing. But the benefits would be apparent immediately. Admittedly, hairstyles and matters of momentary fashion are of no particular significance, but adherence to a standard is an important element of discipline. The military has understood that for five thousand years! If one examines the secret behind a championship football team, a magnificent orchestra, or a successful business, the principal ingredient is invariably discipline. Preparation for this disciplinary lifestyle should begin in childhood. That's why I think it's a mistake to require nothing of children—to place no demands on their behavior—to allow them to giggle, fight, talk, and play in the classroom. We all need to adhere to reasonable rules, and school is a good place to get acquainted with how that is done.

QUESTION 168

You've been somewhat critical of America's public schools in recent years. Whom do you hold accountable for what has gone wrong?

I share the concern of many others about falling test scores, increasing violence on campuses, and the high illiteracy rate, among other serious problems with today's schools. But I am not quick to blame educators for everything that has gone wrong. The teachers and school administrators who guide our children have been among the most maligned and underappreciated people in our society. They are an easy target for abuse. They are asked to do a terribly difficult job, and yet they are criticized almost daily for circumstances beyond their control. Some of their critics act as though educators are deliberately failing our kids. I strongly disagree. We would still be having serious difficulties in our schools if the professionals did everything right. Why? Because what goes on in the classroom cannot be separated from the problems occurring in culture at large.

Educators are not responsible for the condition our kids are in when they arrive at school each day. It's not the teachers' fault that families are unraveling and that large numbers of their students have been sexually and/or physically abused, neglected, and undernourished. They can't keep kids from watching mindless television or from R-rated videos until midnight, or from using illegal substances or alcohol. In essence, when the culture begins to crumble, the schools will also look bad. That's why even though I disagree with many of the trends in modern education, I sympathize with the dedicated teachers and principals out there who are doing their best on behalf of our youngsters. They are discouraged today, and they need our support.

QUESTION 169

What immediate changes would you make in junior and senior high schools to improve the learning environment there?

Most important, we must make schools safer for students and teachers. Guns, drugs, and adolescence make a deadly cocktail. It is unbelievable what we have permitted to happen on our campuses. No wonder some kids can't think about their studies. Their lives are in danger! Yes, we can reduce the violence if we're committed to the task. Armed guards? Maybe. Metal detectors? If necessary. More expulsions? Probably. No-nonsense administrators? Definitely. When schools are blessed by strong leadership, like the legendary Joe Clark at Eastside High School in Paterson, New Jersey, they make dramatic progress academically. Above all, we must do what is required to pacify the combat zones in junior and senior high schools.

We will not solve our pervasive problems, however, with the present generation of secondary school students. Our best hope for the future is to start over with the youngsters just coming into elementary school. We can rewrite the rules with these wide-eyed kids. Let's redesign the primary grades to include a greater measure of discipline. I'm not talking merely about more difficult assignments and additional homework. I'm recommending more structure and control in the classroom.

As the first official voice of the school, the primary teacher is in a position to construct positive attitudinal foundations on which future educators can build. Conversely, she can fill her young pupils with contempt and disrespect. A child's teachers during the first six years will largely determine the nature of his attitude toward authority and the educational climate in junior and senior high school (and beyond).

QUESTION 170

What can we as parents do to improve public schools in our area?

Most educators know that parental involvement is absolutely critical to what public schools are trying to do. Others (fortunately not the majority) see themselves as the professionals and resent parental interference. We should never accede to that idea. Parents are ultimately responsible for the education of their kids, and they should not surrender that authority. Educators are their employees, paid with tax dollars, and are accountable to the school-board members whom parents elect. The best schools are those with the greatest parental involvement and support.

With that understanding, let me urge you to visit your child's school to answer questions of interest to you. Does the staff understand the necessity for structure, respect, and discipline in the classroom? If so, why don't you call your child's teacher and the principal and express your appreciation to them? They could use a pat on the back. Tell them you stand ready to assist in carrying out their important mission. If your school system is not so oriented, get involved to help turn the tide. Meet with parent groups. Join the PTA. Review the textbooks. Work for the election of school-board members who believe in traditional values and academic excellence. Let me say it again: Schools function best when the time-honored principle of local control—by parents—prevails. I believe it is making a comeback!

QUESTION 171

How do you feel about corporal punishment as a deterrent to school misbehavior? Do you believe in spanking our students?

Corporal punishment is not effective at the junior and senior high school levels, and I do not recommend its application. It can be useful for elementary students, especially with amateur clowns (as opposed to hard-core troublemakers). For this reason, I am opposed to abolishing

spanking in elementary schools because we have systematically eliminated the tools with which teachers have traditionally backed up their
word. We're down now to a precious few. Let's not go any further in that
direction.

QUESTION 172

**I have observed that elementary and junior high school
students—even high schoolers—tend to admire the more
strict teachers. Common sense would tell us that they would
like those who are easier on them. Why do you think they are
drawn to the disciplinarians?**

You are right; teachers who maintain order and demand the most from
their students are often the most respected members of the faculty,
provided they aren't mean and grouchy. One who can control a class
without being unpleasant is almost always esteemed by her students.
That is true, first of all, because there is safety in order. When a class
is out of control, particularly at the elementary school level, the
children are afraid of each other. If the teacher can't make the class
behave, how can she prevent a bully from doing his thing? How can
she keep the students from laughing at one of the less-able members?
Children can be vicious to each other, and they feel good about having
a teacher who is strong but kind.

Second, children love justice. When someone has violated a rule,
they want immediate retribution. They admire the teacher who can
enforce an equitable legal system, and they find great comfort in
reasonable social expectations. By contrast, the teacher who does not
control her class inevitably allows crime to pay, violating something
basic in the value system of children.

Third, children admire strict teachers because chaos is nerve-
racking. Screaming and hitting and wiggling are fun for about ten
minutes; then the confusion begins to get tiresome and irritating.

I have smiled in amusement many times as second- and third-grade
children astutely evaluated the relative disciplinary skills of their
teachers. They know how a class should be conducted. I only wish all
of their teachers were equally aware of this important attribute.

164

Q UESTION 173

Can you give us a guideline for how much work children should be given to do?

There should be a healthy balance between work and play. Many farm children of the past had daily chores that made life pretty difficult. Early in the morning and again after school they would feed the pigs, gather the eggs, milk the cows, and bring in the wood. Little time was left for fun, and childhood became a pretty drab experience. That was an extreme position, and I certainly don't favor its return.

Contrast that workaday responsibility with some families today that require nothing of children—not even asking them to take out the trash, water the lawn, or feed the cat. Both extremes, as usual, are harmful to the child. The logical middle ground can be found by giving a boy or girl an exposure to responsibility and work but preserving time for play and fun. The amount of time devoted to each activity should vary with the age of the child, gradually requiring more work as he or she grows older.

Q UESTION 174

Schools are asked to accomplish many things on behalf of our kids today. They are even expected to teach them how to have sex without spreading disease. What part of the curriculum would you give the greatest priority?

Schools that try to do everything may wind up doing very little. That's why I believe we should give priority to the academic fundamentals— what used to be called "readin', writin', and 'rithmetic." Of those three, the most important is basic literacy. An appalling number of students graduating from high school can't even read the employment page of the newspaper or comprehend an elementary book. Every one of those young men and women will suffer years of pain and embarrassment because of our failure. That misery starts at a very young age.

A tenth-grade boy was once referred to me because he was dropping

165

out of school. I asked why he was quitting, and he said with great passion, "I've been miserable since first grade. I've felt embarrassed and stupid every year. I've had to stand up and read, but I can't even understand a second-grade book. You people have had your last laugh at me. I'm getting out." I told him I didn't blame him for the way he felt; his suffering was our responsibility.

Teaching children to read should be "Job One" for educators. Giving boys and girls that basic skill is the foundation on which other learning is built. Unfortunately, millions of young people are still functionally illiterate after completing twelve years of schooling and receiving high school diplomas. There is no excuse for this failure. Research shows that every student, with very few exceptions, can be taught to read if the task is approached creatively and individually. Admittedly, some can't learn in group settings because their minds wander and they don't ask questions as readily. They require one-on-one instruction from trained reading specialists. It is expensive for schools to support these remedial teachers, but no expenditure would be more helpful. Special techniques, teaching machines, and behavior-modification techniques can work in individual cases. Whatever is required, we must provide it. Furthermore, the sooner this help can be given, the better for the emotional and academic well-being of the child. By the fourth or fifth grade, he or she has already suffered the humiliation of reading failure.

QUESTION 175

What causes a child to be a "slow learner"—one who just doesn't learn like other children in the classroom?

There are many hereditary, environmental, and physical factors that contribute to one's intellect, and it is difficult to isolate the particular influences. For many children who have difficulty in school, we will never know precisely why their ability to learn is limited. Let me tell you what is now known about intellectual development that may explain some—but not all—cases of learning deficits.

Accumulating evidence seems to indicate that some children who are slow learners and even those who have borderline retardation may not have received proper intellectual stimulation in their very early years. There appears to be a critical period during the first three to four years when the potential for intellectual growth must be seized. There are enzyme systems in the brain that must be activated during this brief window. If the opportunity is missed, the child may never reach his capacity.

Children who grow up in deprived circumstances are more likely to be slow learners. They may not have heard adult language regularly. They have not been provided with interesting books and puzzles to occupy their sensory apparatus. They have not been taken to the zoo, the airport, or other exciting places. They have not received daily training and guidance from adults. This lack of stimulation may inhibit the brain from developing properly.

The effect of early stimulation on living brains has been studied in several fascinating animal experiments. In one study, researchers divided littermate rats into two identical groups. The first was given maximum stimulation during the first few months of life. These rats were kept in well-lit cages, surrounded by interesting paddle wheels and other toys. They were handled regularly and allowed to explore outside their cages. They were subjected to learning experiences and then rewarded for remembering. The second group lived the opposite kind of existence. These rats crouched in dimly lit, drab, uninteresting cages. They were not handled or stimulated in any way and were not permitted outside their cages. Both groups were fed identical food.

At 105 days of age, all the rats were sacrificed to permit examination of their neurological apparatus. The researchers were surprised to find that the high-stimulation rats had brains that differed in several important ways: (1) the cortex (the thinking part of the brain) was thicker and wider; (2) the blood supply was much more abundant; (3) the enzymes necessary for learning were more sophisticated. The researchers concluded that the stimulation experienced during the first group's early lives had resulted in more advanced and complex brains.[50]

It is always risky to apply conclusions from animal research directly to humans, but the same kinds of changes probably occur in the brains of highly stimulated children. If parents want their children to be capable, they should begin by talking to them at length while they are still babies. Interesting mobiles and winking-blinking toys should be arranged around the crib. From then on through the toddler years, learning activities should be programmed regularly.

Of course, parents must understand the difference between stimulation and pressure. Providing books for a three-year-old is stimulating. Ridiculing and threatening him because he can't read them is pressuring. Imposing unreachable expectations can have a damaging effect on children.

If early stimulation is as important as it now appears, then the lack thereof may be a leading cause of learning impairment among schoolchildren. It is imperative that parents take the time to invest their resources in their children. The necessity for providing rich, edifying experiences for young children has never been as obvious as it is today.

Q UESTION 176

You have told us what kinds of homes produce children with the greatest intellectual potential. Are there other studies that would tell us how to raise kids with the healthiest attitudes toward themselves and others?

A study designed to answer that precise question was conducted some years ago by Dr. Stanley Coopersmith, associate professor of psychology, University of California. He evaluated 1,738 normal middle-class boys and their families, beginning in the preadolescent period and following them through to young manhood. After identifying those boys having the highest self-esteem, he compared their homes and childhood influences with those having a lower sense of self-worth. He found three important characteristics that distinguished them:

1. The high-esteem children were clearly more loved and appreciated at home than were the low-esteem boys.
2. The high-esteem group came from homes where parents had been significantly more strict in their approach to discipline. By contrast, the parents of the low-esteem group had created insecurity and dependence by their permissiveness. Their children were

more likely to feel that the rules were not enforced because no one cared enough to get involved. Furthermore, the most successful and independent young men during the latter period of the study were found to have come from homes that demanded the strictest accountability and responsibility. And as could have been predicted, the family ties remained the strongest not in the wishy-washy homes but in the homes where discipline and self-control had been a way of life.

3. The homes of the high-esteem group were also characterized by democracy and openness. Once the boundaries for behavior were established, there was freedom for individual personalities to grow and develop. The boys could express themselves without fear of ridicule, and the overall atmosphere was marked by acceptance and emotional safety.[51]

QUESTION 177

My six-year-old son has always been an energetic child with some of the symptoms of hyperactivity. He has a short attention span and flits from one activity to another. I took him to his pediatrician, who said he did not have attention deficit disorder. However, he's beginning to have learning problems in school because he can't stay in his seat and concentrate on his lessons. What should I do?

It sounds like your son is immature in comparison with his age-mates and could profit from being retained in the first grade next year. If his birthday is between December 1 and July 1, I would ask the school psychologist to evaluate his readiness to learn. Retaining an immature boy during his early school career (kindergarten or first grade) can give him a social and academic advantage throughout the remaining years of elementary school. However, it is very important to help him "save face" with his peers. If possible, he should change schools for at least a year to avoid embarrassing questions and ridicule from his former classmates. You have very little to lose by holding back an immature boy, since males tend to be about six months behind females in development at that time. The age of a child is the worst criterion

169

on which to base a decision regarding when to begin a school career. That determination should be made according to specific neurological, psychosocial, and pediatric variables.

Let me add one other suggestion that you might consider. Your son appears to be a good candidate for home schooling. Keep him in the safety of your care until he matures a bit, and then if you choose, place him in school one year behind where he would have been otherwise. He will not suffer academically and will be more secure for the experience.

Home schooling is especially helpful for the immature child—usually a boy—who is just not ready for the social competition and rejection often experienced within large groups. It is also beneficial to children who do not have this problem, if the parent is committed to it. That's why home schooling is the fastest growing educational movement in the United States today.[52]

Q UESTION 178

If age is such a poor factor to use in determining the start of the first grade, why is it applied so universally in our country?

Because it is so convenient. Parents can plan for the definite beginning of school when their child turns six. School officials can survey their districts and know how many first graders they will have the following year. If an eight-year-old moves into the district in October, the administrator knows the child belongs in second grade, and so on. The use of chronological age as a criterion for school entrance is great for everybody—except the late bloomer who is developmentally unprepared for formal education.

Q UESTION 179

We have a six-year-old son who is also a late bloomer and is having trouble learning to read. Even though he is immature, I don't understand why this would keep him from reading.

It is likely that your late-maturing youngster has not yet completed a vital neurological process involving an organic substance called myelin. At birth, the nervous system of the body is not insulated. That is why an infant is unable to reach out and grasp an object; the electrical command or impulse is lost on its journey from the brain to the hand. Gradually, a whitish substance (myelin) begins to coat the nerve fibers, allowing controlled muscular action to occur.

Myelinization typically proceeds from the head downward and from the center of the body outward. In other words, a child can control the movement of his head and neck before the rest of his body. Control of the shoulder precedes the elbow, which precedes the wrist, which precedes the large muscles in the hands, which precedes small-muscle coordination of the fingers. This explains why elementary school children are taught block-letter printing before they learn cursive writing; the broad strokes and lines are less dependent on minute finger control than the flowing curves of mature penmanship.

Since visual apparatus in humans is usually the last neural mechanism to be myelinated, your immature child may not have undergone this necessary developmental process by his present age of six years. Therefore, such a child who is extremely immature and uncoordinated may be neurologically unprepared for the intellectual tasks of reading and writing. Reading, particularly, is a highly complex neurological process. The visual stimulus must be relayed to the brain without distortion, where it should be interpreted and retained in the memory. Not all six-year-old children are equipped to perform this task. Unfortunately, however, our culture permits few exceptions or deviations from the established timetable. A child of that age must learn to read or he will face the emotional consequences of failure. This is why I favor either holding an immature child out of school for a year or home schooling him or her for several years.

QUESTION 180

Is retention in the same grade ever advisable for a child who is not a late bloomer? How about the slow learner?

There are some students who can profit from a second year at the same grade level and many who will not. The best guideline is this: Retain only the child for whom something will be different next year. A youngster who is sick for seven months in an academic year might profit from another run-through when he or she is healthy. And as I've indicated, a late-developing child should be held back in kindergarten (or the first grade at the latest) to place him or her with youngsters of comparable development. For the slow learner, however—the child who has below-average ability—a second journey through the same grade will not help. If he was failing the fourth grade in June, he will continue to fail the fourth grade in September. The findings from research on this issue are crystal clear.

It is not often realized that the curricular content of each grade level is very similar to the year before and the year after. There is considerable redundancy in the concepts taught; the students in each grade are taken a little further, but much of the time is spent in review. The arithmetical methods of addition and subtraction, for example, are taught in the primary years, but considerable work is done on these tasks in the sixth grade, too. Nouns and verbs are taught repeatedly for several years.

Thus, the most unjustifiable reason for retention is to give the slow learner another year of exposure to easier concepts. He will not do better the second time around! Nor is there much magic in summer school. Some parents hope that a six-week program in July and August will accomplish what was impossible in the ten months between September and June. They are often disappointed.

QUESTION 181

I've heard that we forget more than 80 percent of what we learn. When you consider the cost of getting an education, I wonder why we put all that effort into examinations, textbooks, homework, and years spent in boring classrooms. Is education really worth what we invest in it?

In fact, it is. There are many valid reasons for learning, even if forgetting will take its usual toll. First, one of the important functions of the learning process is the self-discipline and self-control that it fosters. Good students learn to follow directions, carry out assignments, and channel their mental faculties. Second, even if the facts and concepts can't be recalled, the individual knows they exist and where to find them. He or she can retrieve the information if needed. Third, old learning makes new learning easier. Each mental exercise gives us more associative cues with which to link future ideas and concepts, and we are changed for having been through the process of learning. Fourth, we don't really forget everything that is beyond the reach of our memories. The information is stored in the brain and will return to consciousness when properly stimulated. And fifth, we are shaped by the influence of intelligent and charismatic people who teach us.

I wish there were an easier, more efficient process for shaping human minds than the slow and painful experience of education. But until a "learning pill" is developed, the old-fashioned approach will have to do.

Q UESTION 182

Our junior higher is the most disorganized kid I've ever seen. His life is a jumble of forgotten assignments and missed deadlines. What can I do to help him?

You'll have no trouble believing what educational consultant Cheri Fuller considers to be the most common cause of school failure. She says it is not laziness or poor study skills. The primary problem is what you see in your son—massive disorganization. Show me a student's notebook, Fuller says, and I'll tell you whether that individual is a B student or a D student. An achieving student's notebook is arranged neatly with dividers and folders for handouts and assignments. A failing student's notebook is usually a jumbled mess and may not even be used at all.

Some children are naturally sloppy, but most of them can learn to be better organized. Fuller says this skill should be taught in the elementary school years. Once they enter junior high, students may have as many as five teachers, each assigning different textbooks, workbooks, handouts, and requirements from various classroom subjects. It is foolish to assume that kids who have never had any organizational training will be able to keep such detail straight and accessible. If we want them to function in this system, we need to give them the tools that are critical to success.[53]

You might consider having your child evaluated to see if he has attention deficit disorder or some temperamental characteristic that makes it difficult for him to organize. When you've determined what he is capable of doing, work with an educational consultant or a school psychologist to design a system that will teach him how to live a more structured life.

*Q*UESTION **183**

I've always had an interest in creative writing, primarily because I had a teacher who encouraged me to express myself and gave me the skills to do it. My kids, however, have not had that exposure. The school system just doesn't teach writing skills anymore. How did you come to be a writer, and how might I give my children a nudge in that direction?

It is true that writing skills are seldom taught today. That was evident a while back when I was considering hiring a Ph.D. candidate from a large university. I called her major professor for a recommendation. He spoke highly of this woman and said he was sure she would do a good job for me. I then asked if she was an adequate writer. He said, "Are you kidding? None of my students have strong writing skills. Young people don't learn to put their thoughts on paper these days." He was right!

It hasn't always been that way. I remember diagramming sentences and learning parts of speech when I was in elementary school. It was a major part of the curriculum. Also, my parents encouraged me and helped me grow in this area. I wrote a letter to a friend when I was nine years old. My mother then suggested that we read it together. I had written, "Dear Tom, how are you? I am just fine." My mom asked me if I thought that sounded a little boring. She said, "You haven't said anything. You used a few words, but they have no meaning." I never wrote that phrase again, although that is the typical way a child begins a letter.

Looking back, I can see how, even at an early age, my mother was teaching me to write. In addition, I was also fortunate to have a few English teachers who were determined to teach me the fundamentals of composition. I had one in high school and another in college who insisted that I learn grammar and composition. They nearly beat me to death, but I'm glad they did. I earn a living today, at least in part, with the skills they gave to me. Especially, I would like to say thanks to Dr. Ed Harwood. His classes were like marine boot camp, but what I learned there was priceless.

It's not terribly difficult or time-consuming to encourage and teach kids some of the basics of grammar and composition. One approach is to ask a family member to correspond with your child and encourage him or her to write back. Then when the reply is written, sprinkle a few corrections, such as the one my mother offered, with a generous portion of praise. Finally, entice that youngster to engage in a little creative expression. As for what you can do to compensate for the de-emphasis on writing in school, I really don't know—except to seek instruction outside the classroom.

The ability to write has gone out of style—much like the old "homemaking" classes for girls. But it is an incredibly valuable craft that your child can use in a wide variety of settings. Don't let him or her grow up without developing it.

QUESTION 184

I'm a teacher, and I love my students. There is one kid in my sixth-grade class, however, who drives me nuts. He works overtime trying to make everybody laugh. What drives this impish child? Why does he want to make life miserable for me?

We all remember the kid you're talking about. He's called "the class clown" and some other things that are less flattering. He is a trial to his teachers, an embarrassment to his parents, and an utter delight to every child who wants to escape the boredom of school. There are millions of class clowns on the job today. It's my belief that boards of education assign at least one such kid to every class just to make sure that schoolteachers earn every dollar of their salaries.

These skilled little disrupters are usually boys. They often have reading or other academic problems. They may be small in stature, although not always, and they'll do anything for a laugh. Their parents and teachers may not recognize that behind the boisterous behavior is often the pain of inferiority.

You see, humor is a classic response to feelings of low self-esteem. That's why within many successful comedians is the memory of a hurting little boy or girl. Jonathan Winters's parents were divorced when he was seven years old, and he said he used to cry when he was alone because other children teased him about not having a father. Joan Rivers frequently jokes about her unattractiveness as a girl. She said she was such a dog, her father had to throw a bone down the aisle to get her married. And so it goes.

These and other comedians got their training during childhood, using humor as a defense against childhood hurts. That's usually the inspiration for the class clown. By making an enormous joke out of everything, he conceals the self-doubt that churns inside.

That understanding should help us meet his needs and manage such a child more effectively.

Q UESTION 185

A great deal is being made about something called "school choice" these days. Could you explain this concept and tell me whether or not you are in favor of it?

School choice is an idea whose time has come. It would give parents the right to decide whether to send their children to a public, private, or religious institution and even to select a specific school to which they would be sent.

I favor this idea for several reasons. First, giving parents a choice would improve the quality of education because it would force school personnel to compete for students. That would make them more responsive to parents. Competition always improves the performance of human beings, whether one is selling hamburgers or automobiles. It encourages people to serve more willingly, to operate more efficiently, and to do a good job.

That is the heart of the free-enterprise system. It provides incentives to those who work hard and think creatively. Monopolies, by contrast, become unresponsive and stilted. We've seen that lethargy in the U.S. Post Office, in the various departments of motor vehicles, in Amtrak—and in the present educational system. I believe test scores will rise and parents will be more satisfied when schools that do a great job are allowed to grow. Their budgets will expand and their teachers will be proud, while disorganized and unresponsive schools with poor teachers and halfhearted administrators will wither on the vine. That prospect of competition makes educators nervous—but it makes many of us excited.

The second reason I favor school choice is related to the first: It would put power in the hands of parents. If Dad or Mom became dissatisfied with a particular school, he or she could take the child to a nearby school that better serves their needs. With that youngster would go the voucher and the money it represents. As a bad school began to dwindle under this system, you can bet there would be new motivation among administrators to listen to parents and accommodate their concerns. As it stands today, parents are virtually powerless unless they organize and storm a school-board meeting. There has to be a better way to encourage cooperation between the home and professional educators.

The third benefit of school choice is that it would grant poor people the same options now held by the affluent. Today, if an upper-class family is dissatisfied with their local public schools—or if they prefer Christian education or a first-class prep school—they have the resources to send their children where they wish. An underprivileged family has no such alternative. They are stuck with the school in their neighborhood, even if it is rife with violence and rebellion. President Bill Clinton, who campaigned against school choice in California, sent his daughter to an excellent private school in Washington, D.C. I would like to see everyone have the opportunity he had.

Recently, statistics released by the U.S. Department of Education itself indicated that nearly half of our nation's adult population is functionally illiterate. The future looks even dimmer. The Department of Education has forecast that three out of every five of our current school-age population will either drop out or graduate with an education below the seventh-grade level![54] Given that dismal track record, small wonder the movement to place accountability squarely in the hands of the people to whom it belongs—the staff, parents, and students at each individual school—is gaining ground. Families that care about their children's education are crucial to classroom success. School choice ensures their involvement. It is, I believe, the wave of the future.

QUESTION 186

I've read that it is possible to teach four-year-old children to read. Should I be working on this with my child?

If a youngster is particularly sharp and if he or she can learn to read without feeling undue adult pressure, it would be advantageous to teach this skill. But that's a much bigger "if" than most people realize. There are some parents who find it difficult to work with their children without showing frustration over immaturity and disinterest.

Furthermore, new skills should be taught at the age when they are most needed. Why invest unnecessary effort trying to teach a child to read when he has not yet learned to cross the street, tie his shoes, count to ten, or answer the telephone? It seems foolish to get panicky over preschool reading. The best policy is to provide your children with many interesting books and materials, read to them every day, and answer their questions. You can then introduce them to phonics and watch the lights go on. It's fun if you don't push too hard.

QUESTION 187

Some educators have said we should eliminate report cards and academic marks. Do you think this is a good idea?

178

No, I believe academic marks are valuable for students in the third grade or higher. They reinforce and reward the child who has achieved in school and act as a nudge to the youngster who hasn't. It is important, though, that grades be used properly. They have the power to create or to destroy motivation.

Through the elementary years, I've always felt that a child's grades should be based on what he does with what he has. In other words, I think we should grade according to ability. A slow child should be able to succeed in school just as certainly as a gifted youngster. If he struggles and sweats to achieve, he should somehow be rewarded— even if his work falls short of an absolute standard. By the same token, gifted children should not be given A's just because they are smart enough to excel without working.

Again, the primary purpose of grading in the elementary school years should be to reward academic effort.

However, as the student goes into high school, the purpose of grading shifts. Those who take college preparatory courses must be graded on an absolute standard. An A in chemistry or calculus is accepted by college admission boards as a symbol of excellence, and secondary teachers must preserve that meaning. Students with lesser academic skill need not take those difficult courses.

To repeat, marks for children can be the teacher's most important motivational tool, provided they are used correctly. Therefore, the recommendation that schools eliminate grading is a move away from discipline in the classroom.

QUESTION 188

What would you do if you had an elementary school child in a chaotic classroom with a disorganized teacher?

I would do everything I could to get my child reassigned to a different classroom. Some very bad habits and attitudes can develop in ten months with an incompetent teacher. Home schooling or private education might also be considered, if resources permitted.

QUESTION 189

How do you feel about year-round schools in areas where overcrowding makes them advantageous?

I know there are administrative advantages to year-round schools, especially since the facilities are not standing idle two months a year as they are under the current system. Nevertheless, many parents say year-round schools are very hard on them. Siblings attending different schools may have their vacations at different times, making it impossible for families to take trips together. It is also more difficult to coordinate children's time off with parents' schedules. In short, year-round schools represent just one more hardship on families seeking to do fun and recreational things together each year.

QUESTION 190

How do you feel about homework being given by elementary schools? Do you think it is a good idea? If so, how much and how often?

Having written several books on discipline and being on the record as an advocate of reasonable parental authority, my answer may surprise you: I believe homework for young children can be counterproductive if it is not handled very carefully. Little kids are asked to sit for six or more hours a day doing formal classwork. Then many of them take a tiring bus ride home and guess what? They're placed at a desk and told to do more assignments. For a wiry, active, fun-loving youngster, that is asking too much. Learning for them becomes an enormous bore instead of the exciting panorama that it should be.

I remember a mother coming to see me because her son was struggling in a tough private school. "He has about five hours of homework per night," she said. "How can I make him want to do it?"

"Are you kidding?" I told his mother. "I wouldn't do that much homework!"

Upon investigation, I found that the elementary school he attended vigorously denied giving him that many assignments. Or rather, they didn't give the other students that much work. They did expect the slower boys and girls to complete the assignments they didn't get done in the classroom each day, in addition to the regularly assigned homework. For the plodders like this youngster, that meant up to five hours of work nightly. There was no escape from books throughout their entire day. What a mistake!

Excessive homework during the elementary school years also has the potential of interfering with family life. In our home, we were trying to do many things with the limited time we had together. I wanted our kids to participate in church activities, have some family time, and still be able to kick back and waste an hour or two. Children need opportunities for unstructured play—swinging on the swings and throwing rocks and playing with basketballs. Yet by the time their homework was done, darkness had fallen and dinnertime had arrived. Then baths were taken, and off they went to bed. Something didn't feel right about that kind of pace. That's why I negotiated with our children's teachers, agreeing that they would complete no more than one hour per night of supervised homework. It was enough!

Homework also generates a considerable amount of stress for parents. Their kids either won't do the assignments or they get tired and whine about them. Tensions build and angry words fly. I'm also convinced that child abuse occurs at that point for some children. When my wife, Shirley, was teaching second grade, one little girl came to school with both eyes black and swollen. She said her father had beaten her because she couldn't learn her spelling words. That is illegal now, but it was tolerated then. The poor youngster will remember those beatings for a lifetime and will always think of herself as "stupid."

Then there are the parents who do the assignments for their kids just to get them over the hump. Have you ever been guilty of doing that? Shame on you! More specifically, have you ever worked for two weeks on a fifth-grade geography project for your eleven-year-old— and then learned later that you got a C on it?! That's the ultimate humiliation.

In short, I believe homework in elementary school should be extremely limited. It is appropriate for learning multiplication tables, spelling words, and test review. It is also helpful in training kids to remember assignments, bring books home, and complete them as required. But to load them down night after night with monotonous book work is to invite educational burnout.

In junior high classes, perhaps two hours of homework per night should be the maximum. In high school, those students who are preparing for college must handle more work. Even then, however, the load should be reasonable. Education is a vitally important part of our children's lives, but it is only one part. Balance between these competing objectives is the key word.

*Q*UESTION 191

Boy! Do I understand your perspective on homework. The greatest power struggle in our home is over school assignments. Our fifth grader simply will not do them! When we try to force him to study, he sits and stares, doodles, gets up for water, and just kills time. Furthermore, we never know for sure what he's supposed to be doing. Why is he like that?

Let me offer a short discourse on school achievement, based on years of interaction with parents. I served as a teacher, a high school counselor, and a school psychologist. As such, I became very well acquainted with children's learning patterns. The kind of self-discipline necessary to succeed in school appears to be distributed on a continuum from one extreme to the other. Students at the positive end of the scale (I'll call them Type I) are by nature rather organized individuals who care about details. They take the educational process very seriously and assume full responsibility for assignments given. They also worry about grades, or at least they recognize their importance. To do poorly on a test would depress them for several days. They also like the challenge offered in the classroom. Parents of these children do not have to monitor their progress to keep them working. It is their way of life—and it is consistent with their temperaments.

At the other end of the continuum are the boys and girls who do not fit in well with the structure of the classroom (Type II). If their Type I siblings emerge from school cum laude, these kids graduate "thank you, laude!" They are sloppy, disorganized, and flighty. They have a natural aversion to work and love to play. They can't wait for success, and they hurry on without it. Like bacteria that gradually become immune to antibiotics, the classic underachievers become impervious to adult pressure. They withstand a storm of parental protest every few weeks and then, when no one is looking, they slip back into apathy. They don't even hear the assignments being given in school and seem not to be embarrassed when they fail to complete them. And, you can be sure, they drive their parents to distraction.

Some of these kids have what has become known as attention deficit disorder (ADD) or attention deficit/hyperactivity disorder (ADHD). Those are youngsters who have an unidentified neurological condition that makes them easily distractible, flighty, disorganized, and for some, unable to sit still and concentrate. Trying to make ADD or ADHD children function like other kids without treating them medically is a physical impossibility.

I don't know what is inhibiting your son's school performance, but you should have him seen by a school psychologist or learning specialist. They can diagnose his problem and help you establish a strategy to get the most out of what he has.

QUESTION 192

What else can you tell us about the differences between Type I and Type II kids? I have one of each and want to understand them.

First, you should know that these characteristics are not highly correlated to intelligence. By that I mean there are bright children who are at the flighty end of the scale, and there are slow-learning individuals who are highly motivated. The primary difference between them is a matter of temperament and maturity, although there are more smart kids in the Type I category.

Second, Type II children are not intrinsically inferior to Type I. Yes, it would be wonderful if every student used the talent he or she possessed to best advantage. But each child is a unique individual. Kids don't fit the same mold—nor do they need to. I know education is important today, and we want our boys and girls to go as far as they can academically. But let's keep our goals in proper perspective. It is possible that the low achiever will outperform the academic superstar in the long run. There are many examples of that occurring in the real world (Einstein, Edison, Eleanor Roosevelt, etc.). Don't write off that disorganized, apparently lazy kid as a lifelong loser. He or she may surprise you.

Third, you will never turn a Type II youngster into a Type I scholar by nagging, pushing, threatening, and punishing. It isn't in him. If you try to squeeze him into something he's not, you will only produce aggravation for yourself and anger from the child. That attempt can fill a house with conflict. I have concluded that it is simply not worth the price it extracts.

I am certainly not recommending that children be allowed to float through life, avoiding responsibility and wasting their opportunities. My approach to the underachiever can be summarized in these suggestions: (1) He lacks the discipline to structure his life. Help him generate it. Systematize his study hours. Look over his homework to see that it is neat and complete, etc. (2) Maintain as close contact with the school as possible. The more you and your child's teacher communicate, the better. Only then can you provide the needed structure. (3) Avoid anger in the relationship. It does not help. Those parents who become most frustrated and irritated often believe their child's irresponsibility is a deliberate thing. Usually it is not. Consider the problem a matter of temperament rather than defiance. (4) Seek tutorial assistance if necessary to stay on track. (5) Having done what you can to help, accept what comes in return. Go with the flow and begin looking for other areas of success for your child.

Let me say it once more: Not every individual can be squeezed into the same mold. There is room in this world for the creative souls who long to breathe freely. I'll bet some of you parents approached life from the same direction.

QUESTION 193

I assume that you favor a highly structured curriculum that emphasizes the memorization of specific facts, which I consider to be a very low level of learning. We need to teach concepts to our kids and help them learn how to think—not just fill their heads with a bunch of details.

I agree that we want to teach concepts to students, but that does not occur in a vacuum. For example, we would like them to understand the concept of the solar system and how the planets are positioned in rotation around the sun. How is that done? One way is for them to learn the distances between the heavenly bodies, i.e., the sun is 93 million miles from Earth, but the moon is only 240,000. The concept of relative positions is then understood from the factual information. What I'm saying is that an understanding of the right factual information can and should lead to conceptual learning.

QUESTION 194

But again, you're putting too much emphasis on the memorization process, which is a low academic goal.

The human brain is capable of storing some two billion bits of information in the course of a lifetime. There are many avenues through which that programming can occur, and memorization is one of them. Let me put it this way: If you ever have to go under a surgeon's knife, you'd better hope that the physician has memorized every muscle, every bone, every blood vessel, and every Boy Scout knot in the book. Your life will depend on his ability to access factual information during the operation. Obviously, I strongly oppose the perspective held in some academic circles that says, "There's nothing we know for certain, so why learn anything?" Those who feel that way have no business teaching. They are salesmen with nothing to sell!

QUESTION 195

How can I help my child develop wholesome, respectful attitudes toward people of other racial and ethnic groups?

There is no substitute for parental modeling of the attitudes we wish to teach. Someone wrote, "The footsteps a child follows are most likely to be the ones his parents thought they covered up." It is true. Our children are watching us carefully, and they instinctively imitate our behavior. Therefore we can hardly expect them to be kind to all of God's children if we are prejudiced and rejecting. Likewise, we will be unable to teach appreciativeness if we never say please or thank you at home or abroad. We will not produce honest children if we teach them to lie to the bill collector on the phone by saying, "Dad's not home." In these matters, our boys and girls instantly discern the gap between what we say and what we do. And of the two choices, they usually identify with our behavior and ignore our empty proclamations.

If you never speak derogatorily about racial minorities, and if you absolutely will not tolerate racist jokes and slurs, your children will not fail to notice. It's the best place to begin your teaching process.

QUESTION 196

Many of our friends have begun to home school their children with seemingly positive results. My wife and I are considering this possibility as well but aren't quite sure. What are your views on this educational option? What would you do in my shoes?

This is a subject on which my mind has changed dramatically over the years. There was a time when I subscribed wholeheartedly to the notion that early formal childhood education was vital to the child's intellectual well-being. That was widely believed in the sixties and seventies. I no longer accept that idea and favor keeping kids with their parents for a longer time. Dr. Raymond Moore, author of *School Can Wait*[55] and an early leader of the home-schooling movement, had a great influence on me in this regard.

The research now validates the wisdom of keeping boys and girls in a protected environment until they have achieved a greater degree of maturity. Not only do they benefit emotionally from that delay, but they typically make better progress academically. That's why home-schooled individuals often gain entrance to the most prestigious universities and colleges in the country.[56] What parents can teach young children in informal one-on-one interactions surpasses what their little minds can absorb sitting among twenty-five age-mates in a classroom.

You asked what I would do in your shoes? If Shirley and I were raising our children again, we would home school them at least for the first few years!

186

QUESTION 197

Don't you think home schooling might negatively impact the socialization process? I don't want my children growing up to be misfits.

This is the question home-schooling parents hear most often from curious (or critical) friends, relatives, and neighbors. "Socialization" is a vague, dark cloud hanging over their heads. What if teaching at home somehow isolates the kids and turns them into oddballs? For you and all those parents who see this issue as the great danger of home education, I would respectfully disagree—for these reasons.

First, to remove a child from the classroom is not necessarily to confine him or her to the house! And once beyond the schoolyard gate, the options are practically unlimited! Home-school support groups are surfacing in community after community across the country. Some are highly organized and offer field trips, teaching co-ops, tutoring services, social activities, and various other assistances and resources. There are home-schooling athletic leagues and orchestras and other activities. Even if you're operating completely on your own, there are outings to museums and parks, visits to farms, factories, hospitals, and seats of local government, days with Dad at the office, trips to Grandma's house, extracurricular activities like sports and music, church youth groups, service organizations, and special-interest clubs. There are friends to be invited over and relatives to visit and parties to attend. The list is limitless. Even a trip with Mom to the market can provide youngsters with invaluable exposure to the lives and daily tasks of real adults in the real world. While they're there, a multitude of lessons can be learned about math (pricing, fractions, pints vs. gallons, addition, subtraction, etc.), reading labels, and other academic subjects. And without the strictures of schedule and formal curricula, it can all be considered part of the educational process. That's what I'd call socialization at its best! To accuse home schoolers of creating strange little people in solitary confinement is nonsense.

The great advantage of home schooling, in fact, is the protection it provides to vulnerable children from the wrong kind of socialization.

When children interact in large groups, the strongest and most aggressive kids quickly intimidate the weak and vulnerable. I am absolutely convinced that bad things happen to immature and "different" boys and girls when they are thrown into the highly competitive world of other children. When this occurs in nursery school or in kindergarten, they learn to fear their peers. There stands this knobby-legged little girl who doesn't have a clue about life or how to cope with things that scare her. It's sink or swim, kid. Go for it! It is easy to see why such children tend to become more peer dependent because of the jostling they get at too early an age. Research shows that if these tender little boys and girls can be kept at home for a few more years and shielded from the impact of social pressure, they tend to be more confident, more independent, and often emerge as leaders three or four years later.[57]

If acquainting them with ridicule, rejection, physical threats, and the rigors of the pecking order is necessary to socialize our children, I'd recommend that we keep them unsocialized for a little longer.

QUESTION 198

Why don't you favor letting teachers and administrators pray with their classes and at school functions? That's the way it was when I was a kid.

I know. My public-school teachers were also my Sunday school teachers, and they spoke often of the Bible and Christian concepts in the classroom. But the world has changed since then. Today, if school officials of every belief system are permitted to write and recite prayers, our children will be exposed to a wide variety of theologies—from New Age nonsense to Islamic rituals. In some cities, especially Los Angeles and other large communities with culturally diverse populations, educators might have to develop a kind of "affirmative-action" plan to assure fairness for everyone. A typical week might include prayers to Gaia, the "mother of the earth," on Monday; prayers to Sophia, the feminist "goddess of wisdom," on Tuesday; prayers to Allah on Wednesday; prayers to the "Unknown God of Nature" on Thursday; and prayers to Jehovah, God of Abraham, Isaac, and Jacob, on Friday. Some would say this approach is preferable to today's creeping secularism, but there is another answer.

My vision is for a society that protects religious liberties for people of all faiths. I believe in the concept of pluralism, which acknowledges the widely differing values and beliefs among our citizens. What's needed is a constitutional amendment protecting the rights of students and other citizens to voice their religious convictions and apply their faith to everyday issues.

It would require an amendment to the Constitution of the United States to protect voluntary school prayer and religious liberty generally. The wording should clearly articulate a principle of government neutrality toward religion and should explicitly restore student religious expression in public school. Accordingly, the proposal would prevent the government from forbidding students to mention Jesus in a classroom discussion, sing a religious song at a school recital, draw a nativity scene in art class, share their faith with other students, wear religious clothing, or distribute religious literature. Legal experts on constitutional law have assured me that 80 to 90 percent of religious-liberty court cases could be won if such a measure were to gain passage.

As I write, legislation calling for a religious-liberties amendment is being considered in Congress. Perhaps our leaders will soon give the American people an opportunity to vote on this issue.

11
Sex Education: Where, When, and How

QUESTION **199**

We're told that sex-education programs reduce the incidence of teen pregnancy. Do they work?

Hardly! As the safe-sex ideology has been taught in the nation's schools, the rates of unwed pregnancy and abortion among teens have skyrocketed. A comprehensive study conducted by Stan Weed and Joseph Olson at the Institute for Research and Evaluation confirms that the Planned Parenthood approach actually worsens, rather than lessens, the problem of adolescent sexuality.

Weed and Olson compared rates of pregnancy, abortion, and live births on a state-by-state basis. They concluded that, all things being equal, for every one thousand teens between fifteen and nineteen years of age enrolled in family-planning clinics, we can expect between fifty and a hundred more pregnancies! Their study, based on Planned Parenthood's own data, also revealed significant contradictions between the organization-projected decreases in pregnancy and abortion rates, compared with actual increases in both categories. The researchers concluded that "when a program clearly should work, but apparently doesn't, it is important to find out why."[58]

Q UESTION **200**

You have been critical of the philosophy and intent of Planned Parenthood and similar organizations. What is their program? What are they trying to accomplish with teenagers? What would their leaders do if given free rein in the schools?

As I understand their agenda, it can be summarized in the following four-point plan:

1. *Provide "value-free" guidance on sexuality to teenagers.* Heaven forbid any preference for morality or sexual responsibility being expressed.
2. *Provide unlimited access to contraceptives by adolescents, dispensed from clinics located on junior high and high school campuses.* In so doing, a powerful statement is made to teenagers about adult approval of premarital sexual activity.
3. *Keep parents out of the picture by every means possible.* Staff members for Planned Parenthood can then assume the parental role and communicate their libertarian philosophy to teens.
4. *Provide free abortions for young women who become pregnant, again, without parental involvement or permission.*

Incredibly, millions of Americans and Canadians seem to buy this outrageous plan, which would have brought a storm of protest from yesterday's parents. Imagine how your father or grandfather would have reacted if a school official had secretly given contraceptives to you or arranged a quiet abortion when you were a teenager. The entire community would have been incensed.

Q UESTION **201**

Our local school board is currently trying to decide whether or not boys and girls should be segregated for courses on sexuality and "family life." What are your feelings with regard to coed sex-education programs?

I have severe reservations about highly explicit discussions occurring with both sexes present. To do so breaks down the natural barriers that help to preserve virginity and makes casual sexual experimentation much more likely to occur. It also strips kids—especially girls—of their modesty to have every detail of anatomy, physiology, intercourse, and condom usage made explicit in coed situations. Those who have thereby become familiar and conversant about the most intimate subjects later find themselves watching explicit sexual scenes in movies, rock videos, and hot television programs. It doesn't take a rocket scientist to recognize the combined impact of these influences. Whereas it was a weighty decision to give up one's virginity in decades past, it is but a small step for those whose conditioning began in the school classroom. Familiarity "breeds," as we all know. I am also convinced that the incidence of date rape rises when the barriers that help a girl protect herself are removed.

In some cases, no doubt, school officials have pushed for mixed sex-ed. classes out of a sense of obligation. Somehow, they feel this is what's expected of them—that parents and the community at large want it. Let them know if you disagree! Tell your school-board members about the educational advantages of separated classes. They may see your point if you present it to them from that angle.

QUESTION 202

It seems clear that comprehensive sex-education programs have failed miserably in addressing the problems of teen pregnancy and sexually transmitted diseases, all of which have dramatically increased over the past twenty years. So what is the answer to curbing teenage sexual activity?

One significant study, authored by Stephen Small from the University of Wisconsin-Madison and Tom Luster of Michigan State and published in the *Journal of Marriage and the Family,* demonstrated rather conclusively that parental involvement and the transmitting of the parents' values were significant factors in preventing early sexual activity. In a direct and refreshingly sensible way, Small and Luster put parents back in the driver's seat (or the hot seat) when they said,

"Permissive parental values regarding adolescent sexual behavior emerged as a strong risk factor for both males and females. Not surprisingly, adolescents who perceived their parents as accepting of premarital adolescent sexual activity were more likely to be sexually experienced."[59] The acorn never falls far from the tree.

Another important study, conducted by Drs. Sharon White and Richard DeBlassie (published in *Adolescence*), found that parents who set the most moderate and reasonable rules for their teens in the areas of dating and interaction with the opposite sex actually got the best results—in contrast to those who were overly strict (who experienced a lesser degree of success) and those who provided no guidelines whatsoever (whose position was least efficacious of all).[60]

From these studies and others, we can conclude that the people who are most effective in steering their children away from the precipice of premarital sex are those who understand that parenting adolescents is a delicate art. They are the parents who are present and involved, who communicate and exemplify their own values and attitudes, who ask questions, who carefully supervise their kids' choice of escorts and points of destination, and who insist on a reasonable curfew. But they also keep a light touch as far as it's possible to do so, because they know that the rod of iron comes with problems of its own. The bottom line? There is no sex-education program, no curriculum, no school or institution in the world that can match the power and influence of this kind of parental involvement.

It's worth adding that kids from intact, two-parent homes are less likely to engage in sexual experimentation than their counterparts from single-parent families or less stable backgrounds. And teens who have strong religious convictions and participate actively in church are, as a group, far more likely to practice abstinence than their peers. It's difficult to avoid the conclusion that faith and fidelity in the older generation are the best insurance against promiscuity in the younger.

QUESTION 203

I disagree emphatically with what the local junior high school is teaching my daughter in sex-education class. Do I have a right to object, and how should I go about doing it?

You certainly do. I strongly support the historic American idea that parents are ultimately responsible for raising and educating their children. The school is an important ally in that effort, but the final authority lies in the home. Thus, when educational materials and content are contrary to a family's basic beliefs, parents have the right to ask school personnel to help them protect their children. Most educators are willing to accommodate the needs of individual families in this way. If they refuse, you as parents have two choices—stay and fight for what you believe, or find a new school. If you decide to oppose what is being taught, you will need the support of as many other parents as possible. Eventually you may have to take your case to the local school board. If so, be encouraged. You *can* win there. Parents in New York City became incensed over pro-homosexual materials being used in elementary schools. The superintendent and some board members refused to budge, which proved to be their undoing. Before it was over, the superintendent was fired, some board members lost their seats, and parents reestablished local control over the education of their children.[61] Some things are worth fighting to defend. Our kids are at the top of the list.

QUESTION 204

Since you disapprove of public school sex-education programs as currently designed, who do you think should tell children the facts of life, and when should that instruction begin?

For those parents who are able to handle the instructional process correctly, the responsibility for sex education should be retained in the home. There is a growing trend for all aspects of education to be taken from their hands (or the role is deliberately forfeited by them). This is unwise. Particularly in the matter of sex education, the best approach is one that begins casually and naturally in early childhood and extends through the years, according to a policy of openness, frankness, and honesty. Only parents can provide this lifetime training—being there when the questions arise and the desire for information is evidenced.

Unfortunately, moms and dads often fail to do the job. Some are too sexually inhibited to present the subject with poise, or they may lack the necessary technical knowledge of the human body. Another common mistake is to wait until puberty is knocking at the door and then try to initiate a desperate, tension-filled conversation that embarrasses the kid and exhausts the parent. If this is the way sex education is going to be handled, there has to be another alternative to consider.

QUESTION 205

When parents need help with sex education, who do you think should provide it?

It is my strong conviction that churches believing in abstinence before marriage and in lifelong marital fidelity should step in and offer their help to families sharing that commitment. Where else will moms and dads find proponents of traditional morality in this permissive day? There is no other agency or institution likely to represent the theology of the church better than the church itself. It is puzzling to me that so few have accepted this challenge, given the attack on biblical concepts of morality today.

A few parents who enroll their children in private schools are able to get the help they need with sex education. Even there, however, the subject is often ignored or handled inadequately. What has developed, unfortunately, is an informational vacuum that sets the stage for far-reaching programs in the public schools that go beyond parental wishes, beginning in some cases with kindergarten children.

QUESTION 206

I would like to teach my own child about human sexuality, but I'm not sure I know how to go about it. Talk about the matter of timing. When do I say what?

One of the most common mistakes made by parents and many overzealous educators is teaching too much too soon. One parent told me, for example, that the kindergarten children in her local district were shown films of animals in the act of copulation. That is unwise and dangerous! Available evidence indicates that there are numerous hazards involved in moving too rapidly. Children can sustain a severe emotional jolt by being exposed to realities for which they are not prepared.

Furthermore, it is unwise to place the youngster on an informational timetable that will result in full awareness too early in life. If eight-year-old children are given an understanding of mature sexual behavior, it is less likely that they will wait ten or twelve years to apply this knowledge within the confines of marriage.

Generally speaking, children should be given the information they need at a particular age. Six-year-olds, for example, don't need to understand the pleasures of adult sexuality. They are not ready to deal with that concept at their developmental stage. They *should* be told where babies come from and how they are born. Sometime between six and nine, depending on the maturity and interest of an individual (and what is being heard in the neighborhood), he or she ought to understand how conception occurs. The rest of the story can be told later in elementary school.

Admittedly, this ideal timetable can be turned upside down by exposure to precocious friends, racy videos, or unwise adults. When that occurs, you have to cope with the fallout as best as possible. It is regrettable that we expose our vulnerable children to far too much of the wrong kind of sexuality.

QUESTION 207

How do I get started? Is there a natural way to get into the topic?

Fortunately, most children will ask for information when they need it. You should be ready to grab those opportunities at the drop of a hat. Sometimes very little warning is given. Our daughter asked for very specific details when she was only seven years old, catching her mother off guard. My wife stalled for an hour, during which she alerted me. Then the three of us sat on the bed drinking hot chocolate and talking about matters we hadn't expected to discuss for several years.

You never know when such a moment will arrive, and you need to think it through in advance.

Although those spontaneous conversations are easiest, some children never ask the right questions. Some boys and girls have "inquiring minds that want to know," while others never give the subject of sex a second thought. If your child is one of those who seems disinterested, you're still on the hook. The task must get done. Someone else will do the job if you won't—someone who may not share your values.

QUESTION 208

In one of your early books you talked about something you gave to your daughter that symbolized the importance of moral purity. Describe it again.

Yes, many years ago Shirley and I gave our daughter a small gold key. It was attached to a chain worn around her neck and represented the key to her heart. She made a vow to give that key to one man only—the one who would share her love through the remainder of her life. You might consider a similar gift for your daughter or a special ring for your son. These go with them throughout adolescence and provide a tangible reminder of the lasting, precious gift of abstinence until marriage and then fidelity to the mate for life. I still recommend this approach enthusiastically.

Here is a letter I received from a fifteen-year-old girl describing how much this experience meant to her:

I am writing to share with you a most blessed experience. . . . On my fifteenth birthday my parents gave me a surprise birthday party in which my ring would be presented. When my father put the ring on my finger I stood there looking at unsaved relatives and my peers. Suddenly I realized this was the opportunity I had been waiting for. Saying a quick prayer I said the following: "It is a great honor for me to wear this ring, because it symbolizes the commitment I am making to God, myself, my family, my friends, my future husband, and my future children to remain physically and sexually abstinent from this day until the day I enter a biblical marriage relationship. I know it won't

198

be easy, but as long as I keep my eyes on Jesus, things will be easier. Temptations may and will come, but my heart's prayer is that God will give me the courage and strength to stand my ground. And finally, may I always have the desire to serve, honor, and please the Lord today and forevermore." . . . The people's response was positively incredible . . . God had used my sincere statement to move even the most hardened of hearts. . . . The purpose of my letter is to encourage you when you are in the valley or maybe even feel like quitting (like we all do sometimes); remember me and this letter; remember that because you have been faithful to the call, God has blessed you by helping you reach millions like me around the world.

Question **209**

You've indicated when sex education should begin. When should it end?

You should plan to end your formal instructional program about the time your son or daughter enters puberty (the time of rapid sexual development in early adolescence). Puberty usually begins between ten and thirteen for girls and between eleven and fourteen for boys. Once they enter this developmental period, they are typically embarrassed by discussions of sex with their parents. Adolescents usually resent adult intrusion during this time—unless they raise the topic themselves. In other words, this is an area where teens should invite parents into their lives.

I feel that we should respect their wishes. We are given ten or twelve years to provide the proper understanding of human sexuality. After that foundation has been laid, we serve primarily as resources to whom our children can turn when the need exists. That is not to say parents should abdicate their responsibility to provide guidance about issues related to sexuality, dating, marriage, etc., as opportunities present themselves. Again, sensitivity to the feelings of the teen is paramount. If he or she wishes to talk, by all means, welcome the conversation. In other cases, parental guidance may be most effective if offered indirectly. Trusted youth workers at church or in a club program such as Campus Life or Young Life can often break the ice when parents can't.

I'd also suggest that you arrange a subscription for your kids to magazines that provide solid Christian advice—from the perspective of a friend rather than an authority figure. Examples include *Brio* (for girls ages twelve and up) and *Breakaway* (for boys ages twelve and up), both of which are available through Focus on the Family.

Q UESTION 210

If you were a parent and knew that your son or daughter was thinking about engaging in sexual intercourse, wouldn't you talk to them about condom usage? If our kids are going to have sex anyway, shouldn't we make sure they are properly protected?

I would not, because that approach has an unintended consequence. By recommending condom usage to teenagers, we inevitably convey five dangerous ideas: (1) that "safe sex" is achievable; (2) that everybody is doing it; (3) that responsible adults *expect* them to do it; (4) that it's a good thing; and (5) that their peers *know* they *know* these things, breeding promiscuity. Those are very destructive messages to give our kids.

Furthermore, Planned Parenthood's own data shows that the number one reason teenagers engage in intercourse is *peer pressure!*[62] Therefore, anything we do to imply that "everybody is doing it" results in more—not fewer—teens who give the game a try. What I'm saying is that our condom-distribution programs do not reduce the number of kids exposed to the disease—they radically increase it!

Since the Planned Parenthood–type programs began in 1970, unwed pregnancies have increased 87 percent among fifteen- to nineteen-year-olds.[63] Likewise, abortions among teens rose 67 percent;[64] unwed births went up 83.8 percent.[65] And venereal disease has infected a generation of young people. The statistics speak for themselves.

And consider this: Research indicates that where disease prevention is concerned, the failure rate of condoms is incredibly high, perhaps 50 percent or greater.[66] Condoms also fail to protect against some STDs that are transmitted from areas not covered (the base of the male genitalia, for example). After twenty-five years of teaching safe-sex ideology, and more than 2 billion federal dollars invested in selling this notion, we have a medical disaster on our hands. More than 500,000 cases of herpes occur annually,[67] and the number of reported cases of chlamydia has risen 281 percent since 1987. Forty-six percent of chlamydia cases occur in teenage girls ages fifteen to nineteen.[68] In addition, there are now over 24 million cases of HPV (human papilloma virus) in the United States, with a higher prevalence among teens.[69]

Having acknowledged these problems, why in the world would I recommend this so-called solution to my son or daughter? Look at it this way. Suppose my kids were sky divers whose parachutes had been demonstrated to fail 50 percent of the time. Would I suggest that they simply buckle the chutes tighter? Certainly not. I would say, "Please don't jump. Your life is at stake!" How could I, as a loving father, do less?

I should add that, despite the popular myth to the contrary, teens *can* understand, accept, and implement the abstinence message. It's not true that young people are sexual robots, hopelessly incapable of controlling their own behavior. As a matter of fact, almost 50 percent of all high school students are virgins today,[70] even though hardly anybody has told them it is a good thing. These kids desperately need to be affirmed in their decision and held up as positive examples for others. None of this will be accomplished by pushing condoms.

But there is another reason for talking to teens about abstinence rather than "safe sex." It is even more important than the life-and-death issue cited above. I'm referring, of course, to the Creator's design, God's expressed will for human sexuality "Protected promiscuity" has no part in that plan. Sex within the context for which it was intended—lifelong, monogamous marriage—is *always* safe. *This* is the message our kids need to hear from the earliest days of childhood! Anything less is worse than third-rate!

QUESTION 211

Given the problems with condom usage and the epidemic of STDs that infect the human family, why is there so much

resistance to teaching abstinence-based educational programs in our schools? What do we have to lose by telling kids what's at stake for them?

If you ask the sex-education gurus that question, most will tell you that teenagers are going to be sexually active no matter what we do. Therefore, they say, we should teach them to do it in a safer way. I don't believe that answer is entirely honest, however. It won't explain the blatant and aggressive promotion of promiscuity among the young, or why they would recommend reliance on fragile rubber sheaths to protect against potentially deadly diseases. There is something else behind their motivation. These people become incensed when the word *abstinence* is even mentioned.

I began to understand their passion during the Reagan era when I was appointed by the Health and Human Services secretary, Otis Bowen, to a panel on the prevention of teen pregnancy. I accepted that responsibility because I thought our purpose was to prevent teen pregnancies. But during our first meeting in Washington, D.C., I learned that fifteen of the eighteen panel members had another agenda. They wanted to spend additional millions of federal dollars to put condoms in every pocket and purse of the nation's teenagers. I can't describe how emotional they were about this objective. It didn't take long to figure out their underlying point of view.

Millions of jobs and entire industries are supported by teen sexual irresponsibility. The abortion business alone generates up to one billion dollars annually. Why would physicians and nurses working in abortion clinics, and medical suppliers, and school-based sex-education counselors prefer that adolescents abstain until marriage? And what about the organizations that owe their existence to teen sexual irresponsibility, such as Planned Parenthood and SIECUS? They receive upwards of $600 million per year, domestically and internationally, from the U.S. federal government.[71] Added to that incentive are uncounted millions in corporate grants and individual contributions that flow to the problem. Imagine how many jobs would be lost if kids quit playing musical beds with one another! This is, I'm convinced, why so many professionals who advise young people about sex become angry when abstinence rears its ugly head. If that idea ever caught on, who would need the services of Planned Parenthood and their ilk?

QUESTION 212

Someone told me the other day that there are more than twenty sexually transmitted diseases at an epidemic level, and many of them are incurable. I've been through five years of sex-education classes, and no one has ever told me this. I think that is scandalous!

It *is* scandalous that these facts are withheld from today's young people. That's what motivated our organization, Focus on the Family, to create a full-page advertisement that attempted to get the word out. It presented the dangers of viral and bacterial infections and was documented throughout with respected medical references. That ad, entitled "In Defense of a Little Virginity," has now run in 1,300 newspapers, including *USA Today*. We've received thousands of letters of appreciation from students and from parents thanking us for sharing the truth with them for the first time.

Meanwhile, 56 million Americans—one out of every five—are suffering from incurable viruses.[72] Even more have bacterial and fungal infections that cause infertility and other physical problems. And of course, 1.5 million babies are aborted each year.[73] Clearly, it's time we told young people the truth.

That need for information is especially evident to those of us at Focus on the Family. We receive heartbreaking mail from very young people who have been lured into destructive behavior. Some of them are still children, like the girl who sent us this letter. She wrote:

This has been on my mind for a long time. I've heard that if you have sex during your period you won't get pregnet *[sic]*. If not, I have a problem. I'm only 11.
[signed] Really Worried

What a disgrace that we have permitted innocent kids like this one to be dragged into destructive behavior before they've even gotten

203

started in life. We have to begin giving them the whole truth about premarital sex and the difficulties it can cause.

QUESTION 213

When I've tried to argue the "abstinence" position with the advocates of safe sex, they have said, "You just don't live in the real world. Kids are going to do what comes naturally. It is ridiculous to ask them to abstain, so we might as well show them how to do it right." Is it really a waste of time to try to teach principles of morality to this generation?

I've heard the same rationale from the advocates of safe sex. They don't want kids to abstain, so they tell us it is foolish to promote that behavior. Nothing could be further from the truth.

I remember a reporter from the *New York Times* coming to Focus on the Family several years ago to get a quote from us. She was writing a story about today's sexually active kids, making the point that morality is dead and gone. We disagreed and invited her to come to Lexington, Kentucky, to attend a youth rally we were cosponsoring with local ministries. It offered teenagers straight talk about sex, drugs, their choice of friends, and other concerns.

The reporter accepted our invitation and was blown away by what she saw. The stadium was designed to hold eighteen thousand people, but twenty-six thousand kids showed up for the rally. Several thousand who couldn't get inside stood listening to a speaker system outside the arena as they were urged to live a responsible life and stay out of bed until they were married.

The reporter went back to New York and—you guessed it—wrote that morality is dead among the young. It isn't true. But it will be soon if we continue to promote immoral principles to young people.

QUESTION 214

The spread of sexually transmitted diseases is very unsettling to me. I have three teenage daughters and am afraid they

don't understand how easily these organisms are spread and what they can do to the body. This is a very scary subject.

Like you, I wonder what it will take to awaken our young people. I interviewed Dr. C. Everett Koop in the mideighties while he was surgeon general of the United States. He said, "The AIDS epidemic will soon change the behavior of everyone. When infected young people begin dying around us, others will be afraid to even kiss anyone."[74]

The epidemic has spread since those days, just as Dr. Koop predicted. But he was wrong about the fear of sex. People continue jumping in and out of bed with each other as though they were immune to all the viruses and bacteria that stalk the human family.

QUESTION 215

Why are young people so oblivious to the danger? Why do they put themselves at such risk?

For one thing, their idols in movies, television, and rock music tell them absolutely everyone is having sex. Unfortunately, these voices from the culture never reveal what it's like to have herpes or HPV or the other incurable viruses that are at epidemic proportions today. Also the safe-sex gurus have convinced kids that these terrible diseases can be prevented with the simple use of condoms. So why not?

Thank goodness for a few physicians who are sounding the alarm and trying to get the uncensored facts to our kids. They don't get much press, but someday they will be vindicated. One of the most vocal of these concerned doctors is my good friend Dr. Joe McIlhaney, an obstetrician-gynecologist who heads an organization called Medical Institute for Sexual Health (MISH). A frequent *Focus on the Family* broadcast guest, he talked about the fallacy of "safe sex" on a recent program:

> What you hear mostly from the press is what science is going to do for people who have a sexually transmitted disease (STD), how science is going to come up with a vaccine or treatment for AIDS,

how antibiotics will kill gonorrhea and chlamydia. What is not discussed is how these STDs leave women's pelvic structures scarred for life, and they end up infertile or having to do expensive procedures to get pregnant later on.

I could name patient after patient in the twenty-two years I've been in practice where I've had to perform a hysterectomy before a woman had the children she wanted because of pelvic inflammatory disease, which is caused by chlamydia and gonorrhea. The public announcements about "safe sex" infuriate me, because what they're saying is that you can safely have sex outside of marriage if you use condoms, and you don't have to worry about getting an STD. The message is a lie. The failure rate of condoms is extremely high, and that's why married people don't use them.

He went on to say, "I see the examples of these failures in my office every day. These include victims of chlamydia, probably the most prevalent STD, and of human papilloma virus (HPV), which can cause a lasting irritation of the female organs, as well as cancer of the vulva, vagina, and cervix. It is one of the most difficult diseases to treat and kills more than 4,800 women a year. I also see victims of herpes, which some studies indicate is present in up to 30–40 percent of single, sexually active people, as well as victims of syphilis, which is at a forty-year high."[75]

Rather than expecting science to solve our problems, Dr. McIlhaney said a better solution involves a return to spiritual and moral guidelines that have been with us for thousands of years. Dr. McIlhaney concluded, "The people who made my automobile know how it works best and what I need to do to avoid car problems. They tell me that in my Ford manual. Likewise, God knows how we work best and gave us an 'owner's manual' for the human race: the Bible. In it, He tells us not to have sex until we are married; not to have sex with anybody other than the one man/one woman to whom we are married; and to stay married the rest of our lives. That's the one and only prescription for safe sex."[76]

Note: The Medical Institute for Sexual Health has a variety of materials for physicians and others who have opportunities to teach students and testify before legislators and school-board members. They include photographic slides, a curricular guide, and other helpful aids. They can be contacted at P.O. Box 4919, Austin, TX 78765-4919 or by calling 1-800-892-9484.

QUESTION 216

We've all become aware of the AIDS epidemic, but I recently heard that a college friend of mine who used to sleep around has been diagnosed with something called HPV. I'm not exactly sure what it is, but it sounded serious. Are you familiar with this disease?

Yes, I am—and I'm afraid it's very serious. You've heard that HIV is deadly because it leads to AIDS, but the human papillomavirus (HPV) causes far more deaths among women in the U.S. each year.[77] Thousands of American women die from it every year. It causes genital warts and in some patients leads to cancer of the cervix. In fact, it is estimated that 90 percent of cervical-cancer cases are caused by HPV, and the virus itself cannot be eradicated once it is in the system.[78]

A medical investigation of this virus was conducted at the University of California at Berkeley in 1992. Averaging twenty-one years of age, all the young women coming to the campus health center for routine gynecological examinations for one year were tested for HPV. Would you believe that 47 percent of these female students were found to carry this virus?[79] Every one of them will suffer painful symptoms for the rest of their lives, and some will die of cervical and uterine cancer.

The most disturbing news is that HPV can be transmitted while the male is wearing a condom. The virus lurks around the portion of the genitalia that is not covered by the condom. This is one of the reasons some of us object strenuously to the campaign to get young people to have "protected sex." It gives them a false sense of security. There is no such thing as safe sex when it occurs promiscuously and outside the marital relationship. Abstinence before marriage is the only safe way to go.

207

QUESTION 217

This information about HPV is alarming. If there are really thousands of women dying every year from cancer of the cervix caused by this virus, it seems unconscionable that it isn't being talked about in schools and on today's TV talk shows.

I heartily agree, and I can assure you that the victims of HPV feel the same. Let me share a letter that I received from a woman who has this virus but doesn't yet have cervical cancer. She makes the case very dramatically and asked me to share her story with as many people as possible.

Dear Dr. Dobson,

In one of your radio broadcasts you covered the fact that it [HPV] can cause cervical dysplasia leading to cancer of the cervix. Certainly, that's tragic. But it has many other effects that I have not read anything about.

Let me tell you about this disease and what it's done to my life. I'm a twenty-five-year-old college graduate. I've remained single and childless. That singleness is imposed on me by my physical condition. The last four years of my life have been lived with chronic pain, two outpatient surgeries, multiple office biopsies, thousands of dollars in prescriptions, and no hope. The effect of this problem is one of severe relentless infection. This condition can be so severe that the pain is almost unbearable. A sexual relationship, or the possibility of marriage, is out of the question.

The isolation is like a knife that cuts my heart out daily. Depression, rage, and hopelessness, and a drastically affected social and religious life are the result. Physicians say they are seeing this condition more commonly. Females are being sentenced to a life of watching others live, marry, and have babies. Please take what I have written to the airwaves.

Thank you for listening, Dr. Dobson. This obstacle has been the one that I cannot gain victory over.

12
Spiritual Life of the Family

Q UESTION **218**

Sometimes I wish there were a place where I could go to protect my kids from all the evil in the world—a place where I could raise them like I was brought up. But there is no such place to hide, is there?

No, the negative influences on young people cross all cultural and international boundaries today. As I have traveled in other countries, I've been surprised to see how much teenagers are alike wherever they live. They write the same kind of graffiti on walls and billboards; their values, their attitudes, and even their clothing are similar. Why? Because they watch the same movies, listen to the same music, admire the same idols, play the same video and cyber games, and see the same television shows. For example, MTV is the most-watched cable network in the world. Unbelievably, some little Masai tribal children in Kenya sit in their grass huts and watch the wretched Beavis and Butthead stammer through obscenities and utter foolishness.[80]

Today's youth culture is on display in all the major cities of the world, including London, where my family visited a few years ago. That wonderful and historic city serves as a living museum where more than a thousand years of cultural evolution are on display. But it is also the home of some of the most pitiful young people I've ever seen. Rockers and punkers and druggies are on the streets in search of something. Who knows what? Girls with green-and-orange hair walk by with strange-looking boyfriends. (At least I think they are boys.) They wear blue Mohawk haircuts that stick four inches in the air. While gazing at that sight, a *clang! clang! clang!* sound is heard from the rear. The Hare Krishnas are coming. They dance by with their shaved heads and monklike robes. Gays parade arm in arm, and prostitutes advertise their services. On a recent visit, I stood there in downtown London thinking, *What in heaven's name have we allowed to happen to the next generation?*

The same phenomenon is occurring in the United States, Canada, and other parts of the world, of course. It is shocking to see what has happened to a value system that served us so well. When my daughter was eighteen, I attended a program put on by the music department at her high school. Sitting in front of me was one of Danae's girlfriends. At intermission we chatted about her plans, and she told me she would soon enroll at one of the state universities in California. She had just returned from a visit to the school and mentioned that something had bothered her about the dormitory in which she would reside. She had learned that the men and women lived side by side and that they also shared the same bathrooms. What concerned this pretty young lady was that there was no curtain on the shower stall!

This is the world in which our children are growing up. Obviously, conservative communities still exist, where traditional values are honored. Millions of kids want to do what is right. But dangerous enticements are there, too, and parents know it. So we live with the apprehension that the counterculture will consume our sons and daughters before they have even gotten started in life. That anxiety can take the pleasure out of raising children.

210

Q UESTION **219**

I have heard you say that the most important responsibility for Christian parents is to teach their children about Jesus Christ. We are new Christians and new parents. How do we go about introducing our little girl to what we believe?

The best approach is found in the instruction given to the children of Israel by Moses more than four thousand years ago. He wrote, "Impress them on your children. Talk about them when you sit at home and when you walk along the road, when you lie down and when you get up. Tie them as symbols on your hands and bind them on your foreheads. Write them on the doorframes of your houses and on your gates" (Deuteronomy 6:7-9).

This commandment provides the key to effective spiritual training at home. It isn't enough to pray with your children each night, although family devotions are important. We must *live* the principles of faith throughout the day. References to the Lord and our beliefs should permeate our conversation and our interactions with our kids. Our love for Jesus should be understood to be the first priority in our lives. We must miss no opportunities to teach the components of our theology and the passion that is behind it. As you've said, I believe this teaching task is *the* most important assignment God has given to us as parents.

The reason this is such a critical responsibility is that the world will be giving your children very different messages in the days ahead. It will take them to hell if not counterbalanced by a firm spiritual foundation at home. This is one task about which we can't afford to be lackadaisical.

QUESTION 220

It is difficult for us to have meaningful devotions as a family because our young children seem so bored and uninvolved. They yawn and squirm and giggle while we are reading from the Bible. On the other hand, we feel it is important to teach them to pray and study God's Word. Can you help us deal with this dilemma?

Brevity is the watchword. Children can't be expected to comprehend and appreciate lengthy adult spiritual activities. Four or five minutes devoted to one or two Bible verses, followed by a short prayer, usually represent the limits of attention during the preschool years. To force young children to comprehend eternal truths in an eternal devotional can be eternally dangerous.

QUESTION 221

The concept of who God is has always been difficult for me to comprehend. I'm still not sure I understand Him as I should. How can my children possibly grasp who He really is?

Remember that Jesus said, "Anyone who has seen me has seen the Father" (John 14:9). The best way to introduce our children to the character of God, therefore, is by introducing them to the person of Jesus. Even preschool kids can understand the imagery of Him given in the Gospels. Not only are children capable of comprehending things of the spirit, but Jesus said, "Anyone who will not receive the kingdom of God *like a little child* will never enter it" (Luke 18:17, italics added). They are inherently better at understanding it than are their elders.

The second way children learn about God is from what they see in Mom and Dad. It is a well-known fact that kids identify their parents—and especially their fathers—with God. That makes us grownups uncomfortable, of course, because we are aware of our imperfections and shortcomings. Nevertheless, we have been given the awesome responsibility of representing God to our vulnerable little children. The mistakes we make are often translated into spiritual problems for the next generation. For example, it is tough for the sons and daughters of oppressive or abusive parents to perceive God as being loving and compassionate. Likewise, permissive parents make it hard for children to understand the justice of God.

One of our most difficult tasks as mothers and fathers is to represent these two aspects of God's nature, His love and His justice, to our kids. To show our little ones love without authority is as serious a distortion of God's nature as to reveal an ironfisted authority without love.

If you put your mind and heart to it, I believe you can give your children the understanding they need. You might even get a better grasp of God's nature in the process of conveying it to your kids.

QUESTION **222**

How can a parent ever live up to the perception by a young child that we are Godlike? None of us can match that expectation!

I know. It's scary, isn't it? I remember being shocked when I realized that my two-year-old son, Ryan, identified me with God. He had watched his mother and me pray before we ate each meal, but he had never been asked to say grace. One day when I was out of town on a business trip, Shirley spontaneously turned to our toddler and asked if he would like to pray before he and his sister ate. The invitation startled him, but he folded his little hands, bowed his head, and said reverently, "I love you, Daddy. Amen."

When I returned home and Shirley told me what had happened, the story unsettled me. I hadn't realized the degree to which Ryan linked me with his "heavenly Father." I wasn't even sure I wanted to stand in those shoes. The job was too big, and I didn't want the responsibility. But I had no choice, nor do you. God has given us the assignment of representing Him during the formative years of parenting. That's why it is so critically important for us to acquaint our kids with God's two predominant natures . . . His unfathomable love and His justice. If we love our children but permit them to treat us disrespectfully and with disdain, we have distorted their understanding of the Father. On the other hand, if we are rigid disciplinarians who show no love, we have tipped the scales in the other direction. What we teach our children about the Lord is a function, to a significant degree, of how we model love and discipline in our relationship with them.

QUESTION **223**

What is the most important period in the spiritual training of young children?

Each is important, but I believe the fifth year is often the most critical. Up to that time, a child believes in God because his or her parents say it is the right thing to do. She accepts the reality of Christ like she would a

story about Santa Claus or the Easter Bunny—uncritically and inno-
cently. At about five or six years of age, however, she begins to think more
about what she is told. Some kids come to a fork in the road about that
time. Either they begin to internalize what they've been taught and make
it their own or else the Bible stories become like the fables that don't exist
in the real world. It is a time for careful instruction at home and in church.

I certainly don't mean to imply that parents should wait until the
child is five or six to begin spiritual training. Nor are subsequent years
insignificant. But I am convinced that our most diligent efforts within
the family and our best teachers in Sunday school ought to be assigned
to the child of five or six years. There will be crucial crossroads after
that, but this one is vital.

QUESTION 224

**As a child, Christmas was always my favorite time of the year.
I really enjoyed hearing stories about the birth of the Savior.
I also have special family memories associated with the antic-
ipation of Santa's arrival on Christmas Eve. I would very
much like to offer these same happy experiences to my young
children, but it seems many of my Christian friends think it's
wrong or harmful to include any mythical characters as part
of the Christmas celebration. How do you feel about this?**

My sentiments mirror yours exactly. Christmas memories are among
the most cherished of all my childhood reminiscences. The fantasy of
Santa Claus coming on Christmas Eve was an important part of the
fun. I'm reluctant to deprive today's kids of an experience that was so
exciting for me.

On the other hand, I understand the concerns expressed by many
Christian parents about the pagan celebration of Christmas. They
don't want to link Santa Claus, a mythical figure, with the reality of the
baby Jesus who was born in Bethlehem of Judea. They have good
reason to fear that they might weaken the validity of the Christmas
story by mixing it with fantasy.

So this is the dilemma—Santa is fun, but Santa could be confusing.
What are Christian parents to do? This is a judgment call to be made

by a given family. Shirley and I chose to play the "Santa game" with our kids, and we had no difficulties teaching them who Jesus was and is. Other families regret mixing the two images.

What is best? I don't know. But if I had to do it over, I would still let my children thrill to the excitement of Santa's arrival down the chimney on Christmas Eve.

QUESTION 225

What about Halloween?

Halloween is a rather different story. Whereas it can be argued that Christmas is a Christian holiday with Christian origins that has suffered the effects of growing secularism, Halloween can be traced to distinctly pagan sources. It is reasonable, then, that many believers would find some aspects of its celebration disturbing. I agree with them in that regard. The traditional emphasis upon the occult, witches, devils, death, and evil sends messages to our kids that godly parents can only regard with alarm. There is clearly no place in the Christian community for this "darker side" of Halloween.

Even here, however, there is a place for some harmless fun. Kids love to dress up and pretend. If the Halloween experience is focused on fantasy rather than the occult, I see no harm in it. Make costumes for your children that represent fun characters, such as Mickey Mouse or an elderly grandmother, and then let them go door-to-door asking for treats. This side of Halloween can be thoroughly enjoyable for the little ones.

Let me add, again, that I've given you my personal opinion. I realize that the topic is controversial among committed Christians, and I'm sensitive to the reasons for their misgivings. My final word to parents on the subject would be "Stay true to your own convictions."

QUESTION 226

Should a child be allowed to "decide for himself" on matters related to his concept of God? Aren't we forcing our religion down his throat when we tell him what he must believe?

Let me answer the question with an illustration from nature. A little gosling (baby goose) has a peculiar characteristic that is relevant at this point. Shortly after he hatches from his shell he will become attached, or "imprinted," to the first thing that he sees moving near him. From that time forward, the gosling follows that particular object when it moves in his vicinity. Ordinarily, it becomes imprinted to the mother goose who was on hand to hatch the new generation.

If she is removed, however, the gosling will settle for any mobile substitute, whether alive or not. In fact, a gosling will become most easily attached to a blue football bladder dragged by on a string. A week later, it'll fall in line behind the bladder as it scoots by.

Time is the critical factor in this process. The gosling is vulnerable to imprinting for only a few seconds after it hatches from the shell; if that opportunity is lost, it cannot be regained later. In other words, there is a brief "critical period" in the life of a gosling when this instinctual learning is possible.

Coming back to your question now, there is also a critical period when certain kinds of instruction are easier in the life of children. Although humans have no instincts (only drives, reflexes, urges, etc.), there is a brief period during childhood when youngsters are vulnerable to religious training. Their concepts of right and wrong are formulated during this time, and their view of God begins to solidify. As in the case of the gosling, the opportunity of that period must be seized when it is available. Leaders of the Catholic church have been widely quoted as saying, "Give us a child until he is seven years old, and we'll have him for life"; they are usually correct, because permanent attitudes can be instilled during these seven vulnerable years.

Unfortunately, however, the opposite is also true. The absence or misapplication of instruction through the prime-time period may place a severe limitation on the depth of a child's later devotion to God. When parents withhold indoctrination from their small children, allowing them to "decide for themselves," the adults are almost guaranteeing that their youngsters will "decide" in the negative. If parents want their children to have a meaningful faith, they must give up any misguided attempts at objectivity. Children listen closely to discover just how much their parents believe what they preach. Any indecision or ethical confusion from the parent is likely to be magnified in the child.

After the middle-adolescent age (ending at about fifteen years), children sometimes resent heavy-handedness about anything—including what to believe. But if the early exposure has been properly conducted, they should have an anchor to steady them. Their early indoctrination, then, is the key to the spiritual attitudes they carry into adulthood.

QUESTION 227

You have said that the children of godly parents sometimes go into severe rebellion and never return to the faith they were taught. I have seen that happen to some wonderful families that loved the Lord and were committed to the church. Still, it appears contradictory to Scripture. How do you interpret Proverbs 22:6 (KJV), which says, "Train up a child in the way he should go: and when he is old, he will not depart from it"? Doesn't that verse mean, as it implies, that the children of wise and dedicated Christian parents will never be lost? Doesn't it promise that all wayward offspring will return, sooner or later, to the fold?

I wish Solomon's message to us could be interpreted that definitively. I know that the common understanding of the passage is to accept it as a divine guarantee, but it was not expressed in that context. Psychiatrist John White, writing in his excellent book *Parents in Pain*, makes the case that the proverbs were never intended to be absolute promises from God. Instead, they are *probabilities* of things that are likely to occur.[81] Solomon, who wrote Proverbs, was the wisest man on the earth at that time. His purpose was to convey his divinely inspired observations on the way human nature and God's universe work. A given set of circumstances can be expected to produce a set of specific consequences. Unfortunately, several of these observations, including Proverbs 22:6, have been lifted out of that context and made to stand alone as promises from God. If we insist on that interpretation, then we must explain why so many other proverbs do not inevitably prove accurate. For example:

"Lazy hands make a man poor, but diligent hands bring wealth" (10:4). (Have you ever met a diligent—but poor—Christian? I have.)

"The blessing of the Lord brings wealth, and he adds no trouble to it" (10:22).

"The fear of the Lord adds length to life, but the years of the wicked are cut short" (10:27). (I have watched some beautiful children die with a Christian testimony on their lips.)

"No harm befalls the righteous, but the wicked have their fill of trouble" (12:21).

"Plans fail for lack of counsel, but with many advisers they succeed" (15:22).

"Gray hair is a crown of splendor; it is attained by a righteous life" (16:31).

"The lot is cast into the lap, but its every decision is from the Lord" (16:33).

"A tyrannical ruler lacks judgment, but he who hates ill-gotten gain will enjoy a long life" (28:16).

We can all think of exceptions to the statements above. To repeat, the proverbs appear to represent likelihoods rather than absolutes with God's personal guarantee attached. This interpretation of the Scripture is somewhat controversial among laymen, but less so among biblical scholars. For example, *Bible Knowledge Commentary: Old Testament,* prepared by the faculty of the Dallas Theological Seminary, accepts the understanding I have suggested. This commentary is recognized for its intense commitment to the literal interpretation of God's Word, yet this is what the theologians wrote:

Some parents, however, have sought to follow this directive but without this result. Their children have strayed from the godly training the parents gave them. This illustrates the nature of a "proverb." A proverb is a literary device whereby a general truth is brought to bear on a specific situation. Many of the proverbs are not absolute guarantees for they express truths that are necessarily conditioned by prevailing circumstances. For example, verses 3, 4, 9, 11, 16, 29 of Proverbs 22 do not express promises that are always binding. Though the proverbs are generally and usually true, occasional exceptions may be noted. This may be because of the self-will or deliberate disobedience of an individual who chooses to go his own way—the way of folly instead of the way of wisdom. For that he is held responsible. It is generally true, however, that most children who are brought up in Christian homes, under the influence of godly parents who teach and live God's standards, follow that training.[82]

Those who believe that Proverbs 22:6 offers a guarantee of salvation for the next generation have assumed, in essence, that a child can be programmed so thoroughly as to determine his course inevitably. If they bring him up "in the way he should go," the outcome is guaranteed. But think about that for a moment. Didn't the Creator handle Adam and Eve with infinite wisdom and love? He made no mistakes in "fathering" them. They were also harbored in a perfect environment with none of the pressures we face. They had no in-law problems, no monetary needs, no frustrating employers, no television, no pornography, no alcohol or drugs, no peer pressure, and no sorrow. They had no excuses! Nevertheless, they ignored the explicit warning from God and stumbled into sin. If it were ever possible to avoid the ensnarement of evil, it would have occurred in that sinless world. But it didn't. God in His love gave Adam and Eve a choice between good and evil, and they abused it. Will He now withhold that same freedom from your children? No. Ultimately, they will make their own choices. That time of decision is a breathtaking moment for parents, when everything they have taught appears to be on the line. But it must come for us all.

QUESTION 228

You obviously feel very strongly about this misinterpretation of Scripture. What are its implications?

I am most concerned for dedicated and sincere Christian parents whose grown sons and daughters have rebelled against God and their own families. Many of these mothers and fathers did the best they could to raise their children properly, but they lost them anyway. That situation

produces enormous guilt in itself, quite apart from scriptural understandings. They are led to believe that God has promised—absolutely
guaranteed—the spiritual welfare of children whose parents do their
jobs properly. What are they to conclude, then, in light of continued
rebellion and sin in the next generation? The message is inescapable!
It must be their fault. They have damned their own kids by failing to
keep their half of the bargain. They have sent their beloved children to
hell by their parenting failures. This thought is so terrible for a
sensitive believer that it could actually undermine his or her sanity.

I simply do not believe God intended for the total responsibility for
sin in the next generation to fall on the backs of vulnerable parents.
When we look at the entire Bible, we find no support for that extreme
position. Cain's murder of Abel was not blamed on his parents. Joseph
was a godly man and his brothers were rascals, yet their father and
mothers (Jacob, Leah, and Rachel) were not held accountable for the
differences between them. The saintly Samuel raised rebellious children, yet he was not charged with their sin. And in the New Testament,
the father of the Prodigal Son was never accused of raising his adven-
turesome son improperly. The boy was apparently old enough to make
his own headstrong decision, and his father did not stand in his way.
This good man never repented of any wrongdoing—nor did he need to.

It is not my intention to let parents off the hook when they have been
slovenly or uncommitted during their child rearing years. There is at
least one biblical example of God's wrath falling on a father who failed
to discipline and train his sons. That incident is described in 1 Samuel 2:22-36, where Eli, the priest, permitted his two sons to desecrate
the temple. All three were sentenced to death by the Lord. Obviously,
He takes our parenting tasks seriously and expects us to do likewise.
But He does not intend for us to grovel in guilt for circumstances
beyond our control!

QUESTION 229

**Our three children were prayed for before they were con-
ceived, and we have held their names before the Lord almost
every day of their lives. Yet our middle daughter has chosen**

to reject our faith and do things she knows are wrong. She's living with a twice-divorced man and apparently has no intention of marrying him. She has had at least two abortions that we know about, and her language is disgraceful. My wife and I have prayed until we're exhausted, and yet she has shown no interest in returning to the church. At times, I become very angry at God for allowing this terrible thing to happen. I have wept until there are just no more tears. Tell me what intercessory prayer accomplishes, if anything. Is there a realm into which the Father will not intrude?

I can certainly understand your pain. Perhaps more people have become disillusioned with God over the waywardness of a son or daughter than any other issue. There is nothing more important to most Christian parents than the salvation of their children. Every other goal and achievement in life is anemic and insignificant compared to this transmission of faith to their offspring. That is the only way the two generations can be together throughout eternity, and those parents, like you, have been praying day and night for spiritual awakening. Unfortunately, if God does not answer those prayers quickly, there is a tendency to blame Him and to struggle with intense feelings of bitterness. The "betrayal barrier" claims another victim!

Often, this anger at the Lord results from a misunderstanding of what He will and won't do in the lives of those for whom we intercede. The key question is this: Will God require our offspring to serve Him if they choose a path of rebellion? It is a critically important question.

Let me explain again that God will not force Himself on anyone. If that was His inclination, no person would ever be lost. Second Peter 3:9 says, "He is patient with you, not wanting anyone to perish, but everyone to come to repentance." Nevertheless, to claim this great salvation, there is a condition. An individual must reach out and take it. He or she must repent of sins and believe on the name of the Lord Jesus Christ. Without that step of faith, the gift of forgiveness and eternal life is impossible.

Now let me deal with your question about what intercessory prayer accomplishes. Referring again to Dr. White's insightful book *Parents in Pain,* he wrote:

Here lies a key to understanding how we may pray for our own children or for anyone else. We may ask with every confidence that God will open the eyes of the morally and spiritually blind. We may ask that the self-deceptions which sinners hide behind may be burned away in the fierce light of truth, that dark caverns may be rent asunder to let the sunlight pour in, that self-disguises may be stripped from a man or woman to reveal the horror of their nakedness in the holy light of God. We may ask above all that the glory of the face of Christ will shine through the spiritual blindness caused by the god of this world (2 Corinthians 4:4). All of this we can ask with every assurance that God will not only hear but will delight to answer.

But we may not ask him to force a man, woman, or child to love and trust him. To deliver them from overwhelming temptation: yes. To give them every opportunity: yes. To reveal his beauty, his tenderness, his forgiveness: yes. But to force a man against his will to bow the knee: not in this life. And to force a man to trust him: never.[83]

Said another way, the Lord will not save a person against his will, but He has a thousand ways of making him more willing. Our prayers unleash the power of God in the life of another individual. We have been granted the privilege of entering into intercessory prayer for our loved ones and of holding their names and faces before the Father. In return, He makes the all-important choices crystal clear to that individual and brings positive influences into his or her life to maximize the probability of doing what is right. Beyond that, He will not go.

*Q*UESTION 230

That is deep theological water, isn't it? Who knows exactly how God responds to intercessory prayer and how He deals with a wayward heart?

You are certainly right about that, and I don't claim to have answered all of my own questions. How can I explain the prayers of my great-grandfather (on my mother's side), who died the year before I was born? This wonderful man of God, G. W. McCluskey, took it upon himself to spend the hour between 11:00 A.M. and 12:00 noon every day in prayer specifically for the spiritual welfare of his family. He was talking to the Lord not only about those loved ones who were then alive—McCluskey was also praying for generations not yet born. This good man was talking to the Lord about me, even before I was conceived.

Toward the end of his life, my great-grandfather made a startling announcement. He said God had promised him that every member of four generations—both those living and those not yet born—would be believers. Well, I represent the fourth generation down from his own, and it has worked out more interestingly than even he might have assumed.

The McCluskeys had two girls, one of whom was my grandmother and the other, my great-aunt. Both grew up and married ministers in the denomination of their father and mother. Between these women, five girls and one boy were born. One of them was my mother. All five of the girls married ministers in the denomination of their grandfather, and the boy became one. That brought it down to my generation. My cousin H. B. London and I were the first to go through college, and we were roommates. In the beginning of our sophomore year, he announced that God was calling him to preach. And I can assure you, I began to get very nervous about the family tradition!

I never felt God was asking me to be a minister, so I went to graduate school and became a psychologist. And yet, I have spent my professional life speaking, teaching, and writing about the importance of my faith in Jesus Christ. At times as I sit on a platform waiting to address a church filled with Christians, I wonder if my great-grandfather isn't smiling at me from somewhere. His prayers have reached across four generations of time to influence what I am doing with my life day by day.

What does that say about free moral agency and the right to choose? I don't have a clue. I only know that God honors the prayers of His righteous followers, and we should stay on our faces before Him until each child has been granted every opportunity to repent. We must remember, however, that God will not ride roughshod over the will of any individual. He deals respectfully with each person and seeks to attract him or her to Himself. It is wrong, therefore, to blame God if that process takes years to accomplish—or even if it never comes to pass. That is the price of freedom.

QUESTION 231

Your answer implies that we should continue to pray for our daughter year after year until she comes back to her faith. Does that mean that God will not be offended by our asking Him repeatedly for the same request? Is that what He wants of us on her behalf?

Yes. If what you are requesting is undeniably in the will of God, such as praying for the salvation of your daughter, I think you should keep the matter before Him until you receive the answer. There is a continuing spiritual battle under way for her soul, and your prayers are vital in winning that struggle. Paul admonished us to "pray without ceasing" (1 Thessalonians 5:17, NKJV). Isn't that what Jesus was teaching in the parable of the unjust judge? Let's read it in the book of Luke:

> Then Jesus told his disciples a parable to show them that they should always pray and not give up. He said: "In a certain town there was a judge who neither feared God nor cared about men. And there was a widow in that town who kept coming to him with the plea, 'Grant me justice against my adversary.'
>
> "For some time he refused. But finally he said to himself, 'Even though I don't fear God or care about men, yet because this widow keeps bothering me, I will see that she gets justice, so that she won't eventually wear me out with her coming!'"
>
> And the Lord said, "Listen to what the unjust judge says. And will not God bring about justice for his chosen ones, who cry out to him day and night? Will he keep putting them off? I tell you, he will see that they get justice, and quickly. However, when the Son of Man comes, will he find faith on the earth?" (Luke 18:1-8)

I love that Scripture because it tells us that God is not irritated by our persistence in prayer. He urges us not to give up but to bombard heaven with the desires of our hearts. That is encouragement enough to keep me praying for a lifetime.

Winston Churchill said during World War II, "Never give up. Never, never, never give up!"[84] That advice applies not only to nations under siege but also to believers seeking a touch from the Almighty. I'll say it again: Moms and dads, your highest priority is to lead your children into the fold. Don't stop praying until that objective is fulfilled.

QUESTION 232

My wife and I have been praying for the salvation of our children for more than twenty-five years, and there is no sign that God has even heard those prayers. I know He loves our family, but I'm quite discouraged. Can you tell us anything that will jump-start our faith again?

I *do* have an encouraging word for you and others who have asked the Lord for a miracle that hasn't yet come. It is found in one of my favorite Scriptures located in the book of Genesis. You'll remember that when Abraham was seventy-five years of age he began receiving promises from God that he would become the father of a great nation and that in him, all the nations of the world would be blessed. That was great news to an aging man and his barren wife, Sarah, who longed to be a mother.

Yet these exciting promises were followed by Sarah's continued infertility and many years of silence from God. What she and Abraham faced at this point was a classic case of "God contradicting God." The Lord hadn't honored His word or explained His delay. The facts didn't add up. The pieces didn't fit. Sarah had gone through menopause, effectively ending her hope of motherhood. By then, she and her husband were old, and we can assume that their sexual passion had diminished. There was no realistic probability that they were to be given an heir.

Abraham's response at that discouraging moment was described nearly two thousand years later in the writings of the apostle Paul. These are the inspirational words that he wrote:

Without weakening in his faith, [Abraham] faced the fact that his body was as good as dead—since he was about a hundred years old—and that Sarah's womb was also dead. Yet he did not waver through unbelief regarding the promise of God, but was strengthened in his faith and gave glory to God, being fully persuaded that God had power to do what he had promised. This is why "it was credited to him as righteousness." (Romans 4:19-22)

In other words, Abraham believed God even when He made no sense. The facts clearly said, "It is impossible for this thing to happen." The Lord had made "empty promises" for nearly twenty-five years, and still there was no sign of their fulfillment. Unanswered questions and troubling contradictions swirled through the air. Nevertheless, Abraham "did not waver through unbelief." Why? Because he was convinced that God could transcend reason and factual evidence. And this is why he is called the "father of our faith."

Isn't that a wonderful example of faith under fire? It should give us courage to retain our spiritual confidence even when the pieces don't fit. Remember that with God, even when nothing is happening, something is happening. And if we don't waver, someday we'll understand, and "it will be credited to [us] as righteousness" for our faithfulness.

Stay on your knees. And hang on to your faith like a life preserver! The Lord is at work in the lives of your children, even though you see no evidence of it at the moment.

QUESTION 233

My wife and I are new Christians, and we now realize that we raised our kids by the wrong principles. They're grown now, but we continue to worry about the past, and we feel great regret for our failures as parents. Is there anything we can do at this late date?

Let me deal first with the awful guilt you are obviously carrying. There's hardly a parent alive who does not have some regrets and painful memories of their failures as a mother or a father. Children are infinitely complex, and we can no more be perfect parents than we can be perfect human beings. The pressures of living are often enormous. We get tired and irritated; we are influenced by our physical bodies and our emotions, which sometimes prevent us from saying the right things and being the models we should be. We don't always handle our children as unemotionally as we wish we had, and it's very common to look back a year or two later and see how wrong we were in the way we approached a problem.

All of us experience these failures! No one does the job perfectly! That's why each of us should get alone with God and say:

> "Lord, You know my inadequacies. You know my weaknesses, not only in parenting, but in every area of my life. I did the best I could, but it wasn't good enough. As You broke the fishes and the loaves to feed the five thousand, now take my meager effort and use it to bless my family. Make up for the things I did wrong. Satisfy the needs that I have not satisfied. Wrap Your great arms around my children, and draw them close to You. And be there when they stand at the great crossroads between right and wrong. All I can give is my best, and I've done that. Therefore, I submit to You my children and myself and the job I did as a parent. The outcome now belongs to You."

I know the Father will honor that prayer, even for parents whose job is finished. The Lord does not want you to suffer from guilt over events you can no longer influence. The past is the past. Let it die, never to be resurrected. Give the situation to God, and let Him have it. I think you'll be surprised to learn that you're no longer alone!

> Forgetting what is behind and straining toward what is ahead, I press on toward the goal to win the prize for which God has called me heavenward in Christ Jesus. (Philippians 3:13-14)

227

*Q*UESTION 234

I am a grandmother who is blessed to have fourteen grandchildren. I often take care of them and love just having them over. However, I would like to do more for them than just

baby-sit. What can I do to really make an impact on their lives?

Above all else, I would hope you would help lead your grandchildren to Jesus Christ. You are in a wonderful position to do that. My grandmother had a profound impact on my spiritual development—even greater in my early years than my father, who was a minister. She talked about the Lord every day and made Him seem like a very dear friend who lived in our house. I will never forget the conversations we had about heaven and how wonderful it would be to live there throughout eternity. That little lady is on the other side today, waiting for the rest of her family to join her in that beautiful city.

You can have that kind of impact on your family too. Grandparents have been given powerful influence on their grandchildren if they will take the time to invest in their lives. There is so much to be accomplished while they are young. Another of the great contributions you can make is to preserve the heritage of your family by describing its history to children and acquainting them with their ancestors.

The lyrics of an African folk song say that when an old person dies, it's as if a library has burned down. It is true. There's a richness of history in your memory of earlier days that will be lost if it isn't passed on to the next generation.

To preserve this heritage, you should tell them true stories of days gone by. Share about your faith, about your early family experiences, about the obstacles you overcame or the failures you suffered. Those recollections bring a family together and give it a sense of identity.

I spoke earlier about my grandmother. There was another wonderful lady in our family, my great-grandmother (Nanny), who helped raise me from babyhood. She was already old when I was born and lived to be nearly one hundred years of age. I loved for her to tell me tales about her early life on the frontier. A favorite story involved mountain lions that would prowl around her log cabin at night and attack the livestock. She could hear them growling and moving past her window as she lay in bed. Nanny's father would try to shoot the cats or chase them away before they killed a pig or a goat. I sat fascinated as this sweet lady described a world that had long vanished by the time I came onto the scene. Her accounts of plains life helped open me to a love of history, a subject that fascinates me to this day.

The stories of your past, of your childhood, of your courtship with their grandfather, etc., can be treasures to your grandchildren. Unless you share those experiences with them, that part of their history will be gone forever. Take the time to make yesterday come alive for the kids in your family, and by all means, pass your faith along to the next generation.

13
The Tougher Spiritual Questions

QUESTION **235**

The Lord answered prayer miraculously for my son when he was eight years old. He had open-heart surgery and survived without any permanent problems. But my husband was diagnosed with cancer three years ago, and we prayed for him night and day. Nevertheless, he died last January. I just can't understand why God heard my prayer for our son but allowed my husband to die. Is He there—or isn't He?

I assure you that He is there and that your prayers for your husband received no less attention or compassion than those for your endangered son. What you've experienced is evidence of the sovereignty of God. He will always be the determiner of what is best for those who serve Him.

One of the most dramatic illustrations of this divine nature occurred in the lives of my good friends, Von and Joann Letherer. When Von was just one year old, his parents noticed that he bruised badly whenever he bumped into furniture or even tumbled in his crib. They took him to their doctor, who diagnosed Von with hemophilia—the hereditary "bleeder's disease." His blood lacked the substance necessary to coagulate, actually threatening his life each time he suffered the most minor injury. There was very little treatment for hemophilia in those days, and Von was not expected to live beyond childhood. Indeed, he survived because of prayer, and because of nearly four hundred pints of blood transfused by the time he reached the end of adolescence.

During those teen years, when Von's life repeatedly hung in the balance, there was a young lady standing by his side. Her name was Joann, and she was his childhood sweetheart. Joann understood very well that Von's future was uncertain, but she loved him dearly. Hemophilia, they decided, was not going to determine the course of their lives. The couple was married when he was twenty-two and she was nineteen years old.

A new crisis occurred several years later when Joann was carrying their second child. She became seriously ill and was diagnosed with Hodgkin's disease, a type of cancer that attacks the lymph glands. It was usually fatal in that era. Although a treatment program had been developed, Joann's pregnancy prevented the doctors from prescribing it for her. She and Von could have aborted their baby, of course, but chose instead to place themselves in the hands of the Lord.

They began asking for a miracle—and promptly received one. Several weeks after the initial diagnosis, the hospital repeated the laboratory and clinical tests. Doctors concluded that there was no sign of Hodgkin's disease in Joann. She has been cancer free from that day to this.

Now, notice what occurred in this instance. As we have seen, Von was born with a painful, debilitating illness about which his father, a minister, and his mother prayed diligently. They asked repeatedly for God to heal their son. When Von got older, he began praying on his own behalf. Then Joann came along and joined the chorus. Despite these and many other petitions, the Lord chose not to heal Von's hemophilia. At sixty-three years of age, he is still afflicted with the disorder and suffers daily from immobile joints and related physical difficulties. Von has taken medication every day for many years, just to cope with the pain. Yet his indomitable spirit has been a witness to me and thousands of others through the years.

Why has the Lord been unwilling to heal this good man? I don't know. Some might say that his prayer team lacked faith, except for the fact that Joann was healed in response to their petitions. The same people who asked for intervention in her life were also praying for Von. In one instance the answer was yes, and in the other it was no. And life goes on. The Lord has offered no explanation or interpretation of His response, except, by inference, "This is My will for you."

In this and countless other circumstances that occur within the human family, only one conclusion can be drawn: God will do what is best, and we must continue to trust Him regardless of the outcome.

To the woman whose husband recently succumbed to cancer, let me offer this word of encouragement: The Father has not lost track of your circumstances, even though they seem to be swirling out of control. He is there. Hold on to your faith in the midst of these unanswered questions. Someday His purposes will be known, and you will have an eternity to talk it over. In the meantime, I pray that the Lord will help you cope with this tragic loss of, or should I say temporary separation from, your partner and friend.

QUESTION 236

I know God is able to do miracles and even raise the dead. I have to admit, however, that it is hard to depend on Him when I'm going through dark times. Does this mean I lack faith?

Most of us struggle to "be anxious for nothing" (Philippians 4:6, NKJV) when we are agitated or frightened by events in our lives. Still, we can learn to let God be God and accept His direction and judgment. But in direct response to your question, I think you may be confusing the concepts of faith and trust. There is a very old illustration that brings these two ideas into sharp focus. It goes like this: Imagine yourself near the beautiful and dangerous Niagara Falls on the border between Canada and upstate New York. Suppose a circus performer has strung a rope across the falls with the intention of pushing a wheelbarrow to the other side. If he loses his balance, he will surely drown or be crushed in the churning waters below. Just before stepping on the rope, the stuntman turns to you and says, "Do you think I can accomplish this feat?"

You reply that his reputation has preceded him and that you fully believe he has the ability to walk the tightrope. In other words, you have faith that he will succeed.

But then he says, "If you really believe I can do it, how about getting in the wheelbarrow and crossing to the other side with me?" To accept that invitation would be an example of remarkable trust.

It is not difficult for some of us to believe that God is capable of performing mighty deeds. After all, He created the entire universe from nothingness. He has the power to do anything He chooses. Having faith in Him can be a fairly straightforward thing.

To demonstrate trust, however, takes the relationship a step further. It involves the element of risk. It requires us to depend on Him to keep his promises, even when proof is not provided. It is continuing to believe when the evidence points in the opposite direction. Yes, it is getting into the wheelbarrow and making the perilous journey across the falls. I'm convinced that faith in moments of crisis is insufficient, unless we are also willing to trust our very lives to His care. That is a learned response, and some people find it more difficult than others by reason of temperament.

Q UESTION 237

Do you believe the Lord still performs miracles today, or has the era of supernatural intervention passed?

I have no doubt that miracles still occur every day, although I'm suspicious of people who attempt to market them on demand. I have been privileged to witness some incredible evidences of God's power in my life and in the experience of those with whom I am close. One of the most miraculous events happened to my friend Jim Davis when he and his family visited Yellowstone National Park in 1970. Jim was a guest on the *Focus on the Family* broadcast sometime later, and he shared that story with our listeners. These are his approximate words on that occasion:

> My wife and I were both raised in Christian families, and we were taught the power of prayer. But we were not living very godly lives. We did not pray together or have a family altar in our home. About

that time, she made a wonderful commitment to the Lord and began praying for me. She bought me a research Bible, and I began to get into the Word. Things started to change in my heart, but I still wasn't mature spiritually.

That summer, we went on a vacation to Yellowstone Park with four other couples. Several of these friends went fishing the next day in an aluminum boat, and one of the ladies hooked a trout. She leaned over to net the fish, and her glasses fell off. They immediately sank to the bottom of the lake. She was very disturbed by the loss because it was the beginning of their vacation, and she could not drive or read without the glasses. She also got severe headaches when she didn't wear them.

That night, everyone was talking about the glasses and how unfortunate it was that they were lost. Then my wife said, "No sweat. Jim is a great scuba diver. He'll go out and find them for you."

"Hey, thanks a lot," I said. "Do you know that Yellowstone Lake has 172 miles of shoreline, and every tree is coniferous and looks exactly the same? There's no way I can get a fix on where you guys were when the glasses went overboard. Besides, the water is very, very cold—fifty degrees. They won't even allow you to water-ski out there. And I don't have a wet suit—just a pair of fins and a snorkel."

My objections fell on deaf ears. She told me privately that she intended to pray that the Lord would help me find those glasses.

Yeah, sure, I thought.

The next morning we got in the boat and headed about a half mile out from shore.

"Uh, where do you think you dropped them?" I asked.

"It seems like about here," someone said.

Well, I got in the water, and it was freezing. I took hold of a rope, and the boat dragged me along the surface as I looked at the bottom. The water was about ten feet deep and crystal clear. We made a swath about fifty feet long and then turned and worked our way back. After about twenty minutes of this search, I was just chilled to the bone. I prayed a little prayer and said, *Lord, if You know where those glasses are, I sure wish You'd tell me.* I wasn't convinced He knew. It's a very big lake.

But a little voice in my mind said, *I know exactly where they are. Get in the boat, and I'll take you to them.* Well, I didn't tell anyone about this message because I was too embarrassed to say it. But about twenty minutes later I was just shivering, and I said, *Lord, if You still know where those glasses are, I'll get in the boat.*

I called out to my friends and said, "We're in the wrong place. They're over there."

I got in the boat and pointed to a spot that I thought the Lord was telling me about. The driver said, "No, we weren't out that far." But we kept going, and I said, "Stop. Right here. This is the place."

I jumped back in the water and looked down. We were right on top of those glasses. I dove to the bottom and came up with the prize. It was one of the clearest answers to prayer I've ever experienced, and it set me on fire spiritually. It was also an incredible witness to my wife and all my friends. And I'll never forget those sparkling glasses at the bottom of Yellowstone Lake.

As dramatic as this story is, I can personally vouch for its authenticity as Jim told it. There are many witnesses who remember that remarkable day on Yellowstone Lake. What I don't know is why the Lord chose to reveal Himself in that way or why He doesn't do it more often. Clearly, He has plans and purposes to which we are not privy.

I can't resist sharing another incident that ranks as one of the most interesting examples of God's intervention I've ever heard. It occurred in 1945, shortly after the end of World War II. A young associate pastor named Cliff and his fiancée, Billie, were anxious to get married, even though they had very little money. They managed to scrape together enough funds for a simple wedding and two train tickets to a city where he had been asked to hold a revival with a friend. By combining this responsibility with their honeymoon, they thought they could make it. They planned to stay at a nearby resort hotel.

The couple got off the train and took a bus to the hotel, only to learn that it had been taken over by the military for use as a rehabilitation center. It was no longer open for guests. There they were, stranded in an unfamiliar city with only a few dollars between them. There was little to do but attempt to hitch a ride on the nearby highway. Soon a car pulled over, and the driver asked them where they wanted to go.

"We don't know," they said, and explained their predicament. The man was sympathetic and said perhaps he could offer a suggestion. A few miles down the road was a grocery store that was owned by a woman he knew. She had a couple of empty rooms upstairs and might be willing to let them stay there inexpensively. They were in no position to be choosy.

The lady rented them a room for five dollars, and they moved in. During their first day in residence, the new bride spent the afternoon practicing the piano, and Cliff played the trombone he had brought with him. The proprietor of the store sat rocking in a chair, listening to the music. When she realized they were Christians, she referred them to a friend who invited them to spend the rest of their honeymoon in his home. Several days later, the host mentioned that a young evangelist was speaking at a youth rally at a nearby Christian conference center. They were invited to attend.

That night, it so happened that the regular song leader was sick, and Cliff was asked to take charge of the music for the service. What a historic occasion it was! The evangelist turned out to be a very young Rev. Billy Graham. The groom was Cliff Barrows. They met that evening for the first time, and a lifetime partnership was formed. As the Christian world knows so well, Cliff and his wife, Billie, were members of the Billy Graham Evangelistic Association until Billie's death in 1994.[85] Cliff continues to be used by the Lord in crusades all around the world. I suppose Paul Harvey would say, "And now you know . . . the rest of the story."

Isn't it amazing the lengths to which the Lord went to bring these now inseparable team members together? Some would call their meeting a coincidence, but I disagree. I recognize the hand of God when I see it.

Do miracles still occur today as they did in Bible times? Yes, but they usually take place in such a manner as to preserve the need for faith. Even those who witness them must choose whether or not to believe in their validity. I choose to believe!

QUESTION 238

You've written about human pride and the offense it is to God. I don't fully understand what that means. Shouldn't we be proud of our achievements and discoveries? Do you not admire the accomplishments of modern science, medicine, and the arts? What is wrong with a little self-satisfaction and confidence? Does God, if he exists, want us to grovel like beggars before Him?

Let me clarify what I have attempted to say. As a former professor in a large university medical school, I have marveled at the miracles accomplished through research and scientific inquiry. I'm grateful we live in a day when vast knowledge is available to anyone with a computer or access to a local library. These are remarkable times, to be sure, and we have reason to feel good about the effort to reduce human suffering and make a better life for us all. There is nothing offensive to God about progress per se.

But there is something inherently evil about the prevailing notion that man no longer needs God—that we can get along very well on our own, thank you. Even more odious is the New Age philosophy that grants godlike status to mere mortals. Its followers worship the human mind, as though that pound of wrinkled gray matter somehow produced itself from nothingness. Shirley MacLaine's followers proclaim with awe, "We only use 5 percent of our brains. Imagine what is possible if we would achieve our entire potential." This gee-whiz view of "human potential" is nonsense. If it were possible to employ 95 percent more brainpower, some bright soul among the five billion now living would have found a way to do it. And even if that happened, we would still have peanut brains compared with the wisdom and omnipotence of the Almighty.

The word *arrogance* comes to mind in this context. Though we exist by the graciousness of a loving Lord, mankind is systematically seeking to overthrow Him as the moral authority of the universe. We've jettisoned His commandments and replaced them with our puny notions and ideas. The postmodernists have concluded that

238

there are no eternal truths, no transcendent values, no ultimate rights and wrongs. What seems right at the time *is* right. Morality is determined by public-opinion polls, as though our pooled ignorance will somehow produce verity. In the process, we have forgotten the faith of our fathers that was lovingly handed down to us and entrusted to our care.

Arrogance is not a new phenomenon in human society, of course. Jesus told us about a rich farmer who had no need for God. He had his life nicely laid out. He produced such a bumper crop that year that he couldn't even store it all. In a world of suffering and starvation, that was his biggest problem:

> Then he said, "This is what I'll do. I will tear down my barns and build bigger ones, and there I will store all my grain and my goods. And I'll say to myself, 'You have plenty of good things laid up for many years. Take life easy; eat, drink and be merry.'"
>
> But God said to him, "You fool! This very night your life will be demanded from you. Then who will get what you have prepared for yourself?" (Luke 12:18-20)

That rich farmer who basked in self-sufficiency is reminiscent of today's superstars and miracle men. Pick up any issue of *People* magazine, and the aroma of human pride will waft from its pages.

When I think of arrogance and contempt for God, I am reminded of the deceased rock star John Lennon. He and his fellow Beatles rebelled against everything holy and clean. They were involved in the most wicked homosexual and heterosexual orgies, and they popularized the use of marijuana and hard drugs among a generation of young people.[86] We're still suffering from that plague. Some of their music, as melodic and clever as it was, reflected this decadence and set the stage for the demonic excesses of today's rock industry.

Lennon was also an outspoken atheist. One of his well-known compositions was a song entitled "Imagine," which postulated a world with no religion to wreak havoc on mankind. Lennon felt that patriotism and belief in God were responsible for war and other social ills. He said this in 1966:

Christianity will go. It will vanish and shrink. I needn't argue about that. I'm right and I will be proved right. We're more popular than Jesus now; I don't know which will go first—rock 'n' roll or Christianity. Jesus was all right, but his disciples were thick and ordinary. It's them twisting it that ruins it for me.[87]

As it turned out, Lennon was the one to go, succumbing in 1980 to five bullets fired by a psychopath on the streets of New York City. The wages of John's sin turned out to be death. Now he must deal with the One who said, "Vengeance is mine; I will repay, saith the Lord" (Romans 12:19, KJV).

Any man is a fool, regardless of his intelligence or accomplishments, if he fails to reckon with the God of the universe. It's that simple.

QUESTION 239

How can we determine God's will for our lives? He doesn't speak to us in an audible voice. Do we just have to guess at what He wants?

That is a very important question. You can't obey God if you are hazy about what He wants you to do. But most people lack a clear idea of how to discern His voice. They depend on feelings and impressions, which are unreliable and dangerous, to interpret His will. What they feel is highly subjective. It is influenced by what they want, what is going on in their lives, and even how much sleep they got last night. Some terrible mistakes have been made by believers who thought they had heard the voice of the Lord.

I knew a college student who awakened from a dream in the middle of the night with the strong impression that he should marry a certain young lady. They had dated only once or twice and hardly knew each other—yet "God" had assured him that "this is the one!" The next morning, he called the coed and told her of his impression. The girl felt no such impulse but didn't want to argue with the Lord. The couple was married shortly thereafter and has suffered through the agonies of an unsuccessful and stormy marriage.

I could tell you many similar stories about people who misunderstood what seemed to have been the will of the Lord. Remember that Satan comes "as an angel of light" (2 Corinthians 11:14), which means he counterfeits the voice of God. If he can get you to accept your impressions uncritically and impulsively, then he can confuse and disillusion you.

Determining the will of God by means of feelings or impressions always reminds me of the day I completed my formal education at the University of Southern California and was awarded a Ph.D. My professors shook my hand and offered their congratulations, and I walked from the campus with the prize I had sought so diligently. On the way home in the car that day, I thanked God for His blessing on my life and asked Him to use me in any way He chose. The presence of the Lord seemed very near as I communed with Him in that little red Volkswagen.

Then, as I turned the corner (I remember the precise spot), I had a strong impression that someone very close to me was going to die within the next twelve months. The Lord seemed to be telling me that I should not be dismayed when this loss occurred but should continue trusting and depending on Him.

Since I had not been thinking about death or anything that would have explained the sudden premonition, I was alarmed by it. My heart thumped a little harder as I contemplated who might die and in what manner the end would come. Nevertheless, when I reached my home that night, I told no one about that experience.

One month passed without tragedy or human loss. Two or three months sped by, and still the hand of death failed to visit my family. Finally, the anniversary of my morbid impression came and went without consequence. Ten years went by before my father's death, and I'm certain that it didn't have anything to do with my premonition in the Volkswagen.

Through my subsequent counseling experience and professional responsibilities, I have learned that my phony impression was not unique. Similar experiences are common, particularly for intuitive people who are more susceptible to those thoughts.

For example, a thirty-year-old wife and mother came to me for treatment of persistent anxiety and depression. In relating her history, she described an episode that occurred in a church service when she was sixteen years old. Toward the end of the sermon, she "heard" this alarming message from God: "Jeanie, I want you to die so that others will come to Me."

Jeanie was absolutely terrified. She felt as though she stood on the gallows with a hangman's noose dangling above her head. In her panic, she jumped from her seat and fled through the doors of the building, sobbing as she ran. Jeanie felt she would commit a sin if she revealed her impression to anyone, so she kept it to herself. For years she has awaited the execution of this divine sentence, still wondering when the final moment will arrive. Nevertheless, she appears to be in excellent health today, these many years later.

From these examples and dozens more, I have come to regard the interpretation of impressions as risky business, at best.

QUESTION 240

If you can't always trust what you feel, how can you know what is right?

There are at least five ways you can discern the will of the Lord. First, the apostle Paul wrote in the book of Ephesians, "And this is my prayer. That the God of our Lord Jesus Christ, the all-glorious Father, will give you spiritual wisdom and the insight to know more of him" (Ephesians 1:16-17, Phillips). He wouldn't have said that unless it were possible through prayer to gain spiritual wisdom and insight. Therefore, a search for God's will should begin on your knees. He will meet you there. Remember that Jesus promised, "Ask and it will be given to you; seek and you will find; knock and the door will be opened to you" (Matthew 7:7).

Second, you should examine the Scriptures for principles that relate to the issue at hand. The Lord will never ask you to do anything that is morally wrong or in contradiction to His Word. If what you are considering violates a concept you find in the Word, you can forget it.

Third, it is helpful to seek advice from those who are spiritually mature and solid in their faith. A godly counselor or pastor can assist you in avoiding the common mistakes that confuse many young people.

Fourth, you should pay close attention to what are known as "providential circumstances." The Lord often speaks through doors that open or close. When you begin to be blocked on all sides in a particular pursuit, you might consider the possibility that God has other plans for you. I'm suggesting not that you give up at the first sign of obstacles but that you attempt to "read" the events in your life for evidence of divine influence.

Fifth and finally, do nothing impulsively. Give God an opportunity to speak. Until he does, stall for time and concentrate on the first four approaches.

In addition to these five steps to determine God's specific will, I can tell you now what His general will is for each of us. The Scripture gives all believers the same assignment, and it's called the great commission. We find it in the words of Jesus, who said, "Go ye into all the world, and preach the gospel to every creature" (Mark 16:15, KJV). That responsibility applies to all of us. Our task as believers is to tell as many people as possible that Jesus Christ died for our sins and offers eternal life to those who will believe on His name. So in whatever you do, whether you are a dentist, a truck driver, an artist, a car dealer, or a homemaker, you are expected to use that position as a springboard to witness for the Savior.

Q UESTION 241

Whenever Christians talk about pain and suffering, someone can be counted on to quote Romans 8:28: "And we know that in all things God works for the good of those who love him, who have been called according to his purpose." But how can that be true literally? You have acknowledged that Christians go through the same kind of suffering that unbelieving people do. So how can it be said that all their difficulties somehow "work together for good"?

First, it must be noted from this Scripture that Paul didn't say all things were good. He wasn't claiming that death, sickness, and sorrow were really positives in disguise. But he did tell us that God has promised to take these hardships and bring good from them. As long as what happens to me is within the perfect will of the Father, I have no reason to fear—even if it costs me my life. It is an article of our faith that we can trust Him to do what is best, even if it appears contrary to our own wishes or the prevailing attitudes of the day.

I'll answer the question a different way. The laws of physics tell us that energy in the universe is never lost. It is simply transformed from one state to another. So it is with human experience. Nothing is ever lost entirely. God uses every happening to accomplish His divine purposes. For example, missionary Jim Elliot and his companions were speared to death by Waorani Indians in Ecuador. Their sacrifice seemed like an unmitigated tragedy and a total waste of human life. In God's scheme of things, however, it had a purpose. Each of those Indians came to know Jesus Christ as his personal Savior in the years that followed. The gospel was firmly planted among their tribesmen. Thus, Elliot and his fellow missionaries will rejoice throughout eternity with the men who took their lives. That is "good." Romans 8:28, then, must be interpreted from this eternal perspective, rather than a temporal, earthbound point of view.

There are innumerable other examples. Remember the death of Stephen, the first believer to be martyred in the days following the crucifixion of Jesus? What was accomplished for God by the terrible stoning of this faithful apostle? Well, when Stephen's followers then fled Roman persecution, they spread the news of Jesus' death and resurrection to the far reaches of the known world. The "church" was planted in countless communities and cities where the Good News would not otherwise have been heard.

Let's cite an illustration closer to home. A few months ago, we received a phone call here at Focus on the Family from a Mr. Greg Krebs. He wanted to get a message through to me, and this is what he told our telephone representative. Mr. Krebs and his wife have a twenty-one-year-old son named Chris, whom they had been advised to abort when still in the womb. They chose to give him life, and he was born with cerebral palsy. He is also profoundly retarded. His parents do not regret their decision to bring him into the world because they believe that all life is precious. They are thankful for this son, who has touched their lives in warm and wonderful ways.

"God has used him as he is," Mr. Krebs said.

Then he described something that happened when Chris was just seven years old. He said, "My wife worked in a hospital at the time, and I had taken Chris with me to pick her up. She was late getting off, so Chris and I waited for her in one of the family rooms. There was another man there who was not well dressed and, in fact, was a little smelly. I went to the nurses' station to ask how much longer my wife would be, and when I returned, I saw Chris sitting by the man. The man was sobbing, and I wondered what Chris had done to offend him. I began to apologize.

"'I'm sorry if my son offended you,' I said.

"The man replied, 'Offended me? Offended me? Your son is the only person who has hugged me in the last twenty years!'

"I realized at that moment Chris had a more Christlike love for this man than I did."

Thank you, Mr. and Mrs. Krebs, for loving and valuing your son despite his limitations. I agree wholeheartedly that there is no "junk" in God's value system. He loves every one of us the same, and He uses each person—even the profoundly retarded—to accomplish some part of His purpose. He will also use your pain, although it is not always immediately possible to interpret it.

To repeat my thesis, when we submit ourselves to the sovereign will of the Lord, we can say with confidence that in all things—yes, in all things—"God works for the good of those who love him, who have been called according to his purpose."

QUESTION 242

I've often heard that God will not abandon us when we go through the fiery trial. But I don't know what that really means. You've shown that He still lets us go through some hard times. What can we expect from Him in the stressful moments?

I may lack the words to describe what occurs to the faithful in times of personal crisis. It is virtually inexpressible. Let it be said, simply, that there is often a quiet awareness in the midst of chaos that the Lord is there and He is still in control. Millions of people have reported this persistent presence when life was systematically unraveling. On other occasions, He permits us to see evidence of His love at the critical moment of need.

I recall today that tragic time in 1987 when four very dear friends of mine were killed in a private-plane crash. We had been together the night before, and I had prayed for their safety on the journey home. They took off early the next morning on their way to Dallas but never made it. I can never forget that telephone call indicating that the wreckage had been found in a remote canyon—but there were no survivors! I loved those men like brothers, and I was staggered by the loss.

I was asked by two of the families to speak briefly at their loved ones' funeral. The untimely deaths of such vibrant and deeply loved men seemed to scream for an explanation. Where was God in their passing? Why did He let this happen? Why would He take such godly men from their families and leave them reeling in grief and pain? There were no answers to these agonizing questions, and I did not try to produce them. But I did say that God had not lost control of their lives and that He wanted us to trust Him when nothing made sense. His presence was very near.

As we exited the sanctuary that day, I stood talking with loved ones and friends who had gathered to say good-bye. Suddenly, someone pointed to the sky and exclaimed, "Look at that!" Suspended directly above the steeple was a small rainbow in the shape of a smile. There had been no precipitation that day and no more than a few fleecy clouds. Yet this beautiful little rainbow appeared above the church. We learned later that it had been hovering there through most of the funeral service. It was as though the Lord was saying to the grieving wives and children, "Be at peace. Your men are with Me, and all is well. I know you don't understand, but I want you to trust Me. I'm going to take care of you, and this rainbow is a sign to remember."

One of the people standing there had the presence of mind to take a photograph at that moment. When it was developed, we saw what no one had recognized at the time. There, cradled near the center of the rainbow, was a small private plane.

Cynics and nonbelievers will say the rainbow and the plane are coincidences that have no spiritual significance. They are entitled to their opinion. But for every member of four wounded families, and certainly for me, the Lord used that phenomenon to convey His peace to us all. He has fulfilled His promise to take care of those four courageous widows and their children.

There are other examples that beg to be shared. Sandra Lund and her family survived Hurricane Andrew in south Florida by spending the night in a shelter. Then they returned to their home the next morning to find everything destroyed except some of the interior walls. As a bewildered Sandra strolled through the rubble, she found a note she had taped in what had been the kitchen. It was still in place and read, "For I have learned in whatsoever state I am, therewith to be content." On the remaining bathroom wall was another verse she had penned, "O give thanks to the Lord for He is good." Sandra got the message.[88]

Examples of God's presence and assurance in times of tragedy would fill many books. This is the promise we find in Scripture: "Yet I am always with you; you hold me by my right hand. You guide me with your counsel, and afterward you will take me into glory. Whom have I in heaven but you? And earth has nothing I desire besides you. My flesh and my heart may fail, but God is the strength of my heart and my portion forever" (Psalm 73:23-26).

QUESTION 243

There are times when I feel so close to the Lord, and I can sense His approval on my life. On other occasions, it seems like He is a million miles away. How can I have any stability in my spiritual life when the Lord's assurance and presence are so inconstant?

His presence is not inconstant. It is your perception of Him that comes and goes. If your spiritual walk is dependent on the ebb and flow of emotion, your confidence as a believer will pitch and roll like a ship on a stormy sea. Very little in human experience is as undependable as the way we feel from day to day. That's why our faith must be grounded in a solid commitment of the will, in our prayer life, in the fellowship of believers, and in a careful study of Scripture.

Another factor is extremely important in understanding God's intervention in human affairs. It deals with the natural rhythm to our lives—the regular progression of emotions and circumstances from positive to negative to positive. We are rarely granted more than about two weeks of tranquillity before something goes wrong. Either the roof springs a leak or the Ford throws a rod or the kids get the chicken pox or business reverses occur. Mark Twain said life is just one darn thing after another. That's just the way it goes in this imperfect world.

If it's any consolation to those of you who have also been dragged up and down the emotional roller coaster, it is apparent from Scripture that even Jesus experienced this fluctuation. His ministry began officially at the Jordan River, where He was baptized by John. That must have been the most exhilarating day of his thirty years on earth. Matthew 3:16-17 tells us, "As soon as Jesus was baptized, he went up out of the water. At that moment heaven was opened, and he saw the Spirit of God descending like a dove and lighting on him. And a voice from heaven said, 'This is my Son, whom I love; with him I am well pleased.'"

What an incredible experience that must have been for the young Messiah. There are no words to describe what it meant to be ordained and blessed by the Father in this manner. But note that the next verse says, "Then Jesus was led by the Spirit into the desert to be tempted by the devil" (Matthew 4:1). Isn't it interesting that Jesus was taken from the most emotionally exhilarating experience of His life directly into one of the most terrible ordeals He would ever encounter—a forty-day battle with Satan? Observe, also, that He didn't wander into the desert. He didn't even go there by His own design. He was led there by the Spirit to be tempted by the devil!

The upheaval in Jesus' life was only beginning. In a sense, His entire ministry is characterized by that fluctuation. After His difficult period in the wilderness, He began to receive the adulation of the crowds as word spread that a "prophet" was in their midst. Can't you imagine the scenes of hysteria as sick and deformed people pressed to get near Him?

Then the chief priests and the Pharisees began plotting to kill

Jesus. He became a hated man and, eventually, a wanted criminal. They tried to embarrass and intimidate Him wherever He went. Back and forth came the praise of the common people and the animosity of the religious leaders.

Let's move to the events surrounding Jesus' final days on earth. As He approached Jerusalem, multitudes came to greet Him, shouting, "Hosanna: Blessed is the King of Israel that cometh in the name of the Lord" (John 12:13, KJV). A few days later, however, He went through the terrible ordeal surrounding His persecution and trial. The same people who had worshiped Him now clamored for His execution. Then He was crucified between two thieves on Mount Calvary. This darkest day in human history was followed three days later by the most wonderful news ever given to mankind. Soon, 120 disciples received the baptism of the Holy Spirit at Pentecost, and the church was born. That was followed by incredible persecution of the saints and the martyrdom of many. There was good news one day and bad news the next. James was killed, but Peter was rescued. The early Christians went through high moments and low times as they labored to establish the church.

What I've tried to illustrate through the vicissitudes of Jesus' ministry is that there is no stability or predictability in this imperfect world. It is that way for you and me, too. We must expect the unexpected—the unsettling—the irritating. One day we'll ride high above the fray, and the next we could slide under the door. So whence cometh the stability in such a topsy-turvy world? It is found only by anchoring our faith on the unchanging, everlasting Lord, whose promises never fail and whose love is all-encompassing. Our joy and our hope can be as steady as the sunrise even when the happenings around us are transitioning from wonderful to tragic. That's what Scripture teaches us, and His peace is there for those who choose to take it.

14
Sibling Rivalry

QUESTION 244

Why do my kids have to fight all the time? I have three of them, and they drive me crazy. Why can't they be nice to each other?

Good question! All I can tell you is that sibling rivalry has been going on for a long time. It was responsible for the first murder on record (when Cain killed Abel) and has been represented in virtually every two-child family from that time to this. The underlying source of this conflict is old-fashioned jealousy and competition between children. Marguerite and Willard Beecher, writing in their book *Parents on the Run*, expressed the inevitability of this struggle as follows:

> It was once believed that if parents would explain to a child that he was having a little brother or sister, he would not resent it. He was told that his parents had enjoyed him so much that they wanted to increase their happiness. This was supposed to avoid jealous competition and rivalry. It did not work. Why should it? Needless to say, if a man tells his wife he has loved her so much that he now plans to bring another wife into the home to "increase his happiness," she would not be immune to jealousy. On the contrary, the fight would just begin—in exactly the same fashion as it does with children.[89]

Q UESTION 245

If jealousy between kids is so common, then how can parents minimize the natural antagonism children feel for their siblings?

It's helpful to avoid circumstances that compare them unfavorably with each other. They are extremely sensitive to the competitive edge of their relationship. The question is not "How am I doing?" it is "How am I doing compared with John or Steven or Marion?" The issue is not how fast I can run, but who crosses the finish line first. A boy does not care how tall he is; he is vitally interested in who is tallest. Each child systematically measures himself against his peers and is tremendously sensitive to failure within his own family. Accordingly, parents should guard against comparative statements that routinely favor one child over another.

Perhaps an illustration will help make the case. When I was about ten years old, I loved to play with a couple of dogs that belonged to two families in the neighborhood. One was a black Scottie who liked to chase and retrieve tennis balls. The other was a pug bulldog who had a notoriously bad attitude. One day as I was tossing the ball for the Scottie, it occurred to me that it might be interesting to throw it in the direction of the ol' grouch. It was not a smart move. The ball rolled under the bulldog, who grabbed the Scottie by the throat when he tried to retrieve it. It was an awful scene. Neighbors came running as the Scottie screamed in pain. It took ten minutes and a garden hose to pry the bulldog's grip loose, and by then the Scottie was almost dead. He spent two weeks in the hospital, and I spent two weeks in "the doghouse." I regret throwing that ball to this day.

I have thought about that experience many times and have begun to recognize its application to human relationships. Indeed, it is a very simple thing to precipitate a fight between people. All that is necessary is to toss a ball, symbolically, under the more aggressive of the two and prepare for the battle that ensues. This is done by repeating negative comments one has made or by baiting one in the presence of the other. It can be accomplished in business by assigning overlapping territory to two managers. They will tear each other to pieces in the inevitable rivalry. Alas, it happens every day.

This principle is also applicable to siblings. It is remarkably easy to make them mortal enemies. All a parent must do is toss a ball in the wrong direction. Their natural antagonism will do the rest.

Q UESTION 246

What are the areas of potential conflict that should be handled with care? How can we keep the bulldog and the Scottie apart?

There are three areas that are most delicate. First, children are extremely sensitive about the matter of physical attractiveness and body characteristics. It is highly inflammatory to commend one child at the expense of the other. Suppose, for example, that Sharon is permitted to hear the casual remark about her sister, "Betty is sure going to be a gorgeous girl." The very fact that Sharon was not mentioned will probably establish the two girls as rivals. If there is a significant difference in beauty between the two, you can be assured that Sharon has already concluded, "Yeah, I'm the ugly one." When her fears are then confirmed by her parents, resentment and jealousy are generated.

Beauty is the most significant factor in the self-esteem of Western children. Anything that a parent utters on this subject within the hearing of children should be screened carefully. It has the power to make brothers and sisters hate one another.

Second, the matter of intelligence is another sensitive nerve to be handled with care. It is not uncommon to hear parents say in front of their children, "I think the younger boy is actually brighter than his brother." Adults find it difficult to comprehend how powerful that kind of assessment can be in a child's mind. Even when the comments are unplanned and are spoken routinely, they convey how a child is seen within his family. We are all vulnerable to that bit of evidence.

Third, children (and especially boys) are extremely competitive with regard to athletic abilities. Those who are slower, weaker, and less coordinated than their brothers are rarely able to accept "second best" with grace and dignity. Consider, for example, the following note given to me by the mother of two boys. It was written by her nine-year-old son to his eight-year-old brother the evening after the younger child had beaten him in a race.

Dear Jim:

I am the greatest and your the badest. And I can beat everybody in a race and you can't beat anybody in a race. I'm the smartest and your the dumbest. I'm the best sport player and your the badest sport player. And your also a hog. I can beat anybody up. And that's the truth. And that's the end of this story.

Yours truly,

Richard

This note is humorous to me because Richard's motive was so poorly disguised. He had been badly stung by his humiliation on the field of honor, so he came home and raised the battle flags. He will probably spend the next eight weeks looking for opportunities to fire torpedoes into Jim's soft underbelly. Such is the nature of humankind.

Q UESTION 247

My older child is a great student and earns straight A's year after year. Her younger sister, now in the sixth grade, is completely bored in school and won't even try. The frustrating thing is that the younger girl is probably brighter than her older sister. Why would she refuse to apply her ability like this?

There could be many reasons for her academic disinterest, but let me suggest the most probable explanation. Children will often refuse to compete when they think they are likely to place second instead of first. Therefore, a younger child may avoid challenging an older sibling in his area of greatest strength. If Son Number One is a great athlete, then Son Number Two may be more interested in collecting butterflies. If Daughter Number One is an accomplished pianist, then Daughter Number Two may be a boy-crazy goof-off.

This rule does not always hold true, of course, depending on the child's fear of failure and the way he estimates his chances of successful competition. If his confidence is high, he may blatantly wade into the territory owned by big brother, determined to do even better. However, the more typical response is to seek new areas of compensation that are not yet dominated by a family superstar.

If this explanation fits the behavior of your younger daughter, then it would be wise to accept something less than perfection from her school performance. Every child need not fit the same mold—nor can we force them to do so.

QUESTION 248

Sometimes I feel as though my children fight and argue as a method of attracting my attention. If this is the case, how should I respond?

You are probably correct in making that assumption. Sibling rivalry often represents a form of manipulation of parents. Quarreling and fighting provide an opportunity for both children to "capture" adult attention. It has been written, "Some children had rather be wanted for murder than not wanted at all." Toward this end, a pair of obnoxious kids can tacitly agree to bug their parents until they get a response—even if it is an angry reaction.

One father told me that his son and his nephew began to argue and then beat each other with their fists. Both fathers were nearby and decided to let the fight run its natural course. During the first lull in the action, one of the boys glanced sideways toward the passive men and said, "Isn't anybody going to stop us before we get hurt?!" The fight, you see, was something neither boy wanted. Their violent combat was directly related to the presence of the two adults and would have taken a different form if the boys had been alone. Children will "hook" their parents' attention and intervention in this way.

Believe it or not, this form of sibling rivalry is easiest to control. The parent must simply render the behavior unprofitable to each participant. I would recommend that you review the problem (for example, a morning full of bickering) with the children and then say, "Now listen carefully. If the two of you want to pick on each other and make yourselves miserable, then be my guests [assuming there is a fairly equal balance of power between them]. Go outside and fight until you're exhausted. But it's not going to occur under my feet anymore. It's over! And you know that I mean business when I make that kind of statement. Do we understand each other?"

Having made the boundaries clear, I would act decisively the instant either boy returned to his bickering. If they had separate bedrooms, I would confine one child to each room for at least thirty minutes of complete boredom without radio, computer, or television. Or I would assign one to clean the garage and the other to mow the lawn. Or I would make them take a nap. My purpose would be to make them believe me the next time I asked for peace and tranquillity.

It is simply not necessary to permit children to destroy the joy of living. And what is most surprising, children are the happiest when their parents enforce reasonable limits with love and dignity.

QUESTION 249

I've been very careful to be fair with my children and give them no reason to resent one another. Nevertheless, they continue to fight. What can I do?

The problem may rest in your lack of disciplinary control at home. Sibling rivalry is at its worst when there is an inadequate system of justice among children—where the "lawbreakers" do not get caught or if apprehended, are set free without standing trial. It is important to understand that laws in a society are established and enforced for the purpose of protecting people from each other. Likewise, a family is a minisociety with the same requirement for protection of human rights.

For purposes of illustration, suppose that I live in a frontier community where there is no established law. Policemen do not exist, and there are no courts to whom disagreements can be appealed. Under those circumstances, my neighbor and I can abuse each other with impunity. He can steal my horses and throw rocks through my windows, while I raid the apples from his favorite tree and take his plow late at night. This kind of mutual antagonism has a way of escalating day by day, becoming ever more violent with the passage of time.

When permitted to run its natural course, as in early American history, the end result can be feudal hatred and murder.

As indicated, individual families are similar to societies in their need for law and order. In the absence of justice, "neighboring" siblings begin to assault one another. The older child is bigger and tougher, which allows him to oppress his younger brothers and sisters. But the junior member of the family is not without weapons of his own. He strikes back by breaking the toys and prized possessions of the older sibling and interfering when friends are visiting. Mutual hatred then erupts like an angry volcano, spewing its destructive contents on everyone in its path.

In many homes, the parents do not have sufficient disciplinary control to enforce their judgments. In others, they are so exasperated with constant bickering among siblings that they refuse to get involved. In still others, parents require an older child to live with an admitted injustice "because your brother is smaller than you." Thus, they tie his hands and render him utterly defenseless against the mischief of his bratty little brother or sister. Even more commonly today, mothers and fathers are both working while their children are home busily disassembling each other.

I will say it again to parents: One of your most important responsibilities is to establish an equitable system of justice and a balance of power at home. There should be reasonable "laws" that are enforced fairly for each member of the family. For purposes of illustration, let me list the boundaries and rules that evolved through the years in my own home.

1. Neither child was ever allowed to make fun of the other in a destructive way. Period! This was an inflexible rule with no exceptions.
2. Each child's room was his or her private territory. There were locks on both doors, and permission to enter was a revocable privilege. (Families with more than one child in each bedroom can allocate available living space for each youngster.)
3. The older child was not permitted to tease the younger child.
4. The younger child was forbidden to harass the older child.

257

5. The children were not required to play with each other when they preferred to be alone or with other friends.
6. We mediated any genuine conflict as quickly as possible, being careful to show impartiality and extreme fairness.

As with any plan of justice, this plan requires (1) children's respect for leadership of the parent, (2) willingness by the parent to mediate, (3) occasional enforcement of punishment. When this approach is accomplished with love, the emotional tone of the home can be changed from one of hatred to (at least) tolerance.

15

Help for Single Parents and Stepparents

QUESTION **250**

What encouragement can you offer to those of us who are single parents? Each day seems more difficult than the one before it. Can you help plead our case to those who don't understand what we're facing?

In my view, single parents have the toughest job in the universe! Hercules himself would tremble at the range of responsibilities people like you must handle every day. It's difficult enough for two parents with a solid marriage and stable finances to satisfy the demands of parenting. For a single mother or father to do that task excellently over a period of years is evidence of heroism.

The greatest problem faced by single parents, especially a young mother like yourself, is the overwhelming amount of work to be done. Earning a living, fixing meals, caring for kids, helping with homework, cleaning house, paying bills, repairing the car (if she has one), handling insurance, and doing the banking, the income tax, marketing, etc., can require twelve hours a day or more. She must continue that schedule seven days per week all year long. Some have no support from family or anyone else. It's enough to exhaust the strongest and healthiest woman. Then where does she find time and energy to meet her social and emotional needs—and how does she develop the friendships on which that part of her life depends? This job is no easier for most fathers, who may find themselves trying to comb their daughter's hair and explain menstruation to their preteen girls.

There is only one answer to the pressures single parents face. It is for the rest of us to give them a helping hand. They need highly practical assistance, including the friendship of two-parent families who will take their children on occasion to free up some time. Single moms need the help of young men who will play catch with their fatherless boys and take them to the school soccer game. They need men who will fix the brakes on the Chevy and patch the leaky roof. They need prayer partners who will hold them accountable in their walk with the Lord and bear their burdens with them. They need an extended family of believers to care for them, lift them up, and remind them of their priorities. Perhaps most important, single parents need to know that the Lord is mindful of their circumstances.

Clearly, I believe it is the responsibility of those of us in the church to assist you with your parenting responsibilities. This requirement is implicit in Jesus' commandment that we love and support the needy in all walks of life. He said, "Inasmuch as ye have done it unto one of the least of these my brethren, ye have done it unto me" (Matthew 25:40, KJV). That puts it in perspective. Our effort on behalf of a fatherless or motherless child is seen by Jesus Christ as a direct service to Himself!

The biblical assignment is even more explicitly stated in James 1:27: "Religion that God our Father accepts as pure and faultless is this: to look after orphans and widows in their distress and to keep oneself from being polluted by the world."

Thankfully, churches today are becoming more sensitive to the needs of single parents. More congregations are offering programs and ministries geared to the unique concerns of those with special needs. I'd advise every single parent to find such a church or fellowship group and make himself or herself at home there. Christian fellowship and support can be the key to survival.

Those among my readers who want to help mothers or fathers raising kids alone might start by giving them a subscription to the *Single Parent Family*, from Focus on the Family. Write us in Colorado Springs for information.

Question 251

My husband died three years ago, leaving me to raise my ten-year-old son and nine-year-old daughter alone. For the past year I have been dating a very gentle, godly man who has three kids of his own. We have recently begun to talk about marriage, which really excites me. I have a major concern, however, that my children are not in favor of the relationship, even though Bill has been very good to them and quick to include them in many of our activities. I know Chuck and Laura miss their father and don't want to give up his memory, but I need companionship, and this is definitely a good thing. How should I handle this situation?

If you love Bill and he loves you, I think you should press forward with your marriage plans—especially if you have made it a matter of prayer. I do need to tell you unequivocally that the blending of your two families will not be easy. I have seen fewer than five "reconstituted families" in my professional career that didn't experience major adjustments and struggles. The myth of *The Brady Bunch*—the old television sitcom based on the harmonious blending of six children—just doesn't happen. There are highly predictable points of conflict that must be anticipated and dealt with early in the relationship. One of them is the situation you've described, where the children of one parent refuse to accept the new stepparent. These problems can be sorted out, but you must set your mind to doing it.

Question 252

Where should we start to build this new family? And could you identify the issues that are likely to be most difficult for us?

I would strongly suggest that you get some outside help as you bring your two families together. It is extremely difficult to do that on your own, and for some people, it is impossible. If you can afford professional counseling from a marriage, family, and child counselor who has dealt with blended families, it would be wise to get that assistance. A pastor also might be able to guide you, although there are some tough relationship issues to be handled by a professional who has "been there" before.

You're already experiencing the thorny issue of conflict between Bill and your children, which is common. One of the kids is likely to see him as a usurper. When a mother or father dies or when a divorce occurs, one child often moves into the power vacuum left by the departing parent. That youngster becomes the surrogate spouse. I'm not referring to sexual matters. Rather, that boy or girl becomes more mature than his or her years and relates to the remaining parent more as a peer. The status that comes with that supportive role is very seductive, and he or she is usually unwilling to give it up. The stepfather becomes a threat to that child. Much work must be done to bring them together.

The kids' loyalty to the memory of their dad is another issue that requires sensitive handling. In their eyes, to welcome the newcomer with open arms would be an act of betrayal. That's certainly understandable and something that must be worked through with your children. It will require time, patience, understanding, and prayer.

I would say the greatest problem you will face, however, is the way you and Bill will feel about your kids. Each of you is irrationally committed to your own, and you're merely acquainted with the others. When fights and insults occur between the two sets of children, you will be tempted to be partial to those you brought into the world, and Bill will probably favor his own flesh and blood. The natural tendency is to let the blended family dissolve into armed camps—us against them. If the kids sense any tension between you and Bill over their clashes, they will exploit and exaggerate it to gain power over the other children, etc. Unless there are some ways to ventilate these issues and work through them, battles will occur that will be remembered for a lifetime.

I have painted a worst-case scenario in order to prepare you for what could occur. Now let me encourage you. Many of these problems can be anticipated and lessened. Others can be avoided altogether. It *is* possible to blend families successfully, and millions have done it. But the task is difficult, and you will need some help in pulling it off.

Q UESTION 253

I'd like to leave my children with friends or relatives for a few days and get some time for myself, but I'm worried about how this might affect them. Will they feel deserted again?

Not only is a brief time away from your children not likely to be hurtful—it will probably be healthy for them. One of the special risks faced by single parents is the possibility of a dependency relationship developing that will trap their children at an immature stage. This danger is increased when wounded people cling to each other exclusively for support in stressful times. Spending a reasonable amount of time apart can teach independence and give everyone a little relief from the routine. Therefore, if you have a clean, safe place to leave your children for a week or two, by all means, do it. You'll be more refreshed and better able to handle your usual "homework" when you return.

Q UESTION 254

My former wife and I were married for thirteen years before we divorced two years ago. She has since remarried and has custody of our twelve-year-old daughter. Recently, I've learned that my ex-wife is saying things to our daughter that I feel are damaging to her spirit. She frequently blames her weight problem, smoking addiction, and financial woes on our daughter ("I wouldn't be in this mess if it weren't for you"). She also has no respect for our daughter's boundaries and routinely confiscates cash gifts that are received for birthday or Christmas presents. Since I am no longer recognized as the primary care provider, I am somewhat hesitant to raise objections. Still, she is my daughter, and it pains me to see her subjected to this kind of abuse. Should I step in and make things right?

I'm sure what you are witnessing is extremely distressing, and I wish there were legal remedies to help you protect your daughter. Within certain limits, however, your ex-wife is permitted by the court to be a bad mother and even do things that are harmful to the child. If you attack her or try to place her on the defensive, you could even make things tougher for your daughter. Apart from what you can accomplish with your wife through negotiation and personal influence, then, your hands are tied.

There is, however, so much that you can do directly with your daughter—even though you don't have custody over her. Work hard on that relationship. Be there for her when she needs you. Give her the best of your love and attention when she visits. At twelve years of age, she is at the most vulnerable time of her life, and she needs a father who thinks she is very special. You can have a profound influence on her if you demonstrate your love and concern consistently during this difficult period of her life. Remember, too, that the present situation may be temporary. Teenagers are given greater latitude in deciding which parent they want to live with. By your daughter's choice, you might have custody of her in a year or two. Until then, all you can do is the best you can do. I pray that it will be enough.

QUESTION 255

I am a single mother with a five-year-old son. How can I raise him to be a healthy man who has a good masculine image?

As I think you recognize from your question, your son has needs that you're not properly equipped to meet. Your best option, then, is to recruit a man who can act as a mentor to him—one who can serve as a masculine role model.

In her book *Mothers and Sons,* the late Jean Lush talked about the challenges single mothers face in raising sons. She says the ages four to six are especially important and difficult.[90] I agree. A boy at that age still loves his mother, but he feels the need to separate from her and gravitate toward a masculine model. If he has a father in the home, he'll usually want to spend more time with his dad apart from his mother and sisters. If his dad is not accessible to him, a substitute must be found.

Admittedly, good mentors can be difficult to recruit. Consider your friends, relatives, or neighbors who can offer as little as an hour or two a month. In a pinch, a mature high schooler who likes kids could even be "rented" to play ball or go fishing with a boy in need.

If you belong to a church, you should be able to find support for your son among the male members of the Christian community. Scripture commands people of faith to care for children without fathers. Isaiah 1:17 states, "Defend the cause of the fatherless, plead the case of the widow." Jesus Himself took boys and girls on His lap and said, "And whoever welcomes a little child like this in my name welcomes me" (Matthew 18:5). I believe it is our responsibility as Christian men to help single mothers with their difficult parenting tasks.

Certainly single mothers have many demands on their time and energy, but the effort to find a mentor for their sons might be the most worthwhile contribution they can make.

QUESTION **256**

I am a single mom who is struggling to survive. Of all the things that frustrate me, I am bothered most by having to send my kids to visit their dad for three weeks in the summer. That will happen next month, and I'm already uptight about putting them on the plane. Can you help me accept what I'm about to go through?

Maybe it will help to know that many other single parents have similar feelings. One of these mothers expressed her frustration this way:

> I stand in the terminal, and I watch the kids' airplane disappear into the clouds. I feel an incredible sense of loss. The loneliness immediately starts to set in. I worry constantly about their safety, but I resist the urge to call every hour to see how they're doing. And when they do call me to tell me how much fun they're having, I grieve over the fact that they're living a life completely separate from my own. My only consolation is knowing that they're returning soon. But I'm haunted by the fear that they won't want to come home with me.

If the anxieties of that mother represent your own feelings, let me offer some suggestions for how you might make the most of your days alone. Instead of seeing the next three weeks as a period of isolation, view them as an opportunity to recharge your batteries and reinvigorate the spirit. Single parenting is an exhausting responsibility that can cause burnout if it knows no relief. Take this time to enjoy some relaxed evenings with your friends. Read an inspirational book, or return to a hobby that you've set aside. Fill your day with things that are impossible amidst the pressures of child care, recognizing that your children will benefit from your rehabilitation. They'll return to a reenergized parent, instead of one coming off three weeks of depression.

QUESTION 257

There are several single parents in my church who seem to be so needy. I would like to help them, but, honestly, I am barely able to do everything necessary to care for my own family. What responsibility do you think I have as a Christian woman to help these other families?

Everyone is busy today. I don't know any families that aren't experiencing fatigue and time pressure. None of us need new things to do, certainly, but I do believe it is our duty to reach out to those who are going through hard times. This is especially true of single parents because their vulnerable children are the ones who suffer. I'm sure Jesus would have us care for these little families, financially and with our love and concern.

Many years ago, my wife, Shirley, was working around the house one morning, when a knock came at the front door. When she opened it, there stood a young woman in her late teens, who called herself Sally.

"I'm selling brushes," she said, "and I wonder if you'd like to buy any."

Well, my wife told her she wasn't interested in buying anything that day, and Sally said, "I know. No one else is, either." And with that, she began to cry.

Shirley invited Sally to come in for a cup of coffee, and she asked her to share her story. She turned out to be an unmarried mother who was just struggling mightily to support her two-year-old son. That night, we went to her shabby little apartment above a garage to see how we could help this mother and her toddler. When we opened the cupboards, there was nothing there for them to eat, and I mean nothing. That night, they both had dined on a can of SpaghettiOs. We took her to the market, and we did what we could to help get her on her feet.

Sally is obviously not the only single mother out there who is desperately trying to survive in a very hostile world. All of these mothers could use a little kindness—from baby-sitting to providing a meal to repairing the washing machine or even to just showing a little thoughtfulness.

Raising kids alone is like climbing a mountain a mile high. Can you find it in your heart to baby-sit for that single mother one afternoon a week? Or maybe you can fix extra food when you cook and take it over some evening. Imagine what that kindness will convey to a mom or dad who comes home exhausted and discovers that someone cares about his or her little family. Not only will it bring encouragement to the parent, but one or more children will bless you as well.

16
Living with a Teenager

QUESTION **258**

**Why do you think kids are more sexually active today than
when I was young? Lust is certainly not new. What is causing
this generation to be so promiscuous?**

There are many factors that have brought on the epidemic we're
seeing, not the least of which is the trash that is beamed to teenagers
on television, in movies, and from the rock-music industry. Young
people today are bombarded by immoral entertainment that models
promiscuous behavior and teaches them that "everyone is doing it."
The diminishing influence of traditional Christian teaching is also
responsible for the changing mores of our kids.

There is another extremely important consideration that has been
identified recently by behavioral research. A team of researchers from
the Oregon Social Learning Center has found that parental divorce
plays a direct role in fostering sexual experimentation among adolescents.

The investigators tracked the behavior of 201 junior high and high
school boys who lived in "higher-crime areas." They found that the
boys who had sexual intercourse at an early age tended to be those
who had experienced two or more "parental transitions," (divorce,
remarriage, or repartnering). Only 18 percent of these promiscuous

269

boys came from intact families. By contrast, 57 percent of the virgins came from homes where divorce had not occurred. On average, these abstinent boys had experienced fewer than one parental transition.[91]

A similar study was conducted on young women by sociologist Lawrence L. Wu, of the University of Wisconsin, Madison. He studied 2,441 white women and 1,275 black women, and found that there was a strong correlation between those who bore babies out of wedlock and those who had been through a "change in family structure" when growing up. Wu concluded that the stresses of divorce and/or remarriage on children are directly implicated in out-of-wedlock childbearing.[92]

In study after study now, we are seeing that divorce, single parenting, and family disruption are unhealthy for children. This is not to criticize those who find themselves in those circumstances, but neither can we continue to deny that intact, two-parent families are the most healthy and contribute directly to a stable society. If that is true (and the evidence for it is overwhelming), then our public policies and governmental agencies should favor and encourage traditional families. Anything that undermines or weakens them, such as confiscatory taxes or governmental intrusion, should be viewed with suspicion. The future of the nation depends, quite literally, on millions of strong, committed, and loving families.

To those who remember the vice president's controversial speech on family values during the election of 1992, we can now say unequivocally, "Dan Quayle was dead right!"

Q UESTION 259

Children seem to be growing up at a younger age today than in the past. Is this true, and if so, what accounts for their faster development?

Yes, it is true. Statistical records indicate that our children are growing taller today than in the past, probably resulting from better nutrition, medicine, exercise, rest, and recreation. And this more ideal physical environment has apparently caused sexual maturity to occur at younger and younger ages. It is thought that puberty in a particular child is triggered when he or she reaches a certain level of growth; therefore, when environmental and general health factors propel a youngster upward at a faster rate, sexual maturation occurs earlier.

For example, in 1850 the average age of menarche (first menstruation) in Norwegian girls was 17.0 years of age; in 1950, it was 13.0. The average age of puberty in females had dropped four years in one century. In the United States the average age of menarche dropped from 16.5 in 1840 to 12.9 in 1950.[93] More recent figures indicate that it now occurs on average at 12.8 years of age![94] Thus, the trend toward younger dating and sexual awareness is a result, at least in part, of this "fast-track" mechanism.

QUESTION 260

Are there limits to this trend toward younger and younger sexual development? If not, the kids of the future may enter puberty in the middle of childhood. That could create enormous problems when sexual awareness precedes emotional maturity by a decade or more.

It could happen, but that isn't likely. Actually, studies now indicate that a leveling off and perhaps a reversal of the trend is occurring. As of 1988, the average age of menarche reached a low point of 12.5.[95] By 1993, however, researchers Dann and Roberts found that the curve had begun to swing back in the other direction. Puberty appears to be arriving slightly later again. Why? Well, just as better nutrition and health care caused the average age to drop in the recent past, the present emphasis on ultrathin bodies and intense exercise is apparently delaying development somewhat.[96] Many physicians are concerned about today's obsession with what used to be called "skinniness." Extremes, they say, are rarely beneficial to human beings—whether they be manifested in grossly overweight bodies or those that are bone thin.

A famous biochemist at the University of Southern California, Dr. Sam Bessman, once told me, "Remember that the body never stops eating. If you don't feed it properly, it will begin to consume

itself." That is precisely what happens in the girl who consumes too
few calories; she may have no periods for years at a time.

QUESTION 261

**What is the most difficult period of adolescence, and what is
behind the distress?**

The eighteenth year is the time of greatest conflict between parent and
child, typically. But the thirteenth and fourteenth years commonly are the
most difficult twenty-four months in life for the youngster. It is during this
time that self-doubt and feelings of inferiority reach an all-time high,
amidst the greatest social pressures yet experienced. An adolescent's
sense of worth as a human being hangs precariously on peer-group
acceptance, which can be tough to garner. Thus, relatively minor evidences of rejection or ridicule are of major significance to those who
already see themselves as fools and failures. It is difficult to overestimate
the impact of having no one to sit with on the school-sponsored bus trip
or of not being invited to an important event or of being laughed at by the
"in" group or of waking up in the morning to find seven shiny new
pimples on your forehead or of being slapped by the girl you thought had
liked you as much as you liked her. Some boys and girls consistently face
this kind of social catastrophe throughout their teen years.

Dr. Urie Bronfenbrenner, eminent authority on child development at
Cornell University, told a Senate committee that the junior high years are
probably the most critical to the development of a child's mental health.
It is during this time of self-doubt that the personality is often assaulted
and damaged beyond repair. Consequently, said Bronfenbrenner, it is not
unusual for healthy, happy children to enter junior high school but then
emerge two years later as broken, discouraged teenagers.[97]

272

QUESTION 262

**Talk about the social pressures that beset many early adoles-
cents. Why do they seem to overreact to almost everything at
that time?**

It is common knowledge that a twelve- or thirteen-year-old child suddenly awakens to a brand-new world around him, as though his eyes were opening for the first time. That world is populated by age-mates who scare him out of his wits. His greatest anxiety, far exceeding the fear of death, is the possibility of rejection or humiliation in the eyes of his peers. This ultimate danger will lurk in the background for years, motivating him to do things that make absolutely no sense to the adults who watch. It is impossible to comprehend the adolescent mind without understanding this terror of the peer group.

I'll never forget a vulnerable girl named Lisa who was a student when I was in high school. She attended modern-dance classes and was asked to perform during an all-school assembly program. Lisa was in the ninth grade and had not begun to develop sexually. As she spun around the stage that day, the unthinkable happened! The top of her strapless blouse suddenly let go (it had nothing to grip) and dropped to her waist. The student body gasped and then roared with laughter. It was terrible! Lisa stood clutching frantically at her bare body for a moment and then fled from the stage in tears. Years later she hadn't recovered from the tragedy. And you can bet that her "friends" made sure she remembered it for the rest of her life.

Such a situation would also humiliate an adult, of course, but it was worse for a teenager like Lisa. An embarrassment of that magnitude could even take away the desire to live, and indeed, thousands of adolescents are killing themselves every year. That is how forceful is the need to be respected and accepted during the teen years. Those who are mocked and rejected by the peer group are often devastated well into the adult years.

QUESTION 263

You obviously have a great empathy for kids who are in the junior high years—especially those who are rejected and ridiculed by their peers. Have you always felt that way about that age-group, which many adults don't like to be around?

My concern for early adolescents dates back to the years I spent teaching in junior high school. I was only twenty-five years old at the time, and I fell in love with 250 science and math students. The day I left to accept other responsibilities I fought back the tears. Some of the kids were hurting badly, and I developed a keen sensitivity to their plight. Let me illustrate how I saw them.

Years later, I was sitting in my car at a fast-food restaurant, eating a hamburger and French fries. I happened to look in the rearview mirror. There I saw the most pitiful, scrawny, dirty little kitten on a ledge behind my car. I was so touched by how hungry she looked that I got out, tore off a piece of my hamburger, and tossed it to her. But before this kitten could reach it, a huge gray tomcat sprang out of the bushes, grabbed the morsel, and gobbled it down. I felt sorry for the kitten, who turned and ran back into the shadows, still hungry and frightened.

I was immediately reminded of those kids I used to teach. They were just as needy, just as deprived, just as lost as that little kitten. It wasn't food that they required; it was love and attention and respect that they needed, and they were desperate for it. And just when they opened up and revealed the pain inside, one of the more popular kids would abuse and ridicule them, sending them scurrying back into the shadows, frightened and alone.

We, as adults, must never forget the pain of trying to grow up and of the competitive world in which many adolescents live today. Taking a moment to listen, to care, and to direct such a youngster may be the best investment of a lifetime.

Q UESTION 264

Why are kids so vulnerable? How do you explain this paralyzing social fear at an age when they are notoriously gutsy? There is very little else that scares them. Teenagers drive their cars like maniacs, and the boys make great combat soldiers. Why is it that an eighteen-year-old can be trained to attack an enemy gun emplacement or run through a minefield, and yet he panics in the noisy company of his peers? Why are they so frightened of each other?

I believe the answer is related to the nature of power and how it influences human behavior. Adolescent society is based on the exercise of raw force. That is the heart and soul of its value system. It comes in various forms. For girls, there is no greater social dominance than physical beauty. A truly gorgeous young woman is so powerful that even the boys are often terrified of her. She rules in a high school like a queen on her throne, and in fact, she is usually given some honor with references to royalty in its name (Homecoming Queen, Homecoming Princess, All-School Queen, Sweetheart's Queen, Football Queen, etc.). The way she uses this status to intimidate her subjects is in itself a fascinating study in adolescent behavior.

Boys derive power from physical attractiveness too, but also from athletic accomplishment in certain prescribed sports. Those that carry the greatest status are usually skilled in sports that exhibit sheer physical strength (football) or size (basketball).

Do you remember what the world of adolescence was like for you? Do you recall the power games that were played—the highly competitive and hostile environment into which you walked every day? Can you still feel the apprehension you experienced when a popular (powerful) student called you a creep or a jerk, or he put his big hand in your face and pushed you out of the way? He wore a football jersey that reminded you that the entire team would eat you alive if you should be so foolish as to fight back. Does the memory of the junior-senior prom still come to mind occasionally, when you were either turned down by the girl you loved or were not asked by the boy of your dreams? Have you ever had the campus heroes make fun of the one flaw you most wanted to hide, and then threaten to mangle you on the way home from school?

Perhaps you never went through these stressful encounters. Maybe you were one of the powerful elite who oppressed the rest of us. But your son or daughter could be on the receiving end of the flak. A few years ago I talked to a mother whose seventh-grade daughter was getting butchered at school each day. She said the girl awakened an hour before she had to get up each morning and lay there thinking about how she could get through her day without being humiliated.

Typically, power games are more physical for adolescent males than females. The bullies literally force their will on those who are weaker. That is what I remember most clearly from my own high school years. I had a number of fights during that era just to preserve my turf. The name of the game was power! And not much has changed for today's teenagers.

Q UESTION 265

Explain in greater detail the role of power in the life of a teenager.

Let's begin with a definition. *Power* is the ability to control others, to control our circumstances, and especially, to control ourselves. The lust for it lies deep within the human spirit. We all want to be the boss, and that impulse begins very early in life. Studies show that one-day-old infants actually reach for control of the adults around them. Even at that tender age, they behave in ways designed to get their guardians to meet their needs.

The desire for power is evident when a toddler runs from his mother in a supermarket or when a ten-year-old refuses to do his or her homework or when a husband and wife fight over money. We see it when an elderly woman refuses to move to a nursing home. The common thread between these and a thousand other examples is the passion to run our own lives—and everything else, if given the chance. People vary in the intensity of this urge, but it seems to motivate all of us to one degree or another.

Now, what about your sons and daughters? Have you wondered why they come home from school in such a terrible mood? Have you asked them why they are so jumpy and irritable through the evening? Perhaps they are unable to describe their feelings to you, but they may have engaged in a form of combat all day. Even if they haven't had to fight with their fists, it is likely that they are embroiled in a highly competitive, openly hostile environment where emotional danger lurks on every side. Am I overstating the case? Yes, for the kid who is coping well. But for the powerless young man and woman, I haven't begun to tell their stories.

That's why they are nervous wrecks on the first day of school or before the team plays its initial game or any other time when their power base is on the line. The raw nerve, you see, is not really dominance but self-worth. One's sense of value is dependent on peer acceptance at that age, and that is why the group holds such enormous influence over the individual. If he or she is mocked, disrespected, ridiculed, and excluded—in other words, if that individual is stripped of power—he or she feels it deeply.

QUESTION **266**

If power is so important to teenagers, then it must play a key role in family dynamics. How does it work itself out at home?

You've asked a very perceptive question. It is a wise parent who knows intuitively how to transfer power, or independence, to the next generation. That task requires a balancing act between two equally dangerous extremes. They dare not set their teenagers free before they are mature enough to handle the autonomy—even though they are screaming for it. Adolescents still need parental leadership, and parents are obligated to provide it—that's the law of the land. One of the characteristics of those who acquire power too early is a prevailing attitude of disrespect for authority. It extends to teachers, ministers, policemen, judges, and even to God Himself. Such an individual has never yielded to parental leadership at home. Why should he or she submit himself or herself to anyone else? For a rebellious teenager, it is only a short step from there to drug abuse, sexual experimentation, running away, and so on. The early acquisition of power has claimed countless young victims by this very process.

On the other hand, there is an equally dangerous mistake to be avoided at the latter end of adolescence. We must not wait too long to set our young adults free. Self-determination is a basic human right to which every adult is entitled. To withhold that liberty too long is to incite wars of revolution.

My good friend Jay Kesler observed that Mother England made that specific mistake with her children in the American colonies. They grew to become rebellious "teenagers" who demanded their freedom. Still she refused to release them, and unnecessary bloodshed ensued. Fortunately, England learned a valuable lesson from that painful experience. Some 171 years later, she granted a peaceful and orderly

277

transfer of power to another tempestuous offspring named India. Revolution was averted.[98]

At the risk of being redundant, let me summarize our goal as parents: First, we must not transfer power too early, even if our children take us daily to the battlefield. Mothers who make that mistake are some of the most frustrated people on the face of the earth. On the other hand, we must not retain parental power too long. Control will be torn from our grasp if we refuse to surrender it voluntarily. The granting of self-determination should be matched stride for stride with the arrival of maturity, culminating with complete release during early adulthood.

Sounds easy, doesn't it? We all know better. I consider this orderly transfer of power to be one of the most delicate and difficult responsibilities in the entire realm of parenthood.

QUESTION 267

What guidelines can you offer to help us transfer power at the right time—neither early nor late?

There are some approaches that have been successful in lessening this conflict. The Amish people have developed a unique tradition that has succeeded for them. Their children are kept under very tight control when they are young. Strict discipline and harsh standards of behavior are imposed from infancy. When children turn sixteen years of age, however, they enter a period called "Rumspringa." Suddenly, all restrictions are lifted. They are free to drink, smoke, date, marry, or behave in ways that horrify their parents. Some do just that. But most don't. They are even granted the right to leave the Amish community if they choose. But if they stay, it must be in accordance with the social order. The majority accept the heritage of their families, not because they must, but because they choose to.

Although I admire the Amish and many of their approaches to child rearing, I believe the Rumspringa concept is implemented too quickly for children raised in a more open society. To take a teenager overnight from rigid control to complete emancipation is an invitation to anarchy. It works in the controlled environment of Amish country, but it would be disastrous for most of the rest of us. I've seen families grant "instant adulthood" to their adolescents, to their regret. The result has been similar to what occurred in African colonies when European leadership was suddenly withdrawn. Bloody revolutions were often fought in the power vacuum that was created.

If it doesn't work to transfer power suddenly to young people, how can they be established as full-fledged adults without creating a civil war in the process? I have recommended that parents begin granting tiny elements of independence literally in toddlerhood. When a child can tie his shoes, he should be permitted—yes, required—to do it. When she can choose her clothes, she should make her own selections, within reason. When he can walk safely to school, he should be allowed to do so. Each year, more responsibility and freedom (they are companions) must be given to the child so that the final release in early adulthood is merely a small, final release of authority. This is the theory, at least. Pulling it off is sometimes quite another matter.

In the final analysis, your own son or daughter will let you know when the time is right for independence. You must judge his or her maturity, wisdom, and emotional readiness for full-fledged adulthood. Then you grant it—and pray diligently for the next thirty years.

QUESTION **268**

My thirteen-year-old daughter has become increasingly lazy in the past couple of years. She lies around the house and will sleep half a day on Saturday. She complains about being tired a lot. Is this typical of early adolescence? How should I deal with it?

It is not uncommon for boys and girls to experience fatigue during the years of puberty. Their physical resources are being invested in a rapid growth process during that time, leaving less energy for other activities. This period doesn't last very long and is usually followed by the most energetic time of life.

I would suggest, first, that you schedule your daughter for a routine physical examination to rule out the possibility of a more serious explanation for her fatigue. If it does turn out to be a phenomenon of puberty, as I suspect, you should "go with the flow." See that she gets plenty of rest and sleep. This need is often not met because teenagers feel that they shouldn't have to go to bed as early as they did when they were children. Therefore, they stay up too late and then drag through the next day in a state of exhaustion. Surprisingly, a thirteen- or fourteen-year-old actually needs more rest than when he or she was nine or ten, simply because of the acceleration in growth.

In summary, your daughter is turning overnight from a girl into a woman. Some of the physical characteristics you are observing are part of the transformation. Do everything you can to facilitate it.

Q UESTION 269

We have a very athletic junior high school boy who loves every kind of physical activity. He gets most of his exercise in a P.E. class every morning, but I happen to know that he doesn't shower afterward. The school no longer makes him or the other kids do it. When I was a student we were required to clean up after sweating in the gym. How come this is no longer considered necessary?

Like you, I was required to shower after every gym class. The coach would look us over to make sure we were clean before sending us on our way. Students who didn't shower didn't pass. But those days are just about over. The reason is that because junior highers are so sensitive about their bodies today, it is very painful for them to have to strip in front of one another. They vary so much in development at that age that some are grown-up adults and others are still little prepubescent kids. It is nightmarish for the immature youngster to have to put his or her body on display in front of the wolf pack. They would tear him to pieces. Others feel fat or skinny or hairy or (fill in the blank). Increasingly, they resist having to take it all off in the locker room.

When I was a school psychologist, I met with a high school sophomore who absolutely refused to shower. His recalcitrance violated district policy, and I was asked to identify his problem. After talking to this boy and seeing how vulnerable he was to the ridicule of his peers, I agreed that he should not be required to humiliate himself five days a week. Twenty years ago, this lad was an exception. Now, given the body consciousness of our culture, his attitude is common.

Another factor is that coaches and teachers have become very leery of false charges of sexual abuse. Even if untrue, a person's entire career could go down the drain just by the suggestion that he or she was enjoying looking at the kids. This is another reason mandatory showers in schools are being phased out.

The result? Teachers have to work in a classroom full of sweaty adolescents who smell like a gymnasium—or worse.

QUESTION 270

I hear so much about communicating with our children and making sure we stay on the same wavelength. How can I do that during the teen years?

You can expect communication to be very difficult for several years. I said adolescence was sometimes like a tornado. Let me give you a better analogy. This time of life reminds me in some ways of the very early space probes that blasted off from Cape Canaveral in Florida. I remember my excitement when Colonel John Glenn and the other astronauts embarked on their perilous journeys into space. It was a thrilling time to be an American.

People who lived through those years will recall that a period of maximum danger occurred as each spacecraft was reentering the earth's atmosphere. The fliers inside were entirely dependent on the heat shield on the bottom of the capsule to protect them from temperatures in excess of one thousand degrees Fahrenheit. If the craft descended at the wrong angle, the astronauts would be burned to cinders. At that precise moment of anxiety, negative ions would accumulate around the capsule and prevent all communication with the earth for approximately seven minutes. The world waited breathlessly for news of the astronauts' safety. Presently, the reassuring voice of a man named Chris Craft broke in to say, "This is Mission Control. We have made contact with Friendship Seven. Everything is A-OK. Splashdown is imminent." Cheers and prayers went up in restaurants, banks, airports, and millions of homes across the country. Even CBS news anchor Walter Cronkite seemed relieved.

The application to the teen years should be apparent. After the training and preparation of childhood are over, a pubescent youngster marches out to the launching pad. His parents watch apprehensively as he climbs aboard a capsule called adolescence and waits for his rockets to fire. His father and mother wish they could go with him, but there is room for just one person in the spacecraft. Besides, nobody invited them. Without warning, the mighty rocket engines begin to roar and the "umbilical cord" falls away. "Liftoff! We have liftoff!" screams the boy's father.

Junior, who was a baby only yesterday, is on his way to the edge of the universe. A few weeks later, his parents go through the scariest experience of their lives: They suddenly lose all contact with the capsule. "Negative ions" have interfered with communication at a time when they most want to be assured of their son's safety. Why won't he talk to them?

This period of silence lasts much longer than a few minutes, as it did with Colonel Glenn and friends. It may continue for years. The same kid who used to talk a mile a minute and ask a million questions has now reduced his vocabulary to nine monosyllabic phrases. They are, "I dunno," "Maybe," "I forget," "Huh?" "No!" "Nope," "Yeah," "Who—me?" and "He did it." Otherwise, only static comes through the receivers—groans, grunts, growls, and gripes. What an apprehensive time it is for those who wait on the ground!

Years later, when Mission Control fears the spacecraft has been lost, a few scratchy signals are picked up unexpectedly from a distant transmitter. The parents are jubilant as they hover near their radio. Was that really his voice? It is deeper and more mature than they remembered. There it is again. This time the intent is unmistakable. Their spacey son has made a deliberate effort to correspond with them! He was fourteen years old when he blasted into space and now he is nearly twenty. Could it be that the negative environment has been swept away and communication is again possible?

Yes. For most families, that is precisely what happens. After years of quiet anxiety, parents learn to their great relief that everything is A-OK on board the spacecraft. The "splashdown" occurring during the early twenties can then be a wonderful time of life for both generations.

QUESTION 271

Isn't there some way to avoid this blackout period and the other stresses associated with the adolescent voyage?

Not with some teenagers; perhaps not with the majority. Tension occurs in the most loving and intelligent of families. Why? Because it is driven by powerful hormonal forces that overtake and possess boys and girls in the early pubescent years. I believe parents and even some behavioral scientists have underestimated the impact of the biochemical changes occurring in puberty. We can see the effect of these hormones on the physical body, but something equally dynamic is occurring in the brain. How else can we explain why a happy, contented, cooperative twelve-year-old suddenly becomes a sullen, angry, depressed thirteen-year-old? Some authorities would contend that social pressure alone accounts for this transformation. I simply don't believe that.

The emotional characteristics of a suddenly rebellious teenager are rather like the symptoms of premenstrual syndrome or severe menopause in women or perhaps a tumultuous midlife crisis in men. Obviously, dramatic changes are going on inside! Furthermore, if the upheaval were caused entirely by environmental factors, its onset would not be so predictable in puberty. The emotional changes I have described arrive right on schedule, timed to coincide precisely with the arrival of sexual maturation. Both characteristics, I contend, are driven by a common hormonal assault. Human chemistry apparently goes haywire for a few years, in some more than others, affecting mind as much as body.

QUESTION 272

If that explanation is accurate, then what implications does it have for parents of early adolescents?

First, understanding this glandular upheaval makes it easier to tolerate and cope with the emotional reverberations that are occurring. For several years, some kids are not entirely rational! Just as a severely menopausal woman may accuse her innocent and bewildered husband of infidelity, a hormonally depressed teenager may not interpret his world accurately either. His social judgment is impaired. Therefore, parents shouldn't despair when it looks like everything they have tried to teach their kid seems to have been forgotten. He is going through a metamorphosis that has turned everything upside down. But stick around. He'll get his legs under him again!

I strongly recommend that parents of strong-willed and rebellious females, especially, quietly keep track of the particulars of their daughters' menstrual cycles. Not only should you record when their periods begin and end each month, but also make a comment or two each day about moods. I think you will see that the emotional blowups that tear the family apart are cyclical in nature. Premenstrual tension at that age can produce a flurry of skirmishes every twenty-eight days. If you know they are coming, you can retreat to the storm cellar when the wind begins to blow. You can also use this record to teach your girls about premenstrual syndrome and how to cope with it. Unfortunately, many parents never seem to notice the regularity and predictability of severe conflict with their daughters. Again, I recommend that you watch the calendar. It will tell you so much about your girls.

QUESTION 273

How about adolescent boys? Do they have a hormonal cycle too?

Their emotions and behavior are certainly driven by hormones. Everything from sexual passion to aggressiveness is motivated by the new chemicals that surge through their veins. There is, however, no cyclical fluctuation that parallels a menstrual calendar in girls. As a result, they can be more volatile and less predictable throughout the month than their female counterparts.

QUESTION 274

My fourteen-year-old boy is flighty, mischievous, irresponsible, and lazy. If I don't watch him very carefully, he'll find

ways to get into trouble—not really bad stuff, just stupid kid
behavior. But I'm afraid I could lose him right at this time.
What can I do to keep him on track?

It is most important to keep your rambunctious youngster moving. If
you let him get bored, he'll find destructive ways to use unstructured
and unsupervised time. My advice is to get him involved in the very
best church youth program you can find. If your local congregation
only has four bored kids in its junior high department and seven
sleepy high schoolers, I would consider changing churches. I know
doing that could be disruptive to the rest of your family, but it might
help save your volatile kid. This can be done not only through church
activities but also by involvement with athletics, music, horses or
other animals, and part-time jobs. The hope is that one of those
options will grab his fancy at some point, and his boundless energy
will be channeled into something constructive. Until then, you must
keep that energetic kid's scrawny legs churning!

Q UESTION 275

It is commonly understood that peer pressure causes teenagers to begin smoking or using drugs. Is that what really
motivates them to pick up dangerous habits?

That precise question was the subject of a recent survey. The researchers studied more than sixteen thousand schoolchildren in Orange County, California. They found that it was family members, not
classmates or teachers, who had the biggest influence on whether
children used drugs, alcohol, or tobacco. If teenagers felt that their
parents or siblings approved of smoking, they were likely to follow
suit. And if there was one person who could convince them not to
participate, it was usually a member of their own family. Many parents
feel that this is an area that can be left to the schools, and they neglect
to talk about it at home. But this study and others have shown that
family pressure, not peer pressure, has the greatest effect on children.[99]

Another finding to come out of the investigation is that children are still dangerously unaware of the hazards of smoking. Obviously, the antismoking advertising campaign has not reached their tender ears.

Like other messages we want our children to hear, the responsibility to communicate them lies with parents. Talk to your sons and daughters when they are young about the dangers of cigarette smoking. Tell them that you don't approve of the habit. Discuss the health hazards, including the risk of cancer and lung disease. And offer them professional help in quitting if they've already started. Warn them repeatedly about drug abuse and what it can do to the body. Parents can make a difference in avoiding addictive behavior in their children if they take the time to teach them. Most of them can even counterbalance the peer group.

QUESTION 276

My thirteen-year-old son is in the full bloom of adolescence. I'm suspicious that he may be masturbating when he's alone, but I don't quite know how to approach him about it. Should I be concerned, and if so, what should I say to him?

I don't think you should invade that private world at all unless there are unique circumstances that lead you to do so. I offer that advice while acknowledging that masturbation is a highly controversial subject and Christian leaders differ widely in their perspectives on it. I will answer your question but hope you understand that some Bible scholars will disagree emphatically with what I will say.

First, let's consider masturbation from a medical perspective. We can say without fear of contradiction that there is *no* scientific evidence to indicate that this act is harmful to the body. Despite terrifying warnings given to young people historically, it does not cause blindness, weakness, mental retardation, or any other physical problem. If it did, the entire male population and about half of females would be blind, weak, simpleminded, and sick. Between 95 and 98 percent of all boys engage in this practice—and the rest have been known to lie. It is as close to being a universal behavior as is likely to occur. A lesser but still significant percentage of girls also engage in what was once called "self-gratification."

As for the emotional consequences of masturbation, only four circumstances should give us cause for concern. The first is when it is associated with oppressive guilt from which the individual can't escape. That guilt has the potential to do considerable psychological and spiritual damage. Boys and girls who labor under divine condemnation can gradually become convinced that even God couldn't love them. They promise a thousand times with great sincerity never again to commit this despicable act. Then a week or two passes, or perhaps several months. Eventually, the hormonal pressure accumulates until nearly every waking moment reverberates with sexual desire. Finally, in a moment (and I do mean *a moment*) of weakness, it happens again. What then, dear friend? Tell me what a young person says to God after he or she has just broken the one thousand first solemn promise to Him? I am convinced that some teenagers have thrown over their faith because of their inability to please God at this point of masturbation.

The second circumstance in which masturbation might have harmful implications is when it becomes extremely obsessive. That is more likely to occur when it has been understood by the individual to be "forbidden fruit." I believe the best way to prevent that kind of obsessive response is for adults not to emphasize or condemn it. Regardless of what you do, you will not stop the practice of masturbation in your teenagers. That is a certainty. You'll just drive it underground—or under covers. Nothing works as a "cure." Cold showers, lots of exercise, many activities, and awesome threats are ineffective. Attempting to suppress this act is one campaign that is destined to fail—so why wage it?

The third situation around which we should be concerned is when the young person becomes addicted to pornographic material. The kind of obscenity available to teenagers today has the capacity to grab and hold a boy for the rest of his life. Parents will want to intervene if there is evidence that their son or daughter is heading down that well-worn path.

The fourth concern about masturbation refers not to adolescents but to us as adults. This habit has the capacity to follow us into marriage and become a substitution for healthy sexual relations between a husband and wife. This, I believe, is what the apostle Paul meant when he instructed us not to "deprive" one another as marital partners: "Do not deprive each other except by mutual consent and for a time, so that you may devote yourselves to prayer. Then come together again so that

Satan will not tempt you because of your lack of self-control" (1 Corinthians 7:5).

As for the spiritual implications of masturbation, I will have to defer to the theologians for a more definitive response. It is interesting to me, however, that Scripture does not address this subject except for a single reference in the Old Testament to a man named Onan. He interrupted sexual intercourse with his sister-in-law and allowed his semen to fall on the ground to keep from producing offspring for his brother, which was his "duty" (Genesis 38:8). Though that verse is often cited as evidence of God's disapproval of masturbation, the context doesn't seem to fit.

So, what should parents say to their kids about this subject? My advice is to say nothing after puberty has occurred. You will only cause embarrassment and discomfort. For those who are younger, it would be wise to include the subject of masturbation in the "Preparing for Adolescence" conversation I have recommended on other occasions. I would suggest that parents talk to their twelve- or thirteen-year-old boys, especially, in the same general way my mother and father discussed this subject with me. We were riding in the car, and my dad said, "Jim, when I was a boy, I worried so much about masturbation. It really became a scary thing for me because I thought God was condemning me for what I couldn't help. So I'm telling you now that I hope you don't feel the need to engage in this act when you reach the teen years, but if you do, you shouldn't be too concerned about it. I don't believe it has much to do with your relationship with God."

What a kind thing my father did for me that night in the car. He was a very conservative minister who never compromised his standards of morality to the day of his death. He stood like a rock for biblical principles and commandments. Yet he cared enough about me to lift from my shoulders the burden of guilt that nearly destroyed some of my friends in the church. This kind of "reasonable" faith taught to me by my parents is one of the primary reasons I never felt it necessary to rebel against parental authority or defy God.

Well, those are my views, for what they are worth. I know my recommendations will be inflammatory to some people. If you are one of them, please forgive me. I can only offer the best advice of which I'm capable. I pray that in this instance, I am right.

QUESTION 277

My oldest son is approaching the age when we had previously agreed to allow him to date. The more I think about it, though, the more the whole idea concerns me. It seems that even in the best of dating situations, the negatives exceed the positives. I can't help but feel that I'm setting my son up for failure. Several of my church friends have adopted the concept of "courtship" rather than dating. Could you please explain this idea to me and suggest which of the two arrangements you favor?

Simply put, the "courtship" concept is a reaction to the dating model that is thought by many to be unhealthy. Dating couples go through a series of short-term and often unsatisfying relationships over a period of five or ten years or longer. They are being taught to flit from one relationship to another like a honeybee buzzing from flower to flower. Why would they not be inclined later to bail out on a marriage partner when bored or frustrated? Dating also encourages sexual familiarity and experimentation. It isn't difficult to understand why an increasing number of parents feel this traditional model undermines commitment, exclusivity, and permanence in marriage.

The courtship model, by contrast, seeks to postpone emotional and physical entanglements until they occur with the probable husband or wife. The family is very supportive in helping to choose that special individual for a serious courtship when the time is right. Until then, relationships between the sexes are limited to group situations in carefully controlled settings. Physical intimacy for the sake of titillation and experimentation is considered to be most inappropriate. It is the ultimate in "saving oneself" for the man or woman with whom a lifetime will be spent.

Many parents, and undoubtedly the majority of teenagers, would consider the courtship model to be extreme and terribly restrictive. Not every teenager would tolerate it. I believe it is a good idea in those settings where both generations are committed to it and are willing to work together to make it successful. Courtship is not recommended in cases of adolescent rebellion or where there is great resistance to the idea. Whether or not to take this approach, therefore, is a matter for individual families to determine.

QUESTION 278

How do you feel about the changes in the way boys and girls relate to each other? When I was a kid, guys always did the telephoning. My mother would never have allowed me to call a boy when I was fourteen. Now, girls ask boys for dates and are sometimes very pushy in getting what they want. Does it matter? What should I teach my daughter?

You are right. Relationships between the sexes at all ages have changed radically. Historically, young girls were taught to be reserved—to keep a tight rein on their impulses—especially when it came to matters of the heart. Boys have traditionally been the initiators, and girls were quite content to be the responders. But what we're seeing now is a new sexual aggressiveness among females that has many parents worried. I am one of them.

Some hard-charging girls are so bold that they intimidate the boys they pursue. The male ego is constructed in such a way as to be uncomfortable if in retreat. Even in this day, when the old restrictions and taboos for women have fallen away, I believe it's still appropriate for parents to teach their girls a certain reserve, a certain self-respect, when it comes to romantic relationships. This is especially true during the awkward experiences of early adolescence.

It may be difficult for a girl to cool down a bit, but she'll be more successful and less vulnerable by attracting the object of her affection, rather than trying to run him down. If that is an old-fashioned notion, I still believe in it.

290

QUESTION 279

Do you believe in what is known as "the double standard"? In other words, is it OK for guys to do things that girls can't do?

I emphatically do *not* believe in the double standard. The Scripture makes no distinction between the sexes when it prohibits immoral behavior. It is just as wrong for a boy to engage in premarital sex as it is for a girl to do it. Still, there is a reason why girls have been given a different code of behavior than boys in the past.

The double standard came into being, I would think, because parents understood that girls are more likely to get hurt from premarital sexual encounters. Only females get pregnant, of course, and their complex reproductive system is more vulnerable to venereal diseases and infections. Girls and women also have more to lose emotionally. They often feel wounded and used after casual sex, whereas guys may think of the experience as another trophy to brag about. That is why parents and teachers used to worry more about girls and took steps to guard their virginity. Many still do.

Given these differences between the sexes, the sexual revolution was the biggest joke men ever played on women. By convincing them that the old rules didn't apply, men enticed women to do what men have always wanted women to do. But what a price was paid for the new "freedom." And predictably, women were the ones who got stuck with most of the bill.

Again, the moral significance of sexual promiscuity is the same for both sexes, and sin is devastating to whoever engages in it. Nevertheless, the physical and emotional consequences of immorality are disproportionate. Women are usually the bigger losers.

QUESTION **280**

I was watching an old black-and-white movie on television the other night that was made in the late 1930s. What jumped out at me was the respectful way the teenagers related to their parents. These kids, who appeared to be seventeen or eighteen years old, were downright deferential and looked to their father to make final decisions regarding their own behavior. I know this was just fiction, but I got the impression that that's the way families functioned back then. Today, even "good kids" from strong families are often more independent and

disrespectful to their parents. If I'm right about this change, why has it occurred and how do you see it?

The movie you saw is characteristic of others made during that era, because children in most nations of the world responded that way to their parents. There were exceptions, of course. Rebellion has occurred throughout history—even in biblical times. Remember that King David's son Amnon raped his half sister Tamar and Absalom tried to overthrow the reign of his father. While some of yesterday's families had to deal with upheavals of this nature, they have typically been the exception rather than the rule. But today, as you indicated, children and young people are taught to be disrespectful and rebellious by the culture. One of the most effective teachers is the rock-music industry and the excesses it embraces.

It is difficult to overestimate the negative impact contemporary music is having. Rock stars are the heroes, the idols, that young people want to emulate. And when they are depicted in violent and sexual roles, many teenagers and preadolescents are pulled along in their wake.

What could possibly be wholesome about showing explicit sex scenes—especially those involving perversion—to twelve- and thirteen-year-old kids? Yet videos come into the home via MTV and other channels that feature men and women in blatantly sexual situations, or even in depictions of sadism.

One study showed that more than half of all MTV videos featured violence or implied violence, and 35 percent revealed violence against women.[100] A steady diet of this garbage will pollute the minds of even the healthiest of teenagers.

I believe that this perpetual and pernicious exposure to rock music is responsible, at least in part, for many of the social problems now occurring among the young, including the high suicide rate, the reported willingness of young men to rape women if given an opportunity, and the moral undermining of the next generation.

292

QUESTION 281

Can you illustrate your concerns about the lyrics of contemporary teen music, especially as it relates to attitudes toward parents?

It might be helpful to see how popular music has changed over the years.

Let's go back to 1953, when the most popular song in the United States was sung by Eddie Fisher and was titled "Oh, My Papa." Here's a portion of the lyrics:

Oh, my papa, to me he was so wonderful.
Oh, my papa, to me he was so good.
No one could be so gentle and so lovable.
Oh, my papa, he always understood.
Gone are the days when he would take me on his knee,
And with a smile he'd change my tears to laughter.
Oh, my papa, so funny and adorable,
Always the clown, so funny in his way.
Oh, my papa, to me he was so wonderful.
Deep in my heart I miss him so today.
Oh, my papa. Oh, my papa.[101]

That sentimental song accurately reflected the way many people felt about their fathers at that time in our history. Oh, sure, there were conflicts and disagreements, but family was family. When it was all said and done, parents were entitled to respect and loyalty, and they usually received it from their children.

By the time I had reached college age, things were starting to change. The subject of conflict between parents and teenagers began to appear as a common theme in artistic creations. The movie *Rebel without a Cause* featured a screen idol named James Dean who seethed with anger at his "old man." Marlon Brando starred in *The Wild One*, another movie with rebellion as its theme. Rock-'n'-roll music portrayed it, too.

But what began as engaging drama turned decidedly bitter in the late sixties. Everyone in those days was talking about the "generation gap" that had erupted between young people and their parents. Teenagers and college students vowed they'd never again trust anyone over thirty, and their anger toward parents began to percolate. The Doors released a song in 1968 entitled "The End," in which lead singer Jim Morrison fantasized about killing his father. It concluded with gunshots followed by horrible grunts and groans.[102]

n 1984, Twisted Sister released "We're Not Gonna Take It," which referred to a father as a "disgusting slob" who was "worthless and weak."[103] Then he was blasted out the window of a second-story apartment. This theme of killing parents showed up regularly in that decade. A group called Suicidal Tendencies released a recording in 1983 called "I Saw Your Mommy." Some of the phrases in this song are "I saw your mommy and your mommy's dead . . . chewed-off toes on her chopped-off feet. . . . I saw her lying in a pool of red; I think it's the greatest thing I'll ever see—your dead mommy."[104]

For sheer banality, nothing yet produced can match "Momma's Gotta Die Tonight," by Ice-T and Body Count. The album sold 500,000 copies and featured its wretched lyrics on the CD jacket. Most of them are unfit to quote here, but they involved graphic descriptions of the rapper's mother being burned in her bed, then beaten to death with a baseball bat she had given him as a present, and finally the mutilation of the corpse into "little bitty pieces." What incredible violence! There was not a hint of guilt or remorse expressed by the rapper while telling us of this murder. In fact, he called his mother a "racist b—-h" and laughed while chanting, "Burn, Mama, burn."[105]

My point is that the most popular music of our culture went from the inspiration of "Oh, My Papa" to the horrors of "Momma's Gotta Die Tonight" in scarcely more than a generation. And we have to wonder, *Where do we go from here?*

One thing is certain: The younger generation has been bombarded with more antifamily rhetoric than any that preceded it. When added to equally disturbing messages about drug use, sex, and violence against women, the impact has to be considered formidable. And the most profane and obscene rock stars have become idols to many impressionable teenagers. MTV, which promotes the worst stuff available, is telecast into 231 million households in seventy-five countries, more than any other cable program.[106] Though it will not be popular for me to say it, I believe many of the problems that plague this generation, from suicide to unwed pregnancy to murder, can be traced to the venom dripped into its veins by the entertainment industry in general.

One of the consequences of this shift in the popular culture is a generation that sees itself and its elders less respectfully than those who have preceded it. There are still millions of responsible and respectful teenagers out there, of course, but the culture in which they are growing up has changed—for the worse.

QUESTION 282

I don't believe kids are as easily influenced as you say. What they see does not necessarily determine how they behave.

Well, look at it this way. Back in the early eighties, the most popular movie was a science-fiction film entitled *E.T. The Extra-Terrestrial.* It included a brief scene where the little creature from outer space was given a few pieces of the candy Reese's Pieces. The brand was not named, but children recognized it during its few seconds on the screen. In the months that followed, the sale of Reese's Pieces went through the ceiling. Isn't that a clear example of a movie's influence on children's thinking?

Why do advertisers spend billions of dollars to put their products before the people if what we see and hear does not influence our behavior? Why do schools and colleges purchase textbooks for children and young adults if what they read does not translate into influence of one form or another? *Of course* children are vulnerable to what they witness! We all are. How much greater impact is made by dramatic, sexually oriented, no-holds-barred musical and theatrical presentations that are aimed at the hearts and souls of our kids? Whom are we kidding when we say they are not harmed by the worst of it?

QUESTION 283

I remember adults complaining about the music of my day. Doesn't every generation of parents think their kids have gone too far?

Yes, but we're dealing with something especially vile today. As a case in point, you may remember the flap that occurred over the rap group 2 Live Crew and their album *As Nasty As They Wanna Be.* A Florida judge reviewed the filthy lyrics of this album, and, for the first time ever, a piece of "music" was declared to be obscene and illegal.[107]

Predictably, Phil Donahue (shortly before his show was canceled) and his cronies in the press threw their usual temper tantrums when the news broke. "Censorship!" they cried from the rooftops. Hundreds of newspaper editors and television commentators carried editorials and feature stories about the audacity of the judge who imposed his standard of morality on the rest of us.

Dan Rather, on his show *48 Hours,* made outlandish statements about our loss of freedoms in this era of oppression. And Geraldo Rivera risked getting his nose broken again by bringing 2 Live Crew and their critics face-to-face on his television show.

What the media did not tell the American people, however, was the content of 2 Live Crew's album. They censored that information from the public, choosing instead to talk abstractly about "First-Amendment rights" and "right-wing fundamentalists."

Isn't it interesting that those who were accusing concerned citizens of censorship were themselves editing the truth? Millions of words were spoken about the obscene lyrics to a single album, yet no one would quote them directly. Why not? Because adults would be shocked and outraged by their filth and debauchery. Thus, language that was unfit to print or utter on television was considered perfectly acceptable for the consumption of young minds. That is the logic of Phil, Dan, and Geraldo.

At the risk of upsetting our readers, let me list for you—as discreetly as possible—the words that appeared in the album *As Nasty As They Wanna Be.* They included

- 226 uses of the *f*-word
- 117 explicit terms for male or female genitalia
- 87 descriptions of oral sex
- 163 uses of the word for female dog
- 15 uses of *ho* (slang for *whore*) when referring to women
- 81 uses of the vulgarity *s—t*
- 42 uses of the word *ass*
- 9 descriptions of male ejaculation
- 6 references to erections

- 4 descriptions of group sex
- 3 mentions of rimming (oral/anal sex)
- 2 inclusions of urination or feces
- 1 reference to incest
- over 12 illustrations of violent sex

Please understand that these words did not appear singularly in the album. They were used to describe specific acts and attitudes. Remember, too, that youngsters—some only eight to ten years of age—buying this "music" typically listened to it dozens, or perhaps hundreds, of times.

Descriptions of oral sex and extreme violence against women were thereby memorized and burned into the conscious experience of kids barely out of elementary school. More than two million albums were sold, and with the exception of Florida and a few other locations where it was banned, no restrictions were placed on the album's distribution. A child of any age could purchase it.

This is merely one salvo in an industry that has helped to destroy the moral code of Western civilization. It has been accomplished methodically and deliberately during the past thirty years, in cooperation with television and movie producers. The damage has been incalculable!

I feel like the patriarch Lot when he said of Sodom and Gomorrah more than four thousand years ago: "I am 'vexed with the filthy conversation of the wicked'" (2 Peter 2:7, KJV).

Oh, by the way. The conviction of 2 Live Crew on obscenity charges was overturned by an appeals court.[108] It turns out that the offensive language used in their album is protected by the U.S. Constitution. Imagine what the framers of that document would have thought about that.

*Q*UESTION 284

My sister's daughter went off to college at eighteen and immediately went a little crazy. She had always been a good kid, but when she was on her own, she drank like a lush, was sexually promiscuous, and flunked three of her classes. My daughter is only twelve, but I don't want her to make the same

mistakes when she is beyond our grasp. How can I get her ready to handle freedom and independence?

Well, you may already be twelve years late in beginning to prepare your daughter for that moment of release. The key is to transfer freedom and responsibility to her little by little from early childhood so she won't need your supervision when she is beyond it. To move suddenly from tight control to utter liberty is an invitation to disaster.

I learned this principle from my own mother, who made a calculated effort to teach me independence and responsibility. After laying a foundation during the younger years, she gave me a "final examination" when I was seventeen years old. Mom and Dad went on a two-week trip and left me at home with the family car and permission to have my buddies stay at the house. Wow! Fourteen slumber parties in a row! I couldn't believe it. We could have torn the place apart—but we didn't. We behaved rather responsibly.

I always wondered why my mother took such a risk, and after I was grown, I asked her about it. She just smiled and said, "I knew in one year you would be leaving for college, where you would have complete freedom with no one watching over you. I wanted to expose you to that independence while you were still under my influence."

I suggest that you let your daughter test the waters of freedom occasionally as she's growing up, rather than tossing her into the big wide ocean all at once. It takes wisdom and tact to pull that off, but it can be done. If you do the job properly, the time of release in six or seven years will be a gentle transition rather than a cataclysmic event.

QUESTION **285**

My sixteen-year-old daughter is driving me crazy. She is sassy, noisy, and selfish. Her room looks like a pigpen, and she won't work any harder in school than absolutely necessary to get by. Everything I taught her, from manners to faith, seems to have sailed through her ears. What in the world do my husband and I do now?

I'm going to offer you some patented advice that may not make sense or seem responsive to the problem you've described. But stay with me. The most important thing you can do for your daughter is to "just get her through it." The concept is a bit obscure, so let me make an effort to explain it.

Imagine your daughter riding in a small canoe called "Puberty" on the Adolescent River. She soon comes to a turbulent stretch of white water that rocks her little boat violently. There is a very real danger that she will capsize and drown. Even if she survives today's rapids, she will certainly be caught in swirling currents downstream and plunge over the falls. That is the apprehension harbored by millions of parents with kids bouncing along on the wild river. It's the falls that worry them most.

Actually, the typical journey down the river is much safer than believed. Instead of the water becoming more violent downstream, it eventually transitions from frightening rapids to tranquillity once more. What I'm saying is that I believe your daughter is going to be OK even though she is now splashing and thrashing and gasping for air. Her little boat is more buoyant than you might think. Yes, a few individuals do go over the falls, usually because of drug abuse or other addictive behavior. But even some of them climb back in the canoe and paddle on down the river. Most will regain their equilibrium in a few years. In fact, the greatest danger of sinking a boat could come from . . . parents!

*Q*UESTION **286**

Why do you focus your comments on parents? It's the kids who do crazy things.

I'm particularly concerned about idealistic and perfectionistic moms and dads who are determined to make their adolescent perform and achieve and measure up to the highest standard. In so doing, they rock a boat that is already threatened by the rapids. Perhaps another child could handle the additional turbulence, but the unsteady kid—the one who lacks common sense for a while and may even lean toward irrational behavior—could capsize if you're not careful. Don't unsettle his boat any more than you must!

I'm reminded of a waitress who recognized me when I came into the restaurant where she worked. She was not busy that day and wanted to talk about her twelve-year-old daughter. As a single mother, she had gone through severe struggles with the girl, whom she identified as being very strong willed.

"We have fought tooth and nail for this entire year," she said. "It has been awful! We argue nearly every night, and most of our fights are over the same issue."

I asked her what had caused the conflict, and she replied, "My daughter is still a little girl, but she wants to shave her legs. I feel she's too young to be doing that, and she becomes so angry that she won't even talk to me. This has been the worst year of our lives together."

I looked at the waitress and said, "Lady, buy your daughter a razor!"

That twelve-year-old girl was paddling into a time of life that would rock her canoe good and hard. As a single parent, Mom would soon be trying to keep this rebellious kid from getting into drugs, alcohol, sex and pregnancy, early marriage, school failure, and the possibility of running away. Truly, there would be many ravenous alligators in her river within a year or two. In that setting, it seemed unwise to make a big deal over what was essentially a nonissue. While I agreed with the mother that adolescence should not be ushered in prematurely, there were higher goals than maintaining a proper developmental timetable.

I have seen other parents fight similar battles over nonessentials such as the purchase of a first bra for a flat-chested preadolescent girl. For goodness' sake! If she wants it that badly, she probably needs it for social reasons. Run, don't walk, to the nearest department store, and buy her a bra. The objective, as Charles and Andy Stanley wrote, is to keep your kids on your team.[109] Don't throw away your friendship over behavior that has no great moral significance. There will be plenty of real issues that require you to stand like a rock. Save your big guns for those crucial confrontations.

Let me make it very clear, again, that this advice is not relevant to every teenager. The compliant kid who is doing wonderfully in school, has great friends, is disciplined in his conduct, and loves his parents is not nearly so delicate. Perhaps his parents can urge him to reach even higher standards in his achievements and lifestyle. My concern, however, is for that youngster who could go over the falls. He is intensely angry at home and is being influenced by a carload of crummy friends. Be very careful with him. Pick and choose what is worth fighting for, and settle for something less than perfection on issues that don't really matter. Just get him through it!

QUESTION 287

What does this mean in practical terms? Give me some examples of demands that would rock my daughter's boat unnecessarily.

Well, you will have to decide what the nonnegotiables are to you and your husband. Defend those demands, but lighten up on lesser matters. That may indicate a willingness to let her room look like a junkyard for a while. Close the door and pretend not to notice. Does that surprise you? I don't like lazy, sloppy, undisciplined kids any more than you do, but given the possibilities for chaos that this girl might precipitate, spit-shined rooms may not be all that important.

You have to ask yourself this question: "Is the behavior to which I object bad enough to risk turning the canoe upside down?" If the issue is that important, then brace yourself and make your stand. But think through those intractable matters in advance, and plan your defense of them thoroughly.

Someday, when the river has smoothed out again, you may look back with satisfaction that you didn't add to the turbulence when your daughter was bobbing like a cork on a stormy sea.

QUESTION 288

I think I understand what you're recommending. You're not suggesting that my husband and I let this kid run wild. Instead, we should choose our battles very carefully and not push her into further rebellion by trying to make her something she can't be right now.

That's it. The philosophy we applied with our teenagers (and you might try with yours) can be called "loosen and tighten." By this I mean we tried to loosen our grip on everything that had no lasting significance and tighten down on everything that did. We said yes whenever we possibly could, to give support to the occasional no. And most important, we tried never to get too far away from our kids emotionally.

It is simply not prudent to write off a son or daughter, no matter how foolish, irritating, selfish, or insane a child may seem to be. You need to be there, not only while their canoe is bouncing precariously, but after the river runs smooth again. You have the remainder of your life to reconstruct the relationship that is now in jeopardy. Don't let anger fester for too long. Make the first move toward reconciliation. And try hard not to hassle your kids. They hate to be nagged. If you follow them around with one complaint after another, they are almost forced to protect themselves by appearing deaf. And finally, continue to treat them with respect, even when punishment or restrictions are necessary.

Then wait for the placid water in the early twenties.

QUESTION 289

Give me your shortest answer to the question: How can I best survive the tumultuous years of my three teenagers?

This is my best shot:

1. Keep the family schedule simple.
2. Get plenty of rest.
3. Eat nutritious meals.
4. Keep your teenager involved in nonstop, wholesome activities.
5. Stay on your knees.

When fatigue and ill health lead adults to act like hot-tempered teenagers, anything can happen at home.

QUESTION 290

Would you speak about the impact of what has been called "the absentee father"—especially during the tougher years of adolescence?

It is stating the obvious, I suppose, to say that fathers are desperately needed at home during the teen years. In their absence, mothers are left to handle disciplinary problems alone. This is occurring in millions of families headed by single mothers today, and heaven only knows how difficult their task has become. Not only are they doing a job that should have been shouldered by two, they must also deal with behavioral problems that fathers are more ideally suited to handle. It is generally understood that a man's larger size, deeper voice, and masculine demeanor make it easier for him to deal with defiance in the younger generation. Many mothers raise their teenagers alone and do the job with excellence, but it is a challenging assignment.

Q UESTION 291

As a father, what should I be trying to accomplish with my son in these teen years?

Someone has said, "Link a boy to the right man and he seldom goes wrong." I believe that is true. If a dad and his son can develop hobbies together or other common interests, the rebellious years can pass in relative tranquillity. What they experience may be remembered for a lifetime.

I recall a song, written by Dan Fogelberg, that told about a man who shared his love of music with his elderly father. It is called "Leader of the Band," and its message touches something deep within me. The son talks of a father who "earned his love through discipline, a thundering, velvet hand." The father's "song is in my soul." The son himself has become a "living legacy to the leader of the band."[110]

Can't you see this man going to visit his aged father today, with a lifetime of love passing between them? That must have been what God had in mind when he gave dads to boys.

Let me address your question directly: What common ground are you cultivating with your impressionable son? Some fathers build or repair cars with them; some construct small models or make things in a woodshop. My dad and I hunted and fished together. There is no way to describe what those days meant to me as we entered the woods in the early hours of the morning. How could I get angry at this man who took time to be with me? We had wonderful talks while coming home from a day of laughter and fun in the country. I tried to maintain that kind of contact with my son.

Opportunities to communicate openly and build the father-son relationship have to be created. It's a goal that's worth whatever it takes to achieve.

QUESTION 292

My wife works hard to teach my sons to respect me as their father, and that makes my job with them easier. Even when she is upset with me, she never lets the kids know about it. Don't you think that is generous of her?

She's not only generous—she's a wise woman, too. Mothers can help bond the generations together, or they can drive a wedge between them. This concept was expressed beautifully in a book entitled *Fathers and Sons* by Lewis Yablonsky. The author observed that mothers are the primary interpreters of fathers' personality, character, and integrity to their sons. In other words, the way boys see their fathers is largely a product of the things their mothers have said and the way they feel about their husbands. In Yablonsky's case, his mother destroyed the respect he might have had for his father. This is what he wrote:

> I vividly recall sitting at the dinner table with my two brothers and father and mother and cringing at my mother's attacks on my father. "Look at him," she would say in Yiddish, "his head and shoulders are bent down. He's a failure. He doesn't have the courage to get a better job or make more money. He's a beaten man." He would keep his eyes pointed toward his plate and never answer her. She never extolled his virtues or persistence or the fact that he worked so hard; instead she constantly focused on the negative and created an image to his three sons of a man without fight, crushed by a world over which he had no control.
>
> His not fighting back against her constant criticism had the effect of confirming its validity to her sons. I have to add that my mother's treatment and depiction of my father did not convey to me

that marriage was a happy state of being, or that women were very supportive people. I was not especially motivated to assume the role of husband and father myself from my observations of my whipped father.

My overall research clearly supports the fact that the mother is a basic filter and has enormous significance in the father-son relationship.[111]

Though Yablonsky did not say so, it is also true that a father can do great damage to his wife's relationship with their children. Very early on I found that when I was irritated with Shirley for some reason, my attitude was instantly picked up by our son and daughter. They seemed to feel, *If Dad can argue with Mom, then we can, too.* It became clear to me just how important it was for me to express my love and admiration for Shirley. However, I could never do that job of building respect for my wife as well as she did for me! She made me a king in my own home. If our son and daughter had believed half of what she told them about me, I would have been a fortunate man. The close relationship I enjoy with Danae and Ryan today is largely a product of Shirley's great love for me and the way she "interpreted" me to our kids. I will always be grateful to her for doing that!

*Q*UESTION **293**

How about a little equal time? Talk about a father's impact on his daughter and what he should hope to accomplish through that relationship.

Fathers have an incalculable impact on their daughters. Most psychologists believe, and I am one of them, that all future romantic relationships to occur in a girl's life will be influenced positively or negatively by the way she perceives and interacts with her dad. If he rejects and ignores her, she will spend her life trying to replace him in her heart. If he is warm and nurturing, she will look for a lover to equal him. If he thinks she is beautiful, worthy, and feminine, she will be inclined to see herself that way. But if he thinks she is unattractive

305

and uninteresting, she is likely to carry self-esteem problems into her adult years.

I have also observed that a woman's respect for her husband is significantly influenced by the way she perceived her father. If he was overbearing, uncaring, or capricious during her developmental years, she may disrespect her husband and question his judgment. But if Dad blended love and leadership in a way that conveyed strength, she will be more likely to live harmoniously with him.

None of these tendencies or trends are absolute, of course. Individual differences can always produce exceptions and contradictions. But this statement will be hard to refute: A good father will leave his imprint on his daughter for the rest of her life.

QUESTION 294

My teen daughter, Cynthia, and I have incredible fights sometimes. No one has ever gotten to me in quite the way she can. We actually yell at each other when these battles are going on. How unusual is that kind of conflict between mothers and daughters? And is there hope for us?

Unfortunately, it is very common. Many psychologists have described a "thing" that occurs between some mothers and teenage daughters. Even though they love each other, the friction between them can generate a lot of heat. It probably results from a phenomenon that has been called "two women in the kitchen"—a kind of natural competitiveness that occurs between females in the family. It can also be caused by a mother's inability to cope with an extremely difficult and antagonistic kid. Whatever the source, it can make life unpleasant for several years. I know women who would give their lives for their daughters, yet they say, with fire in their eyes, "I don't even *like* her very much right now." That appears to be what you and your teenager are experiencing at this time.

Is there hope for a better relationship in years to come? Yes, I believe you will overcome it. Getting Cynthia through adolescence and into adulthood will change everything. I wouldn't be surprised if she became one of your best friends down the road. So take heart. A better day is coming.

QUESTION 295

What can we do in the meantime? How can I deal with this wildcat who lives under my roof?

Before I answer, tell me what your husband's relationship with Cynthia is.

QUESTION 296

It's very good. She doesn't pull the same stuff on him that she does with me. What are you getting at?

He may hold the key to the tension in your home. Fathers can play a valuable role as peacemakers and mediators at a time like this. They can help you ventilate anger and find acceptable compromises where they are appropriate. Cynthia may listen to her dad. When teenagers are greatly irritated with one parent, they will sometimes seek to draw closer to the other. It's like a nation at war that seeks supportive allies. If fathers are favored in that way, they can calm the troubled waters and keep two women from killing each other. Without this masculine influence, routine skirmishes can turn into World War III.

QUESTION 297

You have recommended that parents be willing to apologize to their kids when they are wrong and to "stay on your child's team" even when it's a losing team. This is difficult for me because my son is in full-blown rebellion at this time. He's using drugs, flunking his classes, and giving us fits at home. Is there a time to forget the nicey-nice stuff and get tough with a teenager?

No doubt about it. There are moments when it is appropriate to apologize, to accommodate, to compromise, and to negotiate. But there comes a time to draw a line in the dirt and say, "Enough is enough!" For youngsters who have tyrannized their families, their parents' willingness to "forgive and forget" repeatedly is interpreted as weakness. Appeasement, as we know, is never successful in pacifying a bully. It only makes him or her more angry and disrespectful.

Behavioral research has now validated that statement. Dr. Henry Harbin and Dr. Denis Madden, working at the University of Maryland's medical school, studied the circumstances that surround violent attacks on parents by teenagers.[112] They found that "parent battering" usually occurs when "one or both parents have abdicated the executive position" and left no one in charge. No one, that is, except the violent child. Rebellious, mean-spirited teenagers respect strength and disdain weakness—especially that borne of love.

Harbin and Madden also observed that "an almost universal element" in the parent-battering cases was the parents' unwillingness to admit the seriousness of the situation. They did not call the police, even when their lives were in danger; they lied to protect the children, and they continued to give in to their demands. Parental authority had collapsed.

One father was almost killed when his angry son pushed him down a flight of stairs. He insisted that the boy did not have a bad temper. Another woman was stabbed by her son, missing her heart by an inch. Nevertheless, she continued letting him live at home.

Drs. Harbin and Madden concluded that appeasement and permissiveness are related to youthful violence and that both parents should lead with firmness. "Someone needs to be in charge," they said.[113]

I agree wholeheartedly with these psychiatrists. Having been appointed by President Ronald Reagan to serve on the National Advisory Commission to the Office of Juvenile Justice and Delinquency Prevention, I am very familiar with the pattern of youthful violence. I've seen cold-blooded killers who were no more than thirteen years of age. Many of them came from homes where authority was weak or nonexistent. It is a formula for cranking out very tough criminals at an early age.

When you are faced with a potentially violent situation at home, you must weigh your options and take decisive action. The organization

Tough Love, founded by Phyllis and David York, has been helpful to parents whose backs are to the wall. Tough Love is dedicated to helping out-of-control parents regain the upper hand in their own homes. Their basic philosophy is one of confrontation that is designed to bring a belligerent teenager to his or her senses. You might give them a call. To do nothing is to risk the unthinkable.

QUESTION 298

I read in the paper the other day that a fourteen-year-old boy shot a woman in the face for no reason at all. Things like that are happening all around us. When I was a kid I wouldn't even have sassed a teacher, much less assaulted one. Today the level of violence among the young is like nothing I've ever seen! What is going on?

You are right; an epidemic of violence is occurring among the young that is expected to actually worsen in the next few years. During a recent meeting of Prison Fellowship workers in our city, a group of hardened former criminals said the kids growing up today scare them because they have no consciences. They can kill without a hint of remorse. It is true.

In Seattle a few years ago, two boys, twelve and thirteen, beat to death a person coming out of a convenience store. There was no motive except a desire to brutalize someone—anyone—with a baseball bat.[114]

In Virginia, a fourteen-year-old shot the driver of a nearby car six times in the face. Why? "Because he looked at me," the boy said.[115]

In 1995 a family made a wrong turn down a street in Los Angeles and was subjected to a hail of gunfire that killed their little girl. Gang members poured bullets into the car for the sheer fun of it.[116]

And finally, who can forget the five-year-old Chicago boy who was pushed from an upper-story window and fell to his death? His killers were ten and eleven years old.[117]

This kind of random violence is more common among children and adolescents today than ever before in our history.

QUESTION 299

But why? What has caused many members of the younger generation to be so violent?

Hundreds of millions of dollars have been invested in research to answer that question. The findings are startling. In addition to the violence children have seen on television and in the movies, and apart from the drug wars they have witnessed, the tendency toward violence is a function of the neglect and abuse so many have experienced. That is especially true of those raised in the inner city. What has been learned is that millions of children, many of them born to drug- and alcohol-dependent parents, have been subjected to unimaginable deprivation. They were left in cribs for days with dirty diapers burning their buttocks and legs. Some were hit repeatedly, or they were scalded or starved. Others simply had no one to love and hold them when they were frightened. Many were sexually exploited from their earliest days—some even in infancy. If they survived, they grew up on the streets with no adult guidance and care. At night, they slept in bathtubs to avoid bullets sprayed by drive-by shootings.[118] If this description sounds exaggerated, talk to social workers or police officers who work every day in the slums of large cities.

What does it do to a child to experience intense pain, fear, and deprivation at a very early age? The answers are beginning to come in. What has been learned is that kids who go through these traumas in the first year or two of life produce high levels of stress hormones—notably cortisol and adrenaline. Those substances put the body in an "alarm reaction state" in order to cope with the crisis at hand. But in a small child, the brain is a vacuum cleaner for stress-related hormones. Human neurological apparatus is bombarded with chemicals that shouldn't be there in a child that age. The result is impairment of the boy or girl's thinking apparatus and emotional development. Specifically, the "firing mechanism" of certain portions of the brain is rendered inoperable.

What I'm saying is that many of today's abused kids can kill and destroy without pangs of conscience because they are literally brain damaged. They don't feel what you and I feel. They can't empathize with helpless victims the way they should, because the emotion of compassion flows from cognitive functions that no longer operate. Some of them are, at that point, potential killers waiting for the time and place to shoot or stab or bludgeon.

I am not excusing their violent behavior, of course, and society can't afford to tolerate it. But this explains some of the mayhem occurring day after day in inner cities.

The bottom line is this: We are paying a terrible price for the disintegration of the family and for the victimization of children. Any society that doesn't protect the most vulnerable in their midst can expect to suffer at the hands of those abused individuals when they get old enough to strike back.

So lock your doors and avoid eye contact when you drive through certain sections of your city. There are kids there who would just as soon kill you as look at you.

*Q*UESTION 300

You stated earlier that you do not favor spanking a teenager. What would you do to encourage the cooperation of my thirteen-year-old, who deliberately makes a nuisance of himself? He throws his clothes around, refuses to help out with any routine tasks in the house, and pesters his little brother incessantly. If I can't spank him, how can I get his attention?

If any approach will succeed in charging his sluggish batteries or motivating him to live within the rules, it will probably involve an incentive-and-disincentive program of some variety. The following three steps might be helpful in initiating such a system:

1. Decide what is important to the youngster for use as a motivator. Two hours with the family car on date night is worth the world to a sixteen-year-old who has just gotten his or her license. (This could be the most expensive incentive in history if the young driver is a bit shaky behind the wheel.) An allowance is another easily available source of inspiration. Teenagers have a great need for cold

cash today. A routine date with Helen Highschool might cost twenty dollars or more—in some cases far more. Yet another incentive may involve a fashionable article of clothing that would not ordinarily be within your teen's budget. Offering him or her a means of obtaining such luxuries is a happy alternative to the whining, crying, begging, complaining, and pestering that might occur otherwise. Mom says, "Sure you can have the ski sweater, but you'll have to earn it." Once an acceptable motivator is agreed upon, the second step can be implemented.

2. Formalize the agreement. A contract is an excellent means of settling on a common goal. Once an agreement has been written, it is signed by the parent and teen. The contract may include a point system that enables your teenager to meet the goal in a reasonable time period. If you can't agree on the point values, you could allow for binding arbitration from an outside party. Let's examine a sample agreement in which Marshall wants a compact-disc player, but his birthday is ten months away, and he's flat broke. The cost of the player is approximately $150. His father agrees to buy the device if Marshall earns ten thousand points over the next six to ten weeks doing various tasks. Many of these opportunities are outlined in advance, but the list can be lengthened as other possibilities become apparent:

a. For making bed and straightening room each
   morning . . . . 50 points
b. For each hour of studying . . . . 150 points
c. For each hour of housecleaning or yard work
   done . . . . 300 points
d. For being on time to breakfast and dinner . . . . . 40 points
e. For baby-sitting siblings (without conflict) per
   hour . . . . 150 points
f. For washing the car each week . . . . 250 points
g. For arising by 8:00 A.M. Saturday morning . . . . . 100 points

While the principles are almost universally effective, the method of application must be varied. With a little imagination, you can create a list of chores and point values that work in your family. It's important to note that points can be gained for cooperation and lost for resistance. Disagreeable and unreasonable behavior can be penalized fifty points or more. (However, penalties must be imposed fairly and rarely or the entire system will crumble.) Also, bonus points can be awarded for behavior that is particularly commendable.

3. Finally, establish a method to provide immediate rewards. Remember that prompt reinforcement achieves the best results. This is necessary to sustain teens' interest as they move toward the ultimate goal. A thermometer-type chart can be constructed, with the point scale listed down the side. At the top is the ten-thousand-points mark, beside a picture of a compact-disc player or other prize. Each evening, the daily points are totaled and the red portion of the thermometer is extended upward. Steady, short-term progress might earn Marshall a bonus of some sort—perhaps a CD of his favorite musician or a special privilege. If he changes his mind about what he wishes to buy, the points can be diverted to another purchase. For example, five thousand points is 50 percent of ten thousand and would be worth $75 toward another purchase. However, do not give your child the reward if he does not earn it. That would eliminate future uses of reinforcement. Likewise, do not deny or postpone the goal once it is earned.

This system described above is not set in concrete. It should be adapted to the age and maturity of the adolescent. One youngster would be insulted by an approach that would thrill another. Use your imagination and work out the details with your youngster. This suggestion won't work with every teenager, but some will find it exciting. Lots of luck to you.

*Q*UESTION 301

Generally speaking, what kind of discipline do you use with a teenager who is habitually miserable to live with?

The general rule is to use action—not anger—to reach an understanding. Anytime you can get teenagers to do what is necessary without becoming furious at them, you are ahead of the game. Let me provide a few examples of how this might be accomplished.

1. In Russia, I'm told that teenagers who are convicted of using drugs are denied driver's licenses for years. It is a very effective approach.

2. When my daughter was a teenager, she used to slip into my bathroom and steal my razor, my shaving cream, my toothpaste, or my comb. Of course, she never brought them back. Then after she had gone to school, I would discover the utensils missing. There I was with wet hair or "fuzzy" teeth, trying to locate the confiscated items in her bathroom. It was no big deal, but it was irritating at the time. Can you identify?

   I asked Danae a dozen times not to do this but to no avail. Thus, the phantom struck without warning one cold morning. I hid everything she needed to "put on her face" and then left for the office. My wife told me she had never heard such wails and moans as were uttered that day. Our daughter plunged desperately through bathroom drawers looking for her toothbrush, comb, and hair dryer. The problem never resurfaced.

3. A family living in a house with a small hot-water tank was continually frustrated by their teenager's endless showers. Screaming at him did no good. Once he was locked behind the bathroom door, he stayed in the steamy stall until the last drop of warm water had been drained. Solution? In midstream, Dad stopped the flow of hot water by turning a valve at the tank. Cold water suddenly poured from the nozzle. Junior popped out of the shower in seconds. Henceforth, he tried to finish bathing before the faucet turned frigid.

4. A single mother couldn't get her daughter out of bed in the morning until she announced a new policy: The hot water would be shut off promptly at 6:30 A.M. The girl could either get up on time or bathe in ice water. Another mother had trouble getting her eight-year-old out of bed each morning. She then began pouring bowls of frozen marbles under the covers with him each morning. They gravitated to wherever his body lay. The boy arose quite quickly.

5. Instead of standing in the parking lot and screaming at students who drive too fast, school officials now put huge bumps in the road that jar the teeth of those who ignore them. It does the job quite nicely.

6. You as the parent have the car that a teenager needs, the money that he covets, and the authority to grant or withhold privileges. If push comes to shove, these chips can be exchanged for commitments to live responsibly, share the workload at home, and stay off little brother's back. This bargaining process works for younger kids, too. I like the "one-to-one" trade-off for television-viewing time. It permits a child to watch one minute of television for every minute spent reading.

The possibilities are endless, and they depend not at all on anger, threats, and unpleasantries.

*Q*UESTION **302**

Our fourteen-year-old recently came to my husband and me to say, "I'm pregnant." Nothing has ever upset us more than hearing those words. What should our attitude toward her be now?

Responding to a teenage pregnancy is one of the most difficult trials parents are ever asked to face. When the news breaks, it's reasonable to feel anger at the girl who has brought this humiliation and pain into her life. How dare this kid do something so stupid and hurtful to herself and the entire family!

Once you have caught your breath, however, a more rational and loving response is appropriate. This is no time for recrimination. Your daughter needs your understanding and wisdom now more than ever. She'll face many important decisions in the next few months, and you can't afford to alienate yourselves from her. She will also need your spiritual guidance as you point her to the Lord for forgiveness and direction.

If you can summon a measure of strength and love at this stressful time, you should be able to create the bond that often develops between those who have survived a crisis together.

QUESTION 303

I am suspicious that my sixteen-year-old son may be using some kind of illegal drugs. He's just not himself lately, and his friends are some of the weirdest guys you ever saw. Can you summarize the most common symptoms of drug abuse for me? What should I look for?

A complete answer to that question would fill a book, because there are so many illegal substances on the market today and each has its own characteristic "fingerprint." But there are eight common physical and emotional symptoms you might look for in your son:

1. Inflammation of the eyelids and nose is common. The pupils of the eyes are either very wide or very small, depending on the kind of drugs internalized.
2. Extremes of energy may be evident. Either the individual is sluggish, gloomy, and withdrawn or he may be loud, hysterical, and jumpy.
3. The appetite is extreme—either very great or very poor. Weight loss may occur.
4. The personality suddenly changes; the individual may become irritable, inattentive, and confused, or aggressive, suspicious, and explosive.
5. Body and breath odor is often bad. Cleanliness is generally ignored.
6. The digestive system may be upset—diarrhea, nausea, and vomiting may occur. Headaches and double vision are also common. Other signs of physical deterioration may include change in skin tone and body stance.
7. Needle marks on the body, usually appearing on the arms, are an important symptom. These punctures sometimes get infected and appear as sores and boils.
8. Moral values often crumble and are replaced by new, avant-garde ideas and values.

Let me caution you that some kids are able to hide their drug use better than others. You might stop by to see the officer in charge of narcotics enforcement for your local police department. He or she may be able to give you more specific information applicable to your son.

QUESTION 304

What about snooping through my son's room to see what he might be doing? Do you think parents should do that?

There are definitely times when mothers and fathers need to conduct their own quiet investigation, even though it might invade the privacy of the teenager. This issue was discussed widely in the media some years ago when comedienne Carol Burnett discovered that her teenage daughter was a drug user. When the problem finally came to light, Carol was regretful that she hadn't taken steps to inform herself of what was going on. She appeared on many talk shows to say, in effect, that kids desperately need their parents to "catch them" in a moment like that. Don't let your respect for their privacy cause you to stick your head in the sand and fail to notice what is going on right in front of you.[119] I strongly agree.

Of course, parents have to know their children, too. There are some who would never do anything illegal or harmful. It's just not in them. In those cases, I would not recommend snooping through their room and private stuff. But in situations where a secretive boy or girl is doing suspicious things, running with the wrong crowd, and then demanding utter privacy at home, I would gather whatever information I needed in order to know how to respond.

317

QUESTION 305

I heard you say that we have shamefully mismanaged the present generation of children. Explain what you meant by that.

I was referring to the many harmful influences that previous generations didn't have to confront—at least not to the degree that we see
today. That includes safe-sex ideology and violence and sexual imagery in movies, rock music, and television; it refers to gang activity and
drug abuse, and many other dangerous aspects of the culture. I was
speaking also about the extreme emphasis on physical attractiveness
and body consciousness in Western nations that is having a terrible
impact on children. It can even be life-threatening to them.

A study done at the University of California showed that 80 percent
of girls in the fourth grade have attempted to diet because they see
themselves as fat. One elementary school girl justified her dieting by
saying she just wanted to be skinny so that no one would tease her.[120]
How sad it is that children in this culture have been taught to hate
their bodies—to measure their worth by comparison to a standard that
they can never achieve. At a time when they should be busy being
kids, they're worried about how much they weigh, how they look, and
how they're seen by others.

For young girls this insistence on being thin is magnified by the
cruelties of childhood. Dozens of studies now show that overweight
children are held in low regard by their peers, even at an early age.
According to one investigation, silhouettes of obese children were
described by six-year-olds as "lazy," "stupid," and "ugly."[121]

This overemphasis on beauty does not occur in a vacuum, of course.
Our children have caught our prejudices and our system of values. We,
too, measure human worth largely on a scale of physical attractiveness. It's bad enough when adults evaluate each other that way. It's
tragic when millions of children have already concluded that they're
hopelessly flawed, even before life has gotten started.

We must take the blame for the many pressures on today's kids.
Fifty years ago, parents and other adults acted in concert to protect
kids—from pornography, from sexual abuse, from harmful ideas, and
from dangerous substances. Millions of husbands and wives stayed
together "for the benefit of the children." It was understood that tender
minds and bodies needed to be shielded from that which could hurt
them. But now, child abuse, date rape, and sexually transmitted
disease are rampant. As the family unravels and as adults become
more self-centered and preoccupied, children are often left to fend for

themselves in a very dangerous world. It may be our greatest failing as a people.

Q UESTION 306

I'm convinced that mothers of preschoolers should stay home with them if finances and temperaments permit. But what about after they are off to school? Do you feel it is still important to have Mom at home, we'll say, in the teen years?

Many will not agree with my opinion on that subject, but it is borne of experience with thousands of families. All things being equal, I believe Mom is still needed at home as the kids grow. Why? Because the heavy demands of child rearing do not slacken with the passage of time. In reality, the teen years generate as much pressure on the parents as any other era. An adolescent turns a house upside down—literally and figuratively. Not only is the typical rebellion of those years a stressful experience, but the chauffeuring, supervising, cooking, and cleaning required to support a teenager can be exhausting. Someone within the family must reserve the time and energy to cope with those new challenges. Mom is the candidate of choice. Remember, too, that menopause and a man's midlife crisis are scheduled to coincide with adolescence, which can make a wicked soup! It is a wise mother who doesn't exhaust herself at a time when so much is going on at home.

Let me illustrate why moms are needed at home during the teen years. A good military general will never commit all his troops to combat at the same time. He maintains a reserve army that can relieve the exhausted soldiers when they falter on the front lines. I wish parents of adolescents would implement the same strategy. Instead, they commit every moment of their time to the business of living, holding nothing back for the challenge of the century. It is a classic mistake that can be even more difficult for parents of strong-willed adolescents.

This is my point: A woman in this situation has thrown all her troops into frontline combat. There is no reserve on which to call. In that fatigued condition, the routine stresses of raising an adolescent can be overwhelming. Let me say it again. Raising boisterous teenagers is an exciting and rewarding experience but also a frustrating one at times. Their radical highs and lows affect our moods. The noise, the messes, the complaints, the arguments, the sibling rivalry, the missed curfews, the paced floors, the wrecked car, the failed test, the jilted lover, the wrong friends, the busy telephone, the pizza on the carpet, the ripped new blouse, the rebellion, the slammed doors, the mean words, the tears—it's enough to drive a rested mother crazy. But what about our career woman who already "gave at the office," then came home to this chaos? Any unexpected crisis or even a minor irritant can set off a torrent of emotion. There is no reserve on which to draw. In short, the parents of adolescents should save some energy with which to cope with aggravation!

Whether or not you agree with my advice at this point is your business. It is my responsibility simply to offer it. Generally speaking, the working mother has a challenging task before her. Admittedly, many women are able to maintain a busy career and keep the home fires burning, some with the assistance of involved husbands or domestic help. Other low-energy mothers with unhelpful husbands don't cope so well. Each family must decide for itself how best to deal with life's pressure points and opportunities.

17

The Delicate Art of Letting Go

QUESTION 307

We hear so much about mothers being depressed and unable to accept the empty nest when the kids leave home. In our family, however, it was Dad who took it hard. He went into a tailspin for more than a month. Is this unusual?

No, it happens very commonly. In a recent study, 189 parents of college freshmen were asked to report their feelings when their son or daughter left home. Surprisingly, the fathers took it harder than the mothers.[122]

That resistance to the empty nest was the theme of the movie *Father of the Bride,* which was a hilarious and touching tribute to the love of a father for his daughter. When George, the dad, sat across from his daughter at the dinner table and learned that she was engaged, he took the news hard. He couldn't believe what he was hearing. He had to clear his vision when he saw his daughter as a baby girl, and then as a ten-year-old tomboy, and finally as a beautiful young woman of eighteen. His little girl had grown up so quickly, and now she was leaving home. He would never again be the main man in the life of his precious daughter, and there was grieving to be done.

Why do men sometimes take the empty nest so hard? One of the chief explanations is regret. They have been so busy—working so hard—that they let the years slip by almost unnoticed. Then suddenly they realize it is too late to build a relationship with the child who is leaving home forever.

For those of you who still have children or teenagers at home, take a moment regularly to enjoy your remaining time together. Those days will be gone in the blink of an eye.

Q UESTION 308

Why do you think so many parents are reluctant to let their kids go after they are grown?

One reason is that parents fear their children aren't ready to stand on their own, and they worry about what will happen to them. They want to protect them as long as they can. But more important, they hate to see childhood come to an end. I'm convinced that mothers and fathers in North America are among the very best in the world. We care passionately about our kids and would do anything to meet their needs. But we are among the worst when it comes to letting go of our grown sons and daughters. In fact, those two characteristics are linked.

The same commitment that leads us to do so well when the children are small (dedication, love, concern, involvement) also causes us to hold too tightly when they are growing up. I will admit my own difficulties in this area. I understood the importance of turning loose before our kids were born. I wrote extensively on the subject when they were still young. I prepared a film series in which all the right principles were expressed. But when it came time to open my hand and let the birds fly, I struggled mightily! I had loved the experience of fatherhood, and I was not ready to give it up. Now, however, I relate to my grown children as adults and find this an exciting and rewarding era too. "There is a time for everything," Solomon wrote. There is also a time for everything to end.

Q UESTION 309

I have found it very hard to turn my kids loose and face the empty nest. I know I need to release them, but it is so difficult. Can you help me?

Humorist Erma Bombeck described this difficult process in terms that were helpful to me.[123] She said that the task of raising kids is rather like trying to fly a kite on a day when the wind doesn't blow. Mom and Dad run down the road pulling the cute little device at the end of a string. It bounces along the ground and shows no inclination of getting off the ground.

Eventually, and with much effort, they manage to lift it fifteen feet in the air, but great danger suddenly looms. The kite dives toward electrical lines and twirls near trees. It is a scary moment. Will they ever get it safely on its way? Then, unexpectedly, a gust of wind catches the kite, and it sails upward. Mom and Dad feed out line as rapidly as they can.

The kite begins pulling the string, making it difficult to hold on. Inevitably, they reach the end of their line. What should they do now? The kite is demanding more freedom. It wants to go higher. Dad stands on his tiptoes and raises his hand to accommodate the tug. It is now grasped tenuously between his index finger and thumb, held upward toward the sky. Then the moment of release comes. The string slips through his fingers, and the kite soars majestically into God's beautiful sky.

Mom and Dad stand gazing at their precious "baby," who is now gleaming in the sun, a mere pinpoint of color on the horizon. They are proud of what they've done—but sad to realize that their job is finished. It was a labor of love. But where did the years go?

That is where you are today—standing on tiptoes and stretching toward the sky with the end of the string clutched between your fingers. It's time to let go. And when you do, you'll find that a new relationship will be born. Your parenting job is almost over. In its place will come a friendship that will have its own rewards.

Remember: The kite is going to break free one way or the other. It's best that you release it when the time is right!

QUESTION 310

Our twenty-one-year-old daughter came home from college and moved back into her old bedroom. Now, three years later, she's still there. She doesn't work, she has no ambition

or direction, and she seems perfectly content to freeload on her dad and me. I know she ought to get on with her life, but what can I do? I can't just force her out, can I?

Your daughter is not alone. Millions of young adults are living at home and loving it. They have no intention of growing up—and why should they? The nest is just too comfortable there. Food is prepared. Clothes are laundered, and the bills are paid. There's no incentive to face the cold world of reality, and they are determined not to budge. Some, like your daughter, even refuse to work. I know it's difficult to dislodge a homebound son or daughter. They're like furry little puppies who hang around the back door waiting for a saucer of warm milk. But to let them stay year after year, especially if they're not pursuing career goals, is to cultivate irresponsibility and dependency. That's not love, even though it may feel like it. There comes the time when you must gently but forthrightly hand the reins over to your adult daughter and force her to stand on her own. I think it's time to help her pack.

Giving a shove to a twenty-four-year-old woman may seem cruel at the time, but I encourage you to consider emancipating her. The parental gravy train probably should go around the bend. If that never happens, lasting characteristics of dependency and immaturity may ensue.

I suggest you sit down and talk to your daughter, explaining why the time has come for her to make a life of her own. Set a deadline, perhaps two or three weeks ahead, and begin preparing for it. Then give her a big hug, a promise of prayers, and send her on her way.

Q UESTION 311

Our son will be leaving for college next fall. Is there anything we can do to help ease the transition from home to dorm life?

For starters, author Joan Wester Anderson suggests that you make sure that your teen has the basic skills necessary to survive dorm life. Can he operate a washer and dryer, stick to a budget, handle a checkbook, get along with roommates, and manage his time wisely?

It's important as well to prepare your son for the negative aspects of campus life. Too often, adults present a rosy portrait of college as "the best years of life," which creates unrealistic expectations that lead to disappointment. Remind your son that homesickness is to be expected and that he can call home collect anytime, just to chat. At a dime a minute after working hours, the costs of telephone usage should be within everyone's reach financially.

During the first semester away, letters and treats from home can ease the pain of separation anxiety. And be pleasant when that young man returns for visits. If he feels like an intruder, he just might decide to visit someone else's home for future vacations.[124]

Going away to college is a milestone for those who embark on that journey. With proper planning, it can be a positive time of growth for the whole family.

18

Advice to Young Adults

QUESTION 312

I'm twenty-two years old and am still living at home. It's driving me nuts. My folks are in my face every day. They want me to get a full-time job 'cause I only work part-time at a gas station. Why can't they get off my case and leave me alone?

With all respect, I think it's time for you to pack. Many young adults like you continue to hang around the house because they don't know what to do next. That is a recipe for trouble. Your mother and father can't help "parenting" you if you remain under their noses. To them, it seems like only yesterday since you were born. They find it difficult to think of you as an adult.

The way you live probably irritates them, too. They hate your messy room, which would require a tetanus shot just to walk through. They don't like your music. They go to bed early and arise with the sun; you keep the same hours as hamsters. You drive the family car like you've been to Kamikaze Driving School. They want you to get a job—go to school—do something. Every day brings a new argument—a new battle. When things deteriorate to that point, it's time to get out.

QUESTION 313

I am twenty-one and also still at home. I am very comfortable there, and since I'm not going with anyone, I plan to stay with my parents for a long time. Why not? Tell me why you think it is unwise to go on living where it is cheaper and easier than getting out on your own.

There are individual situations when it makes sense to live with your parents for a longer time, and maybe yours is one of them. I would caution you, however, not to overstay your welcome. That would not be in your best interests or those of your folks. Remaining too long under the "parentos" roof is not unlike an unborn baby who refuses to leave the womb. He has every reason to stay a while. It is warm and cozy there. All his needs are met in that stress-free environment. He doesn't have to work or study or discipline himself.

But it would be crazy to stay beyond the nine months God intended. He can't grow and learn without leaving the security of that place. His development will be arrested until he enters the cold world and takes a few whacks on his behind. It is to everyone's advantage, and especially to the welfare of his mother, that he slide on down the birth canal and get on with life.

So it is in young adulthood. Until you cut the umbilical cord and begin providing for yourself, you will remain in a state of arrested development. It is a trap that can hold a person in an immature state for a decade or more. The Scriptures hint at this need to press on. The apostle Paul wrote, "When I was a child, I talked like a child, I thought like a child, I reasoned like a child. When I became a man, I put childish ways behind me" (1 Corinthians 13:11). Remaining at home with Mom and Dad is the perpetuation of childhood. It may be time to put it behind you.

QUESTION 314

My situation is different. I went away to college and then came home to live again. I'll admit there is tension between me and my parents, but we'd be OK if they would just accept me as

a full-fledged adult. Why can't they see that I'm grown and let me live my own life?

Leaving home and then coming back is called "the elastic nest," and as you're finding, it can be very difficult. You've been on your own—you've made your decisions and controlled your own life. You've changed dramatically during your time away, but you returned to find that your parents have not. They are just like you left them. They want to tell you how to run your life—what to eat, what to wear, which friends to cultivate, etc. It is a formula for combat.

I understand your situation because I've been through it. My parents handled me wisely in my late teen years, and it was rare for them to stumble into common parental mistakes. That is, however, exactly what happened when I was nineteen years old. We had been a very close-knit family, and it was difficult for my mother to shift gears when I graduated from high school.

During that summer, I traveled 1,500 miles from home and entered a college in California. I will never forget the exhilarating feeling of freedom that swept over me that fall. It was not that I wanted to do anything evil or forbidden. It was simply that I felt accountable for my own life and did not have to explain my actions to anyone. It was like a fresh, cool breeze on a spring morning. Young adults who have not been properly prepared for that moment sometimes go berserk, but I remained rather sane. I did, however, quickly become addicted to freedom and was not about to give it up.

The following summer, I came home to visit my folks. Immediately, I found myself in conflict with my mom. She was not intentionally insulting. She simply responded as she had done a year earlier when I was still in high school. But by then, I had journeyed down the road toward independence. She was asking me what time I would be coming in at night and urging me to drive the car safely and advising me about what I ate. No offense was intended. My mother had just failed to notice that I had changed, and she needed to get with the new program.

Finally, there was a flurry of words between us, and I left the house in a huff. A friend came by to pick me up, and I talked about my feelings as we rode in the car. "Darn it, Bill!" I said. "I don't need a mother anymore."

Then a wave of guilt swept over me. It was as though I had said, "I don't love my mother anymore." I meant no such thing. What I was feeling was a desire to be friends with my parents instead of accepting their authority over me. Freedom was granted very quickly thereafter.

I hope you will be a bit more patient with your parents than I was with mine. I was only nineteen years old, and I wanted it all. I should have given them another year to adjust. Your mom and dad will also change their thinking if you give them a little time. They'll accept you as an adult much quicker if you'll get out on your own and establish an independent life for yourself.

QUESTION 315

I am nineteen years old, and I have struggled with a bad self-concept all my life. It seems that everyone I know has more to offer than I do. I envy the girls who are better looking, more athletic, or smarter than I am. I just don't measure up to my own expectations. How can I deal with my own insecurities?

Someone said, "Comparison is the root of all inferiority." It is true. When you look at another person's strengths and compare them to your own weaknesses, there is no way to come out feeling good about yourself. That is what you are doing when you pit yourself against the "best and brightest" around you. This destructive game begins in elementary school when we begin to evaluate ourselves critically. Even at that young age, our self-image is shaped by how we stack up against our peers. It's not how tall we are that matters—it's who is tallest. It's not how fast we can run—it's who runs fastest. It's not how smart we are—it's who is smartest. It's not how pretty or handsome we are—it's who is most gorgeous. Thus begins a pattern of self-doubt that often becomes all-consuming during adolescence. For some people it continues well into adult life. This is why millions of women buy fashion magazines and then envy the beauty of the models. It's why we watch Miss America contests and why some men read about successful and powerful businessmen. When we do that, we're weighing ourselves against the most admired assets of others. It is an exercise that brings us nothing but pain, and yet we continue to engage in it.

It appears that you are caught up in this destructive pattern. Perhaps a wise counselor or pastor can help you see that you are a worthy human being exactly the way you are and that God has designed you for a specific purpose. Mental and spiritual health begin with an acceptance of life as it is and a willingness to make the most of what has been given. When that is achieved, comparison with others is no longer an important issue.

Q UESTION 316

My former girlfriend and I were absolutely certain we were in love because we were crazy about each other from the moment we met. We were together every day, and all our friends thought we would get married. But the relationship cooled off very quickly, and now we can hardly stand each other. I don't even like to be around her. What do you think happened to us?

Not knowing either of you, it is difficult to say for sure. But I can tell you that the way your relationship began had something to do with the way it ended. A love affair is usually doomed when it begins with great intensity. It almost always burns itself out in time. You may recall an old song that described a love affair that was "too hot not to cool down." That's the way it often works.

In a manner of speaking, you and your girlfriend ran your race together as though it were a one-hundred-yard dash. It should have been approached like a marathon. That's why you exhausted yourselves before your journey together ever got started. If a love relationship is to go the distance, there needs to be a comfortable pacing that keeps the two parties from consuming each other. That will give the bond a chance to form—and allow "the glue to dry."

Q UESTION 317

I have a great fear that I will someday be divorced. I've been through it with my parents and watched several of my uncles and aunts. It is very hard on everybody. I'd rather not get

married than to run that risk. Is it possible to protect yourself from a divorce today?

You're not the only member of your generation who worries about the odds against successful marriages. That concern showed up in a song popularized a few years ago by Carly Simon. The lyrics are devastating. They say, in effect, "It is impossible to achieve intimacy in marriage, and our life together will be lonely, meaningless, and sterile. But if that's what you want . . . we'll marry."[125]

While I understand the pessimism expressed in this song, I disagree emphatically with its message. The family was God's idea, not our own, and it is still a wonderful institution.

Furthermore, it is a myth that marriages are destined to fail. Sixty-one percent of people living in the United States are married, 23 percent have never been married, 8 percent are widowed, and only 8 percent are divorced.[126] Seventy-five percent of families with children are headed by two married parents.[127] Despite what you hear about disintegrating families, most of us live within them and are happy about that fact. We do have to acknowledge, however, that marriages are fragile. They must be nurtured and protected if they are to survive for a lifetime. If ignored, they will wither and die.

QUESTION 318

You've been happily married for more than thirty years now. Have you ever been tempted to be unfaithful to your wife? What are the danger points that those of us who are younger should watch for?

Honestly, I have never even considered cheating on Shirley. The very thought of hurting her and inviting God's judgment is more than enough to keep me on the straight and narrow. Furthermore, I would never destroy the specialness we shared for all these years. But even marriages that are based on that kind of commitment are not immune to Satan's attacks.

He laid a trap for me during a time of particular vulnerability. Shirley and I had been married just a few years when we had a minor fuss. It was no big deal, but we both were pretty agitated at the time. I got in the car and drove around for about an hour to cool off. Then when I was on the way home, a very attractive girl drove up beside me in her car and smiled. She was obviously flirting with me. Then she slowed down, looked back, and turned onto a side street. I knew she was inviting me to follow her.

I didn't take the bait. I just went on home and made up with Shirley. But I thought later about how vicious Satan had been to take advantage of the momentary conflict between us. The Scriptures refer to the devil as "a roaring lion . . . seeking whom he may devour" (1 Peter 5:8, KJV). I could see how true that description really is. He knew his best opportunity to damage our marriage was during that hour or two when we were irritated with each other. That is typical of his strategy. He'll lay a trap for you, too, and it'll probably come at a time of vulnerability. Beautiful, enticing, forbidden fruit will be offered to you when your hunger is greatest. If you are foolish enough to reach for it, your fingers will sink into the rotten mush on the back side. That's the way sin operates in our lives. It promises everything. It delivers nothing but disgust and heartache.

Q UESTION 319

Do you believe love at first sight occurs between some people?

Though some readers will disagree with me, "love at first sight" is a physical and emotional impossibility. Why? Because love is much more than a romantic feeling. It is more than a sexual attraction or the thrill of the chase or a desire to marry someone. These are responses that can occur "at first sight," and they might even lead to the genuine thing in time. But those feelings are usually very temporary, and they do not mean the person who experiences them is "in love." I wish everyone understood that fact!

The primary difference between infatuation and real love is where the emphasis lies. Temporary romantic attractions tend to be very selfish in nature. A person may say, "I can't believe what is happening to me. This is the most fantastic thing I've ever experienced! I must be in love." Notice that she's not talking about the other person. She's

333

excited about her own gratification. Such an individual hasn't fallen in love with someone else; she has fallen in love with love!

Genuine love, by contrast, is an expression of the deepest appreciation for another human being. It is an intense awareness of his or her needs and strengths and character. It shares the longings, hopes, and dreams of that other person. It is unselfish, giving, and caring. And believe me, these are not attitudes one "falls" into at first sight, as though one were tumbling into a ditch.

I have developed a lifelong love for my wife, but it was not something I fell into. I grew into it, and that process took time. I had to know her before I could appreciate the depth and stability of her character—to become acquainted with the nuances of her personality, which I now cherish. The familiarity from which love has blossomed simply could not be generated on "some enchanted evening, across a crowded room." One cannot love an unknown object, regardless of how attractive or sexy or nubile it is!

Q UESTION 320

Is it possible to love someone and not feel it?

It certainly is—because love is more than a feeling. It is primarily a decision. Married couples who misunderstand this point will have serious problems when the feeling of love disappears for a time. Couples who genuinely love each other will experience times of closeness, times when they feel apathetic, and times when they are irritated and cranky. That's just the way emotions operate. What, then, will hold them steady as feelings bounce all over the landscape? The source of constancy is a commitment of the will. You simply make up your mind not to be blown off the limb by fluctuating and unreliable emotions.

334

Q UESTION 321

My boyfriend and I have been seeing each other for almost a year. Initially, he would freely show me a great deal of respect and affection. Lately, however, I'm seeing less and less of this

attention. I don't want to be overly sensitive, but I don't want to be used as a doormat, either. How can I know for sure what is the case?

Give yourself a little test by answering these questions about the relationship: Are you making all the phone calls to the other person? Does he tell you the truth invariably? Have you been "stood up" without a reasonable excuse? Do you fear he is slipping away, and is that causing you to "grab and hold"? Are you tolerating insults that others would not accept? Does he show evidence of cherishing you and wanting to make you happy? Does he reveal your secrets to others and make comments about you in public that embarrass you? Is he physically abusive at times? Does he ever reach for you instead of your reaching for him? Do your friends ever say, "Why do you put up with the stuff he does?"

These are questions that only you can answer. But if you are honest with yourself, you will have no difficulty identifying disrespectful components to your relationship. If you come up with the wrong answers, the solution is not to beg him to do better. It is to pull back and see if he follows. If he doesn't, you're better off looking for someone else.

QUESTION 322

My boyfriend doesn't talk to me very much. He's just a very quiet and shy person. Will he always be this way? I just wish he'd tell me what he's thinking and feeling.

Your question reminds me of the twelve-year-old boy who had never spoken a word. His parents and siblings thought he couldn't talk because they'd never heard his voice. Then one day the boy's mother placed some soup in front of him, and he ate a spoonful. Then he pushed the bowl away and said, "This is slop, and I won't eat any more of it!"

The family was ecstatic. He'd actually spoken a complete sentence. They all jumped around gleefully, and his father said, "Why haven't you ever talked to us before?"

The boy replied, "Because up until now everything has been OK."

Maybe your boyfriend will surprise you one day with a flurry of words, but I doubt it. Shyness and an introverted personality result primarily from an inborn temperament that tends to be very persistent throughout life. Research shows that approximately 15 percent of children are genetically programmed to be somewhat introverted like your friend and that most of them will always be that way.[128] It appears that some people just seem to be born "noisy," and others prefer to keep their thoughts to themselves. Your boyfriend may be one of the latter.

If you choose to marry him, I hope you'll do so with your eyes wide open. You're probably not going to change him. Many women fall in love with the strong, silent type and then resent their men for the rest of their lives because they won't talk to them. It is a very common source of frustration among women. But that's the way it is.

Q UESTION 323

I'm the boyfriend who doesn't talk very much. I've been that way all of my life. Part of the problem is that I just don't like to reveal what I'm feeling. But also, I don't know how to talk to people. I get really uncomfortable when I'm with people and I'm expected to say things. Can you give me some hints about how to express myself?

It might help you to understand the basics of good conversation. Let me ask you to imagine that the two of us are facing each other about eight feet apart. You have four tennis balls in your hands, and you toss one of them to me. Instead of throwing the ball back, however, I hold it and wait for you to toss another to me. Eventually all four balls are in my hands. We stand there looking at each other awkwardly and wondering what to do next. The game is over.

Good conversation is something like that game of catch. One person throws an idea or a comment to the other, and he or she then tosses it back. But if that second person doesn't return it, the game ends. Both players feel awkward and wish they could be somewhere else. Let me illustrate further.

Suppose I say to my son when he comes home in the afternoon,

"How did it go in school today?" If he answers, "Fine," he has caught the ball and held it. We have nothing more to say to each other unless I can come up with another comment—another "ball" to throw to him.

But if my son says, "I had a good day because I got an A on my history test," he has caught the ball and thrown it back. I can then ask, "Was it a difficult test?" or "Did you study hard for it?" or "I'll bet you're proud of yourself."

If my son replies, "Yes," he has wrecked the game again. To keep the conversation going, he needs to throw back something of substance, such as "It was a tough examination, but it was fair." Then our "game" can continue.

I hope you see that the art of talking to people is really very simple. It's just a matter of throwing the conversational ball back and forth.

As for your relationship with a future wife, it won't be enough to just throw the ball back to her. She's going to want you to be more intimate than that. She'll need to know how you feel about her, what you dream about, things that upset you, what you'd like her to do, how you feel about God, etc. You can learn to put these thoughts into words, even though you will probably never be a big talker. I suggest that you push yourself in this direction rather than saying, "That's just how I am." Your wife will probably have to make some changes to accommodate you, too.

That's what a good marriage is all about.

QUESTION 324

I have always been a good student, and I want to go to either law school or medical school. That means I could be in my mid or late-twenties by the time I graduate and get on with my life. But I also want to be a wife and mother and stay home with my children. I can't figure out how to reach both these goals. How can I be a professional and a mother, too?

You've described a dilemma that millions of young women struggle with today. Three competing choices lie before them—whether to have a career, be a wife and mother, or attempt to do both. It is a decision that will have implications for everything that is to follow.

Since you don't yet have plans to get married, I would recommend that you press ahead with your academic goals. Once your training is complete, you will still have all the options available to you. If by that time you are married and want to become a full-time mother, you can put your career on hold for a few years or leave it altogether. Remember, you can always return to it after the children are older.

Only you can decide what is best for yourself, of course. I would strongly suggest that you make it a matter of prayer as you seek the Lord's will for your life.

QUESTION 325

Let me ask the question another way. Should a college-educated woman feel that she has wasted her training if she chooses not to use it professionally? I mean, why should I bother to go through school to be a professional if I'm going to wind up raising kids and being a full-time homemaker?

A person doesn't go to college just to prepare for a line of work—or at least, that shouldn't be the reason for being there. The purpose for getting a college education is to broaden your world and enrich your intellectual life. Whether or not it leads to a career is not the point. Nothing invested in the cultivation of your own mind is ever really wasted. If you have the desire to learn and the opportunity to go to school, I think you should reach for it. Your career plans can be finalized later.

QUESTION 326

Do you think it is all right for a woman to make it her exclusive career goal to be a wife and mother? Or should there be something else?

You bet it's all right! Motherhood is an honorable profession that didn't have to be defended for thousands of years. But in the last few decades, young women have been made to feel foolish if they even dared to mention homemaking as a goal.

I remember a college senior who came to see me about her plans after graduation. We talked about various job opportunities and the possibility of her going to graduate school. Then she suddenly paused and looked over her shoulder. She leaned toward me and said almost in a whisper, "May I be completely honest with you?"

I said, "Sure, Debbie. There's nobody here but us. You can say anything you want."

"Well," she continued in a hushed tone, "I don't want to have a career at all. What I really want is to be a full-time wife and mother."

I said, "Why do you say that like it's some kind of secret? It's your life. What's wrong with doing whatever you want with it?"

"Are you kidding?" she said. "If my professors and my classmates at the university knew that's what I wanted, they'd laugh me out of school."

Unbelievably, it has become politically incorrect to have babies and to devote a few years to raising them. That is foolish and insulting. There is no more important job in the universe than to raise a child to love God, live productively, and serve humanity. How ridiculous that a woman should have to apologize for wanting to fulfill that historic role!

Not every woman chooses to be a wife and mother, of course. Some are interested only in a career. Others have no plans to marry. That is all right, too. But those who do elect to be full-time, stay-at-home moms should not be ashamed to admit it—even on a university campus.

Q UESTION **327**

Give me some practical suggestions for the selection of a husband. I sure want to get it right and don't think I should depend just on looks or personality. What are the factors I should consider before saying "I do"?

Let me list a few things that you might want to consider:

1. A Sunday school teacher gave me some advice when I was thirteen years of age that I never forgot. He said, "Don't marry the person you think you can live with. Marry the one you can't live without." There's great truth in this advice. Marriage can be difficult even

when two people are passionately in love with one another. It is murder when they don't have that foundation to build on.

2. Don't marry someone who has characteristics that you feel are intolerable. You may plan to change him or her in the future, but that probably won't happen. Behavior runs in deep channels that were cut during early childhood, and it is very difficult to alter them. In order to change a deeply ingrained pattern, you have to build a sturdy dam, dig another canal, and reroute the river in the new direction. That effort is rarely successful over the long haul.

Therefore, if you can't live with a characteristic that shows up during courtship, it may plague you for the rest of your life. For example, a person who drinks every night is not likely to give up that habit after the honeymoon. If he or she is foolish with money or is basically unclean or tends to get violent when irritated or is extremely selfish, these are red flags you should not ignore. What you see is what you get.

Of course, we all have flaws, and I'm not suggesting that a person has to be perfect to be a candidate for marriage. Rather, my point is that you have to decide if you can tolerate a quirky behavior for the rest of your life—because that's how long you may have to deal with it. If you can't, don't bank on deprogramming the partner after you've said "I do." I advise you to keep your eyes wide open before marriage and then half-closed thereafter.

3. Do not marry impulsively! I can think of no better way to mess up your life than to leap into this critical decision without careful thought and prayer. It takes time to get acquainted and to walk through the early stages of the bonding process. Remember that the dating relationship is designed to conceal information, not reveal it. Both partners put on their best faces for the one they seek to attract. They guard the secrets that might be a turnoff. Therefore, many newlyweds get a big surprise during the first year of married life. I suggest that you take at least a year to get beyond the facade and into the inner character of the person.

4. If you are a deeply committed Christian, do not allow yourself to become "unequally yoked" with an unbeliever. You may expect to win your spouse to the Lord at some future date, and that does happen on occasion. But to count on it is risky at best, foolhardy at worst. Again, this is the question that must be answered: "Just how

critical is it that my husband (or wife) shares my faith?" If it is essential and nonnegotiable, as the Scriptures tell us it should be for believers, then that matter should be given the highest priority in one's decision to marry.

5. Do not move in with a person before marriage. To do so is a bad idea for many reasons. First, it is immoral and a violation of God's law. Second, it undermines a relationship and often leads to divorce. Studies show that couples who live together before marriage have a 50 percent greater chance of divorce than those who don't, based on fifty years of data.[129] Those who cohabit also have less satisfying and more unstable marriages. Why? The researchers found that those who had lived together later regretted having "violated their moral standards," and "felt a loss of personal freedom to exit out the back door." Furthermore, and in keeping with the theme of marital bonding, they have "stolen" a level of intimacy that is not warranted at that point, nor has it been validated by the degree of commitment to one another. As it turns out, God's way is not only the right way—it is the healthiest for everyone concerned.

6. Don't get married too young. Those who wed between the ages of fourteen and seventeen are twice as likely to divorce as couples who wait until their twenties. Making it as a family requires some characteristics that come with maturity, such as selflessness, stability, and self-control. It's best to wait for their arrival.

7. Finally, I'll conclude with the ultimate secret of lifelong love. Simply put, the stability of marriage is a by-product of an iron-willed determination to make it work. If you choose to marry, enter into that covenant with the resolve to remain committed to each other for life. Never threaten during angry moments to leave your mate. Don't allow yourself to consider even the possibility of divorce. Calling it quits must not become an option for those who want to go the distance!

Q UESTION 328

Some of my friends got married with the mutual understanding that they could bail out if it didn't work. In nearly

every one of those families, they are divorced today. From what you say, I guess that doesn't surprise you.

Not at all. Marriage succeeds only as a lifetime commitment with no escape clauses. That kind of determination was common for earlier generations. Let me share how my father felt about my mother when they married in 1935. Forty years later, he and I were walking in a park and talking about the meaning of commitment between a husband and wife. With that, he reached into his pocket and took out a worn piece of paper. On it was written a promise he had made to my mother when she agreed to become his wife. This is what he had said to her:

> I want you to understand and be fully aware of my feelings concerning the marriage covenant which we are about to enter. I have been taught at my mother's knee, and in harmony with the Word of God, that the marriage vows are inviolable, and by entering into them I am binding myself absolutely and for life. The idea of estrangement from you through divorce for any reason at all (although God allows one—infidelity) will never at any time be permitted to enter into my thinking. I'm not naive in this. On the contrary, I'm fully aware of the possibility, unlikely as it now appears, that mutual incompatibility or other unforeseen circumstances could result in extreme mental suffering. If such becomes the case, I am resolved for my part to accept it as a consequence of the commitment I am now making, and to bear it, if necessary, to the end of our lives together.
>
> I have loved you dearly as a sweetheart and will continue to love you as my wife. But over and above that, I love you with a Christian love that demands that I never react in any way toward you that would jeopardize our prospects of entering heaven, which is the supreme objective of both our lives. And I pray that God Himself will make our affection for one another perfect and eternal.

342

If that is the way you approach the commitment of marriage, your probabilities of living happily together are vastly improved. Again, the Scriptures endorse the permanence of the marital relationship: "Therefore what God has joined together, let man not separate" (Mark 10:9).

QUESTION 329

The following question was asked during the filming of the video series Life on the Edge, with 175 teenagers in the audience. During the question-and-answer period, one young lady said with tears in her eyes: "It is my desire to follow Jesus Christ in everything I do. But I have no idea what He wants of me or what I'm supposed to do. Is it enough that I'm willing?"

We are told in the Scriptures that God is infinitely loving and compassionate toward us, His children. Psalm 103:13 says, "As a father pities his children, so the Lord pities those who fear Him" (NKJV). Isaiah 66:13 says, "As a mother comforts her child, so will I comfort you." Given those descriptions of God as the ultimate parent, can you imagine Him ignoring your request for direction and guidance in your life? Is there even a possibility that He would say, "I don't care about her. She wants to do My will, but I'm going to conceal it from her. I'll just let her flounder"?

Not a chance! He sees those tears in your eyes. He knows the desire of your heart. And you will hear from Him—just in time to take the next step.

QUESTION 330

I believe God is calling me to be a youth minister when I get out of college, but I am concerned about how I can do that financially. Pastors don't make very much money, and if I have a family by then, I'm not sure I could support them in that profession.

Let me share a very important spiritual principle that has been very helpful to me. We read in Psalm 119:105 that His Word is "a lamp to my feet and a light for my path." Think about the imagery described in that verse. We are not given a three-hundred-watt beam to reveal the entire landscape. There is no headlight on our hats that points toward the horizon. Instead, the Lord provides only a handheld lamp that illuminates the trail on which we are walking. In other words, He shows us where to place the next step, and that is all. We have to trust Him to lead us through the darkness that lies beyond our vision.

There is an application here to your question. You're asking how the Lord is going to sustain you and your family in years to come. But the light you're carrying only shows what you need to know today. That is enough. Just continue to "walk in the light" you have been given, and leave the future in God's hands. If He is calling you to do a job, He will make it possible for you to care for your family and overcome any other barriers to that responsibility.

QUESTION 331

I heard you talk in your Life on the Edge video series about something you called the "line of respect" between a husband and wife. Would you explain that again?

Yes. It involves a system of accountability to keep a marriage healthy. Let me explain how it works.

Suppose I work in my office two hours longer than usual on a particular night, knowing that my wife, Shirley, is preparing a special candlelight dinner. The phone sits there on my desk, but I lack the concern to make a brief call to explain. As the evening wears on, Shirley wraps the cold food in foil and puts it in the refrigerator. Then suppose when I finally get home, I do not apologize. Instead, I sit down with a newspaper and abruptly tell Shirley to get my dinner ready. You can bet there'll be a few minutes of fireworks in the Dobson household. Shirley will rightfully interpret my behavior as insulting and will move to defend the "line of respect" between us. We will talk it out, and next time I'll be more considerate.

Let's put the shoe on the other foot. Suppose Shirley knows I need the car at 2:00 P.M. for some important purpose, but she deliberately keeps me waiting. Perhaps she sits in a restaurant with a lady friend, drinking coffee and talking. Meanwhile, I'm pacing the floor at home wondering where she is. It is very likely that my lovely wife will hear about my dissatisfaction when she gets home. The "line of respect" has been violated, even though the offense was minor.

This is what I mean by mutual accountability. This kind of minor conflict in a marriage plays a positive role in establishing what is and is not acceptable behavior. Some instances of disrespect may seem petty, but when they are permitted to pass unnoticed, two things happen. First, the offender is unaware that he has stepped over the line and is likely to repeat the indiscretion later. In fact, he may go further into the other person's territory the next time. Second, the person who felt insulted internalizes the small irritation rather than dealing with it. As the interpretation of disrespect grows and the corresponding agitation accumulates in a storage tank, the stage is set for an eventual explosion, rather than a series of minor ventilations.

What I'm saying is that some things are worth fighting over, and at the top of the list is the "line of respect." Most of my conflicts with Shirley have occurred over some behavior that one of us interpreted as unhealthy to the relationship. Shirley may say to me, in effect, "Jim, what you did was selfish, and I can't let it pass." She is careful not to insult me in the confrontation, keeping her criticism focused on the behavior to which she objects.

A workable system of checks and balances of this nature helps a couple keep their marriage on course for a marathon rather than a sprint.

QUESTION 332

I'm a junior in high school, and I am starting to think about college. I'm not sure whether I should go to a Christian college, which costs more and offers fewer academic majors, or whether I should go to a big, impersonal state university. What do you think Christian students should do?

I will answer your question, but first I need to admit that I am not unbiased in the advice I'm about to offer. I'm going to give you one man's opinion that may differ from what you'll hear from your parents, your school counselor, or your pastor. At least you know I've laid my cards on the table and confessed my lack of objectivity on this matter.

I believe strongly in Christian education for those of you who are followers of Christ. My wife and I are products of a church-sponsored college that made an incredible contribution to our lives. Both of our children graduated from Christian universities, and we're delighted that they did.

Let me acknowledge that many students thrive academically and spiritually in large, secular schools, and they do not regret their decision to go there. Some get involved in Christian ministries on campus and emerge with their faith intact. Furthermore, there are thousands of dedicated Christian professors in public universities, and they believe God has led them to teach in that environment. In no way do I challenge that assumption or intend any disrespect whatsoever.

Nevertheless, I wouldn't send my son or daughter there unless there were very good reasons for doing so.

QUESTION 333

What, then, do you see as the disadvantages or drawbacks to attending a public university? Why shouldn't I go to an inexpensive school that has a national reputation right in my home city?

That local university might be exactly right for you, but at least you should know what you're likely to experience when you get there. There are several trends going on today in higher education that are disturbing. Let me describe four of them.

1. *Secular universities today are bastions of moral relativism that have no room for the Christian worldview.*

    I doubt if many students or their parents realize just how antagonistic many of our state schools have become to anything that smacks of Christianity. There is simply no place for God in the system. The new god is "diversity," which respects all worldviews and philosophies—except one. The Christian perspective is not only excluded from the classroom, it is often ridiculed and undermined.

The dominant philosophy in today's public university is called relativism, which categorically denies the existence of truth or moral absolutes. Those who are foolish enough to believe in such archaic notions as biblical authority or the claims of Christ are to be pitied—or bullied.

2. *State universities are dominated by "politically correct" (PC) thought that can be contradicted only at great personal sacrifice.*

There is, perhaps, less freedom of thought on today's secular campuses than any other place in society. A student or faculty member is simply not permitted to espouse ideas that are contrary to the approved "group think." This purity is enforced by what has been called the "campus thought police," including feminist extremists on the faculty, homosexual and lesbian activists, leftist professors, minority activists, and bilingual advocates. Donald Kagan, former dean of Yale University, said, "I was a student during the days of Joseph McCarthy, and there is less freedom now than there was then."[130]

Here are a few examples of political correctness in action:

- Pennsylvania State University advised its ten thousand incoming freshmen in 1990 that they might be assigned a homosexual roommate, and if so, they would not be permitted to object.[131]
- At New York University Law School, students refused to debate a moot court case involving a hypothetical divorced lesbian mother trying to win custody of her child—because arguing the con side would be hurtful to gays.[132]
- The University of Michigan has established a "student guide to proper behavior" that indiscriminately lumps racist threats with such conduct as "failing to invite someone to a party because she's a lesbian."[133]

3. *The politically correct philosophy on many campuses disdains Western civilization, with its emphasis on the Judeo-Christian heritage.*

Many of the most prestigious universities, including Stanford, have eliminated their "core curriculum" based on Western civilization. In fact, it is possible to graduate from 78 percent of America's colleges and universities without taking a course in Western civilization.[134] The consequence? Lynne Cheney, former chairperson of the National Endowment for the Humanities, wrote that many students earn bachelor's degrees without knowledge of "basic landmarks of history and thought."[135] For example, in a 1989 Gallup poll, 25 percent of seven hundred college seniors did not know that Columbus landed in the Western Hemisphere before 1500. Most could not identify the Magna Carta.[136]

4. *State universities are breeding grounds, quite literally, for sexually transmitted diseases (including HIV), homosexual behavior, unwanted pregnancies, abortions, alcoholism, and drug abuse.*

As public universities exercise tighter and tighter control on politically correct thought, they seem entirely disinterested in student sexual activity and other behavior with moral implications. Indeed, even the word *morality* implies a value judgment that violates PC "theology."

Consider these illustrations:

- Cornell University's student assembly recently recommended that a dormitory wing be reserved for about sixty students interested in promoting "gay, lesbian and bisexual awareness."[137]
- About twenty students at the University of Massachusetts at Amherst have lived in a gay-lesbian-bisexual "corridor" for several years. The University of California has about forty students living in two gay "theme" dormitories, and Rutgers University started a gay-studies living unit for about ten students a few years ago. The idea is spreading.[138]
- A study at a University of Texas student health center revealed that nearly one in one hundred students seeking medical care is infected with the virus that causes AIDS.[139]
- Seventy-five percent of students visiting the Cowell Health Center at Stanford University describe themselves as "sexually active."[140]

348

These are only a few of my concerns about the state-university system as it is currently operated.

Q UESTION 334

OK, I see the problem. But how about Christian colleges and universities? Are they really all that much better? I've heard that some of them are pretty liberal, too. Why do you recommend them?

Some are and some aren't, so you have to investigate a particular school. But most of them are a breed apart. I thank God for schools that are serious about the gospel of Jesus Christ. They are vital to perpetuating our faith through your generation and beyond.

Here are a few reasons I believe so strongly in Christian education:

1. *It is difficult to overestimate the importance of having godly professors for students in their late teens and early twenties.*

   My great concern for those of you in the young-adult years is that you are extremely vulnerable to the leadership of your professors. One of the primary reasons education changes people is that students admire and identify with those who tower over them in experience, training, maturity, intelligence, and charisma. This makes a young man or woman an easy mark for older adults who want to reorder their basic beliefs and value systems.

2. *Christian education places its emphasis on unity in relationships between people.*

   As we have indicated, secular institutions have been almost obsessed with the concept of diversity in university life. What this means in practical terms is that people become fractionalized into competing self-interest groups. African-Americans are pitted against Hispanics who are at war with Asian-Americans who resent Native Americans who must compete with homosexuals and lesbians for status and territory.

   During an 1858 speech to the Illinois Republican Convention, Abraham Lincoln quoted the Scripture found in Matthew 12:25, "A house divided against itself cannot stand."[141] That, I fear, is where diversity leads. If by that term we refer to love and tolerance for peoples who are different from one another, it has great validity for us. But if by diversity we mean all have been given reason to resent one another, having no common values, heritage, commitment, or hope, then we are a nation in serious trouble.

Whether right or wrong, it is my belief that Christian colleges place their emphasis not on that which divides us but on the substance that binds us together. That commonality is the gospel of Jesus Christ. He commanded us to love one another—to set aside our differences and to care for "the least of these" among us. It is our unity, not our diversity, that deserves our allegiance.

Though Christian professors and administrators have not always succeeded in this effort, unity has been (and continues to be) the goal. In short, they seek to bring students and faculty together rather than dividing them into competing self-interest groups. I think that is a vitally important distinction.

3. *I firmly believe students typically get a better undergraduate education at a Christian institution than at a large public institution.*

Some universities have earned most of their reputations for excellence from the quality of the research conducted in their graduate schools. Much less attention is given to teaching undergraduates. Professors are rewarded and promoted for their scientific findings and the number of publications they produce. Their ability to inspire and teach is of little consequence in advancement. Thus, freshmen and sophomores often find themselves in huge classes of three hundred to two thousand. The instructor may be an inexperienced graduate student whose primary interest is his or her academic pursuit. I know this system well. I taught such a class at USC when I was working on my Ph.D. I didn't do it very well.

The situation on Christian campuses is usually very different. Students often develop close relationships with their professors. The classes are usually smaller, permitting interaction and more opportunity to ask questions. Informal discussions at the professor's home or at a restaurant are not unusual.

4. *A Christian college is the only place where the majority of students are professing Christians. That is vitally important.*

The single greatest influence during the college years does not come from the faculty. It is derived from other students! Thus, being classmates with men and women who profess a faith in Jesus Christ is vital to the bonding that should occur during those four years.

In addition to formal learning in the classroom, a quality education involves a wide variety of experiences with friends who share basic values and beliefs. These include dorm parties, chapel programs, intramural and intercollegiate athletics, debates and seminars, a range of musical and dramatic groups, dorm Bible study groups, and evenings in faculty members' homes.

The friendships that flow from these activities will be remembered for a lifetime. Likewise, if it is important for you to marry someone who shares your Christian faith (and I think that is extremely important), then it seems wise to select a college where more of them will be found.

The students Shirley and I met while attending a Christian college are still among our best friends today—more than thirty years later. There are no friends quite like those made during your younger years, and not one of them can be replaced in later life. I thank God for the experiences we had among guys and gals of like mind, faith, and values when we were very young!

Q UESTION **335**

I would like to attend a Christian college, but my folks can't afford to send me there, and I don't have any money of my own. Do you have any advice for me?

Yours isn't the only family that can't afford high tuition costs at a private college or university. You might be interested to know, however, that many Christian schools charge less than comparable secular institutions. Christian colleges are also accustomed to serving low-income families or those who have gone through financial difficulties. You'd be amazed to hear how God has provided for their needs through financial aid, federal grants and loans, work programs, and special student scholarships.

Before you rule out a private education, therefore, I hope you'll check out the possibilities. I also recommend that you do *not* plan to attend a community college for the first two years unless it's absolutely necessary. The freshmen and sophomore years are the most important in terms of personal growth and development.

If you are thinking about attending a Christian college and don't know how to find the right one, you can buy an inexpensive handbook in Christian bookstores. It's called *Choose a Christian College,* released by Peterson's Guides, one of the largest publishers of college handbooks. While it doesn't describe every Christian college in North America, this volume includes information on eighty-seven member colleges and universities of the Christian College Coalition. Each of these schools meets eight criteria for membership, including a commitment by the administration to hiring as full-time faculty only people with a personal commitment to Jesus Christ. That book also provides information on tuition costs, grants and aid, available majors, entrance requirements, and campus-life factors.

I hope this has been helpful in clarifying your own views on higher education. Now I suggest you seek advice and counsel from others you trust.

QUESTION 336

What do you think about "date rape" when a girl has given a guy the come-on? If she has flirted with him and gone with him to an apartment or to someplace she shouldn't be, doesn't he have the right to have sex with her?

A guy never has a right to force a woman to have sex with him under any circumstances. She should be able to say no at any point, and he must honor that denial. It is criminal that so many girls and women are raped today. Fully 60 percent of all females who lose their virginity before age fifteen say that their first sexual experience was forced![142] That is a tragedy with far-reaching consequences.

What concerns me is that society has taught young men that they have the right to force themselves on young women. In a study conducted by the Rhode Island Rape Crisis Center, 1,700 students between the sixth and ninth grades were asked if a guy should have a right to force a woman to have sexual intercourse with him under certain circumstances. Sixty-five percent of the boys and 47 percent of the girls said boys do have that right if they have dated a girl for six months or longer! And 51 percent of the boys said a guy has a right to force a girl to kiss him if he spent "a lot of money on her"—defined by twelve-year-olds as ten to fifteen dollars.[143]

No wonder women find themselves on the defensive so often today. Some men fully expect them to prostitute themselves if they've spent a few bucks on them.

Let me leave you with this thought, written by my father before he died. If you incorporate it into your system of values, it will serve as a worthy guide to the management of your sexual energy:

"Strong desire is like a river. As long as it flows within the banks of God's will—be the current strong or weak—all is well. But when it overruns those boundaries and seeks its own channels, then disaster lurks in the rampage below."

QUESTION 337

Most colleges and universities permit men and women to live in coeducational dormitories, often rooming side by side. Others allow unrestricted visiting hours by members of the opposite sex. Do you think this promotes more healthy attitudes toward sex?

It certainly promotes more sex, and some people think that's healthy. The advocates of cohabitation try to tell us that young men and women can live together without doing what comes naturally. That is nonsense. The sex drive is one of the strongest forces in human nature, and Joe College is notoriously weak in suppressing it. I would prefer that supporters of coeducational dormitories admit that morality is not very important to them. If morality is something we value, then we should at least give it a wobbly legged chance to survive. The sharing of collegiate bedrooms (and bathrooms!) hardly takes us in that direction.

QUESTION 338

I've just graduated from high school and am highly motivated to make something of myself. Whatever it takes to be successful, I'm willing to do it. I want to reach the top of the field I eventually choose. Do you think God has put this drive in me?

Well, He can certainly use it for His purposes. Your drive will help carry you through those times when the academic challenges are tough and you might be tempted to give up. But there is one caution I would offer. It is important to ask yourself *why* you hunger for success and what the source of that intense motivation is. Do you desire power for selfish reasons, or is it your objective to be of service to God and to humankind? It is a question that every young Christian should ask.

The lust for power for its own sake is a lifelong passion for many people. It takes different forms in the adult years, but the emotional wellspring is the same. Most people want to run things. The desire for money is a function of this longing for control and influence. Why? Because those with the most money are perceived as the most powerful.

Just how important is raw power in your own motivational system? Do you hope to be a doctor, lawyer, military officer, or politician because these professions represent influence in our culture? Are you determined to make a name for yourself because you want people to say, "There goes a great person"? Do you hope they'll want your autograph and your photograph? Do these symbols of significance underlie your desire for success?

If so, your ladder is leaning against the wrong wall. But I don't want to discourage you. God has given you talent, and He wants you to use it productively. You should set your goals high and direct your energies to achieving them. Train your mind. Develop your skills. Discipline your appetites. Prepare for the future. Work hard. Go for it! You can't steal second with one foot on first.

But before you set out to make your mark, you should ask yourself one more question: For *whom* will this be done? If you seek power so you can be powerful, you're on the wrong track. If you crave fame so

354

you can be famous, the journey will be disappointing. If you desire influence so you can be influential, you're making a big mistake. This is what the Lord says about the trappings of success: "Let not the wise man glory in his wisdom, neither let the mighty man glory in his might, let not the rich man glory in his riches" (Jeremiah 9:23, KJV). What then should we glory in? The apostle Paul provides the answer: "So whether you eat or drink or whatever you do, do it all for the glory of God" (1 Corinthians 10:31).

That's very clear, isn't it? Our purposes are not our own. They are His. Thus, the choice of an occupation and "whatever you do" is to be motivated by your service to the kingdom of God. That is the only thing that carries eternal significance. Nothing else will satisfy. Everything else is going to burn.

QUESTION 339

I'm twenty-one years old and still haven't figured out what I want to do with my life. I know I need to choose a profession, but I can't seem to get a fix on what makes sense for me. How can I find an achievable goal and begin moving toward it?

Selecting an occupation and training for it can be a very difficult assignment. It's tough to predict what you'll want to be doing when you're fifty or sixty years old, yet you're obligated to guess. You have to base your decision on very limited information. You may not even know what the work will be like, yet you enroll yourself in a lengthy academic program or otherwise seek ways to train for it.

The decisions you make under these circumstances may lock you into something you will later hate. And there are social pressures that influence your choices. For example, how many young women secretly want to be wives and mothers but are afraid to admit it in today's "liberated" society? Furthermore, how can a girl plan to do something that requires the participation of another person—a husband—who will love and commit himself to her for the rest of his life? Marriage may or may not be in the picture for her. Yes, there is plenty to consider for men and women at your age in life.

I was very fortunate to have stumbled into a profession when I was young that I have been able to do reasonably well. If I had been born in Jesus' time and had been required to earn a living with my hands, perhaps in carpentry or stonemasonry, I probably would have starved to death. I can see myself sitting outside the temple in Jerusalem with a sign that read "Will work for food." Craftsmanship is just not in my nature. I earned my only high school D in woodworking class, and that was a gift from my teacher, Mr. Peterson. I spent an entire semester trying to make a box in which to store shoeshine stuff. What a waste! At least that experience helped me rule out a few occupational possibilities. Carpentry and cabinetry were two of them.

To make an informed decision about a profession, you'll need to get six essential components together, as follows:

1. It must be something you genuinely like to do. This choice requires you to identify your own strengths, weaknesses, and interests.
2. It must be something you have the ability to do. You might want to be an attorney but lack the talent to do the academic work and pass the bar examination.
3. It must be something you can earn a living by doing. You might want to be an artist, but if people don't buy your paintings, you could starve while sitting at your easel.
4. It must be something you are permitted to do. You might make a wonderful physician and could handle the training but can't gain entrance to medical school. I went through a Ph.D. program in graduate school with a fellow student who washed out after seven years of classwork. He made it to the last big exam before his professors told him, "You're out."
5. It must be something that brings cultural affirmation. In other words, most people need to feel some measure of respect from their contemporaries for what they do. This is the one reason women have found it difficult to stay home and raise their children.
6. Most important for the genuine believer, it must be something that you feel God approves of. How do you determine the will of God about so personal a decision?

What makes it so tough to choose an occupation is that all six of these requirements must be met at the same time. If you get five of them down but you don't like what you have selected, you're in trouble. If you can get five together but are rejected by the required professional schools, you are blocked. If you can get five lined up but you can't earn a living at the job of your choice, the system fails. Every link in the chain must connect.

Given this challenge, it isn't surprising that so many young people, like yourself, struggle in their early twenties. They become immobilized for years, not knowing what to do next. They sit around their parents' house plunking on a guitar and waiting for a dish to rattle in the kitchen.

Young adults in this situation remind me of rockets sitting on their launchpads. Their engines are roaring and belching smoke and fire, but nothing moves. The spacecraft was made to blast its way through the stratosphere, but there it sits as if bolted to the pad. I've met many men and women in their early twenties whose rockets just would not lift them off the ground. And yes, I've known a few whose engines blew up and scattered the debris of broken dreams all over the launchpad.

Q UESTION 340

What do you suggest for a person like me? How can I get my rocket to lift off the pad?

First, you need information. You might begin by going to an occupational psychologist or another knowledgeable counselor who can assess your skills and interests. There are excellent psychometric tests available today that will acquaint you with your own abilities. Computers will analyze your responses and correlate them with those of people who are successful and contented in given professions. You might be surprised at what you can learn about yourself from an occupational inventory.

Second, you should begin an energetic exploration of eight or ten occupations that you might find exciting. Visit people who are working in those fields, and ask them for advice and counsel. Attack this problem like a private investigator who is determined to unravel a mystery. Leave no stone unturned.

Third, when you've identified the area of greatest interest, commit to it. Beyond that point there's no looking back. Even if there might be a more attractive goal out there somewhere, there comes a point where you have to get on with life. Take your best shot and stay with it until you have a more secure and certain alternative to chase.

Finally, remember that the Lord is mindful of your decision too. What you do with your life is important to Him because He cares about you. Lean heavily on prayer and godly counsel as you zero in on a choice. There is no other way to make any decision that is of critical significance. The psalmist wrote, "Except the Lord build the house, they labour in vain that build it: except the Lord keep the city, the watchman waketh but in vain" (Psalm 127:1, KJV).

Those words offer incredible meaning for you and your peers at this stage in life. Whatever you try to accomplish will be useless if you do it in your own strength. That may sound very old-fashioned, but I promise you it is true.

Q UESTION 341

I have been reading the Bible and am surprised by how many of the characters in the Old Testament eventually committed terrible sins and displeased God. Saul, Solomon, Samson, Hezekiah, and even King David began with such high ideals and later fell short of them. Although I know I will make mistakes and fail in many ways, I have a strong desire not to displease God and experience moral failure. As a young woman who has kept her life clean to this point, I am determined to live by that standard. What advice would you give me to help me be God's woman throughout my life?

First, let me commend you for this wonderful commitment to moral integrity. You will never regret choosing to walk that path. It is the only way of life that leads to emotional, physical, and spiritual wholeness. May the Spirit of Jesus Christ guide you from now until the moment you greet Him on the other side. I hope to be there to witness that arrival.

There will be many temptations between now and then, of course. The primary danger will come from the intense longings that burn within each of us—many of them tugging us toward what is morally wrong. It has been my observation that whatever a person hungers for, Satan will appear to offer in exchange for a spiritual compromise. If illicit sex is your desire, it will eventually be within easy reach. Don't be surprised when you are beckoned by a willing partner. If your passion is for fame or power for its own sake, that prize will be promised (even if never delivered). Remember that Jesus was offered bread following His forty-day fast in the wilderness. He was promised power and glory after He had been contemplating His upcoming road to the cross. My point is that Satan uses our keenest appetites to tempt us.

Likewise, if you hunger and thirst for great wealth—beware! You are in a very precarious position. If you doubt it, look at 1 Timothy 6:9, which says, "People who want to get rich fall into temptation and a trap and into many foolish and harmful desires that plunge men into ruin and destruction." What incredible insight into the nature of mankind. If you watch people who care passionately about money, you'll observe that many of them are suckers for wild-eyed schemes and shady deals. They are always on the verge of a bonanza that seems to slip through their fingers. Instead of getting rich, they just get taken.

Not only are there pitfalls for those who seek riches, but the few who acquire them are in for a disappointment. They quickly learn that wealth will not satisfy their need for significance. No amount of money will do that. A popular bumper sticker reads "He who dies with the most toys wins." It's a lie. It should read "He who dies with the most toys dies anyway." I hope you will believe me when I say that a lifetime invested in the accumulation of things will have been wasted. There has to be a better reason for living than that.

These are a few of the fundamentals for young people like you who are determined, with the apostle Paul, to fight a good fight, finish the course, and keep the faith (2 Timothy 4:7). I can tell you that you will not be able to accomplish this in your own strength and dedication. But it will be achieved only by dependence on the One who has promised to walk with you every day of your life. Have a great journey!

QUESTION 342

In your book *Love Must Be Tough*, you suggested some ways unmarried people can build healthy relationships and not smother each other. Would you share those again? Would you apply the "tough love" principle to those of us who are not married? How does the issue of respect relate to our romantic relationships, and how can we build and preserve it?

The principles of loving toughness are the same for those who are single as for those who have been married for decades. There are circumstances, however, that are specific to the courtship period. Let me cite seventeen suggestions that will help you avoid the common pitfalls among those who are trying to win the heart of another.

1. Don't let a relationship move too fast in its infancy. The phrase "too hot not to cool down" has validity. Romantic affairs that begin in a frenzy frequently burn themselves out. Take it one step at a time.
2. Don't discuss your personal inadequacies and flaws in great detail when the relationship is new. No matter how warm and accepting your friend may be, any great revelation of low self-esteem or embarrassing weaknesses can be fatal when interpersonal "valleys" occur. And they will occur.
3. Remember that respect precedes love. Build it stone upon stone.
4. Don't call too often on the phone or give the other person an opportunity to get tired of you.
5. Don't be too quick to reveal your desire to get married—or that you think you've just found Mr. Wonderful or Miss Marvelous. If your partner has not arrived at the same conclusion, you'll throw him or her into panic.
6. Most important: Relationships are constantly being tested by cautious lovers who like to nibble at the bait before swallowing the hook. This testing procedure takes many forms, but it usually involves pulling backward from the other person to see what will happen. Perhaps a foolish fight is initiated. Maybe two weeks will pass without a phone call. Or sometimes flirtation occurs with a

rival. In each instance, the question being asked is "How important am I to you, and what would you do if you lost me?" An even more basic issue lies below that one. It wants to know "How free am I to leave if I want to?" It is incredibly important in these instances to appear poised, secure, and equally independent. Do not grasp the other person and beg for mercy. Some people remain single throughout life because they cannot resist the temptation to grovel when the test occurs.

7. Extending the same concept, keep in mind that virtually every dating relationship that continues for a year or more and seems to be moving toward marriage will be given the ultimate test. A breakup will occur, motivated by only one of the lovers. The rejected individual should know that their future together depends on the skill with which he or she handles that crisis. If the hurting individual can remain calm, the next two steps may be reconciliation and marriage. It often happens that way. If not, then no amount of pleading will change anything.

8. Do not depend entirely upon one another for the satisfaction of every emotional need. Maintain interests and activities outside that romantic relationship, even after marriage.

9. Guard against selfishness in your love affair. Neither the man nor the woman should do all the giving. I once broke up with a girl because she let me take her to nice places, bring her flowers, buy her lunch, etc. I wanted to do these things but expected her to reciprocate in some way. She didn't.

10. Beware of blindness to obvious warning signs that tell you that your potential husband or wife is basically disloyal, hateful, spiritually uncommitted, hooked on drugs or alcohol, given to selfishness, etc. Believe me, a bad marriage is far worse than the most lonely instance of singleness.

11. Beginning early in the dating relationship, treat the other person with respect and expect the same in return. A man should open doors for a woman on a formal evening; a woman should speak respectfully of her escort when in public, etc. If you don't preserve this respectful attitude when the foundations of marriage are being laid, it will be virtually impossible to construct them later.

12. Do not equate human worth with flawless beauty or handsomeness! If you require physical perfection in your mate, he or she may make the same demands of you. Neither of you will keep it for long. Don't let love escape you because of the false values of your culture.

13. If genuine love has escaped you thus far, don't begin believing "no one would ever want me." That is a deadly trap that can destroy you emotionally! Millions of people are looking for someone to love. The problem is finding one another!

14. Regardless of how brilliant the love affair has been, take time to "check your assumptions" with your partner before committing yourself to marriage. It is surprising how often men and women plunge toward matrimony without ever becoming aware of major differences in expectation between them.

15. Sexual familiarity can be deadly to a relationship. In addition to the many moral, spiritual, and physical reasons for remaining virgins until marriage, there are numerous psychological and interpersonal advantages as well. Though it's an old-fashioned notion, perhaps, it is still true that men do not respect "easy" women and often become bored with those who have held nothing in reserve. Likewise, women often disrespect men who have only one thing on their minds. Both sexes need to remember how to use a very ancient word. It's pronounced *"no!"*

16. Country singer Tom T. Hall wrote a song in which he revealed an understanding of the concept we have been describing. His lyric read, "If you hold love too loosely then it flies away; if you hold love too tightly, it'll die. It's one of the mysteries of life."[144] Hall's observation is accurate. If the commitment between a man and a woman is given insufficient importance in their lives, it will wither like a plant without water. The whole world knows that much. But fewer lovers seem to realize that extreme dependency can be just as deadly to a love affair. It has been said that the person who needs the other least will normally be in control of the relationship. I believe that to be true.

17. There is nothing about marriage that eliminates the basic need for freedom and respect in romantic interactions. Keep the mystery and the dignity in your relationship. If the other partner begins to

feel trapped and withdraws for a time, grant him or her some space and pull back yourself. Do not build a cage around that person. Instead, release your grip with confidence while never appeasing immorality or destructive behavior.

These are the basics of the "love must be tough" concept. I could list another hundred suggestions, but you get the idea.

QUESTION 343

I am nineteen years old, and I'm proud to say that I'm still a virgin. I plan to stay that way until I get married, even though it is difficult to control what I feel. Do you have any suggestions that will help people like me to be moral in a very immoral world? I mean, almost everyone I know is sleeping with somebody, and I don't want to do that. Still, I need help to do what is right. What do you suggest?

I admire your determination to save yourself for your future spouse. You will never regret that decision. But in order to stick to it, you need to understand that sex is progressive in nature. The relationship between a man and a woman naturally becomes more intimate as they spend time together.

In the early days they may be content to hold hands or have an occasional good-night kiss. But from that beginning, they typically become more physical week by week until they find themselves in bed. That's just the power of sex in our lives.

I read one study that indicated that when a couple has been together for approximately three hundred hours, even most of those who are trying to be moral will do things they didn't intend originally.[145] They may not even realize that is where the relationship is headed until it happens.

What I'm saying is that the decision not to have sexual intercourse should be made long before the opportunity presents itself. Steps can then be taken to slow down the natural progression before it gets started. It doesn't work to allow all the preliminary intimacies and then hope to stop the progression just short of intercourse. Very few people have the willpower to do that.

Instead, a very early decision must be made to delay kissing, fondling, caressing, and other forms of physical contact. Failure to put the relationship on a slower timetable may result in an act that was never intended in the first place.

Another important principle is to avoid the circumstances where compromise is likely. A girl who wants to preserve her virginity should not find herself in a house or dorm room alone with someone to whom she is attracted. Nor should she single-date with someone she has no reason to trust. A guy who wants to be moral should stay away from the girl he knows would go to bed with him. Remember the words of Solomon to his son: "Keep to a path far from her, do not go near the door of her house" (Proverbs 5:8).

I know this advice sounds very narrow in a day when virginity is mocked and chastity is considered old-fashioned. But I don't apologize for it. The Scriptures are eternal, and God's standards of right and wrong do not change with the whims of culture. He will honor and help those who are trying to follow His commandments. In fact, the apostle Paul said, "He will not let you be tempted beyond what you can bear" (1 Corinthians 10:13). Hold that promise and continue to use your head. You'll be glad you did.

QUESTION 344

I have plenty of reasons to resent my parents. They've never abused me or anything like that, but they do such stupid things. My dad's work has been the only thing he cared about. My mom is a perpetual nagger. How can I respect people like that?

Let's assume that your complaints against your parents are valid—that they didn't do a very good job of raising you and your siblings. Nevertheless, I urge you to cut them some slack. First, because the Scriptures command children to respect their parents. It says nothing about whether or not they are worthy of respect. Second, because you'll learn someday just how hard it is to be a good parent. Even those who are highly motivated to do the job right often make a mess of things.

Why? Because children are infinitely complex. There is no formula that works in every case. In fact, I believe it is more difficult to raise children now than ever before. Be assured that you will not do the job perfectly, either. Someday, if you are blessed with children, one or more of them will blame you for your failures, just as you may have criticized your parents.

Let me share one more suggestion with you and others who have been angry at their parents. Given the brevity of life and the temporary nature of all human relationships, can you find it within your hearts to forgive them? Maybe my own experience will be relevant to you. My mother closed her eyes for the last time on June 26, 1988, and went to be with the Lord. She had been so vibrant—so important to each member of our family. I couldn't imagine life without her just a few years earlier. But time passed so quickly, and before we knew it, she had grown old and sick and incompetent. This human experience is like that. In just a brief moment, it seems, our fleeting days are gone, and as King David said, "The place thereof shall know it no more" (Psalm 103:16, KJV).

As I sat at the memorial service for my good mother, I was flooded with memories and a profound sense of loss. But there was not the slightest hint of regret, remorse, or guilt. There were no hurtful words I wished I could have taken back. There were no brawls—no prolonged conflicts—that remained unresolved between my parents and me. Why not? Was I a perfect son born to flawless parents? Of course not. But in 1962, when Shirley and I had been married two years and I was twenty-six years old, I remember saying to Shirley, "Our parents will not always be with us. I see now the incredible brevity of life that will someday take them from us. We must keep that in mind as we live out our daily lives. I want to respond to both sets of parents in such a way that we will have no regrets after they are gone. This is what I believe the Lord wants of us."

Again, to those of you who are in need of this advice, I urge you not to throw away these good, healthy times. Your parents will not always be there for you. Please think about what I have written and be careful not to create bitter memories that will hang above you when the record is in the books. No conflict is worth letting that happen.

QUESTION 345

My dad was an alcoholic, and my mother is a compulsive gambler. I've seen how those problems have messed up my family, and I don't want to make the same mistakes. How can I be sure I won't get hooked on something destructive?

You will not have to deal with addictions if you never open the door to those behaviors in the first place. At the risk of sounding self-congratulatory, my experience might be helpful in this regard. I've not permitted myself to even sample certain vices, knowing that I can never become addicted to something that is not granted a toehold in my life. For example, Shirley and I have gone to Las Vegas without ever putting a nickel in a slot machine, even though two rolls of coins were provided with the hotel reservations. I refused to use them for the same reason the hotel manager gave them to me. He knew if he could open the door to insignificant gambling I might walk through it. But I wouldn't play his game.

Likewise, we have been lifelong teetotalers with regard to alcohol. I know many people enjoy wine with their meals—and that is entirely their business. But we will never have a problem with alcohol if we take an absolutist position in reference to it. I am not so arrogant as to recommend that others do as we have done, but there would be fewer victims of addiction if they did.

As a member of the Attorney General's Commission on Pornography, I listened to testimony by those who thought they could jazz up their sex lives by viewing obscene materials. They discovered that the stuff they were watching quickly seemed tame and even boring. That led them to seek racier, ever more violent depictions. And then they journeyed down the road toward harder and more violent materials. For some, not all, it became an obsession that filled their world with perversion and sickness. They lusted after sex with animals, molestation of children, urinating and defecation, sadomasochism, mutilation of genitals, and incest. And how did it happen? The door was quietly opened to obscenity, and a monster came charging out.

My point is this: The restrictions and commandments of Scripture were designed to protect us from evil. Though it is difficult to believe when we are young, it is true that "the wages of sin is death" (Romans 6:23). If we keep our lives clean and do not permit ourselves to toy with evil, the addictions that have ravaged humanity can never touch us. It's a very old-fashioned idea. I still believe in it.

19
Building Self-Confidence in Children and Teens

QUESTION 346

You have said that children and young people are experiencing an epidemic of self-doubt and feelings of low self-esteem. Why do you think this is true?

It has resulted, in part, from an unjust system of evaluating human worth now prevalent in our society. Not everyone is seen as worthy; not everyone is accepted. Instead, we reserve our praise and admiration for those who have been blessed from birth with the characteristics we value most highly. It is a vicious system, and we, as parents, must counterbalance its impact.

At the top of the list of the most highly respected and valued attributes in our culture is physical attractiveness. Those who happen to have it are often honored and even feared; those who do not may be disrespected and rejected through no fault of their own. This measure of human worth is evident from the earliest moments of life, when an attractive infant is considered more valuable than a homely one. For this reason, it is not uncommon for a mother to be depressed shortly after the birth of her first baby. She had hoped to give birth to a beautiful six-week-old Gerber baby, having four front teeth and rosy, pink cheeks. Instead, they hand her a red, toothless, bald, prune-faced, screaming little individual who isn't exactly what Mom expected.

As the child grows, his or her value as a person will be assessed not only by parents but also by those outside the home. Beauty contests offering scholarships and prizes for gorgeous babies are now common, as if the attractive child didn't already have enough advantages in life. What a distorted system for evaluating human worth. As author George Orwell has written, "All [people] are equal, but some [people] are more equal than others."[146] The real tragedy today is how often this statement is proven true in the lives of our children.

QUESTION 347

What are the prospects for the very pretty or handsome child? Does he or she usually have smooth sailing all the way?

Well, that child has some remarkable advantages, as I have described. She is much more likely to accept herself and enjoy the benefits of self-confidence. However, she also faces some unique problems that the homely child never experiences. Beauty in our society is power, and power can be dangerous in immature hands. A fourteen-year-old young woman, for example, who is prematurely curved and rounded in all the right places may be pursued vigorously by males who would exploit her beauty. As she becomes more conscious of her flirtatious power, she is sometimes urged toward promiscuity. Furthermore, women who have been coveted physically since early childhood often become bitter and disillusioned as they age. I'm thinking particularly of Hollywood's most glamorous sex queens, such as Marilyn Monroe and Brigitte Bardot, who had difficulty dealing with the depersonalization of body worship as the years passed.

Research also indicates some interesting consequences in regard to marital stability for the "beautiful people." In one important study, the more attractive college girls were found to be less happily married twenty-five years later.[147] It is apparently difficult to reserve the "power" of sex for one mate, ignoring the ego gratification that awaits outside the marriage bonds. And finally, the more attractive a person is in his or her youth, the more painful is the aging process.

My point is this: The measurement of worth on a scale of beauty is wrong, often damaging to the haves and have-nots.

QUESTION 348

If beauty is the most important attribute in determining personal worth in this culture, what is in second place?

It is intelligence as expressed in scholastic aptitude. When the birth of a firstborn child is imminent, his parents pray that he will be normal . . . that is, "average." But from that moment on, average will not be good enough. Their child must excel. He must succeed. He must triumph. He must be the first of his age to walk or talk or ride a tricycle. He must earn a stunning report card and amaze his teachers with his wit and wisdom. He must do well in Little League, and later he must be a track star or first-chair trombone player or the valedictorian. His sister must be a cheerleader or the senior-class president or the soloist or the best pupil in her advanced-placement class.

Throughout the formative years of childhood, parents give their kids the same message day after day: "We're counting on you to do something fantastic. Now don't disappoint us!" The hopes, dreams, and ambitions of an entire family sometimes rest on the shoulders of an immature child. And in this atmosphere of fierce competition, the parent who produces an intellectually gifted child is clearly holding the winning sweepstakes ticket.

Unfortunately, exceptional children are just that—exceptions. Seldom does a five-year-old memorize the King James Version of the Bible or play chess blindfolded or compose symphonies in the Mozart manner. To the contrary, the vast majority of our children are not dazzlingly brilliant, extremely witty, highly coordinated, tremendously talented, or universally popular! They are just plain kids with oversized needs to be loved and accepted as they are. Thus, the stage is set for unrealistic pressure on the younger generation and considerable disappointment for their parents.

371

QUESTION 349

I made a little offhanded comment the other day about my daughter's hair, and she cried for an hour. I didn't mean to hurt her. I guess she's just more sensitive than I thought. Do I have to walk on eggshells around her?

You should always be mindful that your daughter is listening to what you say about her and that she's "reading" the subtle attitudes that you might like to conceal. Kids are extremely sensitive to their parents' love and respect. That's why adults must learn to guard what they say in their presence. Many times I have been consulted by a mother regarding a particular problem her child is having. As Mom describes the details of the boy or girl's problems, I notice that the subject of all this conversation is standing about a yard behind her. His ears are ten feet tall as he listens to a candid description of all his faults. The child may remember that conversation for a lifetime.

Parents often inadvertently convey disrespect to a child whom they genuinely love. For example, Mom may become tense and nervous when little Jimmy speaks to guests or outsiders. She butts in to explain what he is trying to say or laughs nervously when his remarks sound foolish. When someone asks him a direct question, she interrupts and answers for him. She reveals her frustration when she is trying to comb her daughter's hair or make her "look nice" for an important event. The daughter knows Mom thinks it is an impossible assignment. If the daughter is to spend a weekend away from the family, the mother gives her an extended lecture on how to avoid making a fool of herself. These subtle behaviors are signals to the child that the mother doesn't trust him or her with her image and that he or she must be supervised closely to avoid embarrassing the whole family. He or she reads disrespect in her manner, though it is framed in genuine love.

The first step in building a strong self-concept in your daughter is to be very careful what you say and do in her presence. Be particularly cautious about the matters of physical attractiveness and intelligence. These are two primary "soft spots" where boys and girls are most vulnerable.

QUESTION 350

How can parents prepare their younger children for the assault on self-esteem that is almost certain to come in adolescence? That was a tough time for me, and I want it to be easier for my kids.

Well, one important approach is to teach boys and girls valuable skills with which they can compensate in years to come. They can benefit from learning something that will serve as the centerpiece of their self-concept during the difficult years. This would include learning about basketball, tennis, electronics, art, music, or even raising rabbits for fun and profit. It's not so much what you teach your child. The key is that he or she learns something with which to feel good when the whole world seems to be saying, "Who are you and what is your significance as a human being?"

The teenager who has no answer to those questions is left unprotected at a very vulnerable time of life. Developing and honing skills with which to compensate may be one of the most valuable contributions parents can make during the elementary school years. It may even be worth requiring your carefree kid to take lessons, practice, compete, and learn something he or she will not fully appreciate for a few more years.

QUESTION 351

You make a convincing case that beauty and brains are false values that demoralize kids who don't think they measure up. But what values do you suggest that I teach to my children?

I believe the most valuable contribution a parent can make to his child is to instill in him or her a genuine faith in Jesus Christ. What greater sense of self-worth could there be than knowing that the Creator of the universe is acquainted with me personally? That He values me more than the possessions of the entire world; that He understands my fears and my anxieties; that He reaches out to me in immeasurable love when no one else cares; that He actually gave His life for me; that He can turn my liabilities into assets and my emptiness into fullness; that a better life follows this one, where the present handicaps and inadequacies will all be eliminated—where earthly pain and suffering will be no more than a dim memory! What a beautiful philosophy with which to "clothe" your tender child. What a fantastic message of hope and encouragement for the broken teenager who has been crushed by life's circumstances. This is true self-worth at its richest, dependent not on the whims of birth or social judgment or the cult of the superchild but on divine decree.

Q UESTION 352

My two kids are as different as night and day. You'd never even know they were born to the same parents. One of them is having trouble in school, and the other is something of a superstar. I'm very worried about the one boy. Do some kids start out doing poorly and then catch fire?

Thank goodness they often do. Let me give you an encouraging illustration. Several years ago I attended a wedding ceremony in a beautiful garden setting, and I came away with some thoughts about parents who are raising a child like yours.

After the minister had instructed the groom to kiss the bride on that day, approximately 150 colorful, helium-filled balloons were released into the blue California sky. Within a few seconds the balloons were just scattered all across the heavens, some of them rising hundreds of feet overhead and others cruising toward the horizon. A few balloons struggled to clear the upper branches of the trees while the show-offs became mere pinpoints of color on their journey to the sky.

How interesting, I thought, and how symbolic of children. Let's face it. Some boys and girls seem to be born with more helium than others. They catch all the right breezes, and they soar effortlessly to the heights, while others wobble dangerously close to the trees. Their frantic folks run along underneath, huffing and puffing to keep them airborne. It is an exhausting experience.

In short, I have a word of encouragement to you and all the parents

374

of low-flying kids. Sometimes the child who has the greatest trouble getting off the ground eventually soars to the highest heights. That's why I urge you as parents not to look too quickly for the person your child will become.

QUESTION 353

Our fifteen-year-old daughter is getting some rough treat-ment at the hands of her peers these days. She wasn't invited to a party given by a girl who had been her best friend, and she cried herself to sleep that night. It's just tearing me up to see her hurt like this. Will this experience leave lifelong scars on her mind?

It's all a matter of degree. Most teenagers experience a measure of rejection like your daughter is experiencing. They typically roll with the punches and eventually get beyond the discomfort. Others, however, are wounded for life by the rejection of those adolescent experiences. I suggest you give your daughter plenty of emotional support, keep her talking, and do what you can to help her cope. I think she'll get her legs under her when the pressure of these years has passed.

Let me address the larger issue here. When we see our children struggling with the teen experience or other frustrations, it's natural to wish we could sweep aside the problems and obstacles. Sometimes we have to be reminded that the human personality grows through adversity. "No pain, no gain," as they say. Those who have conquered their problems are more secure than those who have never faced them.

I learned the value of hard times from my own experience. During my seventh and eighth grades, I lived through the most painful years of my life. I found myself in a social cross fire that gave rise to intense feelings of inferiority and doubt. And yet those two years have contrib-uted more positive qualities to my adult personality than any other span of my life. What I learned through that experience is still useful to me today.

Though it may be hard to accept now, your child needs the minor setbacks and disappointments that come her way. How can she learn to cope with problems and frustrations if her early experiences are totally without trial? Nature tells us this is true. A tree that's planted in a rain forest is never forced to extend its roots downward in search of water. Consequently, it remains poorly anchored and can be toppled by even a moderate wind. By contrast, a mesquite tree that's planted in a dry desert is threatened by its hostile environment. It can only survive by sending its roots down thirty feet or more into the earth, seeking cool water. But through this adaptation to an arid land, the well-rooted tree becomes strong and steady against all assailants.

Our children are like the two trees in some ways. Those who have learned to conquer their problems are better anchored than those who have never faced them.

Our task as parents, then, is not to eliminate every challenge for our children but to serve as a confident ally on their behalf, encouraging them when they are distressed, intervening when the threats are overwhelming, and above all, giving them the tools they need to overcome the obstacles.

QUESTION 354

I've read that you have recommended that parents not give little girls Barbie dolls. They seem harmless to me. Why do you oppose them?

First I should tell you that my daughter played with Barbie for years, despite my views on this subject. My objection was more passive and philosophical than absolute. Nevertheless, let me tell you why I wish Barbie would go away. There could be no better method for teaching the worship of beauty and materialism than is done with these dolls. If we intentionally sought to drill our little girls on the necessity of growing up rich and gorgeous, we could do no better than has already been done. Did you ever see an ugly Barbie doll? Has she ever had even the slightest imperfection? Of course not! She oozes femininity and sex appeal. Her hair is thick and gleaming—loaded with "body" (whatever in the world that is). Her long, thin legs, curvaceous bust, and delicate feet are absolutely perfect. Her airbrushed skin is without flaw or blemish (except for a little statement on her bottom that she was "Made in Hong Kong"). She never gets pimples or blackheads, and there is not an ounce of fat on her pink body. Such an idealized model creates an emotional time bomb set to explode the moment a real live thirteen-year-old takes her first long look in the mirror. No doubt about it—Barbie she ain't!

Yet it is not the physical perfection of these Barbie dolls (and their many competitors) that concerns me most; of much greater harm are the teenage games that they inspire. Instead of three- and four-year-old boys and girls playing with stuffed animals, balls, cars, trucks, model horses, and the traditional memorabilia of childhood, they are learning to fantasize about life as an adolescent. Ken and Barbie go on dates, learn to dance, drive sports cars, get suntans, take camping trips, exchange marriage vows, and have babies (hopefully in that order). The entire adolescent culture, with its emphasis on sexual awareness, is illustrated to tiny little girls who ought to be thinking about more childish things. This places our children on an unnatural timetable likely to reach the peak of sexual interest several years before it is due—with all the obvious implications for their social and emotional health.

QUESTION 355

Barbie isn't the only example of this adolescent influence in our culture, is it?

No, our children are saturated with commercial stuff that has the same impact. More and more, we see adolescent clothes, attitudes, and values being marketed to younger and younger children. And rock and rap music, with adolescent and adult themes, is finding eager listeners among the very young.

I believe it is desirable to postpone the adolescent experience until it is summoned by the happy hormones. Therefore, I strongly recommend that parents screen the influences to which their children are exposed, keeping activities appropriate for each age. While we can't isolate our kids from the world as it is, we don't have to turn our babies into teenyboppers.

QUESTION 356

Does the middle child really have greater adaptive problems than his or her siblings?

The middle child does sometimes find it more difficult to establish his or her identity within the family. She enjoys neither the status of the eldest nor the attention given to the baby. Furthermore, she is likely to be born at a busy period in the life of her parents, especially her mother. Then, during her preschool years, her precious territory is invaded by a cute little newborn who steals Mama from her. Is it any wonder that she often asks, "Who am I, and where is my place in life?"

QUESTION 357

What can I do to help my middle child figure out who she is?

Parents should take steps to ensure the identity of *all* their children but especially the child in the middle. That can be accomplished by relating to each boy or girl as an individual, rather than merely as a member of the group. Let me offer two suggestions that will illustrate what I mean.

1. It is meaningful for Dad to "date" each child, one at a time, every four or five weeks. The other kids should not be told where they are going until it is revealed by the boy or girl in retrospect. They can play miniature golf, go bowling, play basketball, eat tacos or pizza, or visit a skating rink. The choice should be made by the child whose turn has arrived.
2. Ask each offspring to design his or her own flag, which can be sewn in canvas or cloth. That flag is then flown in the front yard on the child's "special" days, including birthdays, after he has received an A in school, when he scores a goal in soccer or hits a home run in baseball, and so forth.

There are other ways to accomplish the same purpose. The target, again, is to plan activities that emphasize one child's individuality apart from his identity within the group.

QUESTION 358

My son is an outstanding gymnast. His high school coach says he has more natural ability than anyone he's ever seen. Yet when he is being judged in a competitive meet, he does terribly! Why does he fail during the most important moments?

If your son thinks of himself as a failure, his performance will probably match his low self-image when the chips are down. In the same way, there are many excellent golfers on the PGA tour who make a satisfactory living in tournament play, but they never win. They may even place as high as second, third, sixth, or tenth. Whenever it looks like they might come in first, however, they "choke" at the last minute, and someone else wins. It is not that they want to fail; rather, they can't conceive of themselves as winners, and their performance merely reflects this image.

I once spoke with a concert pianist with outstanding talent who has resolved never to play in public again. She knows she is blessed with remarkable talent but believes she is a loser in every other regard. Consequently, when she plays the piano on stage, her mistakes and errors creep into her performance. Each time this mortifying experience has occurred, she has become more convinced of her own unworthiness in every area. She has now withdrawn into the secluded, quiet, talentless world of have-nots.

A person's self-concept is instrumental in determining those who are "winners" and those who see themselves as "losers." Professional tennis players call this characteristic "tournament toughness," but it is really nothing more than confidence in action.

QUESTION 359

Is this true of mental ability, too? My twelve-year-old was asked to recite a poem at a school function the other day, and he went completely blank in front of the crowd. I know he knew the poem perfectly because he said it dozens of times at

home. He's a bright child, but he's had this trouble before. Why does his mind "turn off" when he's under pressure?

It will be helpful to understand an important characteristic of intellectual functioning. Your son's self-confidence, or the lack of it, actually affects the way his brain operates. All of us have experienced the frustration of mental "blocking," which you described. This occurs when a name or fact or idea just won't surface to the conscious mind, even though we know it is recorded in the memory. Or suppose we are about to speak to an antagonistic group and our mind suddenly goes blank. This kind of blocking usually occurs (1) when social pressure is great, and (2) when self-confidence is low. Why? Because emotions affect the efficiency of the human brain. Unlike a computer, our mental apparatus only functions properly when a delicate biochemical balance exists between the neural cells. This substance makes it possible for a cell to "fire" its electrochemical charge across the gap (synapse) to another cell. It is now known that a sudden emotional reaction can instantly change the nature of that biochemistry, interfering with the impulse. This blockage prevents the electrical charge from being relayed, and the thought is never generated. This mechanism has profound implications for human behavior; for example, a child who feels inferior and intellectually inadequate often does not even make use of the mental power with which he has been endowed. His lack of confidence produces a disrupting mental inefficiency, and the two factors go around in an endless cycle of defeat. This is seemingly what happened to your son when he "forgot" the poem.

QUESTION 360

What can I do to help him?

Actually, it is not unusual for a twelve-year-old to "choke" in front of a crowd. I once stood before three hundred fellow teenagers with my words stuck in my throat and my mind totally out to lunch. It was a painful experience, but time gradually erased its impact. As your child matures, he will probably overcome the problem if he can experience a few successes to build his confidence. Anything that raises self-esteem will reduce the frequency of mental blocking for children and adults alike.

Q UESTION 361

As an elementary school teacher, I am bothered by what I see my students doing to each other every day. They can be brutal—especially to the child who is a little different. I'm not sure what my role should be. I feel I should step in to defend the underdog, but other teachers say kids should learn to work out their own problems. What do you think?

As a former teacher, I am very familiar with the cruelty of which you speak. Every classroom has a few boys and girls at the bottom of the social hierarchy who are subjected to frequent ridicule. Their ranks include those who are physically unattractive, intellectually challenged, uncoordinated, boys who are very small or effeminate, girls who are taller than all the boys, the foreign child, the stutterer, etc. Anyone who is different is an easy mark for the wolf pack. What is most disturbing is that adults often feel no obligation to come to the aid of these vulnerable children.

I've heard the argument that says, "Kids will be kids—adults should stay out of the conflict and let the children settle it themselves." I disagree emphatically. It is almost criminal for an adult to stand by passively while a defenseless boy or girl is shredded by peers. The damage inflicted in those moments can reverberate for a lifetime.

Some years ago a woman told me about her experience as a room mother for her daughter's fourth-grade class. She visited the classroom on Valentine's Day to assist the teacher with the traditional party on that holiday. Valentine's Day can be the most painful day of the year for an unpopular child. Every student counts the number of valentines he or she is given, which becomes a direct measure of social worth.

This mother said the teacher then announced that the class was going to play a game that required the formation of boy-girl teams. That was her first mistake, since fourth graders have not yet experienced the happy hormones that draw the sexes together. The moment

381

the teacher instructed the students to select a partner, all the boys immediately laughed and pointed at the homeliest and least-respected girl in the room. She was overweight, had protruding teeth, and was too withdrawn even to look anyone in the eye.

"Don't put us with Nancy," they all said in mock terror. "Anybody but Nancy! She'll give us a disease! Ugh! Spare us from Nasty Nancy." The mother waited for the teacher (a strong disciplinarian) to rush to the aid of the beleaguered little girl. But nothing was said to the insulting boys. Instead, the teacher left Nancy to cope with that painful situation in solitude.

Ridicule by one's own sex is distressing, but rejection by the opposite sex is like taking a hatchet to the self-concept. What could this devastated child say in reply? How does an overweight fourth-grade girl defend herself against nine aggressive boys? What response could she make but to blush in mortification and slide foolishly into her chair? This child, whom God loves more than the possessions of the entire world, will never forget that moment (or the teacher who abandoned her in this time of need).

I say again to teachers: Defend the most defenseless child in your classroom. We can do no less.

Q UESTION 362

What would you have done if you had been the teacher on that day?

Those mocking, joking boys would have had a fight on their hands, I promise you that. Of course, it would have been better if the embarrassment could have been prevented by discussing the feelings of others from the first day of school. But if the conflict occurred as described, with Nancy suddenly being humiliated for everyone to see, I would have thrown the full weight of my authority and respect on her side of the battle.

My spontaneous response would have carried this general theme: "Wait just a minute! By what right do any of you boys say such mean, unkind things to Nancy? I want to know which of you is so perfect that the rest of us couldn't make fun of you in some way. I know you all very well. I know about your homes and your school records and some of your personal secrets. Would you like me to share them with the class, so we can all laugh at you the way you just did at Nancy? I could do it! I could make you want to crawl into a hole and disappear. But listen to me! You need not fear. I will never embarrass you in that way. Why not? Because it hurts to be laughed at by your friends. It hurts even more than a stubbed toe or a cut finger or a bee sting.

"I want to ask those of you who were having such a good time a few minutes ago: Have you ever had a group of students make fun of you in the same way? If you haven't, then brace yourself. Someday it will happen to you, too. Eventually you will say something foolish—something that will cause everyone to point at you and laugh in your face. And when it happens, I want you to remember what happened today."

Then addressing the entire class: "Let's make sure that we learn something important from what took place here this afternoon. First, we will *not* be mean to each other in this class. We will laugh together when things are funny, but we will not do it by making one person feel bad. Second, I will never intentionally embarrass anyone in this class. You can count on that. Each of you is a child of God. You were made with His loving hands, and He has said that we all have equal worth as human beings. This means that Susie is neither better nor worse than Wade or Mary or Brent. Sometimes I think maybe you believe a few of you are more important than others. It isn't true. Every one of you is priceless to God, and each of you will live forever in eternity. That's how valuable you are. God loves every boy and girl in this room, and because of that, I love every one of you. He wants us to be kind to other people, and we're going to be practicing that kindness through the rest of this year."

When a strong, loving teacher comes to the aid of the least-respected child in the class, as I've described, something dramatic occurs in the emotional climate of the room. Every child seems to utter an audible sigh of relief. The same thought is bouncing around in many little heads: "If Nancy is safe from ridicule—even Nancy—then I must be safe too." You see, by defending the least-popular child in the room, a teacher is demonstrating (1) that she has no "pets," (2) that she respects everyone, (3) that she will fight for anyone who is being treated unjustly. Those are three virtues that children value highly and that contribute to mental health.

And may I suggest to parents: Defend the underdog in your neighborhood. Let it be known that you have the confidence to speak for the outcast. Explain this philosophy to your neighbors, and try to create an emotional harbor for the little children whose ship has been threatened by a storm of rejection. Don't be afraid to exercise leadership on behalf of a youngster who is being mauled. There is no more worthy investment of your time and energy.

Q UESTION 363

Can boys and girls be taught to treat each other with respect? That seems like a tough assignment.

They certainly can! Young people are naturally more sensitive and empathetic than adults. Their viciousness is a learned response, resulting from the highly competitive and hostile world in which they live—a world we have allowed to develop. They are destructive to the weak and lowly because we adults haven't bothered to teach them to feel for one another.

One of the values children cherish most is justice. They are uneasy in a world of injustice and abuse. Therefore, when we teach children respect for others by insisting on civility in our classrooms, we're laying a foundation for human kindness in the world of adulthood to come. It is a fundamental attitude that should be taught in every classroom and every home.

Q UESTION 364

Before our baby was born last month, our three-year-old daughter, April, was thrilled about having a new brother or sister. Now, however, she shows signs of jealousy, sucking her thumb sullenly when I nurse the baby and getting very loud and silly when friends drop by. Please suggest some ways I can ease her through this period of adjustment.

Your daughter is revealing a textbook reaction to the invasion that has occurred in her private kingdom. It is typical for such a preschooler to throw temper tantrums, wet the bed, suck her thumb, mess her pants, hold tightly to Mama, talk "baby talk," etc. Since the baby gets all the attention by being helpless, the older child will often try to "out-baby the baby"—behaving in immature ways from an earlier stage of development. That pattern seems to be occurring with your little girl. Here's what I would suggest:

1. Bring her feelings out in the open and help her verbalize them. When she is acting silly in front of adults, take her in your arms and say, "What's the matter, April? Do you need some attention today?" Gradually, a child can be taught to use similar words when she feels excluded or rejected. "I need some attention, Dad. Will you play with me?" By verbalizing her feelings, you also help her understand herself better.
2. Don't let infantile behavior succeed. If she cries when the baby-sitter arrives, leave her anyway. A temper tantrum can be greeted by firmness. However, reveal little anger and displeasure, remembering that the entire episode is motivated by a threat to your love.
3. Meet her needs in ways that grant status to her for being older. Take her to the park, making it clear that the baby is too little to go; talk "up" to her about the things she can do that the baby can't—she can use the bathroom instead of her pants, for example. Let her help take care of the baby so she will feel she is part of the family process.

Beyond these corrective steps, give your daughter some time to adjust to her new situation. Even though it stresses her somewhat today, she should profit from the realization that she does not sit at the center of the universe.

QUESTION 365

My thirteen-year-old daughter is still built like a boy, but she is insisting that I buy her a bra. Believe me, she has no need

for it, and the only reason she wants one is because most of her friends do. Should I give in?

Your straight-and-narrow daughter needs a bra to be like her friends, to compete, to avoid ridicule, and to feel like a woman. Those are excellent reasons. I think you should buy her a bra today.

QUESTION 366

Our teenage daughter has become extremely modest in recent months, demanding that even her sisters leave her room when she's dressing. I think this is silly, don't you?

No, I would suggest that you honor her requests for privacy. Her sensitivity is probably caused by an awareness that her body is changing, and she is embarrassed by recent developments (or the lack of them). This is likely to be a temporary phase, and you should not oppose her in it.

QUESTION 367

How do you feel about children wearing uniforms to school? How about schools having other dress codes and clothing requirements?

I rather like the idea of school uniforms because it solves the problem of competition between the haves and have-nots. It also eliminates the provocative clothing that some kids like to wear. But there is a larger issue here. I think it is extremely important for children to be taught adherence to standards that relate to discipline and self-control. In the 1960s, the courts began ruling against educators' efforts to govern hair length, suggestive messages on T-shirts, and other aspects of personal appearance. While these fashion statements were not terribly important in themselves, the impact of the judicial rulings was significant. It is a mistake to shield children from reasonable rules—to place no demands on their behavior. How inaccurate is the belief that self-control is maximized in an environment that places no obligations on children. How foolish is the assumption that self-discipline is a product of self-indulgence. Reasonable standards of conduct are an important part of an educational system, in my view. School uniforms might be a part of such standards.

QUESTION 368

Just how much opportunity do parents have to remake the personalities of their children? Can they change characteristics that they dislike? My son is painfully shy, and I'd like him to be strong and assertive. Can we redesign him?

You can teach new attitudes and modify some behavioral patterns, but you will not be able to redesign the basic personality with which your child was born. Some characteristics are genetically programmed, and they will always be there. For example, some kids appear to be born to lead, and others seem to be made to follow. And that fact can be a cause of concern for parents at times.

One mother told me that her compliant, easygoing child was being picked on and beaten up every day in nursery school. She urged him to defend himself, but it contradicted his very nature to even think about standing up to the bullies. Finally, his frustration became so great that he decided to heed his mother's advice. As they drove to school one day he said, "Mom, if those kids pick on me again today . . . I'm . . . I'm . . . I'm going to beat them up—slightly!"

How does a kid beat up someone slightly? I don't know, but it made perfect sense to this compliant lad.

Like you, some parents worry about an easygoing, passive child—especially if he's a boy. Followers in this society are sometimes less respected than aggressive leaders and may be seen as wimpy or spineless. And yet, the beauty of the human personality is seen in its marvelous uniqueness and complexity. There is a place for the wonderful variety of temperaments that find expression in children. After all, if two people are identical in every regard, it's obvious that one of them is unnecessary.

My advice to you is to accept, appreciate, and cultivate the personality with which your little child is born. He does not need to fit a preconceived mold. That youngster is, thankfully, one of a kind.

QUESTION 369

We're going to move to another state in a few months. I know it's going to be tough for Chuck and Marcie, who have so many little friends at school. How can I get them ready for life in a new city?

Moving to a new school or a new town can be an unpleasant experience for children, but there are some ways to make it easier for them.

Preparation and forethought are the keys. Educator Cheri Fuller recommends those who are about to relocate to call a family meeting to talk about what's going to happen. Begin to lay plans together. It's sad to say good-bye to good friends, and it's hard to make new ones. Try establishing pen pals for your children in the new school long before the move is to occur. Relationships can blossom through the mail so that the kids are not entirely unknown in the new location.

It's also helpful to create curiosity about the new city or neighborhood you're moving to. Write to the state tourist bureau or to the chamber of commerce and ask for brochures and maps. When your children begin to understand the adventure of moving, they may develop a more positive attitude toward leaving.[148]

A bit of preparation and a healthy dose of communication can help clear the way for a smoother journey to a new home.

QUESTION 370

We have always laughed a lot in our family, sometimes at each other. Is that good or bad?

It is healthy to be able to laugh together in a family. We ought to be able to tease and joke with each other without having to worry about getting an angry overreaction in response. But when the laughter is always at the expense of the most vulnerable member of the family, it can be destructive.

Even innocent humor is painful when it's the same child who is the object of ridicule. Unfortunately, that's the way it often happens. When one youngster has an embarrassing characteristic, such as bed-wetting or thumb-sucking or stuttering, the other members of the family should be encouraged to tread very softly on the exposed nerves thereabouts. And a child should never be ridiculed for his or her size, whether he's a small boy or a large girl.

This is the guiding principle: It's wise not to tease a child about the features that he or she is also defending outside the home. If that youngster is hearing about some obvious flaw all day long, he or she certainly doesn't need more flak from the family. And when that child asks for a joke to end, the request should be honored.

Being the butt of everyone's ridicule is a formula for lifelong resentment, and there's just nothing funny about that happening.

20
Making Marriage Work

Q UESTION 371

Do you think women need men more than men need women?
Which sex copes best when living without the other?

That very interesting question is addressed by the brilliant social commentator George Gilder in his classic book *Men and Marriage*.[149] Gilder acknowledges that men and women were designed for each other and often feel incomplete alone. He makes the point, however, that women do better without men than men without women. This is a reversal of conventional wisdom, which refers to single women derogatorily as "old maids," "unclaimed blessings," and worse. They are viewed as the most poorly adjusted and miserable people in society, and hence, are the subject of much ridicule.

Gilder disagrees with that assessment and says it is the unmarried male who is the most "out-of-pocket" socially. He is far more likely than unmarried females to be an alcoholic, a drug user, a convicted criminal, or a general ne'er-do-well. Landlords don't want to rent an apartment to him, insurance companies don't like to underwrite him, and loan companies are reluctant to loan him money. He drives too fast, he is more hot-tempered, and he tends to be impulsive. There are millions of exceptions to this pattern, of course, but the unmarried young man is at risk for many antisocial behaviors. And yes, he earns less money than even the single woman and is more likely to move aimlessly from job to job.

When a man marries and commits himself to a wife and children, however, most of his social liabilities disappear. He has a reason to live responsibly, work hard, and save for the future. Instead of pandering to his own sensual desires, he postpones gratification and sacrifices for those who depend on him. He becomes more future oriented. This "loose cannon" often becomes the "pillar of the community." This transition has been referred to historically as "settling down" after "sewing wild oats." I'm generalizing, of course, but the trend here is well documented by sociological research.

What a woman does for a man, then, is to harness the sexual energy that was unbridled and threatening to society—and focus it on protecting and providing for a family. This transformation is absolutely vital to the well-being of a culture. Gilder believes (and I agree) that society cannot survive the death of marriage. Without it, women lack the security to reproduce; illicit sex, abortion, and out-of-wedlock pregnancies flourish; children grow up in turmoil; drug abuse and alcoholism abound; legitimate businesses suffer; and peace-loving citizens find themselves besieged by violence and lawlessness.

Women need men, to be sure—but not quite like men need women.

QUESTION 372

As a woman, I'm interested in how your description of men and women applies to my relationship with my husband. Would I be correct in assuming that he needs me in ways that I may not have fully understood?

That is probably accurate. Men rarely reveal to women what they need except in a sexual sense. They may not even be aware of the dynamics themselves. To put it in its most simple terms, your husband needs you to help build his confidence. He is probably not as self-assured as he portrays himself to be, since men carefully guard their own insecurities. In general, however, they want to know they are *respected* and *honored* by their wives, just as their wives want to know that they are *loved.*

This vital role that women play is best illustrated by one of my favorite stories told by my friend E. V. Hill. Dr. Hill is a dynamic black minister and the senior pastor at Mount Zion Missionary Baptist Church in Los Angeles. He lost his precious wife, Jane, to cancer a few years ago. In one of the most moving messages I've ever heard, Dr. Hill spoke about Jane at her funeral and described the ways this "classy lady" made him a better man.

As a struggling young preacher, E. V. had trouble earning a living. That led him to invest the family's scarce resources, over Jane's objections, in the purchase of a service station. She felt that her husband lacked the time and expertise to oversee his investment, which proved to be accurate. Eventually, the station went broke, and E. V. lost his shirt in the deal.

It was a critical time in the life of this young man. He had failed at something important, and his wife would have been justified in saying, "I told you so." But Jane had an intuitive understanding of her husband's vulnerability. Thus, when E. V. called to tell her that he had lost the station, she said simply, "All right."

E. V. came home that night expecting his wife to be pouting over his foolish investment. Instead, she sat down with him and said, "I've been doing some figuring. I figure that you don't smoke and you don't drink. If you smoked and drank, you would have lost as much as you lost in the service station. So it's six in one hand and a half-dozen in the other. Let's forget it."

Jane could have shattered her husband's confidence at that delicate juncture. The male ego is surprisingly fragile, especially during times of failure and embarrassment. That's why E. V. needed to hear her say, "I still believe in you," and that is precisely the message she conveyed to him.

Shortly after the fiasco with the service station, E. V. came home one night and found the house dark. When he opened the door, he saw that Jane had prepared a candlelight dinner for two.

"What meaneth thou this?" he said with characteristic humor.

"Well," said Jane, "we're going to eat by candlelight tonight."

E. V. thought that was a great idea and went into the bathroom to wash his hands. He tried unsuccessfully to turn on the light. Then he felt his way into the bedroom and flipped another switch. Darkness prevailed. The young pastor went back to the dining room and asked Jane why the electricity was off. She began to cry.

"You've worked so hard, and we're trying," said Jane, "but it's pretty tough. I didn't have quite enough money to pay the light bill. I didn't want you to know about it, so I thought we would just eat by candle-light."

Dr. Hill described his wife's words with intense emotion: "She could have said, 'I've never been in this situation before. I was reared in the home of Dr. Caruthers, and we never had our lights cut off.' She could have broken my spirit; she could have ruined me; she could have demoralized me. But instead she said, 'Somehow or another we'll get these lights on. But let's eat tonight by candlelight.'"

E. V. continued, "She was my protector. [Some years ago] I received quite a few death threats, and one night I received a notice that I would be killed the next day. I woke up thankful to be alive. But I noticed that she was gone. I looked out the window, and my car was gone. I went outside and finally saw her driving up in her robe. I said, 'Where have you been?' She said, 'I . . . I . . . it just occurred to me that they [could have] put a bomb in that car last night, and if you had gotten in there you would have been blown away. So I got up and drove it. It's all right.'"

Jane Hill must have been an incredible lady. Of her many gifts and attributes, I am most impressed by her awareness of the role she played in strengthening and supporting her husband. E. V. Hill is a powerful Christian leader today. Who would have believed that he needed his wife to build and preserve his confidence? But that is the way men are made. Most of us are a little shaky inside, especially during early adulthood.

It was certainly true for me. Shirley has contributed immeasurably to my development as a man. I've said many times that she believed in me before I believed in myself and that her respect gave me the confidence with which to compete and strive and risk. Most of what I'm doing today can be traced to the love of this devoted woman who stood beside me saying, "I'm glad to be on your team."

You are in a position to do the same for your husband. Give him what he needs, and I'll bet he will return the favor.

QUESTION 373

I think I understand the principle you're describing, but summarize it for me please.

What I've tried to say is that the sexes are designed with highly specific—but quite different—psychological needs. Each is vulnerable to the other in unique ways. When reduced to the basics, women need men to be romantic, caring, and loving. Men need women to be respectful, supportive, and loyal. These are not primarily cultural influences that are learned in childhood, as some would have us believe. They are forces deeply rooted in the human personality. Indeed, the Creator observed Adam's loneliness in the Garden of Eden and said, "It is not good for the man to be alone" (Genesis 2:18). So He made Adam a helpmate, a partner, a love—designed to link with him emotionally and sexually. In so doing, He invented the family and gave it His blessing and ordination.

Unfortunately, millions of marriages are in trouble today because of an inability of the sexes to get along. Perhaps the fundamental problem is one of selfishness. We're so intent on satisfying our own desires that we fail to recognize the longings of our partners. The institution of marriage works best when we think less about ourselves and more about the ones we love. Again, the basic needs of each gender are straightforward. Women need to be loved, all year round, and men need to be respected, especially when the going gets tough.

That understanding is hardly new. In fact, it is ancient. Here's the way the apostle Paul described it nearly two thousand years ago: "Each one of you [men] must love his wife as he loves himself, and the wife must respect her husband" (Ephesians 5:33).

Love and respect. It's an unbeatable combination.

QUESTION 374

Is there an example of a culture in which marriage waned and brought on the consequences you described? Surely, if that hypothesis is accurate, we should have seen it somewhere.

Marital decline has occurred in many other cultures, but there is an example much closer to home. This is precisely what is happening in America's inner cities, where the family has largely disintegrated. More than 70 percent of all black children are born out of wedlock today and millions more are aborted.[150] Alcoholism, drug abuse, violence, and sexually transmitted disease are rampant. Social chaos reigns.

Why? What has gone wrong in these tragic areas? Gilder believes that the welfare system is responsible for a large portion of the problem. Government programs, however well intended, have effectively stripped men of their historic role as providers and protectors of their families. They are rendered obsolete. Who needs 'em? The government assumes most of the responsibility men were designed to carry. It puts bread on the table, a roof overhead, and social workers to intercede when children get into trouble. When maintenance problems occur in tenement buildings, a repairman is sent by Uncle Sam to fix it. The man's role in family life ends with impregnation. According to law, the woman's welfare checks stop coming if he doesn't get out and stay out. Thus, he is left with nothing to do but to stand on a street corner and look for trouble. His masculine energy becomes a destructive force rather than contributing to family stability and the welfare of children.[151]

It is unconscionable what we have done to African-American men who want and deserve a place of service in life and a meaningful role in the family. The inner city today gives us a classic example of what happens when marriage dies and when a matriarchal society disenfranchises and disrespects men.

QUESTION 375

I'm engaged to a beautiful and godly young lady. Spending the rest of my life with her is more than I could have hoped or dreamed for. Still, the possibility of divorce scares me. What can we do to avoid this tragedy?

That question has many answers, but let me give you what I consider to be the foundation—the cornerstone—on which your entire relationship should be constructed. It is the establishment of a Christ-centered home. When newlyweds are deeply committed to Jesus Christ, they enjoy many advantages over families with no spiritual dimension.

This means, among other things, that you and your fiancée need to develop a meaningful prayer life even before the wedding. Commit your home, your relationship, your future children if God grants them to you, and your entire lives to His purposes. My wife, Shirley, and I did that, and the time we have spent on our knees has been *the* stabilizing factor throughout nearly forty years of marriage. In good times, in hard times, in moments of anxiety, and in periods of praise we have shared this wonderful privilege of talking directly to our heavenly Father. What a concept! No appointment is needed to enter into His presence. We don't have to go through His subordinates or bribe His secretaries. He is simply there whenever we bow before Him. Some of the highlights of my relationship with Shirley have occurred in these quiet sessions we've shared with the Lord.

The second dimension to a Christ-centered home is a regular time set aside to study the Scriptures and apply them to everyday life. By reading this inspired and holy Word, we are given a "window" into the mind of the Lord. What an incredible resource! He created the vast reaches of the universe by simply speaking the heavens into being. This same God has also provided us with the secrets to healthy family life. After all, marriage and parenthood were *His* ideas, and He has told us how to live together in peace and harmony. Everything from handling money to sexual attitudes to the discipline of children is discussed in Scripture, with each prescription bearing the personal endorsement of the King of the universe. Why would anyone disregard this ultimate resource?

Finally, the Christian life lends stability to marriage because its principles and values naturally produce harmony between people. When put into action, Christian teaching emphasizes giving to others, self-discipline, obedience to divine commandments, conformity to the law, and love between a husband and wife. It is a shield against addictions to alcohol, pornography, gambling, materialism, infidelity, and other behaviors that could be damaging to the relationship.

Is it any wonder that a Christ-centered relationship is the ground floor of the stable family? If you and your fiancée build your marriage on that solid foundation, you will not face the bitter fruit of divorce. So go for it. My wife and I will be waiting for you at the finish line.

QUESTION 376

When my husband and I were dating, we could talk for hours about anything and everything. Now that we're married, we go out to dinner and have nothing to say to each other. What has gone wrong? Richard just keeps his thoughts to himself.

Millions of couples experience that transformation. They talk end-lessly before marriage but find themselves with little to say a few years after. When the courtship is over, some people find it very difficult to express their feelings openly and honestly. That is more true of men than women as a general rule. Research makes it clear that little girls are blessed with greater linguistic ability than little boys, and it remains a lifelong talent. Simply stated, she talks more than he. As an adult, she typically expresses her feelings and thoughts far better than her husband and is often irritated by his reticence. God may have given her fifty thousand words per day and her husband only twenty-five thousand. He comes home from work with 24,975 used up and merely grunts his way through the evening. He may descend into Monday-night football while his wife is dying to expend her remaining twenty-five thousand words.

Every knowledgeable marriage counselor knows that the inability or unwillingness of husbands to reveal their inner thoughts to their wives is one of the common complaints of women. A wife wants to know what her husband is thinking and what happened at his office and how he sees the children and, especially, how he feels about her. The husband, by contrast, finds some things better left unsaid. It is a classic struggle.

You and Richard can overcome the problem if you will get it out in the open and agree to work together on communication. It is a key to successful marriage.

QUESTION 377

Tell us how to do that. What can a husband and wife do to improve their communication if they have this classic problem?

The solution requires compromise that should begin, I believe, with the man. Under Mosaic law, a newlywed husband had a specific responsibility to "cheer up his wife which he hath taken" (Deuteronomy 24:5, KJV). That still sounds like a good idea. Time must be reserved for meaningful talks. Taking walks and going out to breakfast and riding bicycles on Saturday mornings are conversation inducers that help keep love alive. With a little effort, good communication can occur even in families like yours where the husband leans inward and the wife leans outward.

On the other hand, women must understand and accept the fact that some men cannot be what they want them to be. Masculine emotional structure makes it impossible for these men to comprehend the feelings and frustrations of another—particularly those occurring in the opposite sex. Obviously, women have to do some compromising too.

Q UESTION 378

My husband is somewhat insensitive to my needs, but I believe he is willing to do better if I can teach him how I am different from him. Can you help me communicate my needs to him effectively?

Perhaps I can begin by suggesting how not to handle this objective. Try not to resort to what I have called the "bludgeoning technique," which includes an endless barrage of nagging, pleading, scolding, complaining, and accusing. Avoid the impulse to say at the end of a tiring workday, "Won't you just put down that newspaper, George, and give me five minutes of your time? Five minutes—is that too much to ask? You never seem to care about my feelings, anyway. How long has it been since we went out for dinner? Even if we did, you'd probably take the newspaper along with you. I'll tell you, George, sometimes I think you don't care about me and the kids anymore. If just once—just once—you would show a little love and understanding, I would drop dead from sheer shock," etc., etc., etc.

That is not the way to get George's attention. It's like hitting him with a two-by-four, which is guaranteed to make him mad, silent, or both. Instead of yelling at him, you should look for opportunities to *teach* your husband during moments when he is most likely to be listening. That instruction requires the proper timing, setting, and manner to be effective. Let's look at those three ingredients.

1. *Timing.* Select a moment when your husband is typically more responsive and pleasant. That is most likely to be in the morning—perhaps on a Saturday, when his workday pressures are less. By all means, don't blunder into a depressing, angry diatribe when he is tired and hungry. Give your effort every opportunity to succeed.

2. *Setting.* The ideal situation is to ask your husband to take you on an overnight or weekend trip to a pleasant area. If financial considerations will cause him to decline, save the money out of household funds or other resources. If it is impossible to get away, obtain a baby-sitter and go out to breakfast or dinner alone. If that too is out of the question, then select a time at home when the children are occupied and the phone can be taken off the hook. Generally speaking, the farther you can get him from home, with its cares and problems and stresses, the better will be your chances to achieve genuine communication.

3. *Manner.* It is extremely important that your husband does not view your conversation as a personal attack. We are all equipped with emotional defenses that rise to our aid when we are vilified. Don't trigger those mechanisms. Instead, your manner should be as warm, loving, and supportive as possible under the circumstances. Let it be known that you are trying to communicate your own needs rather than emphasizing his inadequacies as a husband.

400

When the timing, setting, and manner converge to produce a moment of opportunity, express your deep feelings as effectively as possible. And like every good Boy Scout—be prepared.

For those who wonder how I know so much about getting the attention of husbands, it's because my wife approached me in exactly this manner. She got her message through.

Q UESTION 379

What advice would you give to a woman whose husband just won't respond to her emotionally? That's my situation. Darrell is a good man, but he's not romantic, and he'd rather keep his thoughts to himself. How can I deal with the longing inside me?

Some men will never be able to meet the needs of their wives. They don't understand how women think and have never been required to "give" to anyone. Those who are married to these unromantic and noncommunicative men must decide what is reasonable to expect and how they can forge a meaningful life together. Or they can seek an early divorce. I think the former is better!

If Darrell is such a man, my advice is that you attempt to show him, without nagging or becoming angry, how you are different from him and what your unique needs are. Work to change that which can be improved in your relationship, explain that which can be understood, resolve that which can be settled, and negotiate that which is open to compromise. Create the best marriage possible from the raw materials brought by two imperfect human beings with two distinctly unique personalities. But for all the rough edges that can never be smoothed and the faults that can never be eradicated, try to develop the best possible outlook and determine to accept reality exactly as it is. The first principle of mental health is to accept that which cannot be changed. You could easily descend into depression over the circumstances in your life. But you can also choose to hang tough and be contented in spite of them. The operative word is *choose*.

Can you accept your husband just as he is? Seldom does one human being satisfy every longing and hope in the breast of another. Obviously, this coin has two sides: You can't be his perfect woman, either. He is no more equipped to resolve your entire package of emotional needs than you are to become his sexual dream machine every twenty-four hours. Both partners have to settle for human foibles and faults and irritability and fatigue and occasional nighttime "headaches." A good marriage is not one where perfection reigns: It is a relationship where a healthy perspective overlooks a multitude of "unresolvables."

I don't mean to imply that the advice I've given is easy to implement or that it will take away the longing you described, but every human being eventually encounters difficult situations that are beyond his or her control. At that point, a person is either going to collapse, run, become angry, or do all three. I submit that acceptance is a better alternative.

QUESTION 380

Are you suggesting that women should seek to meet some of their emotional needs outside of marriage?

That is precisely what I'm saying, particularly with regard to an emotionally vulnerable woman who is married to a stoic, unromantic man. If she looks to him as the provider of all adult conversation and the satisfier of every emotional need, their marriage can quickly run aground. He has no clue about how to deal with her "soul hunger" or how to make her happy. When she begins to realize that he will never be what she wants of him, discontent begins to brew in the relationship. I have seen thousands of marriages flounder right at that point.

What can be done, then? A woman with a normal range of emotional needs cannot simply ignore them. Something deep within her screams for fulfillment. One answer is for women in this situation to supplement what their husbands can give by cultivating meaningful female relationships. Having lady friends with whom they can talk heart-to-heart, study the Scriptures, laugh and cry, and raise their children can be vital to mental health.

That is precisely how women dealt with social needs in centuries past. Many men worked sixty or seventy hours per week and had little time or energy for what might be called romantic activities. But a well-integrated society of women filled the void. They worked together, had babies together, cooked and canned together, and went to church together. And somehow, it was enough.

Why does feminine society not exist in the same way today? Because many women are employed (the neighborhoods are empty) and because the world has become so mobile. The extended family has disintegrated, and the culture has moved on. Thus, female companionship is often difficult to find, and many younger women, especially those with two or more preschoolers, abandon the search for friendship. It is simply too much trouble.

To the young wives who are reading these words, I urge you not to fall into this pattern. Invest some time in your female friends—even though you are all busy. Resist the temptation to pull into the walls of your home and wish for someone to talk to. Stay involved as a family in a church that meets your needs and preaches the Word. Remember that you are surrounded by many other women with similar feelings. Find them. Care for them. Give to them. And in the process, your own self-esteem will rise. Then when you are content, your marriage will also flourish. It sounds simplistic, but that's the way we are made. We are designed to love God as social creatures who don't do well in isolation. Don't let that isolation happen to you.

QUESTION 381

My uncle and aunt were happily married for nine years before a couple of terrible things happened. First their youngest child drowned in a neighborhood pool, and then my uncle was injured in an automobile accident. Instead of bringing them together, these two events drove them apart. How could they have weathered the storms? How will my fiancée and I stay together through the difficult times in our lives?

Having served on a large medical-school faculty for fourteen years, I watched many families go through the kind of hardship your relatives suffered. All too commonly, I saw marital relationships succumb to the pressures of personal crises. Parents who produced a mentally retarded child, for example, often blamed one another for the tragedy that confronted them. Instead of clinging together in love and reassurance, they added to their sorrows by attacking one another. I didn't condemn them for this human failing, but I did pity them for it. A basic ingredient was lacking in their relationship that remained unrecognized until their world fell off its axis. That missing component is called . . . commitment.

I heard the late Dr. Francis Schaeffer speak to this issue some years ago. He described the bridges that were built in Europe by the Romans in the first and second centuries A.D. They are still standing today, despite the unreinforced brick and mortar with which they were made. Why haven't they collapsed in this modern era of heavy trucks and equipment? They remain intact because they are used for nothing but foot traffic. If an eighteen-wheeled semi were driven across the historic structures, they would crumble in a great cloud of dust and debris.

Marriages that lack an iron-willed determination to hang together are like the fragile Roman bridges. They appear to be secure and may indeed remain upright . . . until they are put under heavy pressure. That's when the seams split and the foundation crumbles. It appears to me that many young couples today are in that precarious position. Their relationships are constructed of unreinforced mud that will not withstand the weighty trials lying ahead. The determination to survive together is simply not there.

It's not only the great tragedies of life but also the daily frustrations that wear and tear a marriage. These minor irritants, when accumulated over time, may even be more threatening to a marriage than the catastrophic events that crash into our lives. And yes, there are times in every good marriage when a husband and wife don't like each other very much. There are occasions when they feel as though they will never be in love again. Emotions are like that. They flatten out occasionally, like an automobile tire with a nail in the tread. Riding on the rim is a pretty bumpy experience for everyone on board.

Let's return to your specific question. What will you do when unexpected tornadoes blow through your home or when the doldrums leave your sails sagging and silent? Will you pack it in and go home to Mama? Will you pout and cry and seek ways to strike back? Or will your commitment hold you steady? If you want your marriage to last a lifetime, you must set your jaw and clench your fists. Make up your mind that nothing short of death will ever be permitted to come between the two of you. Nothing!

QUESTION 382

If you really love each other, won't that hold you steady when the storms come?

Not necessarily—and certainly not if you are thinking of love as a romantic feeling. Feeling wonderful about one another does not make two people compatible over the long haul. Many couples assume that the excitement of their courtship will continue for the rest of their lives. That virtually never occurs! It is naive to expect two unique individuals to mesh together like a couple of machines and to remain exhilarated throughout life. Even gears have multiple cogs with rough edges to be honed before they will work in concert.

That honing process usually occurs in the first year or two of marriage. The foundation for all that is to follow is laid in those critical months. What often occurs at this time is a dramatic struggle for power in the relationship. Who will lead? Who will follow? Who will determine how the money is spent? Who will get his or her way in times of disagreement? Everything is up for grabs in the beginning, and the way these early decisions are made will set the stage for the future.

The apostle Paul gave us the divine perspective on human relationships—not only in marriage, but in every dimension of life. He wrote, "Do nothing out of selfish ambition or vain conceit, but in humility consider others better than yourselves" (Philippians 2:3).

That one verse contains more wisdom than most marriage manuals combined. If heeded, it could virtually eliminate divorce from the catalog of human experience. It will give you stability when the storms begin to howl.

QUESTION 383

Do you recommend premarital counseling for engaged couples? If so, why? My fiancée and I have spent hours getting to know each other over the past year, so why should we bother with the time and expense of counseling?

Premarital counseling is a must and can literally be a marriage saver. Furthermore, these sessions can help young men and women overcome the cultural tendency to marry virtual strangers. Let me explain.

The typical couple spends much time talking, as you and your fiancée have done. Still, they don't know each other as well as they think they do. That is because a dating relationship is designed to conceal information, not reveal it. Each partner puts his or her best foot forward, hiding embarrassing facts, habits, flaws, and temperaments.

Consequently, the bride and groom often enter into marriage with an array of private assumptions about life after the wedding. Then major conflict occurs a few weeks later when they discover they have radically different views on nonnegotiable issues. The stage is then set for arguments and hurt feelings that were never anticipated during the courtship period.

That's why I strongly believe in the value of solid, biblical premarital counseling. Each engaged couple, even those who seem perfectly suited for one another, should participate in at least six to ten meetings with someone who is trained to help them prepare for marriage. The primary purpose of these encounters is to identify the assumptions each partner holds and to work through the areas of potential conflict.

The following questions are typical of the issues that a competent counselor will help the couple address together.

- Where will you live after getting married?
- Will the bride work? For how long?
- Are children planned? How many? How soon? How far apart?
- Will the wife return to work after babies arrive? How quickly?
- How will the kids be disciplined? fed? trained?
- What church will you attend?
- Are there theological differences to be reckoned with?
- How will your roles be different?
- How will you respond to each set of in-laws?
- Where will you spend Thanksgiving and Christmas holidays?
- How will financial decisions be made?
- Who will write the checks?
- How do you feel about credit?

- Will a car be bought with borrowed money? How soon? What kind?
- How far do you expect to go sexually before marriage?
- If the bride's friends differ from the groom's buddies, how will you relate to them?
- What are your greatest apprehensions about your fiancé(e)?
- What expectations do you have for him/her?

This is only a partial list of questions to be discussed and considered. Then a battery of compatibility tests is administered to identify patterns of temperament and personality. Sometimes the findings are quite shocking. Indeed, some couples decide to postpone or call off the wedding after discovering areas of likely conflict down the road. Others begin working through their differences and proceed toward marriage with increased confidence. In either case, men and women typically benefit from knowing each other better.

Someone has said: The key to healthy marriage is to keep your eyes wide open before you wed and half-closed thereafter. I agree. Premarital counseling is designed to help engaged couples accomplish that.

QUESTION 384

How do you feel about "no-fault divorce" laws, which allow for the dissolution of marriage without cause? If one party wants out, he or she can get out. Has that been a good policy?

The concept of "no-fault divorce" was introduced in California in 1969, making it the first jurisdiction in the Western world to radically alter its divorce law. In the next fifteen years, every state in the U.S. adopted some form of no-fault legislation. The idea literally took the nation by storm.

Statistical evidence in the past three decades verifies that no-fault divorce has been a disaster for the family. According to *Statistical Abstract of the United States,* the number of divorces in this country has increased by 279 percent since these laws began taking effect in 1970.[152] The number of children living with a divorced parent has increased 352 percent in that same period.[153] Demographer Dr. Paul Glick has predicted that one-third of all children will live in a stepfamily before they reach their eighteenth birthday.[154] I agree with those who contend that the liberalization of divorce laws undermined the sanctity of the home and condemned millions of children to a life of poverty and heartache.

In essence, no-fault divorce laws have effectively nullified the act of marriage, making it an unenforceable contract. A person can abandon his or her family more easily than he can abrogate any other agreement that bears his or her signature. It matters not that he made a solemn promise before God, friends, relatives, a member of the clergy, or a licensed representative of the state. If he changes his mind, he doesn't even have to explain why. Of greatest concern is the welfare of the husband or wife who is unwillingly confronted with divorce, custody battles, and rejection. That responsible individual has absolutely no power in the dissolution of the family. But the other spouse, even the person who chases after a younger playmate or a "grand new freedom," is the one in charge.

There is a lesson to be learned from this regrettable exercise in social engineering. The institution of the family is the basic unit of society—the ground floor on which the entire culture rests. If it collapses, everything of value will go down with it. We should never tamper with it frivolously or undermine its rationale for existence. Yet liberal activists are at it again. This time they're determined to sanction same-sex marriage, which will reopen the polygamy debate and destroy the legal definition of the family. I pray that they will not succeed.

Q UESTION 385

My wife will not respond to me sexually unless the circumstances are just right. It isn't enough for us to just enjoy each other physically. I have to talk to her and spend time with her before we even go to bed or else she is disinterested. Are other women like this?

The majority are just like that. Sex for a woman is not exclusively a physical experience. It must have a romantic element to satisfy her. Unless a woman feels a certain closeness to her husband at a particular time—unless she believes he respects her as a person—she may be unable to enjoy a sexual encounter with him. When she makes love in the absence of that romantic closeness, she often feels used. In a sense, her husband has exploited her body to gratify himself. Like your wife, she may either refuse to participate, or she will yield with reluctance and resentment.

To the contrary, a man can come home from work in a bad mood, spend the evening slaving over his desk or in his garage, watch the eleven o'clock news in silence, and finally hop into bed for a brief encounter. The fact that he and his wife have had no tender moments in the entire evening does not inhibit his sexual desire significantly. He sees her on her way to bed in her clingy nightgown, and that is enough to throw his switch. But his wife is not so easily moved. She waited for him all day, and when he came home and hardly even greeted her, she felt disappointment and rejection. His continuing coolness and self-preoccupation put a padlock on her desires. Therefore, she may find it impossible to respond to him later in the evening.

The inability to explain this frustration is, I believe, a continual source of irritation to women.

*Q*UESTION **386**

Is the felt need for sex the same in both males and females?

Many men and women differ significantly in their manifestations of sexual desire. Research seems to indicate that the intensity of pleasure and excitation at the time of orgasm in women and ejaculation in men is about the same, although the pathway to that climax takes a different route. Most men can become excited more quickly than women. They may reach a point of finality before their mates get their minds off the evening meal and what the kids will wear tomorrow morning. It is a wise man who recognizes this feminine inertia, and brings his wife along at her own pace.

This coin has two sides, however. Women should also understand how their husbands' needs differ from their own. When sexual response is blocked in males, they experience an accumulating physiological pressure that demands release. Two seminal vesicles (small sacs containing semen) gradually fill to capacity; as maximum level is reached, hormonal influences sensitize the man to all sexual stimuli. Whereas a particular woman would be of little interest to him when he is satisfied, he may be eroticized just to be in her presence when he is in a state of deprivation. A less passionate wife may find it difficult to comprehend this accumulating aspect of her husband's sexual appetite, since her needs are typically less urgent and pressing. Thus, she should recognize that his desire is dictated by definite biochemical forces within his body, and if she loves him, she will seek to satisfy those needs as meaningfully and as regularly as possible. I'm not denying that women have definite sexual needs that seek gratification; rather, I am merely explaining that abstinence is usually more difficult for men to tolerate.

QUESTION 387

Why are some men and women less sensual than others?

Adult attitudes toward sexual relations are a function of genetics and conditioning during childhood and adolescence. It is surprising to observe how many otherwise well-adjusted people still think of married sex as dirty, animalistic, or evil. Such a person who has been taught a one-sided, negative approach to sex during the formative years may find it impossible to release these carefully constructed inhibitions on the wedding night. The marriage ceremony is simply insufficient to reorient one's attitude from "Thou shalt not" to "Thou shalt—regularly—and with great passion!" That mental turnabout is not easily achieved.

Let me address the other related factor. Not all differences in intensity of the sex drive can be traced to errors in childhood instruction. Human beings differ in practically every characteristic. Our feet come in different sizes, our teeth are shaped differently, some people eat more than others, and some are taller than their peers. We are unique individuals. Accordingly, we differ in sexual appetites. Our intellectual "computers" are clearly programmed differently through the process of genetic inheritance. Some of us "hunger and thirst" after our sexuality, while others take it much more casually. Given this

410

variability, we should learn to accept ourselves sexually, as well as physically and emotionally. This does not mean that we shouldn't try to improve the quality of our sex lives, but it does mean that we should stop struggling to achieve the impossible—trying to set off an atomic bomb with a matchstick!

As long as a husband and wife are satisfied with each other, it doesn't matter what popular magazines say their inadequacies happen to be. Sex in this culture has become a statistical monster. "The average couple has intercourse three times a week! Oh no! What's wrong with us? Are we undersexed?" A husband worries if his genitalia are of "average" size, while his wife contemplates her insufficient bustline. We are tyrannized by this preoccupation with sexuality. I hereby make a proposal: Let's keep sex in its proper place; sure, it is important, but it should serve us and not the other way around!

QUESTION 388

Would you say that most marital problems are caused by sexual difficulties?

No, the opposite is more accurate. Most sexual problems are caused by marital difficulties. Or stated another way, couples that have problems in bed often have bigger problems in the other 23 1/2 hours of the day.

QUESTION 389

My husband and I never talk about the subject of sex, and this is frustrating to me. Is this a common problem in marriage?

It is, especially for those who are having sexual difficulties. It is even more important that the doors of communication be kept open in marriage when sex is a problem. When intercourse has been un-enthusiastic, and when anxiety has been steadily accumulating, the tendency is to avoid referring to the topic in everyday conversation. Neither partner knows what to do about the problem, and they tacitly agree to ignore it. Even during sexual relations, they do not talk to one another.

One woman wrote me recently to say that her sex life with her husband resembled a "silent movie." Not a word was ever spoken.

How incredible it seems that an inhibited husband and wife can make love several times a week for a period of years without ever verbalizing their feelings or frustrations on this important aspect of their lives. When this happens, the effect is like taking a hot Coke bottle and shaking it until the contents are ready to explode. Any anxiety-producing thought or condition that cannot be expressed is almost certain to generate inner pressure and stress. The more unspeakable the subject, the greater the pressurization that tends to weaken sexual desire.

Furthermore, when conversation is prohibited on the subject of sex, the act of intercourse takes on the atmosphere of a performance—each partner feeling that he or she is being critically evaluated by the other. To remove these communication barriers, the husband should take the lead in helping his wife verbalize her feelings, her fears, her aspirations. They should talk about the manners and techniques that stimulate—and those that don't. They should face their problems as mature adults, calmly and confidently. There is something magical to be found in such soothing conversation; tensions and anxieties are reduced when they find verbal expression.

QUESTION 390

My husband and I don't get in bed until nearly midnight every evening, and then I'm too tired to really get into lovemaking. Is there something unusual or wrong with me for being unable to respond when the opportunity presents itself?

There is nothing unusual about your situation. Physical exhaustion plays a significant part in many women's inability to respond sexually. Someone said, "By the time I put the cat out, tuck the kids in, and take the telephone receiver off—who cares?!" Good question. A mother who has struggled through an eighteen-hour day—especially if she has been chasing an ambitious toddler or two—may find that her internal pilot light has flickered and gone out. When she finally falls into bed, sex represents an obligation rather than a pleasure. It is the last item on her to-do list for that day. Meaningful sexual relations utilize great quantities of body energy and are seriously hampered when those resources have already been expended. Nevertheless, intercourse is usually scheduled as the final event in the evening.

If sex is important in a marriage, and we all know that it is, then some prime-time moments should be reserved for its expression. The day's working activities should end early in the evening, permitting a husband and wife to retire before exhausting themselves on endless chores and responsibilities. Remember this: Whatever is put at the end of your priority list will probably be done inadequately. For too many families, sex languishes in last place.

Q UESTION 391

Is it inevitable that sexual desire must diminish in the fifth, sixth, and seventh decades of life?

There is no organic basis for healthy women or men to experience less desire as they age. The sexual appetite depends more on a state of mind and emotional attitudes than on one's chronological age. If a husband and wife see themselves as old and unattractive, they might lose interest in sex for reasons only secondary to their age. But from a physical point of view, it is a myth that men and women must be sexually apathetic unless there are disease processes or physical malfunctions to be considered.

Q UESTION 392

What does a woman want most from her husband in the fifth, sixth, and seventh decades of her life?

413

She wants and needs the same assurance of love and respect that she desired when she was younger. This is the beauty of committed love—that which is avowed to be a lifelong devotion. A man and woman can face the good and bad times together as friends and allies.

By contrast, the youthful advocate of "sexual freedom" and non-involvement will enter the latter years of life with nothing to remember but a series of exploitations and broken relationships. That short-range philosophy, which gets so much publicity today, has a predictable dead end down the road. Committed love is expensive, I admit, but it yields the highest returns on the investment at maturity.

QUESTION 393

Can you be more specific regarding the differences in sexual desire and preferences between males and females? Since I'm getting married next July, I would like to know how my future husband's needs will differ from my own. Could you summarize the major distinctions that will occur between us?

You are wise to ask this question, because the failure to understand the differences between male and female can lead to unnecessary frustration and guilt. What I will share with you is not new, yet it is surprising how many husbands and wives do not understand how their spouses differ from themselves in this regard. Let me say that the description I'll give you relates to *typical* responses. Individuals differ in many ways, and you'll need to discuss the particulars with your fiancé.

First, men are primarily aroused by visual stimulation. They are excited by feminine nudity or partial nudity. Women, on the other hand, are typically much less visually oriented than men. Certainly, they are interested in attractive masculine bodies, but the physiological mechanism of sex is usually not triggered by what they see; women are stimulated primarily by the sense of touch and by romantic allure. Thus, we encounter the first common source of disagreement in the bedroom: He may want her to appear unclothed in a lighted room, and she wants him to caress her in the dark.

Second, and much more important, men are not very discriminating in regard to the person living within an interesting body. A man can walk down a street and be sexually stimulated by an approaching female, even though he knows nothing about her personality, her values, or her mental capabilities. He is attracted by her beauty itself.

Likewise, he can become almost as excited over a photograph of an unknown nude model as he can from a face-to-face encounter with someone he loves. Hence, there is some validity to the complaint by women that they have been used as "sex objects" by men. This explains why female prostitutes outnumber males by a wide margin and why few women try to rape men. It explains why a roomful of men can enjoy watching a burlesque dancer "take it all off." These are not very flattering characteristics of male sexuality, but they are well documented in professional literature.

Women, on the other hand, are much more discriminating in their sexual interests. They less commonly become excited by observing a good-looking charmer or by the photograph of a hairy model; rather, their desire is usually focused on a particular individual whom they respect or admire. A woman is stimulated by the romantic aura that surrounds her man and by his character and personality. She is drawn to a man who appeals to her emotionally as well as physically.

Obviously, there are exceptions to these characteristic desires, but the fact remains: Sex for men is a more physical phenomenon; sex for women is a deeply emotional experience.

QUESTION 394

You have said that every healthy married couple should learn how to fight. What do you mean by that?

What I have said is that people need to learn how to fight *fair*, because there is a big difference between healthy and unhealthy combat in marriage. In an unstable marriage, hostility is aimed at the partner's soft underbelly with comments like "You never do anything right!" and "Why did I marry you in the first place?" and "You're getting more like your mother every day!" These offensive remarks strike at the very heart of the mate's self-worth.

Healthy conflict, by contrast, is focused on the issues that cause disagreement. For example: "It upsets me when you don't tell me you're going to be late for dinner." Or: "I was embarrassed when you made me look foolish at the party last night."

Can you hear the difference in these two approaches? The first

415

assaults the dignity of the partner while the second is addressed to the source of conflict. When couples learn this important distinction, they can work through their disagreements without wounding and insulting each other.

QUESTION 395

My wife and I love each other very much, but we're going through a time of apathy. We just don't feel close to each other. Is this normal, and is there a way to bring back the fire?

This happens sooner or later in every marriage. A man and woman just seem to lose the wind in their romantic sails for a period of time.

Their plight reminds me of seamen back in the days of wooden vessels. Sailors in that era had much to fear, including pirates, storms, and diseases. But their greatest fear was that the ship might encounter the Doldrums. The Doldrums was an area of the ocean near the equator characterized by calm and very light shifting winds. It could mean certain death for the entire crew. The ship's food and water supply would be exhausted as they drifted for days, or even weeks, waiting for a breeze to put them back on course.

Well, marriages that were once exciting and loving can also get caught in the romantic doldrums, causing a slow and painful death to the relationship. Author Doug Fields, in his book *Creative Romance,* writes, "Dating and romancing your spouse can change those patterns, and it can be a lot of fun. There's no quick fix to a stagnant marriage, of course, but you can lay aside the excuses and begin to date your sweetheart."[155] In fact, you might want to try thinking like a teenager again. Let me explain.

Recall for a moment the craziness of your dating days—the coy attitudes, the flirting, the fantasies, the chasing after the prize. As we moved from courtship into marriage, most of us felt we should grow up and leave the game playing behind. But we may not have matured as much as we'd like to think.

In some ways, our romantic relationships will always bear some characteristics of adolescent sexuality. Adults still love the thrill of the chase, the lure of the unattainable, excitement of the new and boredom with the old. Immature impulses are controlled and mini-mized in a committed relationship, of course, but they never fully disappear.

This could help you keep vitality in your marriage. When things have grown stale between you and your spouse, maybe you should remember some old tricks. How about breakfast in bed? A kiss in the rain? Or rereading those old love letters together? A night in a nearby hotel? Roasting marshmallows by an open fire? A phone call in the middle of the day? A long-stem red rose and a love note? There are dozens of ways to fill the sails with wind once more.

If it all sounds a little immature to act like a teenager again, just keep this in mind: In the best marriages, the chase is never really over.

Q UESTION 396

Tell me why it is inevitable for couples with good marriages to go through "flat spots" or "the blahs," and can you offer more advice about what to do when those times come?

Romantic love is an emotion, and as such, it has a way of coming and going. Emotions tend to oscillate from high to low to high, etc. One of the best ways to regenerate "that lovin' feeling" in the down times is to talk about the time and place when passion ran high. Do you recall those days when you just couldn't wait to see each other, and how each minute away seemed like an eternity? Recalling those moments to-gether is one way to regenerate what you felt before.

Even better than talking about them is reexperiencing them. My wife and I celebrated a recent wedding anniversary by exploring what we called our "old haunts." On a single evening, we went to the Pasadena Playhouse, where we had our second date; we ate at the same restaurant for dinner, and the next week we visited the Farmer's Market where we used to stroll on lazy summer evenings. We talked about warm memories and relived the excitement of those days. It was a wonderful reprise.

Another suggestion is to return regularly to the kinds of romantic activities that drew you together in the first place. You need to put

417

some fun and laughter into your lives, which otherwise can get dreary and oppressive.

A few years ago, Shirley and I found ourselves in that kind of situation where we had almost forgotten how to play. We finally got fed up and decided to do something about it. We loaded the car and headed for a winter wonderland in Mammoth, California. There we spent the weekend skiing and eating and laughing together. One night we built a fire in the fireplace and talked for hours while our favorite music played on the stereo. We felt like kids again.

The next time you feel that you're losing that closeness you once shared, try talking about your memories of earlier days and revisit the old haunts, sing the old songs, tell the old stories. It's the best bet to rekindle the sparks of romance that first drew you together. To keep a marriage vibrant and healthy, you simply have to give it some attention. Water the plant, place it in the sunlight, and it will grow. If you put it in a cold dark corner, however, it is likely to die.

With a little effort and creativity, you can keep the fireworks in your marriage . . . even when the Fourth of July has come and gone.

Q UESTION 397

My wife and I sometimes get into fights when neither of us really wants to argue. I'm not even sure how it happens. We just find ourselves locking horns and then feeling bad about it later. Why can't we get along even when we want to?

To answer the question, I would need to know more about the circumstances that set off the two of you. The best I can do is describe one of the most common sources of conflict between people who are committed to each other. I call it experiencing "differing assumptions." Let me explain.

When husbands and wives engage one another in angry combat they often feel hurt, rejected, and assaulted by the other person. But when these battles are analyzed objectively, we often see that neither side really meant to wound the other. The pain resulted not from intentional insults but from the natural consequences of seeing things from different angles.

For example, a man might assume that Saturday is his day to play golf or watch a game on television because he worked hard all week and deserves a day off. Who could blame him? But his wife might justifiably assume that he should take the kids off her hands for a few hours because she's been wiping runny noses and changing diapers all week long. She deserved a break today and expected him to give it to her. Again, it's a pretty reasonable assumption. When these unique perspectives collide, about eight o'clock on Saturday morning, the sparks start to fly.

How can you avoid the stresses of differing assumptions at home? By making sure that you and your wife get no surprises. Most of us can cope with anything if we see it coming in time.

QUESTION 398

I've talked and talked to my husband about how I'm different from him and how I need him to be sensitive to my needs. Somehow, he just doesn't "hear" it. I've also gotten mad at him about a hundred times. How can I get my feelings across to him?

One very effective way to express your feelings is to paint a word picture. My good friends Gary Smalley and Dr. John Trent described this technique in their book *The Language of Love*. In it, Gary told a story about his wife, who was very frustrated with him. Gary would come home from work and clam up. He had nothing to say all evening. Finally, Norma told him a story about a man who went to breakfast with some friends. He ate a big meal, and then he gathered up some crumbs and put them in a bag. Then he went to lunch with some business associates and ate a big steak. Again, he put a few crumbs in a doggie bag to take with him. Then when he came home that night, he handed his wife the little bag of leftovers.

"That's what you are doing to me," said Norma. "All day the children and I wait to talk with you when you get home. But you don't share yourself with us. After being gone all day, you hand us a doggie bag and turn on the television set."

Gary said hearing that story was like being hit with a two-by-four.

419

He apologized and began to work on opening himself to his wife and his family.[156]

Try creating a graphic word picture to communicate your needs to your husband. It is far more effective at getting masculine attention than a torrent of hostile comments.

QUESTION 399

Do you think it is healthy for a husband and wife to work together and to be in each other's company twenty-four hours a day?

That sometimes works out fine. It depends on the individual couple. I can tell you, however, what is typical. According to behavioral researchers, the healthiest marriages and those with the highest sexual voltage are those that "breathe"—relationships that move from a time of closeness and tenderness to a more distant posture and then come together for another reunion as the cycle concludes.

This is why it's not always advantageous for a husband and wife to work together or to concentrate exclusively on one another in the absence of friends and colleagues outside the family. There is something about the diversity of interests and activities by each partner that keeps a couple from consuming one another and burning out the relationship in the short run.

Marriage is, after all, a marathon and not a sprint. Husbands and wives need to maintain a regenerating system that will keep love alive for a lifetime. Cultivating a healthy interest in many things is one big step in that direction.

QUESTION 400

You have said that the natural progression of a marriage is to become more *distant* rather than more intimate. Why is that true?

The natural tendency of everything in the universe is to move from order to disorder. If you buy a new car, it will steadily deteriorate from the day you drive it home. Your body is slowly aging and dying. Your house has to be repainted and repaired every few summers. A business that is not managed carefully will unravel and collapse. A brick that is placed on a vacant lot and left there long enough will eventually turn to dust. Indeed, even the sun and all the stars are slowly burning themselves out. We are, in a manner of speaking, in a dying universe where everything that is not specifically being protected and upgraded is in a downward spiral.

The principle that governs this drift from order to disorder might be called "the law of disintegration." (Engineers and scientists sometimes call it "the law of entropy.") The only way to postpone or temporarily combat its influence is to invest creative energy and intelligent design into that which is to be preserved.

Not so surprisingly, human relationships also conform to the principle of disintegration. The natural tendency is for husbands and wives to drift away from each other unless they work at staying together. To provide another analogy, it is as though they were sitting in separate rowboats on a choppy lake. If they don't paddle vigorously to stay in the same neighborhood, one will drift to the north of the lake and the other to the south. That is exactly what happens when marital partners get too busy or distracted to maintain their love. If they don't take the time for romantic activities and experiences that draw them together, something precious begins to slip away. It doesn't have to be that way, of course, but the currents of life will separate them unless efforts are made to remain together.

I wish every newly married couple knew about the law of disintegration and actively protected their relationship from it.

Q UESTION 401

In recent months, there have been two occasions when a woman at work has made a pass at me. I love my wife deeply, have no interest in this lady, and have communicated this to her in no uncertain terms. Do you think I should share these incidents with my wife?

Yes, I do. First, because I believe the healthiest marriages are those that are open and honest on such matters. Second, because sharing important information is a step toward accountability in a situation that could prove dangerous. And third, because your wife should be your best friend with whom you discuss troubling circumstances and how they will be handled.

My only caution is that you be careful not to reveal this disclosure in order to make your wife jealous or to use the incident to manipulate her. Some spouses seize an opportunity like this to play power games with a mate. Check out your motives carefully before you talk to your wife, and share the experience as objectively as possible. She will appreciate you for it.

Finally, I urge you to continue to reject the advances of the lady in your office, regardless of how attractive she is or how flattering her interest in you may be. To pursue her may give your ego a ride now, but only pain and sorrow lie down that road—for her and for you.

QUESTION 402

My family lives together under one roof, and we share the same last name, but we don't "feel" like a family. How can I begin to put a sense of togetherness into this harried household? How do you put meaningful activities into your family?

One way to accomplish that is by creating traditions in your home. By traditions I'm referring to those recurring events and behaviors that are anticipated, especially by children, as times of closeness and fellowship between loved ones.

In our family, the centerpiece of our holiday traditions is food. Each year during Thanksgiving and Christmas, the women prepare marvelous turkey dinners with all the trimmings. Another great favorite at that time is a fruit dish called ambrosia, containing sectioned oranges and grapes. The family peels the grapes together the night before the big day. These holidays are wonderful experiences for all of us. There's laughter and warm family interaction throughout the day. We look forward to that festive season, not just for the food, but for what happens between loved ones who come together on that occasion.

We also have designated foods on the other holidays throughout the year. On New Year's Day, for reasons I cannot explain, we enjoy a southern meal of pinto beans cooked at least eight hours with large chunks of lean ham, served with corn bread and little onions. It's so good! For many years, we invited thirty or more friends to our home on July Fourth and served them barbecued hamburgers and baked beans. This became a prelude to the fireworks display and much fun and laughter.

There are many other traditions. Immediately prior to the Thanksgiving dinner, I read a passage of Scripture and Shirley tells the story of the Pilgrims who thanked God for helping them survive the ravages of winter. Then each person is given two kernels of Indian corn to symbolize the blessings he or she is most thankful for that year. A basket is passed, and every member drops in the corn while sharing their two richest blessings from God during that year. Our expressions of thankfulness inevitably involve people—children, grandparents, and other loved ones. As the basket moves around the table, tears of appreciation and love are evident on many faces. It is one of the most beautiful moments of the year.

The great value of traditions is that they give a family a sense of identity and belonging. All of us desperately need to feel that we're not just part of a busy cluster of people living together in a house but we're a living, breathing family that's conscious of our uniqueness, our character, and our heritage. That feeling is the only antidote for the loneliness and isolation that characterize so many homes today.

QUESTION 403

My husband is a good man, but he gets angry at the kids and says things that he later regrets. Help me convince him to be careful about these off-the-cuff comments.

Psychologist and author Abraham Maslow once said, "It takes nine affirming comments to make up for each critical comment we give to our children."[157] I believe he is right. All normal human beings respond negatively to criticism and rejection. Conversely, some of us crave affirmation so much that we'll do almost anything to get it.

Children are especially vulnerable to those who use affirmation to manipulate them. As someone said, "Whoever gives your kids praise and attention has power over them." That could be a drug dealer, a gang member, or anyone who could harm them. People with evil intentions know how to use praise to get what they want from lonely kids. This is, in fact, the technique routinely used by pedophiles to abuse their victims sexually.

A highly skilled pedophile can enter a room full of children and instantly spot those who are vulnerable to affirmation. They can have those needy kids under their control in five minutes or less.

All human beings have deep psychological needs for love, belonging, and affection. If you don't meet those longings in your children, I can assure you someone else will.

QUESTION 404

How do men and women differ emotionally, and are those differences caused by cultural influences or genetic factors?

No doubt, some of the differences in masculine and feminine characteristics are culturally induced. It is foolish, however, to discount the impact of genetics, physiology, and inborn temperaments in understanding the sexes. Radical feminists in the sixties and seventies tried to sell the notion that males and females are identical except for the ability to bear children. That is nonsense. Let me describe some of the differences between the sexes that appear to be determined, at least in part, by genetics.

The reproductive capacity of women results in greater needs for security and stability. In other words, because of their sense of responsibility for children, females are less likely to take risks and gamble with the future. Though it varies in individual situations, there is typically a healthy tension between a man and woman that interests me. He likes excitement, change, challenge, uncertainty, and the potential for huge returns on a risky investment. She likes predictability, continuity, safety, roots, relationships, and a smaller return on a more secure investment. These contrasting inclinations work to a couple's best advantage. She tempers his impulsive, foolish tendencies, and he nudges her out of apathy and excessive caution. These genetic tendencies have far-reaching implications. Medical science has not begun to identify all the ramifications of sexual uniqueness. We see the wisdom of the Creator in the way the sexes interrelate at this point.

Related to this is a woman's emotional investment in her home, which usually exceeds that of her husband. She typically cares more than he about the details of the house, family functioning, and such concerns. To cite a personal example, my wife and I decided to install a new gas-barbecue unit in our backyard. When the plumber completed the assignment and departed, Shirley and I both recognized that he had placed the appliance approximately six inches too high. I looked at the device and said, "Hmmm, yessir, he sure made a mistake. That post is a bit too high. By the way, what are we having for dinner tonight?" Shirley's reaction was dramatically different. She said, "The plumber has that thing sticking up in the air, and I don't think I can stand it!" Our contrasting views represented a classic difference of emotional intensity relating to the home.

The sexes also typically differ in competitive drive. Anyone who doubts that fact should observe how males and females approach a game of Ping-Pong, Monopoly, dominoes, horseshoes, volleyball, or tennis. Women may use the event as a backdrop for fellowship and pleasant conversation. For men, the name of the game is conquest. Even if the setting is a friendly social gathering in the host's backyard, the beads of sweat on each man's forehead reveal his passion to win. This aggressive competitiveness has been attributed exclusively to cultural influences. I don't believe it. It is a function of testosterone and the working of the masculine brain. As Dr. Richard Restak said in his book *The Brain: The Last Frontier,* "At a birthday party for five-year-olds, it's not usually the girls who pull hair, throw punches, or smear each other with food."[158]

As I've indicated, there has been an effort in the past thirty years to homogenize the personality traits of boys and girls. The behavior of which Restak wrote was perceived to have resulted from unfortunate cultural biases that could be overcome. Therefore, boys were encouraged to play with dolls and tea sets, and girls were given trucks and tools. It didn't work. To the irritation of mothers with strong feminist beliefs, boys turned out to be depressingly masculine, and no amount of "cross training" would change that fact.

425

Finally, a maternal inclination apparently operates in most women, although its force is stronger in some than others. The desire to procreate is certainly evident in those who are unable to conceive. I receive a steady influx of sad letters from women who express great frustration from their inability to become mothers. Although culture plays a major role in these longings, I believe they are rooted in female anatomy and physiology.

These items are illustrative and are not intended to be exhaustive or to represent a scientific delineation of male and female differences. It is clear from even this cursory examination, however, that God made two sexes, not one, and he designed them to fit together hand in glove. Neither is superior to the other, but each is certainly unique.

Q UESTION 405

You've discussed briefly some of the physiological and emotional differences between the sexes. Could you list other physical characteristics unique to males and females?

Men and women differ in countless ways, many of which they aren't even conscious of. Here are just a few of those differences:

1. A woman has greater constitutional vitality, perhaps because of her unique chromosomal pattern. Normally, she outlives a man by three or four years in the U.S. Females simply have a stronger hold on life than males, even in the uterus. More than 140 male babies are conceived for every 100 females; by the time birth occurs, the ratio is 105 to 100, with the rest of the males dying in spontaneous abortions.[159]

2. Men have a higher incidence of death from almost every disease except three: benign tumors, disorders related to female reproduction, and breast cancer.[160]

3. Men have a higher rate of basal metabolism than women.[161]

4. The sexes differ in skeletal structure, women having a shorter head, broader face, less protruding chin, shorter legs, and longer trunk. The first finger of a woman's hand is usually longer than the

third; with men the reverse is true. Boys' teeth last longer than do those of girls.[162]

5. Women have a larger stomach, kidneys, liver, and appendix, and smaller lungs than men.[163]

6. Women have three very important physiological functions totally absent in men—menstruation, pregnancy, and lactation. Each of these mechanisms influences behavior and feelings significantly. Female hormonal patterns are more complex and varied. The glands work differently in the two sexes. For example, a woman's thyroid is larger and more active; it enlarges during menstruation and pregnancy, which makes her more prone to goiter, provides resistance to cold, and is associated with the smooth skin, relatively hairless body, and the thin layer of subcutaneous fat that are important elements in the concept of personal beauty. Women are also more responsive emotionally, laughing and crying more readily.[164]

7. Women's blood contains more water (20 percent fewer red cells). Since red cells supply oxygen to the body, she tires more easily and is more prone to faint. Her constitutional viability is therefore strictly a long-range matter. When the working day in British factories, under wartime conditions, was increased from ten to twelve hours, accidents among women increased 150 percent; the rate of accidents among men did not increase significantly.[165]

8. Men are 50 percent stronger than women in brute strength.[166]

9. Women's hearts beat more rapidly than those of men (80 versus 72 beats per minute). Their blood pressure (ten points lower than men) varies more from minute to minute, but they have much less tendency to high blood pressure—at least until after menopause.[167]

10. Female lung capacity is about 30 percent less than in males.[168]

11. Women can withstand high temperatures better than men because their metabolism slows down less.[169]

12. Men and women differ in every cell of their bodies because they carry a differing chromosomal pattern. The implications of those genetic components range from obvious to extremely subtle. For example, when researchers visited high school and college campuses to study behavior of the sexes, they observed that males and females even transported their books in different ways. The young

men tended to carry them at their sides with their arms looped over the top. Women and girls, by contrast, usually cradled their books at their breasts, in much the same way they would a baby.[170]

Who can estimate how many other sex-related influences lie below the level of consciousness?

QUESTION 406

Are there productive ways older people can remain mentally alert as their bodies age? Is mental decline inevitable in the golden years?

If you live long enough, there will be some loss of intellectual acuity. There is, however, much that a person can do to postpone that deterioration. An article in *Family Circle* magazine suggested five ways to maintain healthy minds through the aging process:

The first rule is to "use it or lose it." The human brain isn't like a calculator that you can plug in and leave idle for a year and find working just as well when you return. It must have constant use and regular input of sensory information.

Second, proper brain function is dependent on a balanced diet with ample supplies of all the essential nutrients.

Third is exercise. Every organ of the body benefits from physical activity, including the package of neural matter with which we think.

Fourth is regular physical examinations and good health care. Untreated disease processes can affect us physically and mentally.

Finally, the fifth way to keep our brains healthy is by having an active social life. Being sick, isolated, and alone is a prescription for rapid mental decline.[171]

Unfortunately, many older citizens are unable to implement these five suggestions for one reason or another. Some are alone and have no one to talk to. Others lack the resources for good medical care and healthy nutrition.

That's why those of us in the younger generation owe today's seniors our time and attention. They cared for us when we were frail and helpless. Now it's our time to return the favor.

21
Money Matters

Q UESTION 407

My wife and I are approaching our retirement years, and we have been very blessed financially. We own several large businesses and will have a sizable estate to pass on to our three children. How do you feel about leaving large amounts of money to the next generation, and is there a right and wrong way to do it?

My views on that subject may not be what you want to hear, but I can only tell you what I've observed and what I firmly believe. In a word, I'm convinced that it is very dangerous to give large amounts of money to kids who haven't earned it. A sociological study published some time ago called *Rich Kids* validated the concerns I have observed. The authors of that study concluded that large trust funds are usually destructive to those who inherit them.[172] The case studies they cited were convincing.

Human history also confirms the dangerous influence of money. Men and women have lusted for it, killed for it, died for it, and gone to hell for it. Money has come between the best of friends and brought down the proud and mighty. And alas, it has torn millions of marriages limb from limb!

It's also been my observation that *nothing* will divide siblings more quickly than money. Giving them a large inheritance increases the probability of tension and disharmony within a family. Your sons and daughters will fight over control of your businesses, and they'll resent those who are designated as decision makers. Some of them will lose their motivation to be responsible and will experiment with various addictive behaviors—from gambling to alcoholism. There are exceptions to these negative consequences, of course, and some people do handle wealth and power gracefully. But it is a difficult assignment at best and one that requires the greatest maturity and self-control.

The question to ask is whether or not leaving large amounts of money to offspring is worth the risk it imposes on those you love. You must decide if you want to remove from your children the challenges that helped you succeed—the obligation to work hard, live frugally, save, build, and produce by the sweat of your brow. Do you feel right about replacing that need for discipline and industry with a ready-made empire that can be mishandled or squandered?

Please understand that I know this view is unconventional. One of the reasons people work so hard is so their children won't have to. They love their kids immeasurably and want to make things easier for them. Further, they've invested a lifetime in the development of a business and the accumulation of wealth. Are they now going to sell it and walk away? That's an unpleasant prospect for any parent.

I can't make that decision for others, of course. My obligation is simply to present the issue as I see it. And in my experience, the inheritance of wealth is threatening to family relationships, self-discipline, spiritual commitment, and responsible living. It should be done only with great care, years of preparation, and much prayer.

QUESTION 408

Would you leave nothing to kids under these circumstances? What would you do with the balance of an estate?

Assuming I had a large estate, I think it would make sense to help children get started in their life's work, and perhaps, to help them buy a home. Thus, it seems appropriate to give them an amount not to exceed the $600,000 tax-free limit allowed by the IRS. I would give the balance to a worthy nonprofit endeavor in which I believed. If I had a choice between paying unnecessary taxes to a bloated and wasteful federal government or supporting a work in which I believe, there's not much doubt which would get priority.

QUESTION 409

Do you think it is wrong to be unusually wealthy?

No, wealth is not an evil in itself. Abraham, David, and other great men of the Bible were blessed with riches. In fact, the Scriptures indicate that God gives to some people the power to get wealth (see Deuteronomy 8:18 and 1 Samuel 2:7). Where, then, is the point of danger? The apostle Paul clarified for us that money is not the problem. He said it is the *love* of money that is the root of all evil (see 1 Timothy 6:10). We get into trouble when our possessions become a god to us.

Jesus' own teachings have great relevance for us at this point. Have you ever wondered what topic He talked about more often than any other? Was it heaven, hell, sin, repentance, love, or His second coming? The answer is none of these. It was money, and most of what He said came in the form of warnings. This caution about possessions and riches appeared throughout Jesus' teachings. Let me cite a few passages just from one of the four Gospels, the book of Luke:

Jesus said to a crowd of His followers, "But woe to you who are rich, for you have already received your comfort" (Luke 6:24).

He also said, "Watch out! Be on your guard against all kinds of greed; a man's life does not consist in the abundance of his possessions" (Luke 12:15).

Jesus told a parable about a rich fool who had no need of God. The man believed he had many years to live and said to himself, "'You have plenty of good things laid up for many years. Take life easy; eat, drink and be merry.' But God said to him, 'You fool! This very night your life will be demanded from you. Then who will get what you have prepared for yourself?'" Jesus ended the parable with this sober warning: "This is how it will be with anyone who stores up things for himself but is not rich toward God" (Luke 12:19-21).

Jesus later visited the home of a prominent Pharisee and said to His host, "When you give a luncheon or dinner, do not invite your friends, your brothers or relatives, or your rich neighbors; if you do, they may invite you back and so you will be repaid. But when you give a banquet, invite the poor, the crippled, the lame, the blind, and you will be blessed" (Luke 14:12-14).

He told a parable of the Prodigal Son who demanded his inheritance early and then squandered it on prostitutes and riotous living (see Luke 15:11-32).

Jesus said to His disciples, "No servant can serve two masters. Either he will hate the one and love the other, or he will be devoted to the one and despise the other. You cannot serve both God and Money" (Luke 16:13).

He told a parable of the rich man who had everything. The man was clothed in fine purple and linen, and he ate the very best food. But he was unconcerned about the misery of the beggar Lazarus, who was hungry and covered with sores. The rich man died and went to hell, where he was tormented, but Lazarus was taken to heaven, where he was comforted (see Luke 16:19-31).

He spoke to a rich young ruler and commanded him to sell all he had and give it to the poor. The man went away very sorrowfully "because he was a man of great wealth" (Luke 18:18-23).

Finally, Jesus turned to His disciples and said, "How hard it is for the rich to enter the kingdom of God! Indeed, it is easier for a camel to go through the eye of a needle than for a rich man to enter the kingdom of God" (Luke 18:24).

Isn't it incredible how many of Jesus' statements dealt with money in one way or another? We must ask ourselves why. Is there a reason the Master kept returning to that theme? Of course there is. Jesus was teaching us that great spiritual danger accompanies the pursuit and the achievement of wealth. He explained why in Matthew 6:21: "For where your treasure is, there your heart will be also."

The Lord will not settle for second place in our lives. That is the threat posed by money. It can become our treasure—our passion— our greatest love. And when that happens, God becomes almost irrelevant.

QUESTION 410

Do you think it is unbiblical to earn a high salary, own a home, have a nice car, and acquire a savings account?

Certainly not. We read in 1 Timothy 5:8, "If anyone does not provide for his relatives, and especially for his immediate family, he has denied the faith and is worse than an unbeliever." Clearly, those responsible for the welfare of their families are obligated to provide for and protect them, which requires that they bring in money from their labors.

QUESTION 411

What, then, is the biblical approach to possessions and money? You've spelled out what is wrong, but what is right?

To answer your question, I will turn to Christian financial counselor and author Ron Blue. He said there are four principles for money management that are foundational. If they are implemented in your life, you'll never have a problem with materialism. Let's look at them quickly:

Principle 1: God owns it all.

Some people have the notion that the Lord is entitled to 10 percent of our income, which is called our "tithes," and that the other 90 percent belongs to us. Not true. I believe strongly in the concept of tithing, but not because God's portion is limited to a tenth. We are but stewards of all that He has entrusted to us. He is our possessor—and sometimes our dispossessor. Everything we have is but a loan from Him. When God took away his wealth, Job had the correct attitude, saying, "Naked I came from my mother's womb, and naked I will depart. The Lord gave and the Lord has taken away; may the name of the Lord be praised" (Job 1:21). If you understand this basic concept, it becomes clear that every spending decision is a spiritual decision. Waste, for example, is not a squandering of our resources. It is a poor use of His.

433

Expenditures for worthwhile purposes, such as vacations, ice cream, bicycles, blue jeans, magazines, tennis rackets, cars, and hamburgers, are also purchased with His money. That's why in my family, we bow to thank the Lord before eating each meal. Everything, including our food, is a gift from His hand.

Principle 2: There is always a trade-off between time and effort and money and rewards.

You've heard the phrases "There's no such thing as a free lunch" and "You can't get something for nothing." Those are very important understandings. Money should always be thought of as linked to work and the sweat of our brow.

Here's how this second principle has meaning for us. Think for a moment of the most worthless, unnecessary purchase you have made in recent years. Perhaps it was an electric shaver that now sits in the garage or an article of clothing that will never be worn. It is important to realize that this item was not purchased with your money; it was bought with your time, which you traded for money. In effect, you swapped a certain proportion of your allotted days on earth for that piece of junk that now clutters your home.

When you understand that everything you buy is purchased with a portion of your life, it should make you more careful with the use of money.

Principle 3: There is no such thing as an independent financial decision.

There will never be enough money for everything you'd like to buy or do. Even billionaires have some limitations on their purchasing power. Therefore, every expenditure has implications for other things you need or want. It's all linked together. What this means is that those who can't resist blowing their money for junk are limiting themselves in areas of greater need or interest.

And by the way, husbands and wives often fight over the use of money. Why? Because their value systems differ and they often disagree on what is wasteful. My mother and father were typical in this regard. If Dad spent five dollars for shotgun shells or for tennis balls, he justified the expenditure because it brought him pleasure. But if Mom bought a five-dollar potato peeler that wouldn't work, he considered that wasteful. Never mind the fact that she enjoyed shopping as much as he did hunting or playing tennis. Their perspectives were simply unique. This is a common problem for husbands and wives, and they just have to work through it.

Again, this third principle involves a recognition that an extravagance at one point will eventually lead to frustration down the road. Good business managers are able to keep the big picture in mind as they make their financial decisions.

Principle 4: Delayed gratification is the key to financial maturity.

Since we have limited resources and unlimited choices, the only way to get ahead financially is to deny ourselves some of the things we want. If we don't have the discipline to do that, then we will always be in debt. Remember too that unless you spend less than you earn, no amount of income will be enough. That's why some people receive salary increases and soon find themselves even deeper in debt.

Let me repeat that important concept: *No amount of income will be sufficient if spending is not brought under control.* Consider the finances of the United States government, for example. It extracts more than a trillion dollars annually from American taxpayers. That's a thousand billion bucks! But our Congress spends hundreds of billions more than that.

Even by the most liberal interpretation, much of this revenue is wasted on programs that don't work and on unnecessary and expensive bureaucracies. Consequently, the size of our national debt is mind-boggling. The point is inescapable: Whether it be within a government or by a private individual, there must be a willingness to deny short-term gratification and to live within one's means. It isn't easy, but it pays big dividends at maturity.[173]

435

22

Families under Fire

Q UESTION 412

Is the "traditional family" a thing of the past? I hear that it is no longer viable and that we ought to begin thinking about what will take its place.

We've certainly heard that perspective often enough from the media and from influential people. For example, First Lady Hillary Rodham Clinton made it the theme of her Mother's Day commencement speech back on May 8, 1994, delivered at George Washington University. She said, "If it ever did, [the American family] no longer does consist of two parents, two children, a dog, a house with a white picket fence, and a station wagon in the driveway. Instead of families looking like the Cleavers on *Leave It to Beaver*, we have families that include test-tube babies and surrogate moms. Instead of Sunday-night family dinners, we now have cross-country telephone conference calls. Instead of aunts and uncles and grandmas and grandpas, we have nannies and day-care centers."

Mrs. Clinton went on to recommend what she called an "extended family" to fill the void as traditional families dwindle. She urged the graduates to look out for their friends, neighbors, and fellow citizens as they would members of their own families, and concluded by saying, "When the traditional bonds of family are too often frayed, we all need to appreciate that in a very real sense we have become an extended family."[174]

Well, the First Lady was correct in reminding us of our responsibilities to help and care for one another. We should be especially attuned to the needs of single parents who are struggling to raise children on their own. But Mrs. Clinton's remarks that day conveyed another message—that the traditional family is ineffectual and no longer viable. She expressed no regret over the social and governmental forces that have assaulted the institutions of marriage and parenthood. She did not urge the graduates to preserve and support the traditional family unit. Nor did she speak of its vital role in the culture. Rather, Mrs. Clinton began with the supposition that families as we have known them are gone forever, and then suggested ways of replacing them.

It was a familiar theme, to be sure. For the past three decades, we've been hearing about the family's imminent demise from politicians, radical feminists, homosexual activists, and liberal journalists. Then they've hurried to tell us how society should be reorganized in the absence of lifelong marriage. This propaganda began to appear in the early seventies with the publication of a book entitled *The Death of the Family,* by British psychotherapist David Cooper. He emphasized the need to abolish the traditional family unit and to substitute new forms of human relationships.

Actress Shirley MacLaine added her two bits in a 1971 interview published in the now-defunct magazine *Look*. She said:

All this goes back as far as Christian culture, to what Mary and Joseph started. . . . You know it's just a million things that have been handed down with the Christian ethic, so when you begin to question the family, you have to question all those things.

I don't think it's desirable to conform to having one mate, and for those two people to raise children. But everyone believes that's the ideal. They go around frustrated most of their lives because they can't find one mate. But who said that's the natural basic personality of man? To whom does monogamy make sense? . . . To a muskrat maybe . . . Why should they then adhere to this state of monogamy? In a democratic family, individuals understand their natural tendencies, bring them out in the open, discuss them, and very likely follow them. And these tendencies are definitely not monogamous.[175]

Alvin Toffler, author of *Future Shock,* the runaway best-seller in the seventies, also predicted the eventual death of his family. In the same *Look* article, Toffler said:

> My own hunch is that most people will try to go blindly through the motions of the traditional marriage, and try to keep the traditional family going, and they'll fail. And the consequence will be a subtle but very significant shift to much more temporary marital arrangements, an intensification of the present pattern of divorce and remarriage and divorce and remarriage to the point at which we accept the idea that marriages are not for life. I'm not endorsing it, but I think it's likely to be the case.[176]

That was the common wisdom of the day. Those predictions of domestic disaster could be heard regularly throughout the seventies on network-television talk programs. One of the most offensive, *The Merv Griffin Show,* often featured vacuous guests who delighted in ridiculing the family. I happened to be watching late one afternoon when a particularly hostile woman said this about marriage licenses: "It's just a two-dollar piece of paper from a rotten government which tries to tell us who we can sleep with." She also said she was married for thirty years and cheated on her husband at least fifty times during that period. She said she wouldn't recognize his voice if he called her on the phone. The guest then concluded by saying that the problem in the world was that we had too much religious fervor. "We need to get rid of that!" she exclaimed.

Given the viciousness hurled at the family through the years, it is amazing that the institution has survived to our day. Unfortunately, the attacks have not abated. More recent critics have begun citing bogus statistics to "prove" that the traditional family is dead. For example, former U.S. Representative Patricia Schroeder (D—Colo.) proclaimed a few years ago that only 7 percent of all families were "traditional."[177] Her statement went unchallenged by the media and was widely quoted in secular literature. Therefore, I invested considerable effort to track down Schroeder's statistic and to determine on what it was based. What I learned is that she defined traditional families as those having a father who supported the family, a mother who chose not to be employed, and precisely two children at home! What nonsense! By that definition, my wife and I would not qualify as a traditional family because our children are grown and because Shirley serves as unsalaried chairman of the National Day of Prayer. My friends Randy and Marcia Hekman are not traditional because they now have twelve children instead of two. A married couple expecting their first child would not satisfy the criteria. A family in which the wife works ten hours a week in the husband's place of business wouldn't make the grade. Come on, Ms. Schroeder! This phony attempt to document the death of the family is nothing short of dishonest!

It is true that the traditional family has been buffeted, damaged, weakened, and undermined in recent years. Congress has legislated against it decade after decade. The divorce rate is far too high, and many still-intact marriages are beset by alcoholism, pornography, infidelity, and other virulent infections. No, I would not deny that there is trouble on the home front, but the reports of family disintegration have been exaggerated greatly.

Thus, when Mrs. Clinton said, "If it ever did, [the American family] no longer does consist of two parents, two children, a dog, a house with a white picket fence, and a station wagon in the driveway," she joined the chorus of those who want us to believe something that is not true. In fact, 75 percent of children live with two parents.[178] Millions of husbands and wives today are deeply committed to one another in bonds of affection that will never be shaken. Many of them even have dogs and houses with white picket fences. Mrs. Clinton was right about one thing: The station wagons in the driveway are long gone; they have been replaced by minivans and campers.

440

QUESTION 413

Early this year, my husband of eleven years announced that he didn't love me anymore. Joe told me that he would be

leaving, though by begging and pleading with him I convinced him to stay for a while. Then one night he became so cruel and said many mean things before walking out. Every time I see him I humiliate myself. I beg him to call the kids and me, but he only says, "I don't want to talk to you." I tell him how much I love him, and he'll reply, "I have no love for you! I don't hate you, but I don't love you either." I was recently told by my doctor that I must have surgery on my eyes next week and that I might lose my vision. Out of fear and panic, I broke down and called my husband, but he responded with indifference to the news. I asked if he would take me to the hospital and stay in the waiting room while I had the surgery. Joe hesitated and then said, "Well, I guess so." Why is Joe acting this way to me? Is there something I am doing wrong?

I'm going to speak very directly to you, although I understand the pain that you're going through. There is no greater heartache in life than to be rejected by the one you love. By God's help, however, you *will* survive the crisis that has beset your home.

With that, let me say that the compulsion that is driving you to plead for Joe's attention and love is systematically destroying your last glimmer of hope for reconciliation. By groveling before him, you are stripping yourself of all dignity and respect. Those two attitudes are critical ingredients in any stable and fulfilling relationship, and you are systematically destroying them.

This is the message you are conveying inadvertently: "Oh, Joe, I need you so badly. I can't make it without you. I spend my days waiting for you to call and am crushed when the phone doesn't ring. Won't you please let me talk to you occasionally? I'll take you any way I can have you—even if you want to walk all over me. I am desperate here without you."

This is a classic panic reaction, and it is leading you to appease your husband. Appeasement is virtually never successful in human relationships. In fact, it often leads directly to war, whether between husbands and wives or between antagonistic nations. Attempts by one side to buy off an aggressor or offender may seem like proposals of peace, but in most cases they merely precipitate further insult and conflict. Nothing destroys a romantic relationship more quickly than for a person to throw himself or herself, weeping and clinging, on the back of the cool partner to beg for mercy. That makes the wayward spouse even more anxious to escape from the leech that threatens to suck his lifeblood. He may pity the wounded partner and wish that things were different, but he can rarely bring himself to love again under those circumstances.

You need to understand that Joe's withdrawal from the relationship is directly linked to his quest for freedom. He is feeling suffocated and wants to escape from the marriage. By humiliating yourself and clinging to his ankles each time you meet, you increase his desire to get away. The more he struggles to gain his freedom, the more he feels your clutches around him. It becomes a vicious cycle.

QUESTION 414

What should I do, then? How should I change my relationship with my husband?

Though I realize it may be the most difficult thing you've ever done, the only promising option at this point is to loosen the bonds, to open the cage door and set Joe free! I'd suggest gathering every ounce of courage and self-respect you can muster and having a serious talk with him along the following lines:

> "Joe, I've been through some very tough moments since you decided to leave, as you know. My love for you is so deep that I just couldn't face the possibility of life without you. To a person like me, who expected to marry only once and to remain committed for life, it is a terrible shock to see our relationship begin to unravel. Nevertheless, I have been doing some intense soul-searching, and I now realize that I have been attempting to hold you against your will. That simply can't be done. As I reflect on our courtship and early years together, I'm reminded that you married me of your own free choice. I didn't blackmail you or twist your arm or offer you a bribe. It was a decision you made without pressure from me. Now you say you want out of the marriage, and obviously, I have to let

you go. I can no more force you to stay today than I could have made you marry me in 1982 (or whenever). So you are free to go. If you never call me again, then I will accept your decision. I admit that this entire experience has been painful, but I'm going to make it. The Lord has been with me thus far, and He'll go with me in the future. You and I had some wonderful times together, Joe. You were my first real love, and I'll never forget the memories that we shared. I will pray for you and trust that God will guide you in the years ahead."

Slowly, unbelievably, Joe will see the cage door vibrate just a bit and then start to rise. He won't be able to believe it. He has felt bound to you hand and foot for years, and now you've set him free! It isn't necessary to fight off your advances—your grasping hands—anymore.

But there must be a catch, he's likely to think. *It's too good to be true. Talk is cheap. This is just another trick to win me back. In a week or two she'll be crying on the phone again, begging me to come home. She's really weak, you know, and she'll crack under pressure.*

It is my strongest recommendation that you prove that your husband is wrong in this expectation. Let him marvel at your self-control in coming weeks. Only the passage of time will convince him that you are serious—that he is actually free.

QUESTION 415

How is Joe likely to respond to the new me?

He may test your resolve in the next few months by showing hostility, being aloof, or by flirting with other women. He'll be watching during this time for signs of weakness or panic. If you continue to show self-confidence, the passage of time will convince him that you are serious—and that he is actually free.

Three things typically happen when you convey that understanding:

1. The trapped partner no longer feels it necessary to fight off the other, and their relationship improves. It is not that the love affair

is rekindled, necessarily, but the strain between the two partners is often eased.

2. As the cool spouse begins to feel free again, the question he has been asking himself changes. After having wondered for weeks or months, *How can I get out of this mess?* he now asks, *Do I really want to go?* Just knowing that he can have his way often makes him less anxious to achieve it. Sometimes it turns him around 180 degrees and brings him back home!

3. The third change occurs not in the cool spouse but in the mind of the vulnerable one. Incredibly, she feels better—somehow more in control of the situation. There is no greater agony than journeying through a vale of tears, waiting in vain for the phone to ring or for a miracle to occur. Instead, the person begins to respect herself and receives small evidences of respect in return. Even though it is difficult to let go once and for all, there are ample rewards for doing so. One of those advantages involves the feeling that she has a plan—a program—a definite course of action to follow. That is infinitely more comfortable than experiencing the utter despair of powerlessness that she felt before. And little by little, the healing process begins.

Does this approach always work? Of course not. Nothing always works in human relationships. Some people will reexamine the decision to leave and decide to return. Others will keep on going. Either way, however, showing respect for yourself in the crisis will maximize the opportunities for your relationship to survive. Even if it's too late to reconnect with Joe, you'll have your self-confidence back and will be able to go on without him.

*Q*UESTION 416

You described the "trapped" feeling that causes some people to withdraw from their spouses. I think that applies to my wife, who has been strangely distant from me in recent years. Can you tell me more about what such a person might be thinking?

The feeling of entrapment begins with disrespect for a partner. For example, a man may think these kinds of thoughts about his wife: *Look at Joan. She used to be rather pretty. Now with those fifteen extra pounds she doesn't even attract me anymore. Her lack of discipline bothers me in other areas, too—the house is always a mess and she seems totally disorganized. I made an enormous mistake back there in my youth when I decided to marry her. Now I have to spend the rest of my life—can you believe it?—all the years I have left—tied up with someone I'm disinterested in. Oh, I know Joanie is a good woman, and I wouldn't hurt her for anything, but man! Is this what they call living?*

Or Joanie may be doing some thinking of her own: *Michael, Michael, how different you are than I first thought you to be. You seemed so exciting and energetic in those early days. How did you get to be such a bore? You work far too much and are so tired when you come home. I can't even get you to talk to me, much less sweep me into ecstasy.*

Look at him, sleeping on the couch with his mouth hanging open. I wish his hair wasn't falling out. Am I really going to invest my entire lifetime in this aging man? Our friends don't respect him anymore, and he hasn't received a promotion at the plant for more than five years. He's going nowhere, and he's taking me with him!

If Joanie and Michael are both thinking these entrapment thoughts, it is obvious that their future together is in serious jeopardy. But the typical situation is unilateral, as in your marriage. One partner (of either gender) begins to chafe at the bit without revealing to the other how his or her attitude has changed. A reasonably compassionate person simply does not disclose these disturbing rumblings to someone who loves him or her. Instead, a person's behavior begins to evolve in inexplicable ways.

He may increase the frequency of his evening business meetings—anything to be away from home more often. He may become irritable or "deep in thought" or otherwise noncommunicative. He may retreat into televised sports or fishing trips or poker with the boys. He may provoke continuous fights over insignificant issues. And of course, he may move out or find someone younger to play with. A woman who feels trapped will reveal her disenchantment in similar indirect ways.

To summarize, the trapped feeling is a consequence of two factors: Disrespect for the spouse and the wish for an excuse to get away.

QUESTION 417

Does the feeling of entrapment only happen late in life, or does it sometimes occur earlier?

Trapped reactions can occur among teenagers during courtship or *anytime* within a marriage—from the first day of the honeymoon to fifty years thereafter. They happen anytime one partner devalues the worth of the other and feels stuck in the relationship. They form the cornerstone of midlife crises among men and are typical of women who feel their husbands are wimpy and lacking in confidence. I believe the majority of divorces can be traced to the twin reactions of disrespect and marital claustrophobia.

QUESTION 418

Shouldn't I fight for what is important to me? Why can't I let my wife know how badly I want her to stay with me? Why should I play cat-and-mouse games when everything inside me is saying, "Go after her"?

All I can tell you is that in romantic affairs, most people tend to want that which is elusive—that which is just out of reach. They don't want what they are stuck with or that which they have to beat off with a stick. Let me illustrate.

I doubt if you could have coerced your wife to marry you during your dating days. It wouldn't have worked. You had to lure, attract, charm, and entice her. This subtle game of courtship unfolded one delicate step at a time. Can you imagine what would have occurred if you had wept violently and hung on her neck saying, "I think I'll die if you don't marry me! I beg you not to turn me down."

That desperate approach might be compared (simplistically) to a persistent used-car salesman. What do you think he would accomplish by telling a potential customer through his tears, "Oh, please buy this car! I need the money so badly, and I've only had two sales so far this week. You just can't walk away."

This is a far-fetched analogy, admittedly, but there is relevance to it. When one has fallen in love with an eligible partner, he attempts to "sell himself" to the other. But like the car dealer, he must not deprive the buyer of free choice in the matter. Instead, he must convince the customer that the purchase is in his own interest. If a person would not buy an automobile to ease the pain of a salesman, how much more unlikely he is to devote his entire life to someone he doesn't love, simply for benevolent reasons. None of us is that unselfish. Each of us intends to select only one person in the course of a lifetime with whom to invest our entire being, and few of us are willing to squander that one shot on someone we merely pity! In fact, it is very difficult to love another person romantically and pity him or her at the same time.

To summarize, if begging and pleading are ineffective methods of attracting a member of the opposite sex during the dating days, why do victims of bad marriages use the same groveling techniques to hold a drifting spouse? They are only increasing the depth of disrespect in the one who is escaping.

QUESTION 419

Is the advice you've offered consistent with Scripture? Is it really appropriate for a Christian to permit a husband or wife to leave without trying to force them to stay?

Yes, letting go of a spouse who wants out of marriage appears to be specifically sanctioned in Scripture. If it were not, I would never offer that advice again. God's Word is the standard for all human behavior, and every recommendation must be run through that screen. In the present context, a passage found in 1 Corinthians 7:12-15 is particularly relevant. Note especially the portion I have italicized.

> If any brother has a wife who is not a believer and she is willing to live with him, he must not divorce her. And if a woman has a husband who is not a believer and he is willing to live with her, she must not divorce him. For the unbelieving husband has been sanctified through his wife, and the unbelieving wife has been sanctified through her believing husband. Otherwise your children

would be unclean, but as it is, they are holy. *But if the unbeliever leaves, let him do so. A believing man or woman is not bound in such circumstances; God has called us to live in peace.*

Those are very straightforward instructions from the apostle Paul. He was talking to Christian men and women who were married to unbelievers—some of whom were undoubtedly involved in bad marriages. He was telling them unequivocally that divorce was not an option. Period. They were required to remain faithful in hopes of winning their ungodly spouses to the Lord. Good counsel! But Paul was also sensitive to those who had no choice in the matter. In instances where divorce was inevitable, believers were advised to let their spouses go. There is no blame in accepting a fate beyond a person's control. And Paul said this release will result in "peace." Here we see the marvelous wisdom of the Creator as expressed in a marital context by the apostle Paul.

QUESTION 420

My wife has been involved in an affair with her boss for six months. I've known about it from the beginning but just haven't been able to confront her. Melanie acts like she doesn't love me anyway. If I give her an ultimatum, I could lose her completely. Can you assure me that won't happen? Have you ever offered the "love must be tough" advice and had it backfire, ending in divorce?

Yes, I have, and I certainly understand your caution. I wish I could guarantee how Melanie will react to a firmer approach. Unfortunately, life offers few certainties, even when all the probabilities point in one direction. Sometimes well-conditioned athletes drop dead from heart attacks. Some outstanding parents raise children who rebel and become drug addicts. Some of the most intelligent, cautious businessmen foolishly bankrupt themselves. Life is like that. Things happen every day that shouldn't have occurred. Nevertheless, we should go with the best information available to us. I saw a sign that said "The fastest horses don't always win, but you should still bet on them." Even as a nongambler, that makes sense to me.

Having offered that disclaimer, let me say that there is nothing risky about treating oneself with greater respect, exhibiting confidence and poise, pulling backward, and releasing the door on the romantic trap. The positive benefits of that approach are often immediate and dramatic. Loving self-respect virtually never fails to have a salutary effect on a drifting lover, unless there is not the tiniest spark left to fan. Thus, in instances when opening the cage door results in a spouse's sudden departure, the relationship was in the coffin already. I'm reminded of the old proverb that says "If you love something, set it free. If it comes back to you, it's yours. If it doesn't come back, it never was yours in the first place." There is a great truth in that adage, and it applies to your relationship with your wife.

Now, obviously, it is risky to precipitate a period of crisis. When explosive individuals are involved in midlife turmoil or a passionate fling with a new lover, great tact and wisdom are required to know when and how to respond. That's why Christian professional counsel is vital before, during, and after the confrontation. It would be unthinkable of me to recommend that victims of affairs indiscriminately pose ultimatums with twenty-four-hour deadlines or that they push an independent partner into a corner. Great caution is needed in such delicate conflicts, and certainly no move should be made without much prayer and supplication before the Lord.

In short, I suggest that you seek the assistance of a competent counselor who can help you deal with the problem of Melanie's affair.

QUESTION 421

If you were the counselor who was helping someone manage a crisis situation, your recommendations to exercise tough love could potentially kill the marriage. Doesn't that make you nervous? Have you ever regretted taking a family in this direction?

Before I answer that question, you need to understand how I see my situation. My role is similar to that of a surgeon who tells a patient that he needs a coronary-artery-bypass operation. The man sits in his doctor's office, hearing the probabilities of success and failure. "If you undergo this operation," the doctor says, "research shows you'll have a 3 percent chance of not surviving the surgery." Wow! Three out of every hundred people who submit to the knife will die on the table! Why would anyone run that risk voluntarily? Because the chances of death are far greater without the surgery.

The "love must be tough" confrontations and ultimatum are like that. They may result in the sudden demise of a relationship. But without the crisis, there is a much higher probability of a lingering death. Instead of bringing the matter to a head while there is a chance for healing, the alternative is to stand by while the marriage dies with a whimper. I'd rather take my chances today, before further damage is done. A blowout is better than a slow leak.

QUESTION 422

My marriage seems beyond repair to me. My husband is running around with other women and threatening to divorce me. Is there really any hope for us?

It's difficult to say without knowing the details, but I can tell you this: I've seen dozens of families who were in your fix but are now happy and whole. I taught a Sunday school class for young married couples for a number of years, and right there under my nose in a conservative church, infidelity was a surprisingly common event. There was one period of time during which I dealt with nineteen different couples where extramarital affairs had either occurred or were seriously threatened. These families are still known to me, and nine of them are apparently happily married ten years later. Though this percentage may seem low, remember that these were families on the verge of divorce that have now survived intact. Loving toughness played a role in their recovery, although their commitment to the Christian faith was the significant factor. So, yes, hope springs eternal, as well it should.

Let me give you a final word of encouragement. Nothing can seem as fixed but change as rapidly as human emotions. When it comes to romantic endeavors, feelings can turn upside down in a day or two. I've seen husbands or wives who expressed hatred for their spouses, saying, "I never want to see you again," only to fall weeping into the other person's arms some hours later.

Hang tough. God isn't through with you and your husband yet.

QUESTION 423

My husband, Paul, has been having an affair for the past three months and is living with the woman. How should I respond in the event that he leaves her and asks me to forgive him and take him back? Should I just throw my arms open and pretend the affair never happened?

Well, you should certainly take him back. That's the point of everything I've written. But your power to negotiate necessary changes will never be greater than in that moment, and you should not deal it away too quickly. I would suggest that you get Paul's written commitment to participate in counseling immediately, not even waiting two or three weeks to get started. Old patterns will persist if serious effort is not made to change them. Your family also has some deep wounds to work through, and they're not likely to complete that healing process on their own. You must make it clear that never again—and I mean never—will sexual unfaithfulness be tolerated. Paul needs this motivation to go straight. He must know, and believe, that the sky will fall if he has one more escapade or even a serious flirtation with another lover. You must convince him that you mean business. If he wavers, even slightly, give him another month or two to sit somewhere wishing he could come home. Better that you continue at the door of matrimonial death now than go through the misery of infidelity again in a few years. Finally, insist on some major spiritual commitments within the family. Your marriage is going to need the healing powers of God and His grace if you are to rebuild what sin has eroded.

451

QUESTION 424

Isn't your recommendation of "tough love" very difficult for a wounded and broken person to implement? It would seem

to be really hard for him or her to square the shoulders and face the possibility of losing the one he or she loves.

Sure, it's hard. Some people have told me flatly that they couldn't do it. Others never quite comprehend what I've said. But to those who make even a small step in the direction of confidence, the rewards are instantaneous. For the person who has cried for days and lost weight and chewed the fingernails into the quick, you can't imagine what a relief it is to gain some self-respect again. Then when his partner also shows a measure of respect for the first time in months, the effect is exhilarating. As a bystander, it is gratifying for me, too.

QUESTION 425

When my wife left me for another man, I felt like the whole thing was my fault. I still feel that way. I had never even looked at another woman, yet here I am taking the blame for her affair. Rationally, I know I'm being very unfair to myself, but I can't help it. Or can I?

It is the typical reaction of a rejected spouse, like yourself, to take the full responsibility for the behavior of an unfaithful spouse. The wounded partner—the person who was clearly the victim of the other's irresponsibility—is the one who suffers the greatest pangs of guilt and feelings of inferiority. How strange that the one who tried to hold things together in the face of obvious rejection often finds herself wondering, *How did I fail him? I just wasn't woman enough to hold my man. I am "nothing" or he wouldn't have left. If only I had been more exciting as a sexual partner. . . . I drove him to it—I wasn't pretty enough. I didn't deserve him in the first place.*

452

The blame for marital disintegration is seldom the fault of the husband or wife alone. It takes two to tangle, as they say, and there is always some measure of shared blame for a divorce. However, when one marriage partner makes up his mind to behave irresponsibly, to become involved extramaritally, or to run from his family commitments and obligations, he usually seeks to justify his behavior by magnifying the failures of his spouse. "You didn't meet my needs, so

I had to satisfy them somewhere else" is the familiar accusation. By increasing the guilt of his partner in this way, he reduces his own culpability. For a husband or wife with low self-esteem, these charges and recriminations are accepted and internalized as indisputable facts.

You must resist the temptation to take all the blame. I'm not recommending that you sit around hating the memory of your wife. Bitterness and resentment are emotional cancers that rot us from within. However, I would encourage you to examine the facts carefully. Ask yourself these questions: *Despite my many mistakes and failures in my marriage, did I value my family and try to preserve it? Did my wife decide to destroy it and then seek justification for her actions? Was I given a fair chance to resolve the areas of greatest irritation? Could I have held her even if I had made all the changes she wanted? Is it reasonable that I should hate myself for this thing that has happened?*

If you examine objectively what has occurred, you might begin to see yourself as a victim of your wife's irresponsibility rather than a worthless failure at the game of love.

QUESTION 426

My wife tried to make me feel guilty when she left. She angrily blamed me for the divorce despite my desperate attempts to hold things together. I'm not a perfect man, but I loved her and would never have left. But in her mind, I failed so miserably as a husband that she was forced to run around with her boss! Can you believe that? She blamed *me* for her adultery!

Your wife is trying to transfer her guilt to you. Nearly every spouse does something similar when engaging in infidelity. Guilt is a very painful emotion, and the person who is in bed with a new lover is very vulnerable to it. Such people must find a way to deal with the condemnation of their own consciences. They have torn up a home, rejected their spouse, wounded their children, and jeopardized their future. Such outrageous behavior demands an explanation of some sort. Thus, they construct a vigorous defense against moral condemnation, usually by shifting blame to the spouse.

Ask any victim of an affair; he or she has probably heard a version of four specific rationalizations designed to handle several sources of guilt. They are:

1. *Marital guilt.* "I know that what I'm doing is difficult for you now, but someday you will understand that it's for the best. I never really loved you, even when we were young. In fact, we should never have gotten married in the first place. Furthermore, this divorce is really your fault. You drove me to it by (insert grievances here, such as frigidity, in-law problems, nagging, overwork, or all the foregoing)."

This message has a transparent purpose. The first sentence, above, marvelously purifies the motives of the unfaithful spouse. It says in effect, "I'm really doing this for your good."

The second sentence is also a beauty. It is designed to serve as an "annulment" to the marriage instead of a cruel abandonment of a loved one. By saying that they should never have gotten married, their union becomes an unfortunate mistake rather than a relationship that God Himself ordained and cemented. (Henry VIII used this approach to eject his first wife, Catherine of Aragon.) Then by putting the remaining responsibility on the other party, the blame is successfully transferred from the guilty to the innocent. So much for wedding vows. Now let's deal with the children.

2. *Parental guilt.* "This will be hard on the kids for a while, but they'll be better off in the long run. It certainly isn't healthy for them to see us fight and argue like we've been doing. Besides, I will spend just as much time with them after things settle down as I do now."

Zap! Zap! Guilt over the children is also tucked away. Would you believe that Dad's escapade with another woman or Mom's flight with Don Juan is actually a constructive thing? Never mind what the children see and comprehend with their big, beautiful eyes. Pay no heed to the conclusions they draw about why Mommy or Daddy left and why he or she doesn't love them anymore and why God let it happen and why the divorce may have been their fault and why life is so painful and scary. Try to ignore the fact that everything stable has just come unstitched in the lives of some very impressionable and sensitive little people. Don't think about it and maybe your pounding heart will settle down. Guilt over the children can be the toughest to rationalize, but, fortunately, hundreds of books and tapes are available today that will help you silence your writhing conscience.

3. *Social guilt.* "I'm sure our friends won't understand at first, and I can hardly wait to hear what your mother will have to say. But it's like I told the pastor last week, our divorce is really no one's fault. We've just outgrown each other. People change as the years go by, and relationships have to change to accommodate them." (If a woman is speaking she may say: "Besides, I am entitled to do what's best for me once in a while. I've given my entire life to everyone else; now it's time for me to think of myself. It's only fair that I fit into the picture at some point, and this is it. Anyway, what's right for me will prove best for you and the children, too.")

This line of reasoning has been provided for women today almost word for word by the more radical elements of the feminist movement. It is only one of many rationalizations by which selfishness can be purified and made to appear altruistic. Three down and one to go.

4. *Divine guilt.* "I've prayed about this decision, and I am now certain that God approves of what I've chosen to do."

There it is in living color—the ultimate rationalization. If the Creator in His infinite wisdom has taken the matter under advisement and judged the divorce to be in the best interest of everyone, who can argue that point further? The conversation is over. Sin has been sanctified. Guilt is expunged. Self-respect is restored, and, alas, evil has prevailed. Having settled the "big four," every moral and spiritual obstacle is removed. The stage is set for further infidelity and eventual divorce.

QUESTION 427

It has always been my understanding that marriage was supposed to be based on unconditional love. That is, the

commitment to one another should be independent of behavior, no matter how offensive or unfaithful. But your concept of accountability seems to be saying, "I will love you as long as you do what I want."

You've misunderstood my point. The limitations of language make it very difficult to express this concept adequately, but let me try again. I certainly believe in the validity of unconditional love, and in fact, the mutual accountability I have recommended is an expression of that love! For example, if a husband is behaving in ways that will harm himself, his children, his marriage, and the family of the "other woman," then confrontation with him becomes an act of love. The easiest response by the innocent partner would be to look the other way and pretend she doesn't notice. But from my perspective, that is tantamount to a parent's refusing to confront a fourteen-year-old who comes home drunk at 4:00 A.M. That mother or father has an obligation to create a crisis in response to destructive behavior. Love *demands* that they do that! I'm trying to say that unconditional love is not synonymous with permissiveness, passivity, weakness, and appeasement. Sometimes it requires toughness, discipline, and accountability.

QUESTION 428

Your tough love contradicts what I have been taught by Christian leaders who say that as believers "we have no rights." If I understand what they say, I should not even notice instances of disrespect because I have no rights to be defended. Do you disagree?

In a manner of speaking. What must be understood is that the person who holds the partner accountable is not defending his "rights." He is defending the marriage. He acts to confront and deal with a behavior that is threatening to the relationship. As such, it is not a selfish thing but something that is designed to protect what they have built together.

That "no-rights" philosophy would be unbeatable if both partners were totally mature, unselfish, and loving. Unfortunately, we are all riddled with imperfection and self-serving desires. Therefore we need reinforcement and accountability in order to do what is right. When only one member of the family buys the "no-rights" concept and tries to implement it, a marriage can be blown apart. Why? Because the nonparticipating spouse begins to crawl all over the "line of respect." He gets the lion's share of everything—money, sex, power, fun and games, etc. Knowing the partner's spiritual obligation, he feels entitled by divine decree to do as he pleases.

The Christian spouse who is clinging desperately to this theological understanding is not made of steel. Nor is he blind. He sees instance after instance of disrespect and does his best to ignore them. But they go straight into a memory bank, whether he wishes to store them or not. That's the way he's made. Then one day when his resistance is down, perhaps when he is exhausted, or in a woman's case, during the pressures of premenstrual tension, a hydrogen bomb can be detonated that may blow off the head of her startled husband. A "no-rights" position would have carried that person through a short race; unfortunately, life is so daily, and the runner staggers on heartbreak hill.

I must hasten to offer an important disclaimer. Any recommendation can be carried to extremes, including defense of the "line of respect." There are millions of women, especially, who need nothing less than an excuse to harangue their spouses over perceived violations of one sort or another. They do that better than anything else in life. Their poor husbands live with a constant barrage of complaints and criticisms, knowing they can do nothing right. Then here comes Dobson advising, "Hold 'em accountable, ladies!"

That's not what I intended to say. Remember that 1 Corinthians 13:5 tells us love "is not easily provoked" (KJV). That tolerance is certainly evident in good marriages. Husbands and wives must overlook a multitude of flaws in one another and not howl over the speck in a partner's eye when the accuser has a log sticking out of his own. Prolonged anger can kill a marriage—especially when it reflects perceived wrongs from the past that have never been forgiven.

Thus, the "love must be tough" concept does not suggest that people become touchy and picky; it does hold that genuine instances of disrespect should be acknowledged and handled within the context of love. And certainly, when major violations occur that threaten the relationship, they should be met head-on.

QUESTION 429

I know that my husband is a "womanizer"—a guy who can't resist anything in a skirt. Will he always be like this? Can I change him?

It is difficult, if not impossible, to change anyone. It certainly cannot be accomplished by nagging and complaining and chastising. That only causes a person to dig in his heels and fight to the finish. What you can do is make it clear to your husband that he can't have you and a harem too, and that he must make a choice between his lust and his love. Unfortunately, merely putting these alternatives before him verbally will not force him to select one over the other. He would rather have both toys. That's why there will probably come a time for loving toughness, when you back your words by firmness and definitive action. Remember in that difficult hour that God can change your husband and that the crisis may be a divine vehicle to bring him to his senses.

QUESTION 430

I've been aware of my husband's unfaithfulness for some time now. I've taken him to task for it, which has resulted in some incredible, horrible battles. I have even made demands that he stop his infidelity, yet no change in his attitude and behavior has happened. What am I doing wrong?

I'm afraid you've made the common mistake of misunderstanding the difference between expressions of anger and loving toughness. Simply becoming angry and throwing temper tantrums is no more effective with a spouse than it is with a rebellious teenager. Screaming and accusing and berating are rarely successful in changing the behavior of human beings of any age. What is required is a course of action—an ultimatum that demands a specific response and results in a consequence. Then you must have the courage to deliver on the promise.

QUESTION 431

Is it harder for a man or for a woman to recover from an affair by a spouse?

I have not observed any appreciable difference between the sexes at the time of disclosure. Both husbands and wives suffer incalculable anguish when a mate is unfaithful. Men do seem to have a cultural advantage after the crisis is over, however. Their work is often a better diversion, and their economic consequences are less severe. They also find it easier to find someone new, as a rule. But no one wins in illicit affairs of the heart.

QUESTION 432

Do you feel that there is a kind of "blindness" that can occur when a victim of an affair denies the truth? I seemed to experience this when my husband was fooling around with my best friend. The affair went on for two years before I could acknowledge it to myself. But why would I deny the truth? Why do victims "choose" to be blind?

That psychological process is called denial, and it is designed to protect the mind from an unacceptable thought or reality. Once a person admits to himself or herself that a beloved spouse has been unfaithful, then he or she is obligated to deal with that circumstance. The extremely painful experiences of grief, anxiety, and insomnia become inevitable once the truth has been faced. Furthermore, the injured person fears that a confrontation with the unfaithful partner might drive the spouse into the arms of the new lover. Given these concerns, the person consciously or unconsciously chooses not to notice the affair in the hope that it will blow over and be forgotten. Obviously, there is ample motivation for a vulnerable person to deny what the eyes are seeing.

When the evidence of unfaithfulness becomes overwhelming, a man or woman will sometimes "ask" the guilty spouse to assist with the denial. This is done by making accusations in the hope of being proven wrong. For example, a wife will say, "Are you and Donna seeing one another?"

"No, I've told you a thousand times that nothing is going on," he lies.

"But where were you until 2:00 A.M. last night?"

"I had car trouble. Now will you get off my back?"

This wife knows her husband's story is phony, but she continually asks him to lie to her. And interestingly, she does not feel obligated to "blow the whistle" on him until he admits his involvement . . . which may never happen. These tacit agreements help her maintain the illusion that all is well and provide a permissive environment in which the husband can play around.

Denial has many applications and uses in human experience. It will permit a woman to ignore a suspicious lump in her breast or the drugs in her son's bedroom or the debt that the family is accumulating. Through this process the mind is protected for a time, but it often permits even greater disasters to gain a foothold in our lives.

QUESTION 433

How should a person respond to someone who is in denial? I have a very good friend whose wife is cheating on him, but he chooses not to see it. Should I make him face reality?

There is no blanket answer to that question, in view of all the thousands of specific situations to which it could be applied. There are times when denial is the only link to sanity or stability, and it must be preserved. On other occasions, to break the bubble of illusion can be a loving thing. Either way, it is risky to awaken a dreamer. If the need for denial is intense, the individual will often lash out at the one who threatens its validity.

QUESTION 434

What disturbs me is that in many of the cases of infidelity of which I'm aware, the unfaithful spouse has claimed to be a Christian. They were seasoned believers—not merely babes

in Christ. How could they cheat on their spouses? What goes on in the mind of someone who violates his own standard of morality in so blatant a manner?

Like you, I'm amazed at the audacity of those who pursue affairs while calling themselves Christians. You talk about moral gymnastics! Such people can cite the seventh commandment by heart ("Thou shalt not commit adultery," KJV), and they fully understand God's promise to punish sinful behavior, yet somehow they expect to break His laws with impunity! Not only is their behavior forbidden by God, but it's also in violation of every moral code in the civilized world. If that isn't heavy enough, an unfaithful spouse has to deal with the responsibility for crushing his or her wife or husband and for warping the children of their union—those innocent and unsuspecting kids who are about to be shredded by one parent's selfishness and shame. All told, it's enough to cool off some of the most passionate playboys and playgirls. In fact, millions have come right to the door of an affair and, having seen what lies just over the threshold, have retreated to the arms of a relieved spouse.

*Q*UESTION 435

What do you say to the woman who tolerates infidelity in her husband because she has no financial resources? What if she is afraid to confront him because he could leave her in poverty?

I have no simple answers for that lady. Life can place us between rocks and hard places where problems seem almost unsolvable! Such is the plight of mothers raising children with little or no financial help from their ex-husbands. According to the Department of Health and Human Services, this is the primary source of poverty in America today. Almost half of all people living below the poverty line are divorced women with children. The same survey revealed that half of the divorced mothers do not receive the court-ordered amount of child support from the ex-husbands.[179] I'm pleased that the federal government is taking steps, at last, to deal with deadbeat dads. It's about time! In a society that is regulated to death with laws and ordinances for virtually every human activity, it has taken us intolerably long to deal with parents who won't care for their kids. For now, impoverished moms are faced with extremely difficult questions when spousal infidelity is disclosed.

Q UESTION 436

Do you believe that a marital separation for reasons other than infidelity is wrong?

I find no biblical prohibition against couples living apart for a time, if their purpose is not to seek divorce and remarriage. Husbands and wives can often trample on one another's nerves and desperately need some time alone to reorient their outlook. From my point of view, the rightness or wrongness of their separation depends entirely on intent, which only God can judge. For example, a wife whose alcoholic husband needs to experience life without the support of his family may find temporary separation to be the only way to get him to seek professional help. This crisis of loneliness may be the last hope to jar the man to his senses, and his wife could be doing a loving thing by making him more miserable! If this is the desire that motivates the more responsible partner to separate, then I find no scriptural condemnation of it. But please be warned! This understanding can also provide an open door to rationalization for those who are unhappy in marriage and are seeking a way out. I am certainly not sanctioning that maneuver.

Q UESTION 437

462

Several months ago my husband announced that he was leaving me for another woman. Since then, he has been seeing her regularly, but he hasn't left home and seems to be in a state of confusion. He's lost fifteen pounds and just looks terrible. What do you think is going on in his mind? He won't talk to me about his feelings, and he becomes angry when I ask him questions.

It is likely that your husband is experiencing intense guilt and conflict that often accompany a selfish and sinful act such as infidelity. God has placed a little voice in the human soul that screams bloody murder at such moments, although some of us have learned to stuff a fist in its mouth. Even when we ignore its condemnation, the conscience is a formidable opponent of irresponsibility, and it will not permit gross violations of moral laws without a struggle. It is not uncommon for a person in this situation to experience a kind of internal war that can only be resolved in one of three ways: (1) the conscience wins and the person returns to the straight life; (2) the person rationalizes so effectively that his behavior begins to seem pure and holy; or (3) the conscience wins but the person persists in doing what he or she wants to do anyway.

People in the third category, which may include your husband, can be some of the most miserable men and women on the face of the earth. Their behavior has contradicted their personal code of ethics, and all attempts to reconcile the two have been futile. Stated another way, these individuals are in a dogfight with their consciences, and the fur is flying in all directions. Not only psychological disorders but physical illness can result from such disharmony! A person who is going through this internal conflict often experiences depression, weight loss, sleepless nights, nail biting, etc. The ordeal is extremely uncomfortable to the sensitive individual.

If we are right about your husband's frame of mind, you can expect him to commit himself very quickly either to you or to the other woman. It is simply too painful to remain in suspended animation between good and evil. I would advise you to seek professional counsel as to whether this is the proper moment to require your husband to make his choice. With the few facts I've been given, I would lean in that direction.

QUESTION **438**

Since almost every couple fights from time to time, what distinguishes a healthy marriage from one that is in serious trouble? How can a husband and wife know when their

conflicts are within normal limits and when they are symptoms of more serious problems?

It is true that conflict occurs in virtually all marriages. That is how resentment and frustration are ventilated. The difference between stable families and those in serious trouble is evidenced by what happens after a fight. In healthy relationships, a period of confrontation ends in forgiveness—in drawing together—in deeper respect and understanding—and sometimes in sexual satisfaction. But in unstable marriages, a period of conflict produces greater pain and anger that persists until the next fight. When that occurs, one unresolved issue is compounded by another and another. That accumulation of resentment is an ominous circumstance in any marriage. Isn't this why the apostle Paul admonished us not to let the sun go down on our wrath (Ephesians 4:26)?

QUESTION 439

What would your recommendation be to a young wife and mother whose husband is extremely violent and frequently abuses her and their children?

She should get herself and her kids out of the home immediately. Abuse of spouses and children simply must not be tolerated. It's against the law, and the law must be enforced. No one has to live in an abusive environment today.

QUESTION 440

Would you recommend that the Christian wife of an abusive husband actually divorce him?

No, I think she should separate in an effort to get him to acknowledge and deal with his abusive behavior. Through prayer and a resolute spirit, she may be able to save the marriage and help her husband overcome his violent tendencies. That is easier said than done, of course, and there are no guarantees that the outcome will be as hoped. But I believe it is best to try.

QUESTION 441

How should she go about dealing with her husband's problem?

The principles of *Love Must Be Tough* offer the best response to an abusive husband. They begin with a recognition that behavior does not change when things are going smoothly. If change is to occur, it usually does so in a crisis situation. Thus, a crisis must be created and managed very carefully.

After moving out and making it clear that the woman has no intention of returning, the ball moves to her husband's court. If he never responds, she never returns. If it takes a year, or five years, then so be it. He has to want her badly enough to face his problem and to reach out to her. When (and if) her husband acknowledges that he has an abusive behavior pattern and promises to deal with it, negotiations can begin. A plan can be agreed upon that involves intensive Christian counseling with a person of the wife's choosing. She should not return home until the counselor concludes that she will be safe and that the husband is on the way to recovery. Gradually, they put their relationship back together.

It's a long shot but one worth working to achieve.

QUESTION 442

Are you suggesting that any woman who is being beaten should take the same course of action? My husband has only hit me once, in a big fight we had. Should I separate from him?

Your situation may represent another category of behavior. A man can become so enraged on a given occasion that he does something he is immediately sorry for and would never do again. That is very different from a repetitive, pathological situation. You will have to decide how you will deal with that exceptional situation, but I would recommend that it become a point of serious discussion between you. If he hit you once, he can hit you again. You need to set some ground rules that will prevent a similar situation from recurring.

QUESTION 443

I notice that you rarely recommend to unhappy and angry spouses that they seek a divorce and get on with their lives. I disagree. My husband and I were always incompatible and should never have married in the first place. Why do you consider divorce to be a last resort?

Divorce often looks like the easy solution to a very unpleasant situation, and indeed, there are situations wherein it is necessary (continued infidelity, etc.). However, divorce and its aftermath are difficult for both partners and rarely deliver on the promise of "a quick fix." It is usually far more painful than advertised. Everyone loses when a marriage turns sour, especially the children involved. Surprisingly, their grandparents struggle too. I read recently that the parents of divorcing children typically suffer as much as their warring sons and daughters. In-laws can do nothing but stand and watch as two people they love begin clawing one another to pieces, leaving wounded grandchildren in their wake. Certainly, there are no winners when a marriage begins to unravel.

Those who contemplate divorce as the answer to "soul hunger" or the lack of romantic attachments in marriage, which may be the majority of families that split up, remind me of a documentary film made during the early days of motion pictures. Near the top of the Eiffel Tower stood a self-styled inventor with a pair of homemade wings strapped to his arms. This fellow was determined to fly. The jerky black-and-white film captures him pacing back and forth, looking down, and trying to work up the courage to jump. Despite the primitive camera work, the viewer today can see the uncertainty of the inventor. "Should I or shouldn't I?" Finally, he climbed on the rail, wobbled for a moment, and then jumped. Of course he fell like a rock. The camera then panned straight downward as the "flier" descended to his death on the street below.

Many depressed and hurting people are like that hapless man on the Eiffel Tower. They are enticed by the lure of freedom—by the promise of glorious and unencumbered flight . . . by an escape from

466

family stresses. They stand on the railing wondering, *Should I or shouldn't I?*

Those who take the plunge usually discover that their wings fail to provide the lift they expect. Instead, they soon tumble headlong into custody battles, loneliness, bitterness, and even poverty. So much for freedom, which was defined in the lyrics to the song "Me and Bobby McGee" as "just another word for nothing left to lose."[180]

Except in unusual cases, divorce is not an easy answer to the stress of a troubled marriage. It usually involves a ripping and tearing of flesh. That fact is now verified by research. Divorce puts people at a high risk for both psychiatric problems and physical disease. Dr. David Larson, psychiatrist and researcher in Washington, D.C., reviewed medical studies on this subject and made some startling observations. For instance, being divorced and a nonsmoker is only slightly less dangerous than smoking a pack or more a day and staying married. Also, every type of terminal cancer strikes divorced individuals of both sexes, both white and nonwhite, more frequently than it does married people. What's more, premature death rates are significantly higher among divorced men and women. Physicians believe this is because the emotional trauma of divorce stresses the body and lowers the immune system's defense against disease.[181]

In the 1960s, the surgeon general declared cigarettes harmful to the smoker's health. More recently, researchers have warned us about the dangers of foods high in fat and cholesterol. In that tradition, maybe a warning should be offered to newlyweds about the consequences of marital breakup. It can be equally dangerous.

Note: I came across an article some time ago that expressed the pain associated with divorce more dramatically than anything I've read. It is entitled "Death of a Marriage," by Pat Conroy (*Atlanta Magazine*). I've obtained permission to quote a short passage in hopes of helping someone who is contemplating a divorce. If you are such a person and you've been asking the Lord for guidance, perhaps this is His answer. If you know someone who is considering that decision, you might let him or her read Conroy's personal experience. I think it is rather typical of those who have been through that nightmare.

Each divorce is the death of a small civilization. Two people declare war on each other, and their screams and tears infect their entire world with the bacilli of their pain. The greatest comes from the wound where love once issued forth.

I find it hard to believe how many people now get divorced, how many submit to such extraordinary pain. For there are no clean divorces. Divorces should be conducted in abattoirs or surgical wards. In my own case, I think it would have been easier if Barbara had died. I would have been gallant at her funeral and shed real tears—far easier than staring across a table, telling each other it was over.

It was a killing thing to look at the mother of my children and know that we would not be together for the rest of our lives. It was terrifying to say good-by, to reject a part of my own history.

When I went through my divorce I saw it as a country, and it was treeless, airless; there were no furloughs and no holidays. I entered without passport, without directions and absolutely alone. Insanity and hopelessness grew in that land like vast orchards of malignant fruit. I do not know the precise day that I arrived in that country. Nor am I certain that you can ever renounce your citizenship there.

Each divorce has its own metaphors that grow out of the dying marriage. One man was inordinately proud of his aquarium. He left his wife two weeks after the birth of their son. What visitors noticed next was that she was not taking care of the aquarium. The fish began dying. The two endings became linked in my mind.

For a long time I could not discover my own metaphor of loss—until the death of our dog, Beau, became the irrefutable message that Barbara and I were finished.

Beau was a feisty, crotchety dachshund Barbara had owned when we married. It took a year of pained toleration for us to form our alliance. But Beau had one of those illuminating inner lives that only lovers of dogs can understand. He had a genius for companionship. To be licked by Beau when you awoke in the morning was a fine thing.

On one of the first days of our separation, when I went to the house to get some clothes, my youngest daughter, Megan, ran out to tell me that Beau had been hit by a car and taken to the animal clinic. I raced there and found Ruth Tyree, Beau's veterinarian. She carried Beau in to see me and laid him on the examining table.

I had not cried during the terrible breaking away from Barbara. I had told her I was angry at my inability to cry. Now I came apart completely. It was not weeping, it was screaming, it was despair.

The car had crushed Beau's spine, the X ray showing irreparable damage. Beau looked up at me while Dr. Tyree handed me a piece of paper, saying that she needed my signature to put Beau to sleep.

I could not write my name because I could not see the paper. I leaned against the examining table and cried as I had never cried in my life, crying not just for Beau but for Barbara, the children, myself, for the death of a marriage, for inconsolable loss. Dr. Tyree touched me gently, and I heard her crying above me. And Beau, in the last grand gesture of his life, dragged himself the length of the table on his two good legs and began licking the tears as they ran down my face.

I had lost my dog and found my metaphor. In the X ray of my dog's crushed spine, I was looking at a portrait of my broken marriage.

But there are no metaphors powerful enough to describe the moment when you tell the children about divorce. Divorces without children are minor-league divorces. To look into the eyes of your children and to tell them that you are mutilating their family and changing all their tomorrows is an act of desperate courage that I never want to repeat. It is also their parents' last act of solidarity and the absolute sign that the marriage is over. It felt as though I had doused my entire family with gasoline and struck a match.

The three girls entered the room and would not look at me or Barbara. Their faces, all dark wings and grief and human hurt, told me that they already knew. My betrayal of these young, sweet girls filled the room.

They wrote me notes of farewell, since it was I who was moving out. When I read them, I did not see how I could ever survive such excruciating pain. The notes said, "I love you, Daddy. I will visit you." For months I would dream of visiting my three daughters locked in a mental hospital. The fear of damaged children was my most crippling obsession.

For a year, I walked around feeling as if I had undergone a lobotomy. There were records I could not listen to because of their association with Barbara, poems I could not read from books I could not pick up. There is a restaurant I will never return to because it was the scene of an angry argument between us. It was a year when memory was an acid.

I began to develop the odd habits of the very lonely. I turned the stereo on as soon as I entered my apartment. I drank to the point of not caring. I cooked elaborate meals for myself, then could not eat them.

I had entered into the dark country of divorce, and for a year I was one of its ruined citizens. I suffered. I survived. I studied myself on the edge, and introduced myself to the stranger who lived within.

Barbara and I had one success in our divorce, and it is an extraordinarily rare one. As the residue of anger and hurt subsided with time, we remained friends. We saw each other for drinks or lunch occasionally, and I met her boyfriend, Tom.

Once, when I was leaving a party, I looked back and saw Barbara and Tom holding hands. They looked very happy together, and it was painful to recognize it. I wanted to go back and say something to Tom, but I mostly wanted to say it to Barbara. I wanted to say that I admired Tom's taste in women.[182]

Reading these powerful words helps explain why I am so thoroughly committed to the concept of lifelong marriage. That's the way it was intended by the Creator when He laid out the blueprint for the family. Of course, we must acknowledge that divorces do occur, and many of my readers have undoubtedly gone through this tragic experience already. In those cases, we must do all we can to care for them, to pray with them, and to help them deal with the pain that Conroy graphically illustrated. But if we can prevent just one unnecessary dissolution from occurring, with its terrible implications for three or more generations, we will have fulfilled a critically important mission.

470

QUESTION 444

My marriage to my husband has been a very unsatisfying thing for me. I would divorce him if it were not for my concern for

our three children. What does the research say about the impact of divorce on kids?

It's now known that emotional development in children is directly related to the presence of warm, nurturing, sustained, and continuous interaction with *both* parents. Anything that interferes with the vital relationship with either mother or father can have lasting consequences for the child.

One landmark study revealed that 90 percent of children from divorced homes suffered from an acute sense of shock when the separation occurred, including profound grieving and irrational fears.[183] Fifty percent reported feeling rejected and abandoned,[184] and indeed, half of the fathers never came to see their children three years after the divorce.[185] One-third of the boys and girls feared abandonment by the remaining parent, and 66 percent experienced yearning for the absent parent with an intensity that researchers described as overwhelming.[186] Most significant, 37 percent of the children were even more unhappy and dissatisfied five years after the divorce than they had been at eighteen months.[187] In other words, time did not heal their wounds.

That's the real meaning of divorce. It is certainly what I think about, with righteous indignation, when I see infidelity and marital deceit portrayed on television as some kind of exciting game for two.

The bottom line is that you are right to consider the welfare of your children in deciding whether or not to seek a divorce. As empty as the marital relationship continues to be for you, it is likely, from what I know of your circumstances, that your kids will fare better if you choose to stick it out.

Q UESTION 445

What about parent-child separation that occurs for reasons other than divorce? Is the pain any less intense for kids when a parent has a good reason to be away?

Research confirms that the consequences of *any* parent-child separation can be severe. In one study of fathers whose jobs required them to be away from their families for long periods of time, the children tended to experience numerous negative reactions, including anger, rejection, depression, low self-esteem, and commonly, a decline in school performance.[188] Those findings have been confirmed in other contexts, as well.

Some of those conclusions were presented at a White House conference at which I spoke a few years ago. The other speaker was Dr. Armand Nicholi, professor of psychiatry at Harvard University. That day, Dr. Nicholi explained how family circumstances that make parents inaccessible to their children produce some of the same effects as divorce itself. Cross-cultural studies make it clear that parents in the United States spend less time with their children than parents in almost any other nation in the world. For decades, millions of fathers have devoted themselves exclusively to their occupations and activities away from home. More recently, mothers have joined the workforce in huge numbers, rendering themselves exhausted at night and burdened with domestic duties on weekends. The result: No one is at home to meet the needs of millions of lonely preschoolers and latchkey children. Dr. Nicholi expressed regret that his comments would make many parents feel uncomfortable and guilty. However, he felt obligated to report the facts as he saw them.

Most important (and the point of his address), Dr. Nicholi stressed the undeniable link between the interruption of parent-child relationships and the escalation of psychiatric problems that we were then seeing and that are even more pronounced today. If the numbers of dysfunctional families and absentee parents continued to escalate, he said, serious national health problems were inevitable. One-half of all hospital beds in the United States at that time were taken up by psychiatric patients. That figure could hit 95 percent if the incidence of divorce, child abuse, child molestation, and child neglect continue to soar. In that event, Dr. Nicholi said, we would also see vast increases in teen suicide, already up more than 300 percent in twenty-five years, drug abuse, crimes of violence, and problems related to sexual disorientation.[189]

I have reason to understand a measure of the pain spoken of by Dr. Nicholi. I experienced it when I was six years old. My mother and father left me with my aunt for six months while they traveled. That last night together, I sat on my mother's lap while she told me how much she loved me and that she and my father would come back for me as soon as they could. Then they drove away as the sun dropped below the horizon. I sat on the floor in the dark for an unknown period of time, fighting back the tears as depression engulfed me. That sorrowful evening was so intense that its pain can be recalled instantly today, more than five decades later.

In short, even when parent-child separation occurs for valid reasons in a loving home, a boy or girl frequently interprets parental departure as evidence of rejection. If we have any choice in the matter, we should not put them through that painful experience.

QUESTION 446

Our children are all on their own now, and my husband and I are free to do some of the traveling we have always planned to do when we got them through college. But lately I feel too tired even to keep the house clean and too depressed to care about planning or doing anything extra. I'm only forty-six, yet some days I can hardly get out of bed in the morning. I just want to put my head under the pillow and cry—for no reason at all. So why do I feel so terrible? My husband is trying to be patient, but this morning he growled, "You have everything a woman could want. . . . What do you have to be blue about?" Do you think I could be losing my mind?

I doubt if there is anything wrong with your mind. The symptoms you describe sound as if you may be entering menopause, and if so, your discomfort may be caused by the hormonal imbalance that accompanies glandular upheaval. I suggest that you make an appointment to see a gynecologist or other physician in the next few days. He or she can help you.

473

QUESTION 447

Can you give me a simple definition of *menopause*?

It is a time of transition in a woman's life when the reproductive capacity is phasing out. Menstruation gradually stops, and hormonal changes occur. Specifically, the ovaries produce only about one-eighth the estrogen that they once did. This affects not only the reproductive system but the emotions as well. If you are having irregular periods, if you frequently cry for no apparent reason, if you are having hot flashes or night sweats, if your interest in sex has diminished, if you have very low self-esteem and are depressed most of the time, and if you lack the energy to get through your day—you need immediate medical attention. There is hope for women who are suffering from symptoms associated with menopause. Estrogen-replacement therapy can help put you on your feet again. There are other disorders that produce symptoms similar to menopause. That's why it is important to have a complete physical exam to get a definitive diagnosis.

QUESTION 448

Is depression more common among men or women?

Depression occurs in both sexes but is less frequent in men. It is also more crisis-oriented in men. In other words, men get depressed over specific problems, such as a business setback or an illness. Typically, however, they are less likely to experience the vague, generalized, almost indefinable feeling of discouragement that some women encounter on a regular basis. Even a cloudy day may be enough to bring on a physical and emotional slowdown, known as the blahs, for those who are particularly vulnerable to depression. That kind of emotional fluctuation is more common in women.

QUESTION 449

474

What are the most common causes of depression in women?

I asked that question of more than ten thousand women who completed a questionnaire entitled "Sources of Depression in Women." The most frequently reported concern was low self-esteem. More than 50 percent of an initial test group placed this problem at the top of the list, and 80 percent put it in the top five. These were primarily young, healthy women with seemingly happy marriages, which should have produced greater contentedness. Nevertheless, the majority struggled with feelings of inadequacy and a lack of confidence. That finding is rather typical of American women in all age categories and in various economic strata.

QUESTION 450

My wife has been severely depressed for nearly three months. What kind of treatment or therapy would you recommend for her?

Get her to a physician, perhaps an internist, as soon as possible. This kind of prolonged depression can have serious medical and psychological consequences, yet it is usually very responsive to treatment. Antidepressant drugs are effective in controlling most cases of depression. She could also be entering menopause and may need estrogen-replacement therapy or some other hormone treatment. Of course, medication will not correct an emotional problem, if that is what underlies her depression. She may need to talk to a psychologist or a psychiatrist after you have approached the problem from a medical perspective. The important thing is to get going. Depression should not be permitted to continue unchecked.

QUESTION 451

I came home one night last week and was so depressed that I just couldn't cope. I was upset at my kids and angry at my husband. There was nothing to do but go to bed, which I did. I slept for nearly ten hours and got up feeling great. Everything looked so much better. Am I correct is assuming from this that my perception of trouble is very influenced by fatigue?

You bet it is! When a person is exhausted, he is attacked by ideas he thought he conquered long ago. The great football coach for the Green Bay Packers, Vince Lombardi, once explained why he pushed his team so hard toward proper physical conditioning. He said, "Fatigue makes cowards of us all."[190] He was absolutely right. As the reserves of human energy are depleted, one's ability to reject distressing thoughts and wild impressions is greatly reduced.

This is why I recommend that couples never talk about depressing, disturbing, and highly emotional topics at night. File them away until the next morning. You'll both handle the problems better when the sun is high in the sky.

QUESTION 452

My stepfather abused me sexually when I was a child. This went on for three years, and it never did come to light. It has been two decades since then, but I just can't get past it. I still hate that man and think about him nearly every day. I know that isn't healthy. But how can I get on with my life despite what was done to me?

It is understandable that you would continue to struggle with the abuse you went through as a child. Our emotions are so intense when we are young that our wounds and injuries often stay with us for a lifetime. The pain is immeasurably worse when the one who wronged us was a parent or a parent surrogate. Nevertheless, the bitterness you feel today is hurting you, not your stepfather. It will continue to haunt you unless you can come to terms with it.

Psychologists and ministers now agree that there is only one cure for the cancer of hate and resentment. It is to forgive, which Dr. Archibald Hart defines as "giving up my right to hurt you for hurting me."[191] Only when we find the emotional maturity to release those who have wronged us, whether they have repented or not, will the wounds finally start to heal.

Jesus said it like this, "And when you stand praying, if you hold anything against anyone, forgive him, so that your Father in heaven may forgive you your sins" (Mark 11:25). Note that Jesus said nothing about who was right and who was wrong. Forgiveness, like love, must be unmerited and unconditional; experiencing it begins the healing process.

Your stepfather has stolen your childhood. Don't let him rob your peace of mind as an adult. Turn him over to the One who said, "Vengeance is mine; I will repay, sayeth the Lord" (Romans 12:19, KJV). If you will give up your right to hurt the one who hurt you, the tragedy of your early years can be overcome. You will probably need the help of a pastor, a counselor, or a psychologist in working your way through these terrible memories. The sooner you can get on with that work, the better.

Q UESTION 453

I have a lot of stress in my life and just don't know how to cope with it. Any suggestions? When the roof caves in at your house, when your little girl gets the measles or your teenager flunks a course in school or your spouse gets laid off at work, how do you cope with the stress?

Your question reminds me of an old baseball story about Bill Clem, a famous National League umpire. He used to have a habit of hesitating a minute before signaling a ball or a strike. It was just a quirk of his. One day there was this hotshot young pitcher on the mound who would fire away, and Bill Clem would take his time calling the pitch.

Finally, in about the sixth inning, the kid was getting irritated. He threw one crucial pitch and then just couldn't help yelling, "Come on, Bill. What is it?"

Clem pulled off his face mask, stared the kid down, and said, "It ain't nothing 'til I call it something."

Well, that's kind of the way it is in life. We can't stop the curveballs from coming our way, but we do get the privilege of deciding what to call them. You can determine whether a stressful time is the most horrible, terrible, unfair thing that ever happened to you or whether it's just another common problem that you'll manage to get through somehow.

Remember, also, that the way you react is being watched carefully by your kids. If we show them that we can cope, they'll also be more likely to handle their stress more easily.

Q UESTION 454

I went through a very troubling adolescence, and I've never gotten over it. Even today I can feel the rejection and the

ridicule. Especially I hate my body with all of its flaws. Is there anything you can say to help me begin to come to terms with myself?

Millions of adults today, like you, experience something that might be called "self-loathing." They go through life weighed down by this unnecessary and debilitating burden. Just as you learned to hate your body when you were in adolescence, they despised themselves as teenagers and continue at war with themselves into the adult years. It is self-imposed ridicule, and there are few experiences in life that are more destructive.

Dr. Maxwell Maltz, the plastic surgeon who authored a classic book on this subject entitled *Psychocybernetics,* said women came to him in the 1920s requesting that their breasts be reduced in size.[192] More recently they wanted them augmented with silicone (until the health risks became understood).

False values!

In King Solomon's biblical love song, he asked his bride to overlook his dark skin that occurred from exposure to the sun. But today he'd be the pride of the beach.

False values!

Modern women are ashamed to admit that they carry an extra ten pounds of weight, yet Rembrandt would have loved to paint their plump bodies.

False values!

The standards by which we measure our acceptability as human beings are arbitrary, temporary, and unfair. It's a system designed to undermine confidence and paralyze its victims. Your personal worth is not really dependent on the opinions of others or the fluctuating values that they represent. Every person alive is entitled to dignity, self-respect, and confidence.

478

The sooner you can accept the transcending worth of your humanness as a gift from God, the sooner you can rid yourself of the burden of low self-esteem. He cares for you, and I believe He will help you end the civil war that rages within. It's about time, don't you think?

23

The Great Marriage Killers

QUESTION 455

Would you identify some of the major "marriage killers" that are most responsible for the high divorce rate that plagues today's families?

It would take perhaps fifty volumes to describe them all, and even then we would only scratch the surface. Any one of the following "dragons" can rip a relationship to shreds if given an opportunity to do so:

Overcommitment and physical exhaustion: Beware of this condition. It is especially insidious for young couples who are trying to get started in a profession or in school. Do not try to go to college, work full-time, have a baby, manage a toddler, fix up a house, and start a business at the same time. It sounds ridiculous, but many young couples do just that and are then surprised when their marriages fall apart. Why wouldn't they? The only time they see each other is when they are worn out! Husbands and wives must reserve time for one another if they hope to keep their love alive.

Excessive credit and conflict over how money will be spent: We've said it before. Pay cash for consumable items or don't buy. Don't spend more on a house or a car than you can afford, leaving too few resources

479

for dating, short trips, baby-sitters, etc. Allocate your funds with the wisdom of Solomon.

Selfishness: There are two kinds of people in the world, the givers and the takers. A marriage between two givers can be a beautiful thing. Friction is inevitable for a giver and a taker. But two takers can claw each other to pieces within a period of weeks. Selfishness will devastate marital partners in short order.

Unhealthy relationships with in-laws: If either the husband or wife has not been fully emancipated from the parents, it is best not to live near them. Autonomy is difficult for some mothers and fathers to grant, and close proximity is built for trouble.

Unrealistic expectations: Some couples come into marriage anticipating rose-covered cottages, walks down primrose lanes, and unmitigated joy. There is no way a marriage between two imperfect human beings can deliver on that expectation. The late counselor Jean Lush believed, and I agree, that this romantic illusion is particularly characteristic of American women, who expect more from their husbands than they are capable of providing. The consequent disappointment is an emotional minefield.

Space invaders: By space invaders, I am not referring to aliens from Mars. Rather, my concern is for those who violate the "breathing room" needed by their partners, quickly suffocating them and destroying the attraction between them. Jealousy is one way the phenomenon manifests itself. Another is a poor self-concept, which leads the insecure spouse to build a cage around the other. It often suffocates the relationship. Love must be free, and it must be confident.

Sexual frustration and its partner, the greener grass of infidelity: It is a deadly combination!

Business collapse: Failure in work does bad things to men especially. Their agitation over financial reverses sometimes precipitates anger within the family.

Business success: It is almost as risky to succeed wildly as it is to fail miserably in business. King Solomon wrote: "Give me neither poverty nor riches, but give me only my daily bread" (Proverbs 30:8). Edward Fitzgerald said it another way: "One of the saddest pages kept by the recording angel is the record of souls that have been damned by success."[193] It's true.

Getting married too young: Girls who marry between fourteen and seventeen years of age are more than twice as likely to divorce as those who marry at eighteen or nineteen years of age. Those who marry at eighteen or nineteen are 1.5 times as likely to divorce as those who marry in their twenties.[194] The pressures of adolescence and the stresses of early married life do not mix well. Finish the first before taking on the second.

Alcohol and substance abuse: These are notorious killers, not only of marriages, but of the people who indulge excessively. Research indicates that 40 percent of all Americans and Canadians are close family members of an alcoholic.[195]

Pornography, gambling, and other addictions: It should be obvious to everyone that the human personality is flawed. It has a tendency to get hooked on destructive behaviors, especially early in life. During an introductory stage, people think they can tamper with various enticements, such as pornography, gambling, hard drugs, etc., without being hurt. Indeed, many do walk away unaffected. For some, however, there are a weakness and a vulnerability that are unknown until too late. Such people then become addicted to something that tears at the fabric of the family. This warning may seem foolish and even prudish to my readers, but I've made a twenty-year study of those who wreck their lives. Their problems often begin in experimentation with a known vice and ultimately end in death . . . or the death of a marriage.

These are a few of the common marriage killers. But in truth, the list is virtually limitless. All that is needed to grow the most vigorous weeds is a small crack in the sidewalk. If you are going to beat the odds and maintain an intimate, long-term marriage, you must take the task seriously. The natural order of things will carry you away from one another, not bring you together.

QUESTION 456

What do you consider to be *the* greatest threat to the stability of families today?

It would be a phenomenon that every marriage counselor deals with regularly. The scenario involves a vulnerable woman who depends on her husband to meet her emotional needs and a workaholic man who has little time for family responsibilities. Year after year she reaches for him and finds he's not there. She nags, complains, cries, and attacks him for his failures—to no avail. He is carrying the load of three men in his business or profession and can't figure out how to keep that enterprise going while providing what his wife needs. As time goes by, she becomes increasingly angry, which drives him even further into his workaday world. He is respected and successful there. And thereafter he is even less accessible to her. Then one day, to her husband's shock, this woman reaches a breaking point and either leaves him for someone else or files for divorce. It is a decision she may live to regret and one that often devastates her children—although by then the marriage is long gone. It was such a preventable disaster, but one that millions of other families will be victimized by in coming months.

QUESTION 457

That description is scary to me because I can see my own marriage in what you said. I'm a student who has to work full-time just to make ends meet, and I rarely see my family. We have a baby and a toddler, and my wife is pretty unhappy with me. But what can I do? If I'm going to get my degree, we have to sacrifice for a while.

Your self-discipline is admirable, and I hope you reach your goals. A word of caution is in order, however. No amount of success is worth the loss of your family. You and your wife are in a high-risk category for marital problems. The bonding that should occur in the first decade requires time together—time that can't be given if it is absorbed elsewhere. My advice is to hold on to your dreams but take a little longer to fulfill them. Success will wait, but a happy family will not.

QUESTION 458

I've always thought a man should be willing to work and sacrifice to reach his goals. Now you're saying to cool the passion and postpone the dream. That isn't the way I was taught.

There's nothing wrong with having a passion and a dream. It should, however, be kept in balance with other valuable components of your life—your family and your relationship with God being chief among them.

Let me illustrate that need to keep the various components of our lives in perspective. I read an article in the *Los Angeles Times* about a man named J. R. Buffington. His goal in life was to produce lemons of record-breaking size from the tree in his backyard. He came up with a formula to do just that. He fertilized the tree with ashes from the fireplace, some rabbit-goat manure, a few rusty nails, and plenty of water. That spring, the scrawny little tree produced two gigantic lemons, one weighing over five pounds. But every other lemon on the tree was shriveled and misshapen. Mr. Buffington is still working on his formula.

Isn't that the way it is in life? Great investments in a particular endeavor tend to rob others of their potential. I'd rather have a tree covered with juicy lemons than a record-breaking but freakish crop, wouldn't you? *Balance* is the word. It is the key to successful living . . . and parenting.

Husbands and wives who fill their lives with never-ending volumes of work are too exhausted to take walks together, to share their deeper feelings, to understand and meet each other's needs. This breathless pace predominates in millions of households, leaving every member of the family frazzled and irritable. Husbands are moonlighting to bring home more money. Wives are on their own busy career track. Their children are often ignored, and life goes speeding by in a deadly routine. Even some grandparents are too busy to keep the grandkids. I see this kind of overcommitment as the quickest route to the destruction of the family. And there simply must be a better way.

Some friends of mine recently sold their house and moved into a smaller and less expensive place just so they could lower their payments and reduce the hours required in the workplace. That kind of downward mobility is almost unheard of today—it's almost un-American. But when we reach the end of our lives and we look back on the things that mattered most, those precious relationships with people we love will rank at the top of the list.

If friends and family will be a treasure to us then, why not live like we believe it today? That may be the best advice I have ever given anyone—and the most difficult to implement.

So keep your dream and your passion. Work hard to achieve the success you crave. But don't let it become a five-pound lemon that destroys the rest of your crop. You'll regret it if you do!

QUESTION 459

I have very little time to spend with my children these days, but I make sure the hours we do get to spend together are meaningful. Do you agree that the quality of time you are with your kids is more important than the quantity?

I'm afraid the logic of that concept is flawed to me. The question is, why do we have to choose between the virtues of quantity versus quality? We won't accept that forced choice in any other area of our lives. So why is it only relevant to our children?

Let me illustrate my point. Let's suppose you've looked forward all day to eating at one of the finest restaurants in town. The waiter brings you a menu, and you order the most expensive steak in the house. But when the meal arrives, you see a tiny piece of meat about one-inch square in the center of the plate. When you complain about the size of the steak, the waiter says, "Sir, I recognize that the portion is small, but that's the finest corn-fed beef money can buy. You'll never find a better bite of meat than we've served you tonight. As to the portion, I hope you understand that it's not the quantity that matters, it's the quality that counts."

You would object, and for good reason. Why? Because both quality and quantity are important in many areas of our lives, including how we relate to children. They need our time and the best we have to give them.

My concern is that the quantity-versus-quality argument might be a poorly disguised rationalization for giving our children—neither.

Q UESTION 460

You listed alcoholism as a marriage killer. My husband has that problem. It has created a great deal of pain in our home, and I am concerned about the emotional welfare of my children. Can it be treated, and is there hope for families like mine?

Alcoholism is a devastating disease, not only for the person who has it, but for his or her entire family. Research shows that 40 percent of people living in Western nations have a close family member who is an alcoholic.[196] That incidence is even higher in Russia and other countries of Eastern Europe. There is no way to calculate the impact of this problem on children, on spouses, and on the culture itself. Fortunately, it can be treated successfully for those who are willing to seek that help.

I discussed the issue of alcoholism with a panel of knowledgeable people on the *Focus on the Family* radio broadcast. Included were Dr. Keith Simpson, a physician who has treated this problem for twenty years, and Jerry Butler, a marriage and family therapist with twenty-five years of counseling experience. His own father had committed suicide during one of his drunken binges. Also with me were "Bob," a recovered alcoholic, and his wife, "Pauline," who preferred that we withhold their real names.

I did not ask these four individuals for a detailed analysis of alcoholism; our listeners already knew how serious it is. Rather, I wanted them to provide us with practical suggestions as to how family members can recognize the disease and then be of help to those they love. The answers they gave were most encouraging and enlightening.

Dr. Simpson was asked whether alcoholism can be treated successfully today. Is it a hopeless condition, or is there a way out for the victim and his family? This was his reply:

"I specialized in the field of internal medicine for many years but found it to be depressing work. I could help my patients with chronic lung disease and severe diabetes and heart disease, but in reality, my efforts were just a delaying action. Over time, conditions worsened and the diseases progressed. I made my rounds in intensive care each day and watched people losing their battle for life, whereas my alcoholic patients were getting well. That's why I deal almost exclusively with alcoholics now, and I find it to be extremely rewarding work. I see people who come in with more horrible problems than you can imagine, but they get into a recovery program, and in a few months the difference is like going from night to day. So, yes, not only is alcoholism treatable, but the medical community does better with this disorder than any other chronic disease. Alcoholics emerge from treatment programs more functionally integrated, more capable, and more effective than before they 'caught' the disease."[197]

That was the theme of the entire discussion: *There is hope for the alcoholic!* But before recovery can begin, the problem has to be acknowledged and treatment sought. That applies to your own family situation, I'm sure. Your husband can be helped if he has "the want to."

Q UESTION 461

486

My husband drinks a lot, but it doesn't affect him very badly. It is amazing just how much he can drink without getting dead drunk. Does that mean he isn't an alcoholic?

I'm afraid you are describing a telltale characteristic of alcoholism. Let me turn again to the physician who specializes in treating alcoholics. I asked him to describe the early symptoms family members should look for. Dr. Simpson said:

"The first red flag is a 'tolerance' for alcohol. The person finds he has to drink more to achieve the same result. He calls this being able to 'hold his liquor'—a status symbol around the world. In reality, it is a danger signal indicating a chemical adjustment has been made. Second, a person reaches a place where he doesn't want to talk about his drinking anymore. He knows he is consuming more alcohol than other people, and he wants to avoid all reference to it. This begins a process of denial that may be with him for years to come. Third, the person begins to experience blackouts. By that I mean that he has brief periods of amnesia that lengthen as time goes by. What is happening is that the brain's recording cells aren't remembering what is being said and done.

"Furthermore, it's a low-dose phenomenon: It happens after one or two drinks. I'm not referring to the process of being stone drunk from the anesthetic effects of great quantities of alcohol. Instead, the person thinks back on the previous night and says, 'Gee! I can't remember a doggone thing after that second drink.' It's a scary experience. Fourth, the person begins to notice that he can't consistently predict how much he's going to drink once he starts. To me, this is the key feature of alcoholism and constitutes the definition of the disease. It occurs when an individual is constantly drinking more than he intended because he can't help it. He sits down to have a beer and wakes up the next afternoon. It may be hard for people to believe, but alcoholics don't drink to get drunk. They merely want to have a drink or two. That's why they can swear they'll never get drunk again and *mean* it. They have no incentive of breaking that promise. Nevertheless, they sit down to have a drink with a friend and bingo, it's morning."[198]

Let me share with you now the words of Pauline, the spouse, and Bob, the alcoholic, about their experience with this family nightmare:

"I couldn't count the times Bob promised he would never drink again. That must be the most frustrating part of the experience—

having Bob look me straight in the eye and tell me he's through—really done with bingeing. He'd say, 'I've seen how it hurts you and the kids, and I've had it. I promise you that I'll never do it again!' Then in a day or two he was dead drunk. I thought he was lying to me. How could he love me and lie so many times to my face? But he wasn't lying. He *couldn't* keep his promise. Bob thought he could whip this problem with willpower. It's like trying to stop diarrhea by making up your mind to do so."[199]

We asked Bob to express what he was feeling during this period of repeated failure. He said he was confused by his inability to overcome the habit.

"I thought the problem might be vodka, so I switched to scotch, and then bourbon. Then I tried meditation. Nothing worked. I tried a dozen approaches to control my drinking, but I always went back to it. Then I tried covering it up. I carried a bottle of Binaca in my pocket, and I always had a green tongue. I drank for six months without Pauline ever knowing it. Every Saturday morning she would wash her hair and then sit under a noisy hair dryer for a half hour. I could hardly wait for her to get preoccupied because I had a fifth of vodka in the cupboard. I would race in and get a can of Fresca from the refrigerator, pour half of it down the drain, and fill the other half with vodka.

"Then I'd drink it in front of the television set with a halo around my head. You really have to be calculating to hide a drinking problem from those you live with. This went on for months. You see, I was addicted to a drug and was completely unaware of it."[200]

488

QUESTION 462

I'm going to have to acknowledge that my husband, Wally, *is* an alcoholic. Our experience is not so different from Bob and Pauline's. Wally isn't willing to admit he has a problem. He won't even talk about it. Tell me what I should do now.

First, let me tell you what you should *not* do and what is generally unhelpful.

1. Do not nag, complain, scream, cry, beg, plead, embarrass, or label your husband. He has a disease that he can't control. It is not within his power to overcome it alone.
2. Do not protect him by lying to his boss, covering for his irresponsibility, bailing him out of jail, and paying his bills. A person who tries to rescue the alcoholic is called an enabler, and she may actually prolong and worsen the problem.
3. Though opinions differ, most authorities do not look on alcoholism as a character weakness or a moral problem. It was a moral problem during earlier days when the person chose to drink excessively. But later, it was not his desire to hurt his family, stay in a drunken stupor, waste his money, etc. The alcoholic has long since lost his capacity for voluntary action.
4. Do not perpetuate your husband's problem for your own selfish reasons. It is not uncommon for family members to resist treatment for what may be unconscious motives. For example, a woman whose husband is usually drunk has power over her family. She is the unrivaled boss—the one who controls the money and makes all of her family's decisions. As her alcoholic husband begins to recover, she may realize she is losing her power and move to sabotage his rehabilitation. Guard against those subtle forces that may undermine recovery in your home.

Q UESTION 463

OK, I know what not to do. Now tell me how to get help for my family.

It is virtually impossible to deal with this problem without outside help. In a very real sense, the entire family shares the sickness of the alcoholic. They are affected by rage, depression, disillusionment, despair, financial fear, denial, low self-esteem, and myriad other emotions that accompany this illness. They are wounded in spirit and need the loving concern of those who have been there. Even if an alcoholic does recover on his or her own, a relapse is almost certain unless the family has been treated too.

That family assistance is available through an organization called Al-Anon, which provides a support program for the families of alcoholics. Pauline credits Al-Anon with saving her family and perhaps her life. She said, "After refusing to attend for a year, I went to Al-Anon in desperation and finally began to get the answers I needed. I'll never forget the first night. They gave no sympathy and no advice. They just shared their experience, their strength, and their hope. I latched onto it with everything I had and within a few weeks, things began to change for me. Al-Anon directed me toward God and helped me to get my eyes off myself and on Him. Then they taught me how to deal with Bob."

Bob's comments about Al-Anon are even more dramatic. He said:

"If you really want to mess up an alcoholic's drinking fun, just get his spouse involved in Al-Anon. Pauline changed her approach in three ways, and it bugged me like crazy. (1) Whereas she previously poured my booze down the drain, she stopped doing that or anything else to keep me from drinking. I really wondered if she loved me anymore. (2) On Mondays, I would ask her to call the office and tell them that I had the flu. She had always done that for me. But after going to Al-Anon, she would simply smile and say, 'No, you'll have to do that yourself.' (3) She seemed to be calmer, more in control. Before, I would come home from drinking with the guys and look for an excuse to leave again. All I had to do was pick a fight with Pauline and then say, 'All right; if that's the way you are going to act, I'll just take off.' Now, she gets in this Al-Anon thing and instead of trying to hold me at home, she smiles and says, 'So long. I'm going to a meeting.'"[201]

490

Q UESTION 464

Aside from getting help for my family, what should I do specifically for my husband? How on earth am I going to get him to go to Alcoholics Anonymous or some similar treatment

program? He is deep in denial, and I'm not even sure he's thinking right now. He couldn't make a rational decision to save his life. How am I going to get him to cooperate?

You're right about the difficulties you face. Begging won't accomplish anything, and your husband will be dead before he admits he has a problem. Indeed, thousands die each year while denying that they are alcoholics. That's why Al-Anon teaches family members how to confront in love. They learn how to remove the support systems that prop up the disease and permit it to thrive. They are shown how and when to impose ultimatums that force the alcoholic to admit his or her need for help. And sometimes they recommend separation until the victim is so miserable that his or her denial will no longer hold up. In essence, Al-Anon teaches its own version of the "love must be tough" philosophy to family members who must implement it.

I asked Bob if he was forced to attend Alcoholics Anonymous—the program that put him on the road to recovery. He said:

"Let me put it this way. No one goes to A.A. just because they've nothing better to do that evening. Everyone there has been forced to attend initially. You just don't say, 'On Monday night we watched a football game, and on Tuesday we went to the movies. So what will we do on Wednesday? How about going over to an A.A. meeting?' It doesn't work that way. Yes—I was forced—forced by my own misery. Pauline allowed me to be miserable for my own good. It was loving duress that moved me to attend."[202]

Though it may sound easy to achieve, the loving confrontation that brought Bob to his senses was a delicate maneuver. I must reemphasize that families should not attempt to implement it on their own initiative. Without the training and assistance of professional support groups, the encounter could degenerate into a hateful, vindictive, name-calling battle that would serve only to solidify the drinker's position.

Al-Anon Family Groups and Alcoholics Anonymous are both listed in local phone books. Also to be found there is a number for the Council on Alcoholism, which can provide further guidance. For teenagers of an alcoholic parent, there is Alateen. Teens can go there and share without their parents' permission or knowledge, and it's free.

QUESTION 465

I know you served on the Attorney General's Commission on Pornography in the 1980s. Update us on the pornography industry today, and tell us what direction it is moving.

It is extremely important to understand what is being produced and sold by pornographers today, although I can't adequately describe it without being more graphic than you would want me to be. If people understood the debauchery of this business, and what pornography does to the individual addicted to it, they would be far more motivated to work for its control. It is commonly believed that mainstream pornography is represented by the centerfolds in today's men's magazines. In fact, that is precisely what the ACLU and the sex industry want us to think. But if a man were to go into the sex shops on Times Square or in other large cities in the United States, he would find very few depictions of normal heterosexual activity. Instead, he would see a heavy emphasis on violent homosexual and lesbian scenes, on excrement, mutilation, enemas, oral and anal sex, instrumentation for the torture of men and women, and depictions of sex between humans and animals. Amazingly, there is a huge market for disgusting materials of this nature.

What has changed since the 1980s is the invasion of obscenity on the Internet. All of the terrible images that we witnessed during the commission, and worse, are now accessible to any twelve-year-old with a modem and a high-resolution printer. Much of it comes from Holland and other countries where there are no limitations on obscenity. It is disturbing to realize that many kids whose parents think they are doing constructive work on their computers are actually witnessing depictions that would sicken a normal adult. As technology advances, the pornography industry adapts to skirt the law and invade the heartland of the home.

QUESTION 466

Talk briefly about the impact of pornography on the family.

Raising healthy children is the primary occupation of families, and anything that warps childhood and twists the minds of boys and girls must be seen as abhorrent to the mothers and fathers who gave them birth. Furthermore, what is at stake here is the future of the family itself. We are sexual creatures, and the physical attraction between males and females provides the basis for every dimension of marriage and parenthood. Thus, anything that interjects itself into that relationship must be embraced with great caution. Until we know that pornography is not addictive and progressive . . . until we are certain that the passion of fantasy does not destroy the passion of reality . . . until we are sure that obsessive use of obscene materials will not lead to perversions and conflict between husbands and wives . . . then we dare not adorn them with the crown of respectability. Society has a solemn obligation to protect itself from material that crosses the line established by its legislators and judges. This is not sexual repression. This is self-preservation.

QUESTION 467

I know that for the sake of my marriage and family I should not overcommit myself. But we attend a church that schedules activities and events six or seven nights a week. My husband and I are asked, and expected, to accept leadership in many of these functions. Frankly, I feel guilty when I don't do what my pastors ask of me. As a result, we have very little time together as a family. How do we accommodate these competing needs?

493

I can personally identify with your dilemma. Shirley and I went through a similar era in the first decade of our marriage. At that time, I believed I was obligated as a young Christian to accept anything asked of me by my church. I served as superintendent of youth, as a member of the church's governing board, as an adult Sunday school teacher, and as someone who was available for whatever special assignments came along. Shirley was heavily involved in church activities too, leading the children's choir and serving as director of women's ministries. I was also finishing a Ph.D. program and carrying very heavy professional responsibilities. It was a breathless time, to be sure. At one point I remember being scheduled seventeen straight nights away from home at a time when we had a little toddler who loved to play with her daddy.

Gradually, I came to understand that the Lord wanted me to use good judgment and common sense in the things I agreed to do—even if they involved very worthwhile causes. There will always be more good things to do than one man or woman can get done. I realized I needed to maintain a healthy balance between Christian duty, work responsibilities, recreation, social obligations, and meaningful family life.

Then I came across two Scripture references that helped clarify this issue. The first is found in Matthew 14:13-14, as follows: "When Jesus heard what had happened [to John the Baptist], he withdrew by boat privately to a solitary place. Hearing of this, the crowds followed him on foot from the towns. When Jesus landed and saw a large crowd, he had compassion on them and healed their sick."

Jesus was undoubtedly grieving at that time over the beheading of His cousin and friend, John the Baptist. He needed to "withdraw privately to a solitary place." Nevertheless, the people learned of His whereabouts and came seeking His healing touch. Even in that painful time of loss, Jesus took compassion on the people and reached out to those in need. From this I concluded that there are times when we, too, must give of ourselves even when it is difficult or inconvenient to do so.

But there was another occasion when thousands of people sought to be healed by Jesus. After spending some time with them, He got in a boat with His disciples and rowed away. Mark 4:36 says, "Leaving the crowd behind, they took [Jesus] along, just as he was, in the boat." Undoubtedly, the large following that day included individuals with cancer, blindness, physical deformities, and every other kind of human misery. Jesus could have stayed there through the night and healed them all, yet He had apparently reached the end of His strength and knew He needed to rest. He and His disciples rowed away, apparently leaving some of the needy people standing on the bank.

A similar event is described in Matthew 14:23, where we read, "And when he had sent the multitudes away, he went up into a mountain apart to pray: and when the evening was come, he was there alone" (KJV).

Just as there is a time to give, there is also a time to be alone, to pray and to escape from the pressures of the day—even though there are worthy things yet to be accomplished. Those who fail to reserve some downtime for rest and renewal—as Jesus did—are risking even the good things they want to accomplish. That is like installing a new sprinkler system in a yard and putting too many outlets on the line. When that occurs, nothing is watered properly.

Let me offer another illustration. Did you know that grape growers not only trim dead branches from their vines but they also eliminate a certain number of the fruit-producing branches? They sacrifice a portion of the crop so that the fruit that survives will be better. Likewise, we need to eliminate some of our breathless activities to improve the overall quality of the other things we do.

Having said that, let me offer a word of caution. This need to maintain balance can become an excuse for not carrying our share of responsibility in the church. Pastors tell us that a few of their members do most of the work while most others get a free ride. That is wrong. We shouldn't go from one extreme to the other in our search for common sense.

24

The Sanctity of Life

QUESTION 468

My husband and I have been through four years of infertility testing and treatments, to no avail. It has been a terribly frustrating experience. We've spent thousands of dollars on medical bills and have nothing to show for it. We want a child so badly but have now been told that it isn't going to happen unless we use the procedure known as in vitro fertilization. Our doctor has access to fertilized eggs that will be destroyed if they aren't implanted in a recipient woman. A couple whom we don't know had their eggs frozen for future use but decided not to use them. How do you think God would view our accepting the eggs and giving life to one of them? Can you tell me whether or not it is right to "create" a child in this way?

You have asked a very difficult question that reflects advancing medical technology. Issues are arising today that were unheard of a few years ago, and many of them carry moral and ethical considerations that can be very troubling. This is certainly true of in vitro fertilization (IVF), which is the subject of considerable uncertainty and disagreement even among the most respected of conservative theologians. I will give you my own interpretation with the caution that I am not a theologian. The following thoughts are simply my best attempt to ferret out the theological issues as I see them and as others have advised me.

First, I am strongly opposed to the practice of creating fertilized eggs from "donors" outside the immediate family (this would include the donation of sperm or eggs from a brother or sister of the husband and wife wishing to conceive). In my opinion, to engage in such activity would be to "play God"—to create human life outside the bonds of marriage. I believe most conservative Christians would agree that this practice is morally indefensible from a biblical perspective.

On the other hand, I feel that in vitro fertilization is less problematic when the donors are husband and wife—*if* all the fertilized eggs are inserted into the uterus (i.e., no ova are wasted or disposed of after fertilization and no selection process by doctors or parents occurs). As the woman's body then accepts one or more eggs and rejects the others, the process is left in God's hands. This seems to violate no moral principles. I would recommend that no more than three eggs be fertilized and inserted, so that even if the woman's body accepts them all, no more than triplets will be born. To fertilize and implant more than three would unacceptably increase the risk of pregnancies of quadruplets or more, pregnancies which carry high risk for both mother and babies.

The dilemma you and your husband now face is different from ordinary IVF, of course. It involves the relatively new and complex issue arising from implantation of "leftover" embryos from a couple who had them frozen for future use but then decided to abandon them. Your acceptance of them would provide an opportunity for life for at least one embryo that presumably would otherwise be destroyed (as happened to more than three thousand embryos in England in 1996).[203] I believe this procedure is quite different than an infertile couple seeking out an egg or sperm donor, which, as I indicated, is creating life from outside the family.

I would tend to see the option you've been offered as "adoption" at an earlier stage of development. The idea of embryo adoption is a new concept, but one which may become increasingly common as in vitro fertilization is more widely employed. For an infertile couple such as yourselves to participate in this type of procedure may not be a violation of God's law. From a theological standpoint, I believe the fertilized eggs in question already have an eternal soul (which occurred at the moment of fertilization). Most important, you and your husband had nothing to do with the decision to fertilize the eggs. By implanting them, you would merely be rescuing embryos that have no other possibility of life.

I have discussed this idea at some length with Dr. Joe McIlhaney, a gynecologist and infertility specialist who is a frequent *Focus on the Family* broadcast guest. He is also president of the Medical Institute for Sexual Health. We would recommend considering the adoption of the eggs only after serious prayer and consideration of the following points: (a) Make sure the potential donors have been screened for HIV, sexually transmitted diseases, and other health facts; (b) insist that your physician thaw only one to three living embryos (some embryos do not survive the thawing process). We recommend no more than three embryos be implanted because of the risk of multiple pregnancy; (c) insert all living embryos and be prepared to accept the possibility of twins or triplets if that is what happens; and (d) an attorney should handle the relinquishing of rights by the donor couple and the formal adoption process, etc. (The legal climate concerning this procedure is not settled, so it would be wise to secure legal counsel familiar with these issues.)

Let me stress again that this procedure is very controversial. I realize that equally committed Christians may see it in a different light, and I certainly don't claim to have the final word on the subject. There are deeply rooted moral and theological ramifications that will undoubtedly be discussed in the religious and scientific communities for years to come. In the meantime, I would encourage you to seek the mind of the Lord as you endeavor to make your decision. I know this has been a terribly difficult time for you and trust that He will give you peace about whatever direction you're led to take.

QUESTION 469

My friend says she favors a liberal abortion policy because it prevents child abuse in some cases. What are your thoughts?

Perhaps one day we'll hear the argument that murdering your husband or wife should be legalized to prevent spouse abuse. Ridiculous as it is, this is the rationale behind the argument that abortion—killing a baby in the womb—will reduce the chances of that child being abused after birth. Seen in context, it's simply illogical. The incidence of abused, abandoned, neglected, and mistreated children has sky-rocketed since the 1970s, when the radical feminists told us that abortion would make every baby wanted and loved. What it actually did was cheapen life at every stage of development.

While there may be unexpected, unplanned pregnancies, there are no unwanted babies. The list of couples wanting to adopt literally runs into the millions. Across the country prospective parents are pleading for the opportunity to take a child into their hearts and homes. Unfortunately, the desire to adopt is often frustrated by the lack of available babies.

Murder is not the answer for the so-called unwanted child. I must agree with Mother Teresa, who has said, "The greatest destroyer of peace today is abortion. Any country that accepts abortion is not teaching the people to love but to use any violence to get what they want."[204]

QUESTION 470

I've been hearing a great deal about fetal experimentation and some of the possible medical breakthroughs that could be realized as a result of this research. Do you think it is ethical to "harvest" tissue from fetuses if it means we'll find the medical solution to debilitating diseases?

There is no hypothetical medical discovery that will justify the horrible procedure by which organs are "harvested" from a tiny human being. If most of us had to watch the grisly task of cannibalizing the body of a baby, it would sicken and outrage us. At the risk of distressing my readers, I am going to describe that procedure. Be forewarned! What I'm about to write will be disturbing.

First, it is important to remember that a child born alive presents a major problem to an abortionist. It is the ultimate "complication," because legally, every effort must be made to keep a breathing newborn alive. That's why the physician usually crushes the fetus's head while still in the uterus. However, a baby who is born dead is of less value to researchers because brain tissue and other organs quickly deteriorate when deprived of oxygen. Thus, the abortionist must employ a means of extracting the body parts and brain matter from a living baby who is not yet expelled from the birth canal.

The method is called "dilatation and extraction," or "partial-birth abortion." It is grotesque beyond imagination. It occurs on fully viable babies, weighing as much as six to eight pounds. Over a period of two days, the cervix is dilated. Then an ultrasound device and forceps are used to reach in and grab the baby's feet. The little body is pulled into the birth canal until only the head remains in the cervix. Next the abortionist grasps the nape of the neck and stabs the back of the skull with blunt scissors. A device called a cannula is then inserted into the wound, and the brain material is sucked out. If kidneys or other organs are desired, they are removed while the child is still partially in the vagina. Initially at least, these surgical procedures are performed on a live baby who has not specifically been anesthetized. The dismembered and lifeless body is then delivered the other few inches.

If puppies or kittens were subjected to such cruel treatment, the protests of the animal-rights people would be heard around the world—and I would be one of the most vocal.

In this instance, however, we're dealing not with animals but with human beings of inestimably greater worth, who are created in the image of the Creator. How anyone with the remotest sympathy for the sanctity of life could play God with the destiny of these little ones is beyond all comprehension. Without question, they comprise the most disadvantaged and defenseless segment in our culture today. And the excuse for this evil? It is the remote possibility of some distant medical breakthrough—or more commonly—for the convenience of the physician in late-term abortions! I will oppose it for as long as I have breath within my body.

501

*Q*UESTION 471

There are those who think your position on abortion is extreme because you wouldn't even permit it in cases of incest, rape, or when the child is defective. How do you justify such a position?

Only in rare instances when the life of the mother is literally at stake do I feel we have the moral authority to destroy a developing fetus. My reasoning is based on this simple question: Is there any fundamental difference between a baby who resides in his mother's uterus and one who has made an eight-inch journey down the birth canal? If so, what is that difference? At what point in the birth process does God's mantle of humanness fall upon an individual? Is there anything particularly mystical about the expulsion from the mother's body that could account for a transformation from mere protoplasm to a human being with an eternal soul? I think not. Surely the Lord does not look upon the baby inside the uterus with any less love and concern than one who enters the world a few minutes later. The only difference between them is that one can be seen and the other cannot.

If that premise can be accepted, then it is equally immoral to kill either those born or those yet to be born. Physical and intellectual health and the nature of conception are irrelevant to the issue. Even most pro-abortionists would not propose that we destroy children arriving in the delivery room with unexpected deficiencies. Indeed, the authorities would charge them with murder for killing a neonate who lacked adequate cognitive function or who had only a few weeks to live. We would be obligated morally and legally to let nature take its course, regardless of the severity of the baby's condition. Likewise, we would not kill a one-day-old infant who was conceived in a rape or an incident of incest.

Once born, the deliberate destruction of life is unthinkable. Why, then, is such a baby considered "fair game" when he resides within his mother's uterus? It is true that the law sometimes recognizes a different status for those born versus those unborn, but the law in those instances is wrong. There is no biological or moral basis for this distinction. Infanticide merely seems acceptable when we don't have to witness the death process of a tiny victim we have not yet met.

Therefore all the arguments in favor of terminating the defective or handicapped unborn child must be weighed against this understanding, including, "he's going to die anyway," "he'll only suffer if we let him live," "his life will only bring pain to his parents," "he has no chance of living a normal life," and "this is really the best way out for everyone concerned." When applied to the baby who has managed to limp into this world, the evil of these rationalizations becomes apparent. No justification will permit us to give a newborn a lethal injection of cyanide. But hours earlier, when the mother's contractions have not yet begun, some would feel righteously justified in tearing the same defective or ill-conceived infant to pieces. The proposition is categorically immoral in my view.

I am aware that these views are infinitely easier to articulate from a philosophical or theological perspective than they are for the mother or father who must face them personally. Of special concern is the woman who is carrying a baby conceived during a rape. Her pain and agony are beyond expression. I am convinced, however, that such a mother, if she carries the baby to term and either keeps her baby or places it up for adoption, will never regret her decision. What is right and moral for the unborn child is ultimately best for the mother and father, too. I know this statement will be inflammatory to some, but it is what I sincerely believe.

QUESTION 472

Give us, then, a statement of your position on civil disobedience in the prevention of abortions.

Life magazine asked me that same question a few years ago, and I prepared the following statement for them. They chose to publish only a sentence or two out of context, leaving uncertainty in the mind of the reader. Here is the position in its entirety:

After World War II, German citizens living around Nazi extermination camps were required to visit the facilities to witness the atrocities they had permitted to occur. Though it was technically "legal" to kill Jews and other political prisoners, the citizens were blamed for not breaking the law in deference to a higher moral code. This is the way we feel about the slaughter of thirty-five million unborn children. Some of them are being burned to death by a salt solution only days before normal delivery would have occurred. Others are delivered except for the head and then their brains are sucked out with a high-powered device. This is a moral outrage that transcends the law which sanitizes the killings. We are law-abiding people and do not advocate violence or obscene and disrespectful behavior, but to be sure, we will follow that higher moral code nonviolently to rescue innocent, defenseless babies. And someday, the moral issues involved here will be as clear to the world as the Nazi holocaust is today.

QUESTION 473

Why is there such concern about the euthanasia movement? If a sick, elderly person wants to die with dignity, I don't see why that should threaten anybody. Why shouldn't we permit a quiet suicide when the quality of life is no longer there?

Your question is so important in today's cultural environment that I must answer at some length.

You have offered a very seductive argument, especially to those of us who know of older people who are suffering a slow, painful death. It does seem more humane to allow them to go to sleep quietly and escape their misery. It is my firm conviction, however, that untold sorrow for thousands of people and eventual social chaos lie down that road.

The problem, aside from the moral issue of taking human life, is that euthanasia is inevitably progressive in nature. Once you let that snake out of the basket, it will be impossible to control where it slithers! Allow me to illustrate.

Suppose physician-assisted suicide eventually is legalized for elderly people who are terminally ill. How would it be limited thereafter for those who were neither sick nor severely handicapped? How about an older but healthy man who was simply tired of living? Could we really require a note from his physician in order to permit his suicide?

Then if old but healthy people can choose to die, what about the not-so-old? Could a fifty-year-old person take the plunge? If not, why not? How about a forty-year-old woman in menopause or a man in midlife crisis? When you stop to think about it, age has nothing to do with the decision. A twenty-year-old depressed but healthy student would be as entitled to "death with dignity" as the terminally ill.

If euthanasia is legal for anyone, it will soon become legal for everyone. Neither age, health factors, nor quality of life could be defended as qualifiers. The Hemlock Society, which actively promotes euthanasia, certainly understands that fact. They speak confidently about a "right to die" . . . for every human being.

Let's extend that concept now to its worst-case scenario, as suggested by anti-euthanasia activist Rita Marker. Suppose Diane is an eighteen-year-old high school senior who is loved greatly by her family. One day, she fails to come home from school when expected. By six-thirty that evening, her mother is starting to worry. When eight o'clock rolls around, her father calls the police. There's been no report of an accident, he is told. None of the local hospitals have a patient named Diane. Mom then begins making frantic telephone calls and finally reaches Diane's best friend, Rene. "Oh, Mrs. Johnson," Rene says with compassion. She begins to cry. "I wanted so much to call you, but I promised Diane I would let the clinic tell you."

"Clinic? What clinic?!" says Mrs. Johnson.

"You know," says Rene. "The Life Choice Clinic downtown. I think you'd better call them."

Diane's mother gets the clinic administrator on the line, who says, "I'm terribly sorry, Mrs. Johnson, we were just getting ready to call you. I know this will be hard for you, but please sit down. Diane came in this afternoon and asked to be assisted in her passing. You may know that she had been very depressed about her grades and because of the rejection letter she received from the state university. Then when her boyfriend let her down . . . well, she just didn't want to go on living. And as you know, 'right to die' laws now apply to every adult eighteen years old and over.

"Try to understand that this is what Diane most wanted. It was her choice, and she is entitled to control her own body. I assure you she was very peaceful as she left us, and her last words were an expression of love for her family."[205]

Does that story seem too far-fetched to be credible? Perhaps. But who would have thought in 1950 that we would soon be filling garbage bags with perfectly formed premature babies who were mangled or burned to death with salt? Could we have imagined that nearly forty million of those precious children would be torn from their mothers' wombs?

Can anyone believe that we are incapable of killing *any* population of people—especially those who want to die—when we have wreaked such violence on the most defenseless in our midst?

Historically, those nations that have opened the door to the monster of euthanasia have slid into a nightmare of murder. This is precisely what happened in Nazi Germany. They began by killing the sick and old; then they destroyed the mentally ill, mentally retarded, and infants born with deformities. From there, it was but a small step to begin exterminating "undesirables"—the Jews, Poles, Gypsies, the nonproductive, political prisoners, homosexuals, and others. Euthanasia was the first small step down the road toward the extermination camps.

Even if this epidemic of murder did not occur, it is certain that "right to death" laws would result in a dramatic increase in the number of suicides occurring annually. Each death would represent incalculable grief, guilt, and sorrow for those left behind.

Suicide may look like an easy way out for the one who dies, but it is perhaps the most painful experience in living for loved ones and relatives—many of whom would certainly be children. We draw the same conclusion from every angle. Yet the Ninth Circuit Court of Appeals in California, citing the U.S. Supreme Court's ruling in *Planned Parenthood v. Casey,*[206] has unleashed it on the American culture. God help us!

Q UESTION 474

Other than the Nazi example, are there modern nations that have legalized euthanasia? If so, what has been the result?

The nation of Holland has embraced "physician-assisted suicide" with predictable consequences. Although euthanasia is technically illegal, it has been practiced openly for years, with impunity. The killing began with a few terminally ill patients requesting help in dying from their doctors, much like the "service" Dr. Kevorkian performs in the U.S. But in Holland today, more than 2,300 people die at the hands of their physicians every year, and the number is growing steadily.[207] Even more alarmingly, an estimated one thousand citizens are killed who did not request assistance in dying. The doctors made the decision on their own or else with the prompting of family members.[208] The Dutch Committee to Investigate the Medical Practice of Euthanasia reported 14,691 cases where doctors acted on their own initiative to kill a patient—without the individual's knowledge or consent.[209] Elderly patients can never be sure what their doctors have in mind when they come calling.

Recently, a physician in the Netherlands killed an infant with spina bifida at the parents' request. He was absolved of any wrongdoing.[210] Another doctor was acquitted after assisting in the death of a woman who wasn't even ill.[211]

This is where the slippery slope leads. Whenever the law begins to tolerate the killing of individuals, even those who are terminally ill, that practice will spread and cheapen the value of all human life.

QUESTION 475

Why do you think the Dutch experience will be repeated in the U.S. and Canada?

Former surgeon general Dr. C. Everett Koop once told me why he believes the euthanasia movement will someday dwarf the abortion phenomenon. It is because of what he called "the squaring of the pyramid."[212]

Through the centuries, age patterns of populations have been triangular in nature. The greatest number of people in a society were the youngest, represented by the base of the pyramid. The fewest number were the oldest, symbolized by the peak. In our society, however, these classic demographics have been modified. The huge number of babies born after World War II are moving through the midlife years and will soon square off the top of the pyramid.

Conversely, the effect of abortion on demand has thinned the ranks of the young. These unusual patterns will soon create enormous problems. As the large number of baby boomers move into their sixties and seventies, we will experience a serious crisis in the provision of health care. There just aren't as many baby busters as boomers, and the Generation X crowd is outnumbered as well. The upshot is that there will be fewer younger workers to support this crowd of retirees. The newer generation will be saddled with a weighty financial burden it may not be willing or able to bear.

A scenario like this one will be commonplace in that day: A forty-year-old husband and wife will be asked to support their seventy-five-year-old grandmother who has terminal cancer. Because of the shortage of health-care services in the aging population, the family will be saddled with enormous medical costs for Grandma's treatment. If they have to continue paying for her care, they will lose their home and their eighteen-year-old daughter will not be able to go to college. But if the grandmother will do the responsible thing and take an early exit, the family's financial integrity will be preserved and the people she loves can go on with their lives. Some members of the older generation will feel obligated to commit suicide. After all, they've lived a full life, and they shouldn't be selfish at this late date. Why not do the honorable thing?

For this reason, said Dr. Koop, the pressure on many in the older generation to accept physician-assisted suicide will be irresistible.

The former governor of Colorado Richard D. Lamm made no secret of his support for suicide among the elderly. He has argued that they have a moral responsibility to get out of the way and make room for the younger folks.[213] What a warped perspective—and yet one that continues to gain a foothold in Western nations.

25
Other Issues Facing the Family

QUESTION 476

My husband and I have been married for twelve years, and I've known for the past eight years that he is a practicing homosexual. We have one little girl, but she was kind of a miracle. I didn't know about this problem until after we were married. We rarely have sexual relations, and he says he has no interest in me. I'm starting to not care anymore. Even when I learn he's had sex with a guy again, I just feel nothing. It happens so often that I have come to expect it. What I really want to know now is if I have scriptural grounds to divorce my husband. I just don't know which way to turn. I want the kind of family that God describes in the Bible. I don't think my husband has a right to continue in the gay lifestyle and stay married to me. Does he?

I don't blame you for feeling betrayed by the man who promised to "love and cherish" you for life. I can imagine nothing much more painful than discovering that your mate is living the gay lifestyle.

As to whether you have scriptural grounds for a divorce, I believe you do. Keep in mind that I am not a theologian, and there are differing opinions on the interpretation of Scripture. But I see no difference between heterosexual and homosexual infidelity. They are both condemned in the Bible and should be considered in the same classification morally.

Despite the fact that you appear to have grounds for divorce, only you can determine what God wants you to do now. He cares about your husband and wants him to turn from his sin. But He also loves you and has seen your pain and depression. It is not reasonable that you should have to endure the present situation for long. In addition to the emotional stress it causes, there are health implications to consider— for your husband, for yourself, and perhaps for your child. The issue must come to a head soon.

My advice is that you make this decision a matter of intense and persistent prayer in coming days. Then if you feel so led by the Lord, establish a point of crisis with your husband and confront him with a choice between two lifestyles—between a recommitment to marital fidelity versus the lure of that other world. If he decides to reestablish his relationship with you, then he will need competent counseling to address his problem. And contrary to what you may have heard, homosexuality can often (but not always) be treated successfully.

May the Lord be very near to you and your little girl during this difficult time.

QUESTION 477

Homosexual activists claim their lifestyle, which in some cases includes thousands of sexual partners, should be sanctioned, protected, and granted special rights by society. Their rationale is that since their sexual nature is inherited, it is involuntary and therefore should be considered morally neutral. Would you critique this stance?

Let me answer that question by asking two of my own: *"What if?"* and *"So what?"*

What if it could be demonstrated beyond a shadow of a doubt that homosexuality is, as activists claim, genetic, biochemical, and neurological in origin? We would still want to know, *so what?* The homosexual activist community would have us believe that because their behavior is genetically programmed and beyond their control, it is morally defensible. That is not supportable. Most men have inherited a lust for women. Their natural tendency is to have sex with as many beautiful girls as possible, both before marriage and after. Abstinence before marriage and monogamy afterward are accomplished by discipline and commitment. If men did what they are genetically programmed to do, most would be sexually promiscuous from about fourteen years of age onward. Would that make such behavior any less immoral? Of course not.

What if a pedophile (child abuser) could claim that he inherited his lust for kids? He could make a good case for it. Certainly his sexual apparatus and the testosterone that drives it are creations of genetics. Even if his perversion resulted from early experiences, he could accurately claim not to have chosen to be what he is. But *so what?* Does that make his abuse of children any less offensive? Should society accept, protect, and grant special civil rights to pedophiles? Is it blatant discrimination that they are tried, convicted, and imprisoned for doing what they are "programmed" to do? No! The source of their sexual preference is irrelevant to the behavior itself, which is deemed to be immoral and reprehensible by society.

What if it could be demonstrated conclusively that alcoholics inherit a chemical vulnerability to alcohol? Such is probably the case, since some races have a much higher incidence of alcoholism than others. But *so what?* Does that mean alcoholism is any less a problem for those families and for society in general? Hardly!

I hope the point is apparent. Being genetically inclined to do immoral things does not make immoral behavior right. There are many influences at work within us, but they are irrelevant. I know of no instance in Scripture where God winked at evildoers because of their flawed inheritance or early experiences. In fact, the opposite is implied. In the book of Genesis we are told that an angel informed Ishmael's mother that the child she was carrying would be "a wild donkey of a man; his hand will be against everyone and everyone's hand against him, and he will live in hostility toward all his brothers"

(Genesis 16:12). In other words, Ishmael was genetically inclined toward violence and rebellion. Yet there is no indication that he enjoyed a special dispensation from God that excused his sinful behavior. Each of us is accountable for what we do, without excuses and rationalizations. That's why we all need a Savior who died to eradicate our sins, regardless of their source.

There is one other "so what" with which we must deal. If homosexuals can claim to be genetically predisposed to lust after their own sex, why does that make their circumstances different from unmarried heterosexuals? Single individuals are certainly programmed by heredity to desire fulfillment with the opposite sex, but they are called to a world of purity. I know that is a tough requirement—especially for those who will never marry—yet this is my understanding of Scripture. Promiscuity for unmarried heterosexuals is the moral equivalent of promiscuity for homosexuals. Liberal ministers who are revising church standards to sanction sexual expression by homosexuals must, I would think, extend the same concession to heterosexual singles. But before they do, some scriptural justification should be found to support the "new morality." I think none exists.

QUESTION 478

Now that you've made the point that the origin of homosexuality has little moral significance, would you indicate whether or not you believe it is inherited? I have reviewed studies conducted in recent years that seemingly indicate it is in the genes and is therefore involuntary. Do you agree?

No one can say definitively what causes a person to be homosexual. We have to acknowledge that there could be inheritable tendencies (which does not make homosexuality "involuntary") in some individuals. There is no proof of such influence to this point, but we can't rule it out in specific cases. It could also result from the presence or absence of hormonal "spiking" that typically occurs before birth. It is more likely to be related to one or more of the following: (1) confusion of role models seen in parents, including, but not limited to, a dominant mother and a weak or absent father; (2) serious family dysfunction that wounds and damages the child; (3) early sexual abuse; (4) the influence of an older homosexual during a critical period of adolescence; (5) conscious choice and cultivation; and/or (6) homosexual experimentation, such as mutual masturbatory activity, by boys in early adolescence. How do these and other forces interplay in individual circumstances? I don't know. I don't think anyone knows.

On the other hand, I am certain that homosexuality does not result from irresistible genetic influences, as some would have us believe. First, if it were specifically a genetic trait, then all identical twins would either have it or not have it. Their genes are exact duplicates, so anything deriving specifically from their DNA would express itself identically in the two individuals. Such is not the case. There are thousands of identical twins with whom one is gay and the other is straight.[214]

Second, inherited characteristics that are not passed on to the next generation are eliminated from the gene pool. Since homosexuals and lesbians reproduce less frequently than heterosexuals, there should be a steadily decreasing number of people in the population with homosexual tendencies—especially over the many thousands of years mankind has been on the earth. There is, however, no indication that its numbers are in decline.

Third, and related to the same point, Scripture refers to epidemics of homosexuality and lesbianism that occurred in specific cultures. For example, in Romans 1:26-27 the apostle Paul describes such a time in Corinth: "Because of this, God gave them over to shameful lusts. Even their women exchanged natural relations for unnatural ones. In the same way the men also abandoned natural relations with women and were inflamed with lust for one another. Men committed indecent acts with other men, and received in themselves the due penalty for their perversion." (That final sentence sounds like the transmission of sexually transmitted diseases, doesn't it?)

Again, if homosexuality were inherited within the human family, it would be constant over time and within cultures. There would not be surges and epidemics as the apostle Paul referred to and as we appear to be seeing today.

Fourth, God is infinitely just. I don't believe He would speak of homosexuality in the Scriptures as an abominable sin and list it among the most despicable of human behaviors if men and women bore no

513

responsibility for engaging in it (see 1 Corinthians 6:9-10). That is not how He does business.

While homosexuality and lesbianism are not exclusively induced by heredity, it is important to emphasize that it often occurs in those who did not choose it. Some individuals are drawn toward the gay lifestyle in the absence of any known related influences. Such individuals need our care and compassion as they struggle to deal with the forces that lie within. We can accept them without approving of behavior the Bible condemns.

QUESTION 479

I heard a theologian say that the Bible does not condemn homosexual behavior and that those who say it does are nothing more than right-wing fundamentalist homophobes. What do you think Scripture says on this subject?

It doesn't really matter what I think. What matters are the inspired words written on that subject in both the Old and New Testaments. Let me quote a few of them, and then you can draw your own conclusions:

LEVITICUS 18:22

Do not lie with a man as one lies with a woman; that is detestable.

LEVITICUS 20:13

If a man lies with a man as one lies with a woman, both of them have done what is detestable.

JUDGES 19:22-23

While they were enjoying themselves, some of the wicked men of the city surrounded the house. Pounding on the door, they shouted to the old man who owned the house, "Bring out the man who came to your house so we [Benjamites living in Gibeah] can have sex with him." The owner of the house went outside and said to them, "No, my friends, don't be so vile."

1 KINGS 14:24

There were even male shrine prostitutes in the land [Rehoboam was king at the time]; the people engaged in all the detestable practices of the nations the Lord had driven out before the Israelites.

514

1 KINGS 15:12

He [King Asa] expelled the male shrine prostitutes from the land [Judah] and got rid of all the idols his fathers had made.

1 KINGS 22:46

He [King Jehosophat] rid the land [Judah] of the rest of the male shrine prostitutes who remained there even after the reign of his father Asa.

2 KINGS 23:7

He [King Josiah] also tore down the quarters of the male shrine prostitutes, which were in the temple of the Lord and where women did weaving for Asherah.

1 CORINTHIANS 6:9-10

Do you not know that the wicked will not inherit the kingdom of God? Do not be deceived: Neither the sexually immoral nor idolaters nor adulterers nor male prostitutes nor homosexual offenders nor thieves nor the greedy nor drunkards nor slanderers nor swindlers will inherit the kingdom of God.

1 TIMOTHY 1:9-11

We also know that law is made not for the righteous but for lawbreakers and rebels, the ungodly and sinful, the unholy and irreligious; for those who kill their fathers or mothers, for murderers, for adulterers and perverts, for slave traders and liars and perjurers—and for whatever else is contrary to the sound doctrine that conforms to the glorious gospel of the blessed God, which he entrusted to me.

JUDE 1:7

In a similar way, Sodom and Gomorrah and the surrounding towns gave themselves up to sexual immorality and perversion. They serve as an example of those who suffer the punishment of eternal fire.

515

Obviously, these Scriptures leave little room for debate, especially when considered in the light of Romans 1, quoted earlier. The only way their message can be negated is to reject the authority of God's Word. Please note, however, that many similar texts condemn *hetero-*

sexual promiscuity with equal fervor as homosexual behavior. Immorality is immoral whether it occurs between people of the same sex or those of the opposite sex. In both cases, our responsibility is to call sin by its name and to admonish men and women to live in purity and holiness.

QUESTION 480

What should be the attitude of Christians toward those who are gay?

That is a very important question considering the related turmoil going on around us. I feel strongly that Christians have a scriptural mandate to love and care for all the people of the world. Everyone is entitled to be treated with respect and dignity, even those who are living in immoral circumstances. There is no place for hatred, hurtful jokes, or other forms of rejection toward those who are homosexual. We cannot hope to win others to Jesus Christ if we insult and wound them.

Remember, too, that Jesus was more compassionate toward the adulterous woman caught in the very act of intercourse—a capital offense in those days—than He was to hypocrites in the church. That is our model for how to respond to a person living in sin. Indeed, we should be trying to reach out to those who don't know Jesus Christ, which is impossible in an atmosphere of hostility and fear.

Also, it should be remembered that there are celibate homosexuals who are trying desperately to live godly lives. Many of them struggle every day to do what is right, fighting inner battles that rage like wildfires. These men and women need every ounce of compassion and support they can get from Christian people who know of their tendencies. Often, however, they are rejected and excluded from the church community because of fear and misunderstanding by those who find them repulsive. This is wrong! These individuals need the community of Christ and the fellowship it can provide. They must be embraced as fellow believers who are trying to please the Lord and conform to a standard of moral purity. How can we do less?

QUESTION 481

I am glad to hear you talk about the need for Christians to be caring and compassionate to homosexuals and lesbians. I think many of my church friends are homophobic and cruel to those who have these tendencies.

Let me say again, every human being is entitled to respect and acceptance, including those who are caught in the grip of sin. But I must emphasize that while we are expressing compassion to homosexuals as individuals, we are morally obligated to call sin by its name and to oppose the radical agenda of the gay-rights movement. What activists are trying to accomplish in the culture is wrong, and it must be resisted.

That agenda includes teaching prohomosexual concepts in the public schools, redefining the family to represent "any circle of people who love each other," approval of homosexual adoption, legitimizing same-sex marriage, and securing special rights for those who identify themselves as gay. Those ideas must be opposed, even though to do so is to expose oneself to the charge of being "homophobic."

QUESTION 482

Is AIDS God's plague sent to punish homosexuals, lesbians, and other promiscuous people?

I would think not, because little babies and others who bear no responsibility for their disease are also suffering. But consider this: If a person chooses to leap off a ten-story building, he will die when his body crashes to the ground below. It is inevitable. Gravity was not designed by God to punish human folly. He established physical laws that can only be violated at great peril. So it is with His moral laws. They are as real and predictable as the principles that govern the physical universe. Thus, it should have been obvious with the onset of the sexual revolution back in 1968 that today's epidemics would come. That time is here, and what we do with our moral crisis will determine how much we and our children will suffer in the future.

517

By the way, did you know that God created the moral basis for the universe before he made the heavens and the earth? That's what we read in Proverbs 8:22-36, referring to the universal moral law in first person:

> The Lord brought me ["me" here refers to "wisdom," or God's moral perspective] forth as the first of his works, before his deeds of old; I was appointed from eternity, from the beginning, before the world began. When there were no oceans, I was given birth, when there were no springs abounding with water; before the mountains were settled in place, before the hills, I was given birth, before he made the earth or its fields or any of the dust of the world. I was there when he set the heavens in place, when he marked out the horizon on the face of the deep, when he established the clouds above and fixed securely the fountains of the deep, when he gave the sea its boundary so the waters would not overstep his command, and when he marked out the foundations of the earth. Then I was the craftsman at his side. I was filled with delight day after day, rejoicing always in his presence, rejoicing in his whole world and delighting in mankind. Now then, my sons, listen to me; blessed are those who keep my ways. Listen to my instruction and be wise; do not ignore it. Blessed is the man who listens to me, watching daily at my doors, waiting at my doorway. For whoever finds me finds life and receives favor from the Lord. But whoever fails to find me harms himself; all who hate me love death.

Isn't that a fascinating Scripture? It tells us that the moral foundation existed prior to the Creation, because it is an expression of God's very nature. It didn't come along with the Ten Commandments after God saw the need for rules. The moral law is as eternal as God Himself, and it actually outranks physical laws in significance. The universe will wear out like a garment and be rolled up like a scroll, but the moral foundation will exist forever.

This understanding is directly applicable to homosexual *and* heterosexual immorality, and to every other form of sinful behavior common to humankind. If we conform to God's ancient moral prescription, we are entitled to the sweet benefits of life. But if we defy its clear imperatives, then death is the inevitable consequence. AIDS is only one avenue by which sickness and death befall those who play Russian roulette with God's moral imperatives.

*Q*UESTION 483

What is the responsibility of the person who wants to live a Christian life but struggles with a deeply ingrained attraction to members of his or her own sex?

If I interpret Scripture properly, persons with homosexual inclinations have the same obligation as heterosexual single adults. They are required to refrain from immoral sexual behavior. I understand the implications of this position, and I'm not being glib about the issue. It is far easier to write about purity than it is to live by it day by day. But I didn't make the rules. I can only report the standard of behavior given to us in Scripture. Fortunately, those who feel besieged by temptation are also assured that "God is faithful, and he will not let you be tempted beyond your strength, but with the temptation will also provide the way of escape, that you may be able to endure it" (1 Corinthians 10:13, RSV).

Note: Following is an actual letter sent to me by a practicing homosexual and my subsequent reply:

*Q*UESTION 484

I am gay, and I am writing on behalf of many thousands of gay people in this country who have grown to hate the church because of organizations like yours. First, however, I would like to give you a quick background on myself.

I grew up in the home of a minister. It was a very happy, nondysfunctional environment. I grew up as a Bible-believing Christian, and I always tried to put Christ first in my life and live by His commandments. Most of my childhood was spent where I knew of no other gay people.

I loved the Lord, the church, and my family—in that order. I left home and attended college, where I spent hundreds of hours studying the Bible, theology, and the history of the church. My parents were proud and thought that everything had turned out perfectly when I graduated. That's when I told them I was gay. They were devastated!

You see, from day one of puberty, I was attracted to the same sex. I never changed. Of course, I tried to change because I thought I was the only one in the world like this, and my father preached against it. So from the sixth grade to my junior year in college, I tried everything I could to go straight—counselors, prayer vigils, reading countless books on the evils of homosexuality, and attending Homosexuals Anonymous; nothing worked. The more I tried to change, the more it seemed just natural for me to be gay.

I decided to come out of the closet. The first person I met in a gay club was the choir director's son at my parents' church! He introduced me to many other gays—students in seminary, Sunday school teachers, church pianists, ushers, and many preachers' sons. There were gay people all throughout the church, but no one really knew because, like me, they were silently living their lives far from the minority of loud activists that you see on the evening news.

In the next few months, I took a course at college in Pauline Epistles, and one of our textbooks had a lengthy chapter regarding what the Bible says and does not say about homosexuals. To oversimplify a complex argument, it concluded that the Bible did not take a definite position on what we know today as committed gay relationships. I am sure you have read some of the discussions, and they are quite sophisticated. Nothing to be dismissed lightly, I'm sure you'll agree—especially when people's lives are at stake.

I write this letter on behalf of my many friends who come from a similar background but hate the church because of organizations like yours. Sprinkled throughout all your programs are derogatory and demeaning references to gay people. You support legislation to take away our rights and spread misleading, inaccurate information.

If you are really concerned about winning people to Christ, then look to the gay community. They are ripe for harvest. They would be attentive to a voice that preaches hope, forgiveness, acceptance, and sexual morals—as long as you understand we are not perverted in our feelings of love for one another.

Dr. Dobson, I remember watching your first videotape series in my dad's church, and I felt so strong for your message. I still do—basically. My partner and I, as well as thousands of other gay people, just wish you would be more inclusive.

Dear (Name),

More than anything else, I appreciate the respectful and conciliatory attitude you conveyed in broaching an extremely emotional and controversial subject with me. You have made your case sensitively and intelligently. Thank you for that. I honestly believe that if more of us would adopt your approach, we might begin to make some headway in the business of understanding one another!

In response, I want to begin by telling you how strongly I feel about the mandate we have as Christians to love and care for people from all walks of life. Even those with whom we disagree. Even those involved in lifestyles we believe to be immoral. My first reaction to your honest sharing of yourself is a sense of acceptance for you as an individual. I mean that sincerely.

Regardless of what the media may say, Focus on the Family has no interest in promoting hatred toward homosexuals or any other group of our fellow human beings. We have not supported, and will never support, legislation aimed at depriving them of their basic constitutional rights—rights they share with every citizen.

On the contrary, we want to reach out to gay and lesbian people whenever and wherever we can. If I had the time, I could describe for you many situations in which we've done exactly that. It's a commandment we've received from the Lord Jesus.

Beyond that, I have to acknowledge that you and I have a very different understanding of Scripture. It is my firm conviction that sex outside of marriage (whether homosexual or heterosexual) is not permitted by those who call themselves "believers."

Yes, I'm aware that some biblical scholars have conducted elaborate studies to show that Scripture takes no decisive position on the issue. This is neither new nor surprising. Biblical studies have been done to support a wide variety of unbiblical ideas!

But from our perspective, the truth remains clear. You've obviously been over that ground, and I will not use this reply to belabor the point.

Let me simply say that the same Scriptures that condemn homosexuality and premarital heterosexuality also tell us to accept those who are in violation of these ordinances. Jesus was more compassionate toward the woman caught in the very act of intercourse—a capital offense in those days—than He was toward the hypocrites in the church. This is our model and our mandate.

Whereas we have never attempted to hurt or ridicule the individual homosexual or lesbian, I do find myself in sharp disagreement with the more radical elements of the movement. The effort to redefine the family, qualify for adoption, promote the homosexual lifestyle in the schools, etc., are objectives with which I disagree. And I will oppose them when the issues are raised. Does that make me a hatemonger? I think not.

Concerning the passage of Amendment 2 here in Colorado (which would have prohibited ordinances and legislation creating "special rights" for homosexuals, equating them with those needing civil rights protection), let me explain why we strongly favored that legislation. To understand our position, you must know that many Christians also feel they have been victimized by society's hostility to traditional religious views.

A dear friend of mine, Bob Vernon, former assistant chief of the Los Angeles Police Department, was driven from office because of his faith. No charges were ever brought against him. The pressure was political, resulting solely from his fundamental beliefs. He is but one of thousands of people being discriminated against today because of their Christian beliefs.

How would you and your homosexual companions feel if we, as Christians, began lobbying for special, protected legal status? How would you react if we asserted that we should be given a job and shielded from termination just because we are Christians? I can predict that you would fight such ordinances tooth and nail. Why?

Because when one person wins in these kinds of struggles, someone else (the nonbeliever) loses. Thus, we must be very careful before creating new "minorities" based on behavior or beliefs—as opposed to those who have been discriminated against historically based on their race.

That raises the question: Have homosexuals faced this kind of uphill battle? Perhaps in the past, but there is no evidence of which I'm aware that they are disadvantaged now. The average homosexual earns $55,000 per year, compared with $32,000 for heterosexuals.[215]

Gays also have a much higher percentage of college degrees than the straight population.[216] And when it comes to political clout, how can they claim to be shortchanged? Dozens of objectives of the gay and lesbian community are being achieved today.

Look at the issue of funding for AIDS research and treatment. I had a heart attack several years ago, and I am very concerned about support for research on coronary artery disease. After all, heart attacks and strokes kill more people than AIDS, cancer, TB, and several other diseases combined. But as you may know, the federal government spent thirty-nine times as much on AIDS last year as it did on heart disease.[217] Why? Because of the clout of homosexuals who turned their powerful guns on Congress and the White House.

My point is not to decry money being spent on the horrible AIDS epidemic. I'm simply making the point that the homosexual community is hardly an oppressed, powerless minority seeking protection under the law. You have Hollywood, the press, the media, the universities, the publishers, the professionals (in the American Bar Association, American Medical Association, etc.), and the judiciary enforcing your "politically correct" agenda.

Conservative Christians, by contrast, are stranded pretty much on their own. Given this undergirding, I hope you can see that our opposition to the gay and lesbian tidal wave is not an expression of hate but one of social justice and common sense.

One more thought about expressions of hatred. The question is: Who is endeavoring to hurt whom? Have we brought caskets to your front door? Have we thrown bricks through your windows? Have we left bloody animal parts on your property? Have we spread untrue rumors about your activities and motives? Have we spray-painted your buildings or made bomb threats at your offices?

No, but all of these hostilities have been inflicted on us by the homosexual community and its supporters in Colorado Springs. Nevertheless, we have not returned evil for evil, nor do we intend to do so. Thus, the charge that we are hateful is simply not rooted in fact.

I hope this clarifies my position for you. Again, I'm grateful that you cared enough to write, and I want you to know that we're here for you if you need us. God bless you.

QUESTION 485

I read recently that the definition of the family needed to be revised in light of cultural changes. The writer said a family should be thought of as "a circle of love," including any individuals who were deeply attached to each other. Somehow I know this is wrong but can't articulate why. How do you see it?

I am familiar with the effort to redefine the family. It is motivated by homosexual activists and others who see this institution as a barrier to the social engineering they hope to accomplish. But what is the traditional definition of the family? It is a group of individuals who are related to one another by marriage, birth, or adoption—nothing more, nothing else. The family was divinely instituted and sanctioned in the beginning, when God created one man and one woman, brought them together, and commanded them to "be fruitful and multiply." This is where we begin, and this is where we must stand.

By contrast, if the term *family* refers to any group of people who love each other, then the term ceases to have meaning. In that case, five homosexual men can be a "family" until one feels unloved, and then there are four.

Under such a definition, one man and six women could be regarded as a legal entity, reintroducing the debate over polygamy. We thought we settled that issue in the last century.

524

It would also be possible for parents who dislike a rebellious teenager to opt him out of the "circle of love," thus depriving him of any legal identity with the family. With such amorphous terms, wives would have no greater legal protection than female acquaintances with whom men become infatuated. We end up with an unstable social structure rife with potential for disaster.

There is good reason, then, to defend the narrow legal definition of the family as understood over the centuries. After all, the family as I have characterized it is not merely human in origin. It is God's marvelous creation. And He has not included casual social relationships—even the most loving ones—within that bond of kinship. Nor should we.

QUESTION 486

Why have so many parents forgotten the commonsense approach to child rearing that has worked for generations? Why look for something new?

Good question. People began losing confidence in the traditional approach to child rearing during the 1920s and 1930s. Science was making great contributions to their lives through inventions and discoveries, so it was reasonable to think that the experts could provide a better approach to parenting. An array of gurus—educators, psychiatrists, and psychologists—rose to the challenge. They began passing off their personal biases and opinions as scientific fact. Dr. J. B. Watson, the first and most bizarre of the lot, became enormously influential in that era. Known as the father of behaviorism, he offered what he called a foolproof method of child rearing, and mothers bought it hook, line, and sinker. If only they would follow his advice, he said, they could produce any kind of child they wanted: "a doctor, lawyer, artist, merchant-chief, and—yes—even a beggarman and a thief."[218]

Watson believed that the mind does not exist—that the human brain functions as a simple switchboard connecting stimuli and responses. From that ridiculous foundation, he went on to offer parents advice that was truly off-the-wall. He wrote:

525

Never hug and kiss [your children], never let them sit in your lap. If you must, kiss them once on the forehead when they say good night. Shake hands with them in the morning. Remember when you are tempted to pet your child that mother love is a dangerous instrument—an instrument which may inflict a never-healing wound, a wound which will make infancy unhappy, adolescence a nightmare, an instrument which may wreck your adult son or daughter's vocational future and their chances for marital happiness.[219]

Unbelievably, millions of parents followed these notions explicitly for nearly two decades. A generation of mothers and fathers worked diligently to condition their children the way Watson recommended. This strange era in child rearing illustrates the way public confidence shifted from the time-honored wisdom of the Judeo-Christian ethic to the bizarre rumblings of pseudoscientific claptrap.

Unfortunately, Watson was succeeded by a long line of self-appointed "experts" who dreamed up and promoted their own concoctions. Included among their conclusions were the beliefs that loving discipline is damaging, authority is "undemocratic," religious instruction is hazardous, defiance is a valuable ventilator of anger, premarital sex is healthy, "children's rights" should supersede parental leadership, and on and on it went.

In recent years, this humanistic perspective has become even more extreme and anti-Christian. It encompasses everything from "sex equality training" for three-year-olds to teaching homosexual and lesbian propaganda to elementary school children. In short, the twentieth century spawned a generation of professionals who ignored what has been learned in two thousand years of parenting and offered what they considered "better ideas." Most of what they cooked up was ridiculous at best and dangerous at worst.

Given that background, you can understand why I have never tried to invent new concepts or methodology. Instead, my purpose has been simply to reconnect us with the traditional wisdom of the ages. I didn't concoct it, nor have I sought to change it. My task has been merely to report what I believe to be the prescription of the Creator Himself. And I am convinced that this understanding will remain viable as long as mothers and fathers and children cohabit the face of the earth.

QUESTION 487

Why are people who believe in traditional values less involved in public issues than the secular humanists? Do conservative Christians care less about their ideas than the liberals do?

I have been troubled by that question for several years. Many Christians would give their lives for their faith if necessary, and yet they consistently get whipped in the public arena. Their philosophical opponents get there first, fight better when the heat is on, and remain on the battlefield after the pro-family people have gone home. How can this be? Why is our army so tentative?

After giving the matter much thought, I believe I now understand the problem. The difference is that the other side earns a living by fighting policy battles, while we are merely motivated by ideology. Antifamily organizations receive multiplied millions of dollars in subsidies each year. It is no wonder they fight like fanatics when those funds are threatened in Washington.

Likewise, the abortionists, the pornographers, liberal educators, and empire-building bureaucrats all feed at the public trough. Their livelihood depends on it, which helps explain the tenacity of the left. They don't give up, even after years of defeat and disappointment. How about pro-family troops? Well, they're not quite so tough. They get discouraged and embarrassed by a single setback. They're up to their ears in responsibility at home and just can't afford more than a quick skirmish. Obviously, conservative Christians must learn to go the distance if they're to defend the things in which they believe. Votes are what it's all about, and yet half the Christians are not even registered. No wonder they get whipped year in and year out.

527

QUESTION 488

You've talked about the bias against homemakers by today's legislatures. Do you believe such an attitude could be changed if conservative women would become better organized?

To be sure! Women are the key to cleaning up the mess we are facing in this family-unfriendly nation! If we ever get conservative women concerned enough to stand up for what they believe, we could reverse much of the damage done in this half-century. If they would simply band together to vote a few liberal senators and congressmen out of office, word would spread like wildfire on the Hill. Henceforth, when the New Traditionalist Women showed up in their outer offices, the yawns and snickers would vanish. Oh, how I wish! We have the numbers! But who will forge them into one mighty voice?

QUESTION 489

You have been outspoken about the need for citizens to get involved in the political process. Explain why that is important and how I can go about doing it.

You can start by participating in the electoral process. I think it is a disgrace that half the Christians in America aren't even registered to vote, and of those who are, only half go to the polls. America is not ruled by a dictatorship; it is blessed to have a representative form of government that Abraham Lincoln described as being "of the people, by the people, and for the people."[220] The Constitution declares that you and I *are* the government. When we withhold our influence and participation, we yield by default to those who promote immoral and destructive policies. We owe it to our children and to future generations to defend the principles in which we believe—the glorious freedom bought with the blood of so many brave young men and women. Shame on us for failing to do our duty to God and country. It is unconscionable that so many Christians today have concluded that it is somehow immoral to "get political." I don't believe the Founding Fathers intended to exclude people of faith from the process. There is not a scrap of evidence to indicate such.

There are many ways to participate in public policy besides voting. Letters and phone calls to our local officials, congressmen, and senators do make a difference. They certainly need to hear from us. When you write or call, be brief, and restrict each letter to one subject or one piece of legislation. This makes it easier for the person you're writing to to respond and for their staff to organize correspondence. If the letter is about a specific bill, identify it by name and number. Second, make your letter personal. Form letters and postcards do have a place, but personal letters get more attention. Describe how the proposed bill or course of action would affect you or your family or your community. Give the essential background information as well. And third, remember that elected officials receive thousands of letters of complaint and very few positive responses.

If a public official says or does something that you like, respond with a quick note of appreciation, and by all means, remember that democracy works best when the people make their wants and wishes known. Finally, heed the words of the apostle Paul when he wrote, "I urge, then, first of all, that requests, prayers, intercession and thanksgiving be made for everyone—for kings and all those in authority, that we may live peaceful and quiet lives in all godliness and holiness. This is good, and pleases God our Savior" (1 Timothy 2:1-3).

QUESTION 490

Perhaps I'd be more inclined to vote if I felt it would really make a difference, but I'm skeptical, to say the least. Can you give me any evidence that would convince me otherwise?

Our nation's recent political history is sprinkled with examples of when election outcomes hinged on a handful of votes. I recall former senator Bill Armstrong, who invested twenty-eight years of his life in public office, relating the story of his good friend Representative Lou Wyman's campaign. When Wyman ran for a Senate seat, he lost by twelve votes statewide. Other instances in which candidates squeaked through by the narrowest of margins include Averill Harriman's gubernatorial election in 1954, George McGovern's senatorial campaign in 1960, and John Warner's run for the Senate in 1978. All were decided by one vote or less per precinct.[221] And don't forget the Nixon/Kennedy electoral results of 1960; when the dust had settled, the presidential prize was awarded based on an average margin of only one-half vote per precinct nationwide.

Even when elections do not appear to be closely contested, it is a moral outrage that more Christians do not take their voting responsibilities seriously. If they did, this would be a very different nation,

529

and a better one. But for reasons beyond my comprehension, evangelicals are either too involved, too preoccupied, or too disinterested to hold our elected officials accountable and keep our democracy on track.

Because so few citizens vote, many of us are unaware that a small minority actually dominates national politics (not to mention local elections). To illustrate, let's hypothesize that the country as a whole goes to the polls at the rate of ten out of every twenty people. If evangelicals stepped up their voting involvement to thirteen out of every twenty, instead of accounting for only 20 percent of the overall vote, their proportion of the votes cast would increase to nearly 25 percent. Did you know that if most of that additional 5 percent vote had been directed to the loser in four of the presidential elections that have taken place since World War II, it would have tipped the scales in favor of the loser?[222] And obviously, more is at stake than merely the influence of chief-executive policy for a four-year term—judicial appointments made by the president can directly impact our culture and our families for half a lifetime or more.

Your vote is crucial if we are to reintroduce the traditional, family-friendly values on which our nation was founded. A great member of the British Parliament, Edmund Burke, said something 250 years ago that still resonates today: "All that is necessary for evil to prevail in the world is that good men do nothing."[223] So get involved! The same Jesus who multiplied the young lad's loaves and fishes will be faithful to multiply the efforts of those of us who honor His name in the political arena.

Q UESTION 491

You have said on several occasions that a society can be no more stable than the strength of the individual family units. Specifically, you said sexual behavior is directly linked to survival of nations. Explain how that principle works.

A book could be written on that topic, but let me give you a short answer to it. This linkage you referred to was first illuminated by J. D. Unwin, a British social anthropologist who spent seven years studying the births and deaths of eighty civilizations. He reported from his exhaustive research that every known culture in the world's history has followed the same sexual pattern: During its early days of existence, premarital and extramarital sexual relationships were strictly prohibited. Great creative energy was associated with this inhibition of sexual expression, causing the culture to prosper. Later in the life of the society, its people began to rebel against the prohibitions, demanding the freedom to express their internal passions. As the mores weakened, the social energy abated, eventually resulting in the decay or destruction of the civilization.

Dr. Unwin concluded that the energy that holds a society together is sexual in nature. When a man is devoted to one woman and one family, he is motivated to build, save, protect, plan, and prosper on their behalf. However, when male and female sexual interests are dispersed and generalized, their effort is invested in the gratification of sensual desires. Dr. Unwin wrote: "Any human society is free either to display great energy, or to enjoy sexual freedom; the evidence is that they cannot do both for more than one generation."[224]

It is my belief that the burgeoning social ills seen in Western nations, including rising crime rates, drug abuse, sexual exploitation of children, and the disintegration of families, can be traced to the disintegration of traditional values and biblical standards of morality.

There is another reason widespread immorality and avant-garde attitudes are dangerous to the stability of nations. Human beings are sexual creatures, both physically and psychologically. Our very identity ("Who am I?") begins with gender assignment and the understanding of what it means to be masculine or feminine. Virtually every aspect of life is related to this biological foundation. Who can deny the hormonal forces and the neurological wiring that shape the way we think and behave? Given this nature and the vast significance it carries, even the most promiscuous playboy should understand the implications of sexual license and the upheaval it can foment. Any revolution of such proportions is certain to have far-reaching consequences for the family and the culture in which it exists. How can we expect to preserve social order when the rules governing our sexual behavior are turned upside down?

531

QUESTION 492

**I understand you're opposed to legalized gambling. Person-
ally, I think it's a great way to increase state revenues while
at the same time providing recreation for people who enjoy
this kind of activity. What are your concerns?**

My concerns about gambling were almost universally understood in
the culture a generation ago. People recognized that it was a snake in
the grass that threatened families and the stability of society. They
knew it was an addictive behavior that had to be regulated tightly or
prohibited altogether. Then suddenly in the early nineties, the nation
had a change of heart. Folks decided gambling not only provided good
clean fun but was also a wonderful source of income for the state.
Buying a lottery ticket became almost a patriotic act. It promised to
fund schools and help to support government, without pain to anyone.
At last, a "something for nothing" formula had been discovered. What
a deal!

This new attitude, combined with court rulings granting Indians the
right to open casinos on their land, produced an epidemic that is
sweeping the nation. In 1988, only two states had legal casinos.[225] By
1994, there were forty-eight states that legalized gambling.[226] Citizens
in the state of Mississippi legalized gambling in 1993. In 1995, they
spent more money on gambling than they did on all retail sales
combined![227]

Regrettably, state governments have seized upon the concept of
legalized gambling as a revenue-generating gold mine—a kind of
voluntary tax paid by the gullible in search of quick riches. To keep
the cash rolling in, governments now spend approximately $300
million annually in lottery advertisements,[228] effectively reversing
their historic position as a gambling regulator. Most state politicians
have become so addicted to their "fix" from gambling that they feel
they can't turn back. Both Democrats and Republicans in Washington
are heavily funded by gambling interests.

Despite public approval of legalized gambling by a three-to-one
margin,[229] this activity leads to a host of social ills. New Jersey's

record is appalling. From 1976 to 1992, Atlantic City's police budget tripled to $24 million while the local population *decreased* by 20 percent. And despite spending $59 million yearly to monitor casinos during their first three years in operation, Atlantic City jumped from fiftieth to first on the nation's per capita crime chart.[230] This fallout from gambling is not the exception but the norm. John Kindt, Ph.D., professor of commerce and legal policy at the University of Illinois, asserts that for every dollar of revenue generated by gambling, taxpayers must dish out at least three dollars in increased criminal-justice costs, social-welfare expenses, high regulatory costs, and increased infrastructure expenditures.[231] Gambling is a social cancer that ravages the communities in which it metastasizes.

Equally troublesome are the compulsive gamblers who turn to crime to finance their involvement. According to experts, an estimated five to ten million Americans are afflicted with serious gambling addictions.[232] In one survey of pathological gamblers who sought treatment, 75 percent indicated that they had committed a felony to finance gambling activity.[233] And the cash drain often crosses over into the legitimate business sector; in spite of popular conceptions centering on economic windfall and creation of much-needed jobs, evidence indicates that the net economic effects of gambling are negative. Overlooked amid the hype is the fact that gambling-related jobs tend to be low paying and that other businesses suffer from the introduction of gambling. To illustrate again from the Atlantic City debacle, 40 percent of the city's restaurants were forced to shut their doors in the decade following the introduction of casinos.[234] Money that would have been spent on food is squandered on slot machines, card games, and the other contrivances designed to grab people's money.

Most disturbing of all, however, is the cost in broken lives and shattered families. It is estimated that each compulsive gambler adversely affects the lives of ten to twenty relatives, friends, and business associates.[235] Those who are addicted to gambling show a pattern of substance abuse,[236] suicide attempts,[237] and child abuse and neglect that warp and scar the lives of children growing up near them.[238] Indeed, 7 percent of teenagers are estimated to be pathologically addicted to gambling at their young age.[239]

As if the family didn't have enough enemies to deal with, now we have unleashed yet another monster to assault the institutions of marriage and parenthood.

QUESTION 493

I recently read a report that suggested that censorship was growing at an alarming rate in the U.S. An organization called People for the American Way cited 375 "censorship attempts" as having taken place within a recent one-year span. This would appear to be a very disturbing trend. Shouldn't we be concerned?

You have been victimized by a carefully crafted distortion of the facts. Let me explain. Traditionally, *censorship* has been defined as the "prior restraint of free expression by a government agency, preventing or rescinding publication of material." In other words, when the government prevents something from being published, that is censorship.

Unfortunately, the ultraliberal organization People for the American Way (PAW) bases its annual report on a contrived and ridiculous definition of *censorship*. They would have us believe that censorship occurs whenever anyone questions the appropriateness of a book or curriculum, even one intended for children, regardless of how extreme it is and even if it remains in use. Incredibly, a parent who acts to protect his or her own youngster from offensive material has become, according to this definition, a dreaded censor. People for the American Way would assert that any disagreement with professional educators or other public officials is inappropriate and reprehensible. Their judgments and decisions must be accepted uncritically. What distortion! What utter nonsense!

The lifeblood of effective democratic government has always been the freedom to speak one's mind and lobby for one's point of view. Does not the First Amendment, which People for the American Way professes to value, guarantee that right of every citizen to advocate his or her views in the marketplace of ideas? Of course it does!

Another aspect of the censorship issue is particularly irritating to me. The liberal media in the United States gives significant coverage to PAW's phony press release each year—as though it were a legitimate news story. A big press conference is held, and a dozen reporters rush out to write their stories. The casual reader would conclude that America is besieged by hordes of bluenoses who roam the countryside in search of books to burn. But look at the numbers in PAW's own report. Even if the incidents they cite were valid, their conclusion would still be ridiculous. There are 15,000 school districts in the United States, yet PAW could identify only 375 examples of "censorship" in a twelve-month period.[240] That means only one parent in forty school districts lodged a complaint. One person out of 666,666 citizens is a censor. Yes, sir! We have an alarming problem with censorship in this land.

QUESTION 494

Tell me why you support the "rescue movement" and groups that violate trespassing laws in order to block the entrance to abortion clinics. Isn't this a contradiction of scriptural precepts?

I don't think so. It is true that we Christians are instructed in Scripture to obey civil laws and those in authority over us. But we are also commanded to "rescue those being led away to death; hold back those staggering toward slaughter" (Proverbs 24:11). Remember, too, that the apostle Paul and other early Christian leaders disobeyed laws and orders requiring them to remain silent about the teachings of Jesus. There are other biblical examples of godly men and women, including Daniel in ancient Babylon, who refused to obey unjust laws that contradicted their beliefs. Obviously, there are times when we are expected to resist civil authority.

Applying that understanding of Scripture to the abortion movement, we must ask, "Is this such an occasion?" A better question is, Do we believe our own rhetoric about the unborn child? Are the abortionists killing babies or aren't they? If 1.5 million infants are being murdered in the United States every year, how can we stand around debating whether or not it is appropriate to oppose the laws that permit their slaughter?

To illustrate the point, suppose the euthanasia movement catches

535

on in days ahead, making it legal for parents to decide whether or not they wish to continue raising their children. Suppose they could take any child under five years of age to a "Life Clinic," where the boy or girl could be put to sleep. Suppose children were walking in the front door of clinics and going out the back in coffins.

If such a horrible day ever dawned, what do you think the response of Christians would be? Would they thumb carefully through the pages of Scripture to find justification for their civil disobedience? Of course not! The moral issue would be so clear that trespassing to prevent the killing would be of no relevance. The murdering of innocent children would be so abhorrent to what we know of God's nature that many of us would give our lives to rescue the little ones. In a very real sense, we are confronted by that same issue today. We are killing babies, although we can't see them or wrap our arms around them.

I simply do not understand why some Christian leaders, whom I respect, continue to split hairs over subtle scriptural understandings, wondering whether there is a real difference between Daniel's civil disobedience and the insignificant act of trespassing by today's rescuers.

To those Christians who feel prohibited from stepping across a property line to save a baby, I would ask, How would you have responded to the slavery issue in the mid-1800s? Would you have harbored a runaway slave who sought sanctuary from his or her "master"? What would you have done as a citizen of Germany in World War II? The Nazi extermination camps were legal. Would you have broken your country's unjust laws in order to protect millions of people marked for death? Was Corrie ten Boom's father in violation of Scripture for protecting Jews from the murderers in the SS?

Certainly not! Nor are "rescue" participants in violation of any moral law, in my opinion. They seek to prevent violence against a powerless minority, and that is a principle supported throughout Scripture.

QUESTION 495

What is meant by "multiculturalism," which I keep hearing about?

I wish I could say that this term referred to respect for the entire human family, regardless of nationality, race, or ethnic identification. In years past it might have recalled images of the Ballet Folklorico, French crepes, Swedish fiddles, Zulu masks, Tahitian drums, Chinatown, Little Italy, and Armenian delicatessens. Every culture has a rich heritage from which we may gain something beautiful and valuable, and many of them have been assimilated in the land of the "Great Melting Pot."

Unfortunately, the terms *multiculturalism* and *diversity* have come to have very different meanings when used by the cultural elite. They are a kind of Trojan horse in which to smuggle the concept of moral relativism into the heartland of Western culture. They are code words for the proposition that there is no such thing as right and wrong.

The argument runs like this. Because our nation is composed of people from widely diverse cultural and ethnic groups, each having its own unique value system or ethical code, we must conclude that there is no such thing as truth or certainty. In the final analysis, anything goes. Somehow, the existence of many different standards proves that there is no standard. Amoralists, particularly, are attracted to that redefinition and promote it with vigor. Nothing is really right or wrong. Everything depends on one's point of view. The highest form of good, therefore, is tolerance of anything and everything (except traditional Christianity, which is the chief source of intolerance).

That line of reasoning has found its way into every crevice of the culture, and certainly it is represented in the educational system from kindergarten through graduate school. During school-board elections in Littleton, Colorado, for example, one outspoken principal disagreed that graduates should be taught something about the Great Depression, the Holocaust, and World War II. Why? Because he asserted that any attempt to define our cultural landmarks is arbitrary and therefore arrogant and presumptuous.[241] It is wrong to teach our children that an American perspective on world history is more valid than any other—even for Americans.

Similar to this notion is an educational objective recently established by Pennsylvania educators for all graduating seniors. There, where the Declaration of Independence was signed and the Constitutional Convention sat, this became the guiding principle: "[Students

537

should achieve] mastery of the concept that no one form of government is better than any other."[242]

Multiculturalism was the excuse for a curriculum written for children in New York City's elementary schools. It came to be known as "Children of the Rainbow," which taught thousands of wide-eyed kids to regard homosexuality as an "alternative lifestyle." One of the textbooks used was *Daddy's Roommate*, a tale in which Daddy leaves Mommy for his gay lover. Another, entitled *Heather Has Two Mommies*, described lesbian motherhood in glowing terms. Fortunately, parents in that school district got enough of multiculturalism and threw out the superintendent who tried to jam these concepts down the throats of their children.[243]

The bottom line? Multiculturalism is all about moral relativism—not respect for differing cultures.

26

Principles and Concepts Drawn from Dr. Dobson's Books and Statements through the Years

Listed below are the quotations from the writings of Dr. James Dobson that best reflect his perspective on various aspects of family life. Most of these statements were originally included in his books, beginning with Dare to Discipline *and continuing through the most recent to date,* Life on the Edge. *Some of the comments were made during the* Focus on the Family *radio broadcast. References are provided for each quotation.*

1. I have concluded that the accumulation of wealth, even if I could achieve it, is an insufficient reason for living. When I reach the end of my days, a moment or two from now, I must look backward on something more meaningful than the pursuit of houses and land and machines and stocks and bonds. Nor is fame of any lasting benefit. I will consider my earthly existence to have been wasted unless I can recall a loving family, a consistent investment in the lives of people, and an earnest attempt to serve the God who made me. Nothing else makes much sense. —*What Wives Wish Their Husbands Knew about Women,* p. 108

2. Someone observed, "Values are not taught to our children; they are 'caught' by them." —*Straight Talk to Men,* p. 64

3. If we want to see honesty, truthfulness, and unselfishness in our offspring, then these characteristics should be the conscious objectives of our early instructional process. —*The Strong-Willed Child,* pp. 55–56

4. I believe the most valuable contribution a parent can make to a child is to instill in him or her a genuine faith in Jesus Christ. —*Hide or Seek*, p. 169

5. Our task as parents is to begin very early to instruct our children on the true values of life: Love for all mankind, kindness, integrity, trustworthiness, truthfulness, and devotion to God. —*Hide or Seek*, p. 88

6. Guard your family relationships against erosion as though you were defending your very lives. —*Love for a Lifetime*, p. 111

7. Don't permit the possibility of divorce to enter your thinking. Even in moments of great conflict and discouragement, divorce is no easy solution. —*Love for a Lifetime*, p. 103

8. Grandmothers and grandfathers can be invaluable to little people. In today's world, they are often the only grown-ups who have time for them. —*What Wives Wish Their Husbands Knew about Women*, p. 49

9. Every child is entitled to hold up his or her head, not in haughtiness and pride, but in confidence and security. —*Hide or Seek*, p. 57

10. Children just don't fit into a "to-do" list very well. It takes time to be an effective parent when children are small. It takes time to introduce them to good books—it takes time to fly kites and play punchball and put together jigsaw puzzles. It takes time to listen. —*Hide or Seek*, p. 64

11. Those who control what young people are taught and what they experience—what they see, hear, think, and believe—will determine the future course for the nation. —*Children at Risk*, p. 27

12. A family should maintain a variety of traditions that give each member a sense of identity and belonging. —From the *Focus on the Family* broadcast, "Let's Make a Memory," December 2, 1983

13. If there is one lesson parents need to learn most urgently, it is to guard what they say about beauty and intelligence in the presence of their children. —*Hide or Seek*, p. 61

14. The only true source of meaning in life is found in love for God and his Son, Jesus Christ, and in love for mankind, beginning with our own families. —*Straight Talk to Men*, p. 13

15. Every move we make directly affects our future; irresponsible behavior eventually produces sorrow and pain. —*The New Dare to Discipline*, p. 116

16. The solutions to the problems of modern parenthood can be found through the power of prayer and personal appeal to the Creator. —*The New Dare to Discipline,* p. 247

17. Parents who recognize the inevitable war between good and evil will do their best to influence the child's choices—to shape his or her will and provide a solid spiritual foundation. —*The Strong-Willed Child,* p. 174

18. Be willing to let your child experience a reasonable amount of pain or inconvenience when he behaves irresponsibly. —*The New Dare to Discipline,* p. 116

19. The slow learner needs parents' help in finding his compensating skills, coupled with the assurance that his personal worth does not depend on productivity or successes in academia. —*Hide or Seek,* p. 102

20. Parental warmth after discipline is essential to demonstrate that it is the behavior—not the child himself—that the parent rejects. —*The New Dare to Discipline,* p. 36

21. Men and women should recognize that depression can become nothing more than a bad habit—a costly attitude of negativism that can rob them of life's pleasures. —*The New Dare to Discipline,* p. 246

22. The objective of parenting is to take the raw material with which our babies arrive on this earth and then gradually mold it into mature, responsible, and God-fearing adults. —*The New Dare to Discipline,* p. 34

23. Nothing invested in a child is ever lost. —From the *Focus on the Family* broadcast, "Let's Hide the Word," November 2, 1994

24. A husband and wife should have a date every week or two, leaving the children at home and forgetting their problems for an evening. —*The New Dare to Discipline,* p. 245

25. Parents cannot require their children to treat them with dignity if they will not provide the same respect to them in return. —*The New Dare to Discipline,* pp. 25–26

26. Give your child an exposure to responsibility and work, but also preserve time for play and fun. —*The New Dare to Discipline,* p. 155

27. Make no important, life-shaping decisions quickly or impulsively, and when in doubt, stall for time. —*What Wives Wish Their Husbands Knew about Women*, p. 93

28. The quickest way to destroy a romantic love between a husband and wife is for one partner to clamp a steel cage around the other. —*The Strong-Willed Child*, p. 220

29. Many confrontations can be avoided by building friendships with kids and thereby making them *want* to cooperate at home. —*The New Dare to Discipline*, p. 75

30. A family is defined as a group of individuals who are related to one another by marriage, birth, or adoption—nothing more, nothing less. —*Children at Risk*, p. 57

31. The parent-child relationship is the first and most important social interaction a youngster will have, and the flaws and knots experienced there can often be seen later in life. —*The New Dare to Discipline*, p. 18

32. If we ask, the Lord will place key individuals in the paths of our sons and daughters for whom we pray—people of influence who can nudge them in the right direction when they are beyond our reach and care. —*Parenting Isn't for Cowards*, p.77

33. If the strong-willed child is allowed by indulgence to develop "habits" of defiance and disrespect during his early childhood, those characteristics will haunt him and his parents for the next twenty years. —*Parenting Isn't for Cowards*, p. 90

34. After a time of conflict it is extremely important to pray with the child, admitting to God that we have all sinned and no one is perfect. Divine forgiveness is a marvelous experience, even for a very young child. —*The Strong-Willed Child*, p. 33

35. Your contributions to your children and grandchildren could rank as your greatest accomplishments in life—or your most oppressive failures. —*Parenting Isn't for Cowards*, p. 166

36. Both good marriages and bad marriages have moments of conflict, but in healthy relationships, the husband and wife search for answers and areas of agreement because they love each other. —*Preparing for Adolescence*, p. 100

37. Screaming, accusing, and berating are rarely successful in changing the behavior of human beings of any age. —*Love Must Be Tough*, p. 123

38. If a husband and wife are deeply committed to Jesus Christ, they enjoy enormous advantages over the family with no spiritual commitment. —*Love for a Lifetime*, p. 49

39. The best source of guidance for parents can be found in the wisdom of the Judeo-Christian ethic, which originated with the Creator and was then handed down generation by generation from the time of Christ. —*The New Dare to Discipline*, p. 16

40. The Christian way of life lends stability to marriage because its principles and values naturally produce harmony. —*Love for a Lifetime*, p. 54

41. Two distinct messages must be conveyed to every child during his first forty-eight months: (1) "I love you more than you can possibly understand," and (2) "Because I love you I must teach you to obey me." —*Dr. Dobson Answers Your Questions about Raising Children*, p. 16

42. The proper programming of the conscience is one of the most difficult jobs associated with parenthood, and the one that requires the greatest wisdom. —*Emotions: Can You Trust Them?* p. 44

43. When a nation is composed of millions of devoted, responsible family units, the entire society is more stable, healthy, and resilient. —*Emotions: Can You Trust Them?* p. 77

44. Children, yours and mine, are the true wealth of any nation, and in them lies the hope of the future. A society that is too busy or too preoccupied for its children is just a nation of aging, dying people who feed on their own selfish interests. —*Children at Risk*, p. 17

45. Raising kids properly is one of life's richest challenges. It is not uncommon to feel overwhelmed by the complexity of the parental assignment. —*The New Dare to Discipline*, p. 244

46. Fortunately, we are permitted to make a few mistakes with our children. No one can expect to do everything right, and it is not the few errors that destroy a child. It is the consistent influence

of conditions throughout childhood. *—The New Dare to Discipline*, pp. 75–76

47. The vast majority of America's founding fathers revered the Lord and looked to him for strength and wisdom. Today we cling to the same source of confidence and hope. *—Children at Risk*, p. 270

48. The love of money is the root of all evil. That's why Jesus issued more warnings about materialism and the lust for wealth than any other sin. *—Values in the Home*, p. 6

49. In the matter of sex education, the best approach begins in early childhood and extends through the years, according to the policy of openness, frankness, and honesty. Only parents can provide this lifetime training. *—The New Dare to Discipline*, p. 217

50. Our sons and daughters will be grown so quickly and these days at home together will be nothing but a distant memory. Let's make the most of every moment. *—Parenting Isn't for Cowards*, p. 17

51. Where does your marriage rank on your hierarchy of values? Does it get the leftovers and scraps from your busy schedule, or is it something of great worth to be preserved and supported? It can die if left untended. *—What Wives Wish Their Husbands Knew about Women*, p. 99

52. There is a brief period during childhood when youngsters are vulnerable to religious training. Their concepts of right and wrong are formulated during this time, and their view of God begins to solidify. *—The New Dare to Discipline*, p. 232

53. The strong-willed adolescent simply must not be given large quantities of unstructured time. He or she will find destructive ways to use such opportunities. Get that youngster involved in the very best church youth program and other healthy activities you can find. *—Parenting Isn't for Cowards*, p. 150

54. Overcommitted parents must ask themselves three questions about every new activity that presents itself: (1) Is it worthy of our time? (2) What will be eliminated if it is added? (3) What will be its impact on our family life? *—What Wives Wish Their Husbands Knew about Women*, p. 54

55. Marital problems are almost inevitable when couples overcommit themselves during the early years. The bonding that should occur in the first decade requires time together—time that cannot be

given if it is absorbed elsewhere. Success will wait, but a happy family will not. —*Parenting Isn't for Cowards,* p. 189

56. Married life is a marathon. It is not enough to make a great start toward long-term marriage. You will need the determination to keep plugging. Only then will you make it to the end. —*Love for a Lifetime,* p. 120

57. A child's will is a powerful force in the human personality. It is one of the few intellectual components which arrives full strength at the moment of birth. Whereas the self concept is delicate and wobbly, the will is made of steel. —*The Strong-Willed Child,* p. 76

58. A family is literally a "museum of memories" to those who have been blessed with children. —*Straight Talk to Men,* p. 33

59. Laughter is the key to survival during the special stresses of the child rearing years. —*Parenting Isn't for Cowards,* p. 101

60. Minor irritants, when accumulated over time, may even be more threatening to a marriage than the catastrophic events that crash into our lives. —*The Strong-Willed Child,* p. 61

61. Nothing could be more dangerous than to permit our emotions to rule our destinies. They can't be trusted! —*Straight Talk to Men,* p. 187

62. Children naturally look to their fathers for authority. —*Straight Talk to Men,* p. 65

63. A personal relationship with Jesus Christ is the cornerstone of marriage, giving meaning and purpose to every dimension of living. —*Love for a Lifetime,* p. 52

64. Children should grow up seeing their parents on their knees before God, talking to Him. —*Parenting Isn't for Cowards,* p. 104

65. The parent who is willing to bail his child out of every difficulty may be doing him or her a devastating disservice. —*Dare to Discipline,* p. 103

66. We can make no greater mistake as a nation than to continue this pervasive disrespect shown to full-time homemakers who have devoted their lives to the welfare of their families. —*Dr. Dobson Answers Your Questions about Marriage and Sexuality,* p. 41

67. Committed love is expensive, but it yields the highest returns on the investment at maturity. —*What Wives Wish Their Husbands Knew about Women,* p. 176

68. This is the way to be successful in life: Treat every person as you want to be treated; look for ways to meet the physical, emotional, and spiritual needs of those around you. —*Values in the Home*, pp. 4–5

69. Love in the absence of discipline will not produce a child with self-discipline, self-control and respect for his fellow man. —*Dare to Discipline*, p. 10

70. The last prayer which I heard my father pray was: "Thank you, God, for what we have . . . which we know we cannot keep." —*Love for a Lifetime*, p. 111

71. Discipline and love are not antithetical; one is a function of the other. —*Dare to Discipline*, p. 18

72. Our only hope as a nation is to return to the scriptural underpinnings on which our laws, our understanding of morality, and the institution of the family are based. —Personal correspondence, September 1988

73. Adolescence can be a more tranquil experience for the family that has prepared properly for its arrival. —*Hide or Seek*, p. 136

74. The events of today that seem so important are not really very significant, except for those matters that will survive the end of the universe. —*Values in the Home*, p. 4

75. Every day that goes by without spiritual training for your children is a day that can never be recaptured. —*Straight Talk to Men*, p. 71

76. The parent must be convinced that loving discipline is not something he or she does *to* the child; it is something done *for* the child. —*Dare to Discipline*, p. 18

77. No job can compete with the responsibility of shaping and molding a new human being. —*What Wives Wish Their Husbands Knew about Women*, p. 165

78. Growth in the Christian life depends on obedience in times of crisis. —*Emotions: Can You Trust Them?* p. 104

79. When a parent loses the early confrontations with the child, the later conflicts become harder to win. —*Dare to Discipline*, p. 21

80. One of your most important responsibilities as parents is to establish an equitable system of justice and a balance of power between siblings. —*The Strong-Willed Child*, p. 132

81. My most important reason for living is to get the gospel of Jesus Christ safely in the hands of my children. —*Straight Talk to Men,* p. 51

82. Honesty which does not have the best interest of the hearer at heart is a cruel form of selfishness. —*What Wives Wish Their Husbands Knew about Women,* p. 41

83. It is better to be single and unhappy than unhappily married. —*Values in the Home,* p. 10

84. Men typically derive self-esteem by being respected; women feel worthy when they are loved. —*What Wives Wish Their Husbands Knew about Women,* p. 64

85. Bitterness and resentment are emotional cancers that rot us from within. —*Dr. Dobson Answers Your Questions about Confident, Healthy Families,* p. 72

86. If we only realized how brief is our time on this earth, then most of the irritants and frustrations which drive us apart would seem terribly insignificant and petty. —*Love for a Lifetime,* p. 116

87. It has been my observation that whatever a person hungers for, Satan will appear to offer it in exchange for a spiritual compromise. —*Straight Talk to Men,* p. 144

88. Christian men pass on to their children a spiritual heritage that is more valuable than any monetary estate they could have accumulated. —*Emotions: Can You Trust Them?* p. 48

89. Nothing justifies an attitude of hatred or a desire to harm another person, and we are treading on dangerous ground when our thoughts and actions begin leading us in that direction. —*Emotions: Can You Trust Them?* p. 91

90. To a power-hungry tyrant of any age, appeasement only inflames his or her lust for more power. —*Parenting Isn't for Cowards,* p. 168

91. Conceit is a weird disease—it makes everybody sick except the person who has it. —*Values in the Home,* p. 9

92. It may be surprising to learn that human conflict, if properly managed, can be the vehicle for transforming an unstable relationship into a vibrant, healthy marriage. —*Love Must Be Tough,* p. 8

93. Every husband should seek to keep the romantic fires aglow in the relationship, by the use of love notes and surprises and

candlelight dinners and unexpected weekend trips. —*Straight Talk to Men*, p. 125

94. The reason the average woman would rather have beauty than brains is because she knows that the average man can see better than he can think. —*What Wives Wish Their Husbands Knew about Women*, p. 28

95. The philosophy of "me first" has the power to blow our world to pieces, whether applied to marriage, business, or international politics. —*Hide or Seek*, p. 186

96. Love is not defined by the emotional highs and lows, but is dependent upon a steady and unchanging commitment of the will. —*What Wives Wish Their Husbands Knew about Women*, p. 91

97. We should give conscious thought to the reasonable, orderly transfer of freedom and responsibility, so that we are preparing the child each year for the moment of full independence which must come. —*Dr. Dobson Answers Your Questions about Confident, Healthy Families*, p. 55

98. There's no doubt about it, raising children as a single parent can be the loneliest job in the world! —*What Wives Wish Their Husbands Knew about Women*, p. 159

99. Prescription for a happier, healthier life: Resolve to slow your pace; learn to say no gracefully; resist the temptation to chase after more pleasures, hobbies, and social entanglements. —*What Wives Wish Their Husbands Knew about Women*, p. 54

100. If America is going to survive the incredible stresses and dangers it now faces, it will be because husbands and fathers again give their families high priority, reserving a portion of their time and energy for leadership within their homes. —*Straight Talk to Men*, p. 21

101. It is impossible to overstate the need for prayer in the fabric of family life. —*Love for a Lifetime*, p. 54

102. We quickly cease to make sense when we abandon the wisdom of the Creator and substitute our own puny ideas of the moment. —*Children at Risk*, p. 25

103. A good marriage is not one where perfection reigns; it is a relationship where a healthy perspective overlooks a multitude

of "unresolvables." —*What Wives Wish Their Husbands Knew about Women,* p. 185

104. Comparison is the root of all feelings of inferiority. —*Values in the Home,* p. 5

105. While yielding to the loving leadership of their parents, children are also learning to yield to the benevolent leadership of God himself. —*The Strong-Willed Child,* p. 171

106. Respect, the critical ingredient in human affairs, is generated by quiet dignity, self-confidence, and common courtesy. —*Love Must Be Tough,* p. 70

107. The greatest delusion is to suppose that our children will be devout Christians simply because their parents have been. —(Letter to his son by James Dobson, Sr.) *Straight Talk to Men,* p. 76

108. The overall objective during the final preadolescent period is to teach the child that actions have inevitable consequences. —*The Strong-Willed Child,* p. 61

109. If a woman is to have the contentment and self-satisfaction necessary to produce a successful family, she needs the constant support and respect of the man she loves. —*What Wives Wish Their Husbands Knew about Women,* p. 162

110. If Christian parents are perceived by a child as not being worthy of respect, then neither is their God, or their morals, or their government, or their country, or any of their values. —*Dr. Dobson Answers Your Questions,* p. 119

111. You can hardly become greedy or selfish when you are busily sharing what you have with others. —*Love for a Lifetime,* p. 82

112. Marital discord almost always emanates from the poison of disrespect somewhere in the relationship! —*Love Must Be Tough,* p. 45

113. Infidelity and marital conflict are cancers that gnaw on the soul of mankind, twisting and warping innocent family members who can only stand and watch. —*Love Must Be Tough,* p. 142

114. We should make it clear to our children that the merciful God of love whom we serve is also a God of justice. —*The New Dare to Discipline,* p. 228

115. Link a boy to the right man and he will seldom go wrong. —*Parenting Isn't for Cowards,* p. 165

116. Parents today are much too willing to blame themselves for everything their children or adolescents do. —*Parenting Isn't for Cowards,* p. 68

117. Because mothers and fathers represent "God" to their children, the fundamental element in teaching morality can be achieved through a healthy parental relationship during the early years. —*The New Dare to Discipline,* p. 228

Endnotes

1. John Locke, *An Essay Concerning Human Understanding,* 1690 and John-Jacques Rousseau, *Emile, ou de'l Education,* 1762.
2. Dr. Stella Chess and Dr. Alexander Thomas, *Know Your Child: An Authoritative Guide for Today's Parents* (New York: Basic Books, 1987).
3. Blake Morrison, "From the Chill of Cold Steel to the Iron Laws of History," *The Independent* (10 February 1991): 31.
4. APA Monitor, American Psychological Association, Washington D.C. 7:4 (1976).
5. Morton Edwards, ed., *Your Child from Two to Five* (New York: Permabooks, 1955), 95–96.
6. Ibid.
7. Willard and Marguerite Beecher, *Parents on the Run: A Commonsense Book for Today's Parents* (New York: Crown Publishers, 1955), 6–8.
8. Focus on the Family, "Helping Your Kids Say No," Josh McDowell, guest, 16 October 1987.
9. Dr. N. J. Sheers, *Infant Suffocation Project—Final Report,* U.S. Consumer Product Safety Commission, January 1995.
10. Dr. Daniel Pine, Dr. Patricia Cohen, and Dr. Judith Brook, "Emotional Problems during Youth as Predictors of Stature during Early Adulthood: Results from a Prospective Epidemiologic Study," *Pediatrics* 97; no. 6 (June 1996): 1–8.
11. Beth Ashley, "Bedwetting Often Medical, Parents Wrong to Punish," *USA Today,* 17 December 1996, 1D.
12. Ray Reed, "Abusers Often Start with Animals," *Roanoke Times and World News,* 19 January 1995, C1.
13. Harold M. Voth and Gabriel Nahas, *How to Save Your Kids from Drugs* (Middlebury, Vt.: Paul S. Ericksson, 1987).
14. Fetal Alcohol Syndrome Factsheet, Missouri Department of Mental Health, Division of Alcohol and Drug Abuse.
15. Mildred Goertzel, *Three Hundred Eminent Personalities* (San Francisco: Josey-Buss Publishers).
16. Tim Friend, "Heart Disease Awaits Today's Soft-Living Kids," *USA Today,* 15 November 1994, 1D.
17. DuPont Hospital for Children, "The Child Who St-St-Stutters," 1996, The Nemours Foundation.
18. Kim Painter, "Pre-Teens Want to Be Close to Their Parents," *USA Today,* 11 May 1995, 1D.
19. Dr. Edward M. Hallowell and Dr. John J. Ratey, *Driven to Distraction* (New York: Simon and Schuster, 1995), 73–76.
20. Hannah Bloch, "Life in Overdrive," *Time,* 18 July 1994, 46.
21. Ibid., 48.
22. Ibid., 44.

23. Ibid., 45.
24. Grant Martin, *The Hyperactive Child* (Wheaton, Ill.: Victor Books, 1992).
25. Bloch, 48.
26. Hallowell and Ratey, 238.
27. Domeena Renshaw, *The Hyperactive Child* (Chicago: Nelson-Hall Publishers, 1974), 118–120.
28. Dr. David Larson, "Is Mild Spanking Abusive or Helpful for Young Children?" Physicians Research Forum Research Summary, 1993.
29. Edwards, 182–184.
30. Christina Hoff Sommers, Professor of Philosophy, Clark University, Worchester, Mass.
31. Sigmund Freud, "Three Essays on the Theory of Sexuality," 1905.
32. Focus on the Family, "The Family from Shore to Shore," 26 March 1996.
33. *TV Guide*, 22–28 August 1992.
34. Ibid.
35. Mary Ellen McNeil, "The Jury Is Still Out But Video Games Are Sure to Be in for a Long Time," *Los Angeles Times*, 21 September 1989, 1E.
36. Ibid.
37. *Information Bank Abstracts*, 18 April 1976.
38. Kathleen Seligman, "More Children Than Cops Are Shot in the U.S.," *San Francisco Examiner*, 21 January 1994, A16.
39. K. Freund and R. J. Watson, "The Proportions of Heterosexual and Homosexual Pedophiles among Sex Offenders against Children: An Exploratory Study," *Journal of Sex and Marital Therapy* 18, no. 1 (spring 1992): 34–43.
40. Ibid.
41. "Your Baby's Language," *Psychology Today*, May 1977.
42. Focus on the Family, "Rebellious Teenagers," Rev. Raul Ries, Pastor Mike MacIntosh, Rev. Franklin Graham, guests, 19–20 October 1988.
43. National Clearinghouse on Child Abuse and Neglect, Department of Health and Human Services, Washington, D.C.
44. Beecher, 6–8.
45. Ben Sherwood, "Even Spanking Is Outlawed: Once-Stern Sweden Leads Way in Children's Rights," *Los Angeles Times*, 11 August 1985, 2A.
46. Kathleen Engman, "Corporal Punishment v. Child Abuse: Society Struggles to Define 'Reasonable' Force," *The Ottawa Citizen*, 30 December 1996, C8.
47. Dr. David W. Fleming, Dr. Stephen L. Cochi, Dr. Allen W. Hightower, and Dr. Claire V. Broome, "Childhood Upper Respiratory Tract Infections: To What Degree Is Incidence Affected by Attendance?" *Pediatrics* (January 1987): 55–60.
48. Donna Partow, *Homemade Business* (Colorado Springs, Colo.: Focus on the Family, 1991).
49. Speech given by Max Rafferty, former California state superintendent of public instruction, 1967.
50. Research performed at the University of Illinois Urbana-Champaign, reported by J. Madeline Nash, "Fertile Minds: The First Three Years Are Critical," *Time*, 3 February 1997. (Note: While this study is over twenty years old, its findings were also reported in this article.)

51. Dr. Stanley Coopersmith, former associate professor of psychology, University of California, Berkeley.

52. Amy Kaslow, "Learning at Home," *Christian Science Monitor*, 26 February 1996, 9.

53. Focus on the Family, "Preparing Children for Learning," Cheri Fuller, guest, 29–30 August 1991.

54. David Kearns, "How to Revitalize Our Schools," *The Record*, 30 April 1991, B10.

55. Dr. Raymond Moore, *School Can Wait* (Provo, Utah: Brigham Young University Press, 1980).

56. Ibid.

57. Kaslow, 9.

58. Dr. Stan Weed and Dr. Joseph Olson, "Effects of Family Planning Programs for Teenagers on Adolescent Birth and Pregnancy Rates," *Family Research Council*, 1988.

59. Dr. Stephen A. Small, University of Wisconsin-Madison, 1992.

60. Sharon D. White and Richard R. DeBlassie, "Adolescent Sexual Behavior," *Adolescence* 27 (1992): 183–191.

61. Eleanor Rudolph, "New York City's Controversial Schools Chancellor Ousted," *Washington Post*, 11 February 1993, A3.

62. Tom Hess, "They Call This Abstinence?" *Focus on the Family Citizen*, May 1992, 1–4.

63. "Condom Roulette," *Family Research Council, In Focus*, 1992, 1.

64. Gilbert L. Crouse, Office of Planning and Evaluation, U.S. Department of Health and Human Services, t.i., 12 March 1992, based on data from Planned Parenthood's Alan Guttmacher Institute.

65. *Monthly Vital Statistics Report*, National Center for Health Statistics, 41:9, supplement, 25 February 1993.

66. Source: Alan Guttmacher Institute. Reported by Kim Painter in "Few Changes in Profile of Women Getting Abortions," *USA Today*, 8 August 1996, 4A.

67. U.S. Department of Health and Human Services, Public Health Service, Centers for Disease Control, *1991 Division of STD/HIV Prevention*, Annual Report, 13.

68. Centers for Disease Control, U.S. Department of Health and Human Services, reported in "Chlamydia Infections Rising," *Reuters News Service*, 10 March 1997.

69. Kay Stone, Sexually Transmitted Diseases Division, Centers for Disease Control, U.S. Department of Health and Human Services, t.i., 20 March 1992.

70. "Condom Roulette," 1.

71. Ibid.

72. Felicity Barringer, "Viral Sexual Diseases Are Found in One in Five in the U.S.," *New York Times*, 1 April 1993, A1.

73. Dr. Richard Glascow, "The Most Commonly Asked Questions about RU-486," *National Right to Life News*, 28 April 1993, 12–13.

74. Focus on the Family, "A Visit with the U.S. Surgeon General," Dr. C. Everett Koop, guest, 20 January 1984.

75. Focus on the Family, "A Doctor Speaks Out on Sexually Transmitted Diseases," Joe McIlhaney, M.D., guest, 26–27 March 1991.

76. Ibid.
77. Dr. Barbara Reed, "Factors Associated with Human Papillomarvirus Infection in Women Encountered in Community-Based Offices," *Archives of Family Medicine* 2 (December 1993): 1239.
78. Ibid.
79. Heidi M. Bauer, "Genital HPV Infection in Female University Students as Determined by a PCR-Based Method," *Journal of the American Medical Association* 265, no. 472 (1991).
80. Jill Brookes, "Its Empire Stretches Worldwide," *Los Angeles Times*, 22 April 1993, 21.
81. John White, *Parents in Pain* (Downers Grove, Ill.: InterVarsity Press, 1979), 44.
82. John Walvoord and Roy Zuck, eds., *Bible Knowledge Commentary: Old Testament* (Wheaton, Ill.: Victor Books, 1985), 953.
83. White, 47.
84. Address at Harrow School, 29 October 1941.
85. Dr. James Dobson, *When God Doesn't Make Sense* (Wheaton, Ill.: Tyndale House Publishers, 1993), 127.
86. Albert Goodman, *The Lives of John Lennon* (New York: William Morrow and Co., 1988).
87. Interview in *London Evening Standard*, 4 March 1966.
88. Dobson, *Sense*, 127.
89. Beecher, 128.
90. Jean Lush and Pamela Vredevelt, *Mothers and Sons* (Pomona, Calif.: Focus on the Family, 1988).
91. Deborah M. Capaladi, Lynn Crosby, and Mike Stoolmiller, "Predicting the Timing of First Sexual Intercourse for At-Risk Adolescent Males," *Child Development* 67 (1996): 344–259.
92. Lawrence L. Wu, "Effects of Family Instability, Income, and Income Instability on the Risk of a Premarital Birth, *American Sociological Review* 61 (1996): 386–406.
93. Dr. Dorothy V. Whipple, *Dynamics of Development: Euthenic Pediatrics* (New York: McGraw-Hill, 1966), 98.
94. Margaret Rees, "Menarche When and Why?" *The Lancet* (journal of the British Medical Association) 342, no. 8884 (4 December 1993): 1375.
95. "Growing Needs, Diverse Needs: Discussion of Reproductive Health and Sexuality Needs of Today's Youth," *Population Reports*, Johns Hopkins University 23, no. 3 (October 1995): 4.
96. Rees, 1375.
97. Urie Bronfenbrenner, "The Social Ecology of Human Development" in *Brain and Intelligence: The Ecology of Child Development*, ed. Fredrick Richardson (Hyattsville, Md.: National Educational Press, 1973).
98. Focus on the Family, "Too Big to Spank," Jay Kesler, guest, 5–6 December 1984.
99. Lily Eng, "Study Measures Drug Abuse by Orange County Students," *Los Angeles Times*, 16 January 1992, A1.

100. William A. Davis, "Flesh for Fantasy: Women Are Often Depicted in Music Videos as Powerless and Decorative," *Montreal Gazette*, 25 August 1991, F2.

101. Eddie Fisher, "Oh, My Papa," copyright 1953, RCA-Victor Records, English words by John Turner and Geoffrey Parsons; music and original lyric by Paul Burkhard; copyright 1948, 1950 Musikverlag und Buhnenvertrieb Zurich A.G. Zurich, Switzerland; copyright 1953, Shapiro, Bernstein, & Co. Inc., New York. Copyrights renewed. All rights reserved. Used with permission.

102. The Doors, "The End," copyright 1968, Viva Records.

103. Twisted Sister, "We're Not Gonna Take It," copyright 1984, Atlantic Records.

104. Suicidal Tendencies, "I Saw Your Mommy," written by Michael Muir, copyright 1984, You'll Be Sorry Music (BMI)/American Lesion Music (BMI)/Administered by BUG. All rights reserved. Used by permission.

105. Ice-T and Body Count, "Momma's Gotta Die Tonight," copyright 1992, Sire Records.

106. Brookes, 2.

107. Margaret Cronin Fisk, "1990 Was a Year of Uncertainty for the Profession," *National Law Journal*, 31 December 1990, 53.

108. Ibid.

109. Dr. Charles Stanley, *How to Keep Your Kids on Your Team* (Nashville: Thomas Nelson, 1991).

110. Dan Fogelberg, "The Leader of the Band," copyright 1981, April Music, Inc. and Hickory Grove Music, Inc.

111. Lewis Yablonsky, *Fathers and Sons* (New York: Simon and Schuster, 1982), 134.

112. "'Giving In' Often Seen When Kids Hit Parents," *Omaha World-Herald*, 6 July 1979.

113. Ibid.

114. Focus on the Family, "The Family at the End of the 20th Century," 8–9 June 1995.

115. Ibid.

116. Sonia Nazari, "Wrong Turn Ends in Deadly Gang Ambush; Violence: Child, 3, Dies. Two Others Hurt As Youths Block Car's Escape from Dead End Street and Open Fire," *Los Angeles Times*, 18 September 1995, 1A.

117. Susan Kuczka and Flynn McRoberts, "5-Year-Old Was Killed Over Candy; Boy Refuses to Shoplift and Is Dropped 14 Floors to His Death, Police Say," *Chicago Tribune*, 15 October 1994, 1.

118. Jerry Adler, "Growing Up Scared," *Newsweek*, 10 January 1994, 44.

119. Bob Thomas, "Television and Movie Viewers Are Used to a Happy, Laughing, Carol Burnett on Screen. But at Home, Things Have Been a Lot Different Since She and Her Husband Revealed Their Daughter's Addiction to Drugs," *Associated Press*, 10 December 1979.

120. Sandra Boodman, "Researchers Study Obesity in Children," *Washington Post*, 13 June 1995, Z10.

121. Patricia Long, "Kids with a Lot to Lose," *Hippocrates*, November 1988.

122. Marilyn Elias, "Nest Is Emptier for Dad," *USA Today*, 23 January 1985, 1D.

123. Erma Bombeck, "Fragile Strings Join Parent, Child," *Arizona Republic*, 15 May 1977.

124. Joan Wester Anderson, "Preparing Your Child for Those College Years," *Focus on the Family*, May 1992, 8.

125. Carly Simon, "That's the Way I've Always Heard It Should Be," copyright 1971, Jacob Brackman, Warner Brothers Music, Inc.

126. U.S. Bureau of the Census, *Statistical Abstract of the United States*, 1993, 53.

127. Ibid.

128. Chess and Thomas, 33.

129. Larry L. Bumpass, James A. Sweet, and Andrew Cherlin, "The Role of Cohabitation in Declining Rates of Marriage," *Journal of Marriage and the Family* 53 (1991): 913–927.

130. Dinesh D' Souza, "The Visigoths in Tweed," *Forbes*, 1 April 1992, 82.

131. Carol Innerst, "'Sensitivity' Is the New Buzzword at Colleges," *Washington Times*, 29 August 1990, A1.

132. John Leo, "The Academy's New Ayatollahs," *U.S. News and World Report*, 10 December 1990, 22.

133. Steven Chapman, "Campus Speech Codes Are on the Way to Extinction," *Chicago Tribune*, 9 July 1992, 21.

134. Dennis Kelly, "A Call for a Return to Liberal Arts Education," *USA Today*, 4 March 1991, 4D.

135. William Celis, "College Curriculums Shaken to the Core," *New York Times*, 10 January 1993, 4A.

136. Ibid.

137. Hilary Appleman, "Cornell University President Considering Gay Living Unit Proposal," *Associated Press*, 24 March 1993.

138. Ibid.

139. Scott W. Wright, "One in 100 Tested at UT Has AIDS Virus," *Austin American-Statesman*, 14 July 1991, A14.

140. Robin Wilson, "Sexually Active Students Playing Russian Roulette," *Seattle Times*, 6 February 1992, A9.

141. Abraham Lincoln, "Government Cannot Endure Half-Slave and Half-Free," Republican State Convention, Springfield, Illinois, 16 June 1858. See also Matthew 12:25 and Luke 11:17.

142. *The Alan Guttmacher Institute 1994 Report:* "Sex and America's Teenagers," 28.

143. Adelle Banks, "Some Kids Agree in Survey: Rape OK If Date Costs Money," *Los Angeles Herald Examiner*, 8 May 1988, A14.

144. Tom T. Hall, "I Left Some Kisses on the Door," copyright 1979, Hallnote Music.

145. Jim Talley and Bobbie Reed, *Too Close, Too Soon* (Nashville: Thomas Nelson, 1982), 129–134.

146. George Orwell, *Animal Farm* (London: Longman, 1945), chapter 10.

147. "Attractive Women Less Happy, Study Says," *Psychology Today*, September 1971.

148. Focus on the Family, "Preparing Children for Learning," Cheri Fuller, guest, 29–30 August 1991.

149. George Gilder, *Men and Marriage* (New York: Bantam Books, 1986).

150. Charles Murray, "Bad News about Illegitimacy," *The Weekly Standard*, 5 August 1996, 24.

151. Gilder, op. cit.

152. *Statistical Abstract*, 53.

153. "Families First," *Report of the National Commission on America's Urban Families*, John Ashcroft, chairman, Washington, D.C., 1993, 19.

154. Paul C. Glick, "Remarried Families, Stepfamilies, and Stepchildren: A Brief Demographic Profile," *Journal of Marriage and the Family* 53 (1989): 261–270.

155. Doug Fields, *Creative Romance* (Eugene, Oreg.: Harvest House Publishers, 1991), 15.

156. Gary Smalley and John Trent, *The Language of Love* (Pomona, Calf.: Focus on the Family, 1988), 81–82.

157. Abraham Maslow, *Toward a Psychology of Being* (London: Regency Gateway, 1970).

158. Dr. Richard Restak, *The Brain: The Last Frontier* (Garden City, N.Y.: Doubleday and Company, 1979), 197.

159. Whipple, 19.

160. Ibid.

161. Dr. Paul Popenoe, "Are Women Really Different?" *Family Life* 31, no. 2 (February 1971).

162. Ibid.

163. Ibid.

164. Ibid.

165. Ibid.

166. Ibid.

167. Ibid.

168. Ibid.

169. Ibid.

170. Ibid.

171. *Family Circle*, 26 February 1985.

172. John Sedgwick, *Rich Kids: America's Young Heirs and Heiresses, How They Love and Hate Their Money* (New York: William Morrow and Company, 1985).

173. Ron and Judy Blue, *Money Matters for Parents and Their Kids* (Nashville: Thomas Nelson, 1986), 46.

174. Hillary Rodham Clinton, commencement address at George Washington University, 8 May 1994.

175. John Kronenberger, "Is the Family Obsolete?" *Look* (26 January 1971): 35.

176. Ibid.

177. James Q. Wilson, "The Family Values Debate," *Commentary* (April 1993): 24.

178. *Statistical Abstract*

179. U.S. Commission on Child and Family Welfare Final Report, Department of Health and Human Services, Washington, D.C., 1995.

180. "Me and Bobby McGee," performed by Janis Joplin, Columbia Records, 1971.

181. David Larson, "Divorce: A Hazard to Your Health?" *Focus on the Family Physician*, May/June 1990, 13–17.

182. Pat Conroy, "Death of a Marriage," *Atlanta Magazine*, November 1978. Excerpted by permission.

183. Judith S. Wallerstein and Joan B. Kelly, *Surviving the Breakup* (New York: Basic Books, 1980), 33.

184. Ibid., 48.

185. Ibid., 236.

186. Ibid., 46.

187. Ibid., 211.

188. Ibid.

189. Presentation given by Dr. Armand Nicholi, psychiatrist at Harvard Medical School and Massachusetts General Hospital, at White House Conference on the State of the American Family, May 3, 1983. Copies of the presentation are available in the *Congressional Record*, Extension of Remarks, 3 May 1983.

190. Ron Fimrite, "A Team for All Time," *Sports Illustrated*, 27 January 1986, 56.

191. Focus on the Family, "Resentment: Cancer of the Emotions," Dr. Archibald Hart, guest, 20 December 1982.

192. Maxwell Maltz, *Psychocybernetics* (North Hollywood, Calf.: Wilshire Books, 1973).

193. Edward Fitzgerald, *The Letters of Edward Fitzgerald* (Princeton, N.J.: Princeton University Press, 1980).

194. Mike McManus, *Marriage Savers* (Grand Rapids: Zondervan, 1993).

195. "40 Percent Have Alcoholic Relative," *Copley News Service*, 13 October 1991.

196. Ibid.

197. Focus on the Family, "Help for the Alcoholic," Jerry Butler, Dr. Keith Simpson, and guests, Bob and Pauline, 23–24 June 1983.

198. Ibid.

199. Ibid.

200. Ibid.

201. Ibid.

202. Ibid.

203. Terence Mahoney, "By Law, Britain to Destroy 3,000 Embryos," *Los Angeles Times*, 27 July 1996, 1A.

204. National Prayer Breakfast, Washington, D.C., 3 February 1994.

205. Focus on the Family, "Euthanasia: The Dark Side of Compassion," Rita Marker, guest, 13–14 March 1989.

206. "Court Backs Assisted Suicide," *Reutere*, 7 March 1996.

207. P. J. van der Maas, J. J. M. van Delden, and L. Pijenbrog, *Euthanasia and Other Medical Decisions Concerning the End of Life: An Investigation Performed upon the Request of the Commission of Inquiry into the Medical Practice Concerning Euthanasia* (Amsterdam: Elsevier Science Publishers, 1992), 178.

208. Ibid., 181.

209. Ibid., 73, 75, 183.

210. "Doctor Freed in 'Justified' Mercy Killing," *Chicago Tribune*, 27 April 1995, N21.

211. "Doctor Unpunished for Dutch Suicide," *New York Times*, 22 June 1994, 10A.

212. Focus on the Family, "A Visit with the U.S. Surgeon General," Dr. C. Everett Koop, guest, 20 January 1984.

213. "Governor Swamped with Reaction to Remarks about Terminally Ill," *United Press International*, 28 March 1984.
214. Michael J. Bailey and Richard C. Pillard, "A Genetic Study of Male Sexual Orientation," *Archives of General Psychiatry* 48 (December 1991): 1089–96.
215. Joan E. Rigdon, "Overcoming a Deep-Rooted Reluctance, More Firms Advertise to Gay Community," *Wall Street Journal*, 18 July 1991, 1B.
216. Ibid.
217. "Invest in Heart and Stroke Research: Ensure the Future Health of Our Nation, Our Families, Our Children," American Heart Association Office of Public Affairs, 1996.
218. J. B. Watson, *Psychological Care of Infant and Child, Family in America Series*, 1972 (reprint of 1928 edition).
219. Ibid.
220. Abraham Lincoln, "Address at Gettysburg," 19 November 1863.
221. Focus on the Family, "Being a Responsible Citizen," Senator William Armstrong, guest, 4 November 1994.
222. Anne Marie Morgan, "Election 88: Why You Should Vote," *Focus on the Family*, September 1988, 2–3.
223. Paraphrase of Edmund Burke quote from *Thoughts on the Cause of the Present Discontents*, 23 April 1770.
224. Joseph Daniel Unwin, "Sexual Regulations and Cultural Behavior," address given on 27 March 1935, to the medical section of the British Psychological Society, printed by Oxford University Press (London, England).
225. Robert Goodman, *The Luck Business* (New York: The Free Press, a division of Simon and Schuster, 1995), 2.
226. Patricia A. McQueen, "American Gaming at a Glance," *International Gaming and Wagering Business*, September 1996, 52–53.
227. "Resist Expansion of Casino Gambling," *Northeast Mississippi Daily Journal*, 30 September 1995, 6A.
228. Robert Goodman, "Legalized Gambling as a Strategy for Economic Development," March 1994, 10.
229. *Reuter Business Report*, 11 April 1994.
230. Goodman, *The Luck Business*, 57–58.
231. John Warren Kindt, statement before a hearing of the U.S. House of Representatives Committee on Small Business, 21 September 1994.
232. Earle Eldridge, "Nation's Steamy Love Affair with Gambling Still Growing," *Gannett News Service*, 19 May 1994.
233. Arnold Wexler, "Statistical Information on Compulsive Gamblers," Council on Compulsive Gambling of New Jersey, Inc.
234. Michael deCourcy Hinds, "Riverboat Casinos Seek a Home in Pennsylvania," *New York Times*, 7 April 1994, 18A.
235. Joseph A. Dunne, "Increasing Public Awareness of Pathological Gambling Behavior: A History of the National Council on Compulsive Gambling," *Journal of Gambling Behavior* 1:1 (spring/summer 1985): 15.
236. Henry R. Lesieur, "Compulsive Gambling," *Society*, May/June 1992, 46.
237. National Council on Problem Gambling, Inc., "The Need for a National Policy on Problem and Pathological Gambling in America," 1 November 1993, 7.

238. Ibid.
239. J. Taylor Buckley, "Nation Raising 'A Generation of Gamblers,'" *USA Today*, 5 April 1995, 1D.
240. People for the American Way, "Attacks on the Freedom to Learn," 1993–94.
241. Carol Innerst, "What's Lacking in the Classroom," *Washington Times*, 11 November 1995, C1.
242. Ibid.
243. Rudolph, A3.

Index

Numbers indicate question numbers, not page numbers.

A

Aaron, Dr. Leonard D., 99
abortion, 5, 200, 212, 469, 471
   and civil disobedience, 494
   and the rescue movement, 494
   in case of incest or rape, 471
   and sex education, 211
   prevention of, 472
Abraham and Sarah, 232
absent fathers, 18, 290
abstinence, 205, 208, 210–211, 213, 216
abstinence-based educational programs, 211
academic disinterest, related to sibling
   rivalry, 247
academic freedom, 333
academic marks, 187
Action for Children's Television, Peggy
   Charren, 99
action versus anger in discipline, 116, 301
Adam and Eve, 227
ADD, 65, 67–69, 73, 75, 182, 191
   and discipline, 74
   and high-risk behavior, 70
   and prescription drugs, 73
   in adolescence, 70
   in adulthood, 70
   attention deficit disorder, 65, 68, 182,
      191
addictions, 345
   effect on marriage, 455
   and legalized gambling, 492
ADHD, 65, 71
   and self-concept, 72
   medication for, 72
   treatment of, 72
adolescence, 43, 261, 454
   and communication at home, 270
   and rebellion, 6, 140
   preparation for, 62
adolescents
   and sexual behavior, 202
   and self-esteem, 350
   and sex education, 209
   need for mothers, 306
adopted children, 87–90
   and discipline, 87
adoption by homosexuals, 481
adrenaline, related to violence, 299
adult children

and independence, 313
living at home, 310, 312, 314
adult leadership 27
adultery, *see* sexual infidelity
advice, and God's will, 240
Advice to Young Adults, chapter 18,
   ques #312–345
affirmation, 403
age as factor in school placement, 178
age and maturity in children, 177
aggressiveness, 143
   linked to violence on television, 99
AIDS, 214–216, 482
Al-Anon, 463–464
Al-Anon Family Groups, 464
alcohol consumption during pregnancy, 56
Alcoholics Anonymous, 464
alcoholism, 345, 460–464
Allens, Dr. Hugh, 60
ambition, 338
anger, 27
   inappropriate use in discipline, 116
   toward children, 403
anorexia, 57
antidepressant drugs as treatment for
   depression, 450
antifamily organizations, 487
anxiety
   in children, 46, 165
   in parents, 78, 81
apologies, parents to children, 139, 297
athletic abilities related to sibling rivalry,
   246
athletic accomplishment and peer pressure,
   264
attention deficit disorder, 65, 68, 182, 191
Attention Deficit Disorder in Children
   and Adults, chapter 5, ques #65–75
attention deficit hyperactive disorder, 65,
   191
attention getting, related to sibling rivalry,
   248
attitude chart, 123
attitudes, 123
   of children toward themselves, 176
Attorney General's Commission on
   Pornography, 345, 465
authoritarian parenting, 27
authority figures, 112

authority of parents, 109, 111
  according to Scriptures, 134
authority, 266
  challenged, 39
  in the home, 25
  tested by children, 33

B
babies
  moral state, 12
  personalities of, 5
  temperaments of, 5
baby-sitters, and children's safety, 103
balance of power in the home, 249
  related to sibling rivalry, 249
Barbie dolls, 354
Barkley, Russell, 68
beauty contests, 346
bedwetting, 48–50
Beecher, Marguerite *(Parents on the Run),* 32, 244
Beecher, Willard, *(Parents on the Run),* 32, 244
behavior, 1
  affected by consequences, 126
  indicative of ADD, 66
behavioral boundaries, 14, 104, 108, 137, 248,
Bessman, Dr. Sam, 260
Bible Knowledge Commentary: Old Testament, 227
Bible
  interpretation of, 227
  on authority of parents, 134
  on discipline misused, 134
  on discipline of children, 134
  on homosexuality, 479
  on nature of discipline, 134
biblical principles in parenting, 82
bladder control, 48
blended families, 251–252
Blue, Ron, 411
body image, 305, 454
boredom, 274
brain damage
  related to child abuse, 299
  related to violence in children, 299
Bronfenbrenner, Dr. Urie, 261
Building Self-Confidence in Children and Teens, chapter 19, ques #346–370
bulimia, 57
burnout, of mothers, 160
business success, effect on marriage, 455
business trouble, effect on marriage, 455
Butler, Jerry, 460

562

C
Cain and Abel, 244
cancer of the cervix, related to HPV, 217
car trips, 138
career, 324–326, 339–340
  and motherhood, 161
censorship, 283, 493
Charren, Peggy, 99
checkpoints used to modify behavior, 127
Cheney, Lynne, 333
Chess, Stella *(Know Your Child),* 3
child abuse, 88, 148, 254, 469
  and the law, 146
  and violence, 299
  related to spanking, 145
child care, church programs, 159
child development, 1
child neglect, related to violence, 299
child rearing, philosophy of, 141
child-care centers, 17, 158
child-care support, 159
childhood depression, 58
childhood trauma, 59
childish behavior, 39, 104
children
  and divorce, 443
  and family traditions, 86
  and information about sex, 206–207
  and responsibility, 24
  differences between, 352
  learning from mistakes, 24
  salvation of, 232
  temperaments of, 6
children's rooms, 249
Children's Health and Well-Being, chapter 4, ques #44–64
chlamydia, 215
choice of belief, in children, 226
Choose a Christian College, 335
choosing a spouse, 327
Christ-centered home, 375
Christian colleges, 332, 334
  financing, 335
Christian education, 332
Christmas, 224
church activity and adolescent sexual involvement, 202
church-run child care, 159
churches' involvement in sex education, 205
churches' responsibility to single parents, 250
citizen involvement, 489
civil disobedience
  and the rescue movement, 494
  and prevention of abortion, 472
civility, 363
class clown, 184

classroom discipline, 167, 170
classroom disorder, 188
classroom structure, 167, 170
Clinton, Hillary Rodham, 412
Coalition on Television Violence, 100
Columbia Children's Hospital (Ohio), 60
coeducational dormitories, 337
college, preparation for, 311
Columbia University College of Physicians, 46
commitment in marriage, 328, 381
communication skills, 376
   and dating, 322
   and shyness, 323
   between men and women, 398
   during adolescence, 270
   in marriage, 376–379, 398
   with children, 270
compassion, as a response to homosexuals, 480–481
competition, 348
compliant child, 3, 6, 9
condoms, 210–211, 215
   and disease prevention, 210
   distribution of, 210
confidence, 358
conflict
   between parent and child, 261
   between siblings, 246
   in marriage, 394, 397, 438
   in the family, 407
confrontation, 33, 39, 420, 427, 476
   in discipline, 104
   of an alcoholic, 464
Conroy, Pat, 443
consequences, 126
contempt of God, 238
contraceptives
   and adolscents, 63, 200
"contracts" and teen behavior, 300
Coopersmith, Dr. Stanley, 176
coping skills, 353
Cornell University, 261
corporal punishment, 30, 80, 143–144, 148–151, 153–154, 156, 171
   and age of child, 154
   and the law, 156
   in schools, 171
cortisol, related to violence, 299
counseling, marriage, 423, 441
counselors, and God's will, 240
courtship, 277
Cradles of Eminence study, 59
Creative Romance, 395
creative writing, 183
crime and legalized gambling, 492
criticism, 403

cruel behavior in children, 51
cruelty to animals, 51
crying
   after punishment, 152
   in children, 34
   in infants, 15
cultural influences, 404
culture and marriage, 374
curriculum, 174, 193
cursing, 136
custody, 254
Cylert, 72

D

Daddy's Roommate, 495
Dallas Theological Seminary, 227
Dare to Discipline, 27
date rape, 201, 336
dating, 277–278, 316, 321–322, 342, 383
Death of a Marriage, 443
DeBlassi, Richard, 202
debt, effect on marriage, 455
defiance, 25, 29, 39–40, 87, 106, 114, 118, 125, 130, 149
defined limits, 14
Delicate Art of Letting Go, The, chapter 17, ques #307–311
demanding children, 34
denial
   and alcoholism, 464
   and infidelity, 432–433
dependency, 27, 32
   created by overprotection, 126
   in marriage, 456
depression, 448, 450
   and fatigue, 451
   in children, 58
   in parents, 34
   in women, 449
   related to menopause, 450
   treatment for, 450
deprivation and its effect on intellectual development, 175
destructive behavior in marriage, 427
development in infants, 16
developmental years, 29
devotions in the family, 220
Dexedrine, 72
dieting among girls, 305
differences between children, 352
dilation and extraction, 470
dinnertime battles, 47
disabled children, and discipline, 87
discipline, 30, 39, 80, 104, 116, 176
   agreement between father and mother, 112
   and adopted children, 87

and disabled children, 87
and sick children, 87
and teenagers, 301
for children's welfare, according to
    Scripture, 134
for infants, 31
for one-year-olds, 33
for toddlers, 40
in balance, 28
in schools, 166, 169
in the classroom, 170
misused, 143
most common error in, 155
not to be harsh, according to Scripture, 134
of others' children, 23, 120
of the ADD child, 74
purpose of, 28
related to dress codes, 367
related to safety, 40
related to Scriptures, 134
related to sibling rivalry, 249
too much, 42
disciplinary techniques, 110
**Disciplining the Elementary School
    Child, chapter 7, ques #104–142**
**Disciplining the Preschool Child,
    chapter 3, ques #25–43**
disease prevention, and condoms, 210
dishonesty, 20
disobedience, 39–40, 107, 114, 144, 149
disorganization
    and school achievement, 191
    and school problems, 182
disrespect, 115, 125
distractibility, 67
divine forgiveness, 104
divine purposes, 241
divorce, 328, 375, 419, 425–426, 443, 455
    and health of children, 258
    and homosexuality, 476
    and illness, 443
    and marriage, 317
    and poverty, 435
    effect on children, 443–444
    effect on discipline, 121
    impact on teen sexual involvement, 258
domination, 27
Doors, The, 281
double standard, relating to sexual behavior,
    279
dress codes, 367
dressing, schoolchildren, 83
Driven to Distraction, 66, 72
drug abuse
    and family influence, 275
    and peer pressure, 275
    symptoms, 303

DuPont Hospital for Children, 61
Dutch Committee to Investigate the Medical
    Practie of Euthanasia, 474

E
eating disorders, 57, 260
eating habits in children, 47, 60
**Education: Public, Private, and Home
    Schooling, chapter 10,
    ques #166–198**
educational burnout in children, 190
**Effective Parenting Today, chapter 6,
    ques #76–103**
electronic media, 21
emotional needs, 380
emotions, expression of, 115
emotions, related to premenstrual tension,
    272
employment outside the home, 163
empty nest, 307, 309
engagement, 375, 383
entertainment, 21
enuresis, 48–50
environment, and human behavior, 4
ethnic groups, 195
euthanasia, 473, 475
    legalization of, 474
evil, 10, 218
exercise in children, 60
exhaustion, effect on marriage, 458
expectations, related to marriage, 455
expression of emotions, 115
extinction, in behavior modification, 132, 165

F
failures, in parenting, 233
faith, 236, 351
family, definition of, 485
    conflict, 407
    devotions, 220
    disruption, and health of children, 258
    dynamics, and power, 266
    dysfunction, related to homosexuality, 478
    heritage, 234
    traditions, 86, 402, 412
    unit, related to national stability, 491
fantasy, 225
    in children, 20
**Families under Fire, chapter 22,
    ques #412–454**
Father of the Bride, 307
father, child's need for, 254
father-daughter relationship, 93, 293
father-son relationship, 291–292
fatherhood, 76
fatherless sons, and mentors, 255

Index

Fathers and Sons, 292
fathers
  absent, 18, 290
  as peacemakers, 296
  dates with their children, 357
fatigue
  and depression, 451
  during puberty, 268
  in parents, 34
fear, 27, 118
  of failure, 247
  of the dark, 165
feelings, and God's will, 240
female companionship, important for
  married women, 380
female sexuality, 393
fetal alcohol syndrome, 56
fetal experimentation, 470
fetal tissue harvesting, 470
Fields, Doug, 395
fighting fair, 394
fighting
  with parents, 14
  in marriage, 394, 397
financial principles, 411
forgiveness, 452
  taught in the home, 139
free choice, 1
free will, 229–230
freedom, preparing children for, 284
frustrations of parenting, 77
Fuller, Cheri, 182, 369
fun, as a family, 86
Future Shock, 412
future, 330, 339–340

G

gambling, 345, 492
gay-rights movement, 481
  influence on public schools, 481
genetic factors, 404
genetic heritage, 4
genetics and homosexuality, 477
genetics and immorality, 477
Gilder, George, 371
girls and dieting, 305
Glick, Dr. Paul, 384
goals in life, 339–340
God's presence, 242–243
God's sovereignty, 241
God's will, 231, 239, 241, 329–330
  and advice, 24
  and counselors, 240
  and personal impressions, 240
  and providential circumstances, 240
  and Scriptures, 240

God
  as moral authority, 238
  concept of, 221
  concept of, taught to children, 226
  guidance from, 237
  love and justice, 222
  parents represent to children, 221
  promises of, 236
  represented by earthly fathers, 222
  sovereignty of, 235
Goertzel, Victor and Mildred (Cradles of
  Eminence study), 59
gonorrhea, 215
Graham, Rev. Franklin, 140
grandparents, 82, 148
  and spanking, 148
  impact on grandchildren, 234
great commission, 240
**Great Marriage Killers, The, chapter
  23, ques #455–467**
growth, 45
growth hormones, 45
guidance, from God, 237
guilt, feelings in parents, 78, 228
guilt, related to infidelity, 426

H

Halloween, 225
Hallowell, Edward, M.D., 72
Hammond, Dr. Vince, 100
Harbin, Dr. Henry, 297
harshness, 118, 147
Hart, Archibald, 452
Harvard University Preschool Project, 16
Harvard University, 445
healing, 235
health of children
  related to divorce, 258
  related to family disruption, 258
  related to single parenting, 258
  related to group-setting child care, 158
Heather Has Two Mommies, 495
height, related to anxiety, 46
height in children, 45
**Help for Single Parents and
  Stepparents, chapter 15,
  ques #250–257**
Hemlock Society, The, 473
heredity, and human behavior, 4
heritage, passed on by grandparents, 234
high-risk behavior, associated with ADD,
  70
holidays, 138
Holland, euthanasia policies, 474
home schooling, 177, 188, 196–197
  and socialization, 197

for immature children, 177
  support groups, 197
home-based business, 163
Homemade Business, 163
homemakers, and legislation, 488
homemaking, 164, 325–326
homework, 190
  in elementary schools, 190
homosexual activism, 477
homosexual adoption, 481
homosexual experience during adolescence,
  478
homosexual experimentation, 478
homosexuality, 476
  and biochemical factors, 477
  and Christian attitudes, 480
  and Christian lifestyle, 483
  and divorce, 476
  and genetics, 477
  and sexual infidelity, 476
  causes of, 478
  Focus on the Family position, 484
  Scriptures related to, 479
honesty, 195
HPV (human papilloma virus), 215–217
  related to cancer of the cervix, 217
human papilloma virus (HPV), 215–217
human suffering, 101
human will, 105
humanism, effect on discipline, 105
humiliation, 27
humor in the home, 37, 370
husband, support of mother at home, 161
Hyperactive Child, The, 72, 75
hyperactivity, 67, 177
hysterectomies, related to sexually
  transmitted diseases, 215

I

idealism in parenting, 286
idols of the young, 215
idols, and teenagers, 218
illiteracy, 168, 174, 185, 179
illness, related to divorce, 443
immaturity, in relation to age, 177
immorality
  and genetics, 477
  and homosexuality, 477
impulse control, 143
in-laws, 82
  impact on marriage, 455
in-vitro fertilization, 468
incentive-and-disincentive program, 300
independence, 32
  preparing children for, 284
infants

crying, 15
  early development, 16
  fussiness, 15
infatuation, 319
infertility, 468
  related to sexually transmitted diseases,
    212, 215
inheritance, 407–409
innocence
  in children, 26
  of babies, 10
insecurity, in children, 46
Institute for Research and Evaluation, 199
instruction, in early years, 26
intellectual capabilities in children, 16
intellectual skills, development during
  infancy, 16
intellectual stimulation, during child's early
  years, 175
intelligence, related to sibling rivalry, 246
intercessory prayer, 229–230
Internet, and pornography, 465
intimacy in marriage, 400, 416
irresponsibility, 133
isolation, of mothers of small children,
  160

J

JCD's Principles and Concepts,
  chapter 26
jealousy
  between children, 245
  over new baby, 364
Jesus Christ
  attitude toward sinners, 480
  faith in, 351
  ministry of, 243
  teaching children about, 219
Josh McDowell, 43
Journal of Marriage and Family, 202
Judeo-Christian heritage, and college
  education, 333
junior high, problems, 263
justice, 363
  in the home, 249
  related to sibling rivalry, 249

K

Kagan, Donald, 333
kidnapping, 103
Kindt, John, Ph.D., 492
Know Your Child, 3
Koop, Dr. C. Everett, 475
  comments on AIDS, 214

L

Lamm, Richard D., 475
language learning, in children, 64
language development in infants, 16
Language of Love, The, 398
Larson, Dr. David, 80
late bloomers, 179–180
  and retention, 180
law of disintegration, and marriage, 400
laziness, 268
leadership, in the home, 25
learning environment in schools, 169
learning, related to self-discipline and
  self-control, 181
legalized gambling, 492
  and addictions, 492
  and crime, 492
Lennon, John, 238
letting go of our children, 308–309
Levine, Dr. Milton, 90
Life on the Edge, 329, 331
limits, used in training children, 8, 108,
  127, 248
"line of respect" in marriage, 331, 428
Living with a Teenager, chapter 16,
  ques #258–306
loneliness, and motherhood, 157
love at first sight, 319
Love Must Be Tough, 342, 441
love versus emotion, 320
low self-esteem, in ADD or ADHD children,
  65
Lush, Jean *(Mothers and Sons),* 255
Luster, Tom, 202
lying, in children, 20
lyrics, profanity in, 283

M

MacIntosh, Mike, 140
Madden, Dr. Denis, 297
magic, 21
Making Marriage Work, chapter 20,
  ques #371–405
male sexuality, 393
male-female differences, 372–373, 398
  emotional, 404
  physical, 405
  sexual, 386, 393
Maltz, Dr. Maxwell, 454
manipulation, 129
  of parents, related to sibling rivalry, 248
manners, 22, 85
marijuana, 55
marital problems, 388, 413–419, 422–425,
  428
marital separation, 436

marriage, 327–328
  accountability, 427
  and commitment, 381
  and communication, 376–379, 398
  and culture, 374
  and divorce, 317
  and fighting, 394, 397
  and intimacy, 400
  and law of disintegration, 400
  and romance, 379, 395–396
  and trials, 381
  conflict resolution, 394, 397, 438
  counseling, 423, 441
  feeling trapped, 413–418, 420
  intimacy, 416
  need for good foundation, 382
  of homosexuals, 481
  sexual problems, 388
"marriage killers," 455
Martin, Grant, Ph.D., 72
masturbation, 276
  and guilt, 276
  and pornography, 276
materialism, and rewards, 131
maturity, 32
  in relation to age, 177
McIlhaney, Dr. Joe, 215, 468
media, influence of, 282
medical exams, for adolescents, 63
Medical Institute for Sexual Health (MISH),
  215
medical suppliers, in relation to sex
  education, 211
medication
  and night terrors, 53
  and ADD, 72
memories, related to romance, 395
memorization, in learning process, 194
Men and Marriage, 371
men, and marriage, 371
men's needs, 373, 378
  in marriage, 372
Menninger Foundation (Topeka, KS), 55
menopause, 446–447
  related to depression, 450
mental abilities, 16
  in later years, 406
mental block, 359–360
mental retardation, related to alcohol use
  during pregnancy, 56
mentors, for boys without fathers, 255
Michigan State, 202
middle child, 355–356
miracles, 236–237
mistakes in parenting, 81, 104, 116–117,
  228, 233
mistakes, role in teaching children, 24

modesty, 366
Mom's Day Out, 157
Moms in Touch, 157, 160
money, 407–409
    impact on marriage, 455
Money Matters, chapter 21,
    ques #407–411
moodiness, 122
Moore, Dr. Raymond *(School Can Wait)*, 196
MOPS (Mothers of Preschoolers), 157, 160
moral authority, of God, 238
moral failure, 341
moral integrity, 341
moral laws, related to AIDS, 482
moral purity, 208
moral relativism, 495
    in secular universities, 333
morality, defined by postmodernism, 238
mother's impact on infant development, 16
mother-daughter conflict, 294
mother-daughter relationship, 294
motherhood and career, 161
Mothers and Sons, 255
mothers
    and child rearing, 158
    at home, 162
    feelings of isolation, 160
    of adolescents, 306
    of preschoolers, 306
    of small children, 164
Mothers of Preschoolers (MOPS), 157, 160
Mothers on the Move, 157
movies, 305
    and teenagers, 218
    and violence, 101, 299
    youth idols, 215
moving, effect on children, 369
MTV, 281
    and teenagers, 218
    and violence, 280
multiculturalism, 495
music, 283
    and teenagers, 218
    lyrics, 281
    related to rebellion, 280–281
    rock, 84
mutual accountability in marriage, 331
myelinization, stage of neurological
    development, 179

N

name-calling, 125
National Advisory Commission to the Office
    of Juvenile Justice and Delinquency
    Prevention, 297

National Endowment for the Humanities,
    333
National Institutes of Health, 80
needs, in men, 372–373, 378
needs, in women, 372–373, 378
    later years, 392
negativism, 41
negativity, 123
neighbors, 120
neurological damage, caused by shaking
    infants, 30
New Age, 21, 238
New York Longitudinal Study, 3
newborns, personality of, 3
Nicholi, Armand, 445
night terrors, 52–53
    medication for, 53
nightmares, 52
no-fault divorce, 384
nonessentials in parent-child conflicts, 286
nonissues in parent-child conflicts, 286
nonnegotiables in parent-child conflicts, 287
nuclear family, 16

O

obedience, 13
occult, 21, 225
occupation, 339–340
Olson, Joseph, 199
Oregon Social Learning Center, 258
Other Issues Facing the Family,
    chapter 25, ques #476–495
overcommitment
    effect on family, 467
    effect on marriage, 455
overprotection, 126
overweight, 305
    in children, 60
overwork, effect on marriage, 458

P

pain, 241
parent battering, 297
parent-child conflicts
    choosing the right battles, 286–288
    nonessentials, 286
    nonissues, 286
    nonnegotiables, 287
parent-child separation, 445
parental authority, 25
parental guidance, 12
parental guilt, 228
parental involvement in public schools, 170
parental involvement in sex education, 202
parental leadership, 25, 31–32, 39, 266

parental mediation, related to sibling rivalry, 249
parental mistakes, 104, 116–117, 228, 233
parental pressure, 348
parental values, 7
parenting, 76
 biblical principles of, 82
 frustrations of, 77
 inadequacies, 77, 81
Parenting Isn't for Cowards, 6
parents, identified with God, 29
Parents in Pain, 227, 229
Parents on the Run, 244
parents' role, in children's behavior, 4
partial-birth abortion, 470
Partow, Donna *(Homemade Business),* 163
pedophiles, 103
peer groups
 and power games, 264
 during adolescence, 262
peer-group acceptance, 261
peer pressure, 210, 264
 and athletic accomplishment, 264
 and physical attractiveness, 264
 and substance abuse, 275

peers, and preschoolers, 197
People for the American Way, 493
perfectionism in parenting, 286
permissive parenting, 27
permissiveness, 25, 147
 related to violence in youths, 297
personal responsibility, 59, 128, 228
personal worth, 348
personality, 1–2, 368
 effect on marriage, 383
 in babies, 5
 in newborns, 3
physical abuse, in marriage, 439–442
physical attractiveness, 305, 346–347, 354
 and peer pressure, 264
 related to sibling rivalry, 246
physical development in children, 259
physical exhaustion, effect on marriage, 455
physical punishment, 30, 60, 143–144,
 148–151, 153–154, 156
 and age of child, 154
 and the law, 156
physician-assisted suicide, 473, 475
Pine, Dr. Daniel, 46
Planned Parenthood, 199–200, 210
 and sex education, 211
pluralism, in schools, 198
political correctness, in secular universities, 333
pornography, 345
 and masturbation, 276
 impact on the family, 466
 on the Internet, 465
pornography industry, 465
possessions, 410–411
postmodernism, 238
Poussaint, Dr. Alvin, 62
poverty, related to divorce, 435
power
 given to children, 267
 importance to teenagers, 266
 lust for, 338
 meaning for teenagers, 265
 need for, 265
 role in family dynamics, 266
power games, 125
 and peer groups, 264
 in marriage, 401
power plays, 13
power struggles in marriage, 382
prayer, 231, 235, 237
 for children, 8, 229
 intercessory, 229–230
 persistence in, 231–232
prayer in schools, 198
prayer partners, and single parents, 250
pregnancy, 18
 and alcohol consumption, 56
premarital adolescent sexual activity, 202
premarital counseling, 383
premarital sex, 63, 200
 and sexually transmitted diseases, 212
premature marriage, 455
premenstrual tension, effects on adolescent emotions, 272
"Preparing for Adolescence" weekend, conversation, 62, 276
prescription drugs, and ADD, 73
presence of God, 242–243
pride, 238
privacy, 366
 and teenagers, 304
private education, 188
profanity, 136
 in lyrics, 283
professors, influence on students, 334
promiscuity, 347, 477
 among teens, 211
promises, of God, 227, 236
proverbs in the Bible, nature of, 227
providential circumstances, and God's will, 240
puberty, 209, 285
 and fatigue, 268
public behavior, 38
public schools, 168
 and gay-rights movement, 481
 and parental involvement, 170

public universities, 333
punishment, 31, 37, 111, 118, 152
  and crying, 152
  appropriate, 40
  corporal, 30
  physical, 30
  related to bed-wetting, 49
punishment and reward, 123–124, 129

R

racial groups, 195
**Raising the Preschool Child, chapter
  2, ques #15–24**
rape, related to rock music, 280
Ratey, John, M.D., 72
rationalization, related to infidelity, 426
reading
  and preschoolers, 186
  as a family activity, 86
reading difficulty, 179
reassurance with discipline, 104
Rebel without a Cause, 281
rebellion, 12, 25, 27, 88, 114, 140,
  227–229, 286, 297
  during adolescence, 6, 43, 140, 271–272
  related to culture, 280
  related to music, 280
rebellious nature, 107
reconciliation, 413, 423
regressive behavior in children, 364
Reid, Dr. Robert, 72
reinforcement, 132,
  and report cards, 187
  in behavior modification, 165
rejection 403, 413, 454
  by peers, 353
  by opposite sex, 361
relationships, 342
  mothers' need for, 157
religious liberty, 198
religious training, 226
remarriage, 251
Renshaw, Dr. Domeena, 75
report cards, 187
rescue movement, 494
  as civil disobedience, 494
respect, 29, 115, 266, 363
  in the classroom, 170
  of parents toward children, 349
  for children, 111
  for parents, 110–111, 280, 344
  related to racial and ethnic groups, 195
responsibility, 32, 126–127
  in children, 24
  of church to single parents, 250
retention, when appropriate, 180

reward and punishment, 123–124, 129
rewards, 128, 132
  and materialism, 131
  and report cards, 187
  and teen behavior, 300
  misuse of, 130
Rhode Island Rape Crisis Center, 336
ridicule, 105, 111, 361–362, 370, 454
Ries, Rev. Raul, 140
risky behavior in young people, 215
Ritalin, 72–73
rock music, 84, 305
  related to rape, 280
  related to suicide, 280
  youth idols, 215
role models, 21
  masculine, 255
  related to homosexuality, 478
romance, in marriage, 379, 395–396
routine, change of, 137

S

safe sex, 210, 213, 215–216
safety
  for children, 103
  related to order, 172
salvation, 227
  of children, 229, 232
same-sex marriage, 481
**Sanctity of Life, The, chapter 24,
  ques #468–475**
Santa Claus, 224
sassiness, 40, 285
Schaeffer, Dr. Francis, 381
scholastic aptitude, 348
School Can Wait, 196
school choice, 185
school uniforms, 367
schoolchildren, clothing, 83
schools, 166, 169
  and corporal punishment, 171
scientific inquiry, 238
Scripture
  and God's will, 240
  and homosexuality, 479
  misinterpretation of, 228
searching of teen's room, 304
secular universities, 333
segregation, of boys and girls for sex
  education, 201
self-arousal in children, 95–96
self-concept, 111, 315, 349, 358
  in children, 105
self-confidence, 359
self-control, 113, 176
  related to dress codes, 367

Index

related to learning, 181
self-discipline, 32, 113, 128
  and school achievement, 191
  as goal of structure in the classroom, 167
  related to learning, 181
self-doubt, 346
  during adolescence, 261
  in parents, 78
self-esteem, 176, 184, 346
  during adolescence, 350
  related to depression, 449
  related to sibling rivalry, 246
self-image, 358, 454
self-loathing, 454
self-reliance, 113
self-respect, 424
  in marriage, 420
selfishness, related to marriage, 455
separation between parent and child, 445
separation in marriage, 436
separation related to abuse in marriage, 440
sex
  on television, 99
  and communication, 389
  and fatigue, 390
  as priority in marriage relationship, 390
  designed for marriage, 215
sex education 199–201, 203, 205, 209,
    211–212
  in public schools, 204
sex-education counselors, 211
sex-education programs, 202
**Sex Education: Where, When, and
  How, chapter 11, ques #199–217**
sexes, differences between, 92
sexual abuse, 51, 103, 452
  and homosexuality, 478
sexual activity among teens, 213
sexual attitudes of children, 94
sexual desire
  causes of variability, 389
  in later years, 391
sexual development, 260
sexual differences between men and women,
    279, 393
sexual difficulties, 388–389
sexual experimentation, 201
  related to dating, 277
sexual frustration, related to marriage, 455
sexual infidelity, 318, 419, 423, 425–426,
    429, 431–432, 434–435, 437, 455
  and homosexuality, 476
sexual intercourse, 210
sexual involvement among teens, related to
    divorce, 258
sexual molestation, 103
sexual nature of children, 94

sexual promiscuity, 279
sexual revolution, 279
sexual temptation, 401
sexuality, 62
  and cultural conditioning, 92
  in women, 385
  information to children, 206–207
  progressive nature of, 343
  variations in, 387
sexually transmitted diseases, 202,
    211–212, 214–215
  in public universities, 333
shaking, dangers of with infants, 30
shyness, 323, 368
**Sibling Rivalry, chapter 14,
    ques #244–249**
sibling rivalrly, 245–249
  and parental mediation, 249
sick children, and discipline, 87
SIECUS, in relation to sex education, 211
Simpson, Keith, 460
sin, 228
sin nature in children, 11, 26
single-parent families and adolescent sexual
    involvement, 202
single parenting and health of children, 258
single parents, 158, 250
  and prayer partners, 250
  support for, 257
singleness, 342
sleep, in infants, 34
Slonecker, Dr. Bill, 31
slow learners, 175
  and retention, 180
Small, Stephen, 202
Smalley, Gary, 398
smoking
  and family influence, 275
  and peer pressure, 275
  dangers of, 275
social pressure, 359
  during adolescence, 262
social skills, development during infancy, 16
Society for Pediatric Research, 44
Sommers, Christina Hoff, 92
sovereignty of God, 235, 241
**Spank or Not to Spank, To, chapter 8,
    ques #143–156**
spanking, 37, 80, 143, 145, 149, 150, 153,
    155
  and age of child, 154
  and teenagers, 300
  and the ADHD child, 155
  and the law, 156
  follow-up, 151
spirit, versus will, 134

Spiritual Life of the Family, chapter 12, ques #218–234
spiritual training, 219, 223, 226
spouse selection 327
stammering, 61
standards, inappropriate, 286
Stanley, Andy, 286
Stanley, Charles, 286
STDs, 202, 211–212, 214–215
stimulation
    effect on intellectual development, 175
    in formative years, 16
stress, 453
    in girls, 46
stress hormone cortisol, 46
stress hormones, 299
strong-willed child, 3, 6–8, 14, 25, 34, 38, 47, 105, 108–109, 125, 142
structure
    in schools, 166
    in the classroom, 170
structured time, 274
stuttering, 61
substance abuse
    and family influence, 275
    and peer pressure, 275
    effect on marriage, 455
sudden infant death syndrome (SIDS), 44
suffering, 241
Suicidal Tendencies, 281
suicide, 473
    among teens, 262, 280
    related to rock music, 280
summer school, 180
supernatural intervention, 237, 243
supervision, 274
support, for child care, 159
surrogate spouse, children of single parents, 252
swear words, 136
syphilis, 215

T

targets, in behavior, 127
teachers, 168, 172
teaching through discipline, 104
teen pregnancy, 199, 202, 211, 302
teen sexual involvement, related to divorce, 258
teen suicide, 262, 280
teen years, 29
teenage behavior, across cultures, 218
teenage rebellion, 25
teenagers, 43
    and marijuana use, 55
    and need for power, 265–66

and rebellion, 271–272
and sexual activity, 211, 213, 258
and television, 218
television, 97–99, 305
    advertisers, 98
    and teenagers, 218
    and violence 101–102
    and youth idols, 215
temper tantrums, 25, 35, 37
temperament, 368
    categories of, 3
    effect on marriage, 383
    in babies, 2, 5
terrible twos, 41
test scores, 168
testing authority, 33
Thomas, Alexander (Know Your Child), 3
time away from children, for single parents, 253
time with children, 459
toddlerhood, 41
toddlers, 105, 132
    and discipline, 37, 40
    and temper tantrums, 35
    eating habits, 47
    nature of, 19
    stage of development, 19
Toffler, Alvin, 412
toilet training, 36
Topeka Veterans Administration Medical Center, 55
Tough Love, 297
tough love, 420, 424, 428–430
Tougher Spiritual Questions, The, chapter 13, ques #235–243
traditional values, 487
traditions in the family, 86, 402, 412
transition from home to college, 311
trapped feelings, 413–418, 420
traumas during childhood, 59
Trent, Dr. John, 398
trials, 242
    in marriage, 381
trust, of parents toward children, 349
Twisted Sister, 281
2 Live Crew, 283
Type I children, 191–192
Type II children, 191–192

U

unconditional love in marriage, 427
Understanding the Nature of Children, chapter 1, ques #1–14
uniqueness of babies, 2
University of California, 176, 305
University of Illinois, 492

Index

University of Maryland Medical School, 297
University of Massachusetts Medical Center, 68
University of Nebraska, 72
University of Southern California, 260
University of Wisconsin, 258
University of Wisconsin-Madison, 202
unplanned pregnancies, 469
Unwin, J. D., 491
use of time, 467

V

vacations, 137–138
values, 29
   taught to children, 351
verbal rejection, 105
video games, 100, 218
violence, 101, 143
   among the young, 297–299
   in cartoons, 21
   in schools, 168
   on television, 99, 102
   related to MTV, 280
   related to toys, 21
virginity, 201, 343
   among teens, 210
virtues, 20
visitation rights, 256
Voth, Harold, M.D., 55
voting, as citizen involvement, 490
voucher system, 185

W

wealth, 407–411
Weed, Stan, 199

What's a Mother to Do? chapter 9, ques #157–165
whining, 132
White, Dr. Burton, 16
White, Dr. Sharon, 202
White, John *(Parents in Pain)*, 227, 229
Who Stole Feminism? 92
Wild One, The, 281
will of God, 231, 239, 241, 329–330
will, as differentiated from spirit, 105, 134
willful defiance, in toddlers, 105
willful disobedience, 144
women and sexuality, 385
women's needs, 373, 378–379
   in later years, 392
   in marriage, 372
Woodward, Dr. Luther, 25–26
work, appropriate for children, 173
work, husband and wife working together, 399
workaholism, effect on marriage, 456
writing skills, 183
Wu, Lawrence, L., 258

Y

Yablonsky, Lewis, 292
Yale University, 333
year-round schools, 189
York, David *(Tough Love)*, 297
York, Phyllis *(Tough Love)*, 297
Your Child from Two to Five, 25, 90
youth culture, 218, 354

Index of Scripture References

Numbers refer to question numbers, not page numbers.

Genesis 2:18— *marriage* . . . 373
Genesis 16:12—*sin* . . . 475
Genesis 25:22-27—*personhood in the womb* . . . 5
Genesis 38:8— *sex misused* . . . 27

Leviticus 18:22—*homosexuality* . . . 479
Leviticus 20:13—*homosexuality* . . . 479

Deuteronomy 6:7-9—*child discipline and training* . . . 219
Deuteronomy 8:18—*money/possessions* . . . 409
Deuteronomy 24:5—*marriage* . . . 377

Judges 19:22-23—*homosexuality* . . . 479

1 Samuel 2:7—*money/possessions* . . . 409
1 Samuel 2:22-36—*parental guilt* . . . 228

1 Kings 14:24—*homosexuality* . . . 479
1 Kings 15:12—*homosexuality* . . . 479
1 Kings 22:46—*homosexuality* . . . 479

2 Kings 23:7—*homosexuality* . . . 479

Job 1:21—*money/possessions* . . . 411

Psalm 37:7, 10-11—*reward and punishment* . . . 124
Psalm 51:5— *sin nature.* . . 11
Psalm 73:23-26—*God's presence* . . . 242
Psalm 103:13—*God's love* . . . 329
Psalm 103:16—*brevity of life* . . . 344
Psalm 119:105—*God's Word* . . . 330
Psalm 127:1—*God's will* . . . 340

Proverbs 5:8—*sexual temptation* . . . 343
Proverbs 6:16-19—*truthfulness* . . . 20
Proverbs 8:22-36—*moral law* . . . 482
Proverbs 10:4, 22, 27—*nature of proverbs* . . . 227
Proverbs 12:21—*nature of proverbs* . . . 227
Proverbs 15:22—*nature of proverbs* . . . 227
Proverbs 16:31, 33—*nature of proverbs* . . . 227
Proverbs 22:6— *child discipline and training.* . . 134

Proverbs 22:3-4, 6, 9, 11, 16, 19—*nature of proverbs* . . . 227
Proverbs 24:11—*civil disobedience* . . . 494
Proverbs 28:16—*nature of proverbs* . . . 227
Proverbs 29:17—*child discipline and training* . . . 134
Proverbs 30:8—*wealth* . . . 455

Ecclesiastes 8:11-12—*reward and punishment* . . . 124

Isaiah 1:17—*helping others* . . . 255
Isaiah 66:13—*God's love* . . . 329

Jeremiah 1:5—*personhood in the womb* . . . 5
Jeremiah 9:23—*ambition* . . . 338

Matthew 3:16-17—*Jesus' baptism* . . . 243
Matthew 4:1—*Jesus' temptation* . . . 243
Matthew 6:21—*money/possessions* . . . 409
Matthew 7:7—*prayer* . . . 240
Matthew 12:25—*unity/diversity* . . . 334
Matthew 14:13-14, 23—*rest* . . . 467
Matthew 18:5 *welcoming children* . . . 255
Matthew 25:40—*helping others* . . . 250

Mark 4:36—*rest* . . . 467
Mark 10:9 *marriage* . . . 328
Mark 11:25—*forgiveness* . . . 452
Mark 16:15—*the great commission* . . . 240

Luke 6:24—*money/possessions* . . . 409
Luke 12:15—*money/possessions* . . . 409
Luke 12:18-20—*arrogance* . . . 238
Luke 12:19-21—*money/possessions* . . . 409
Luke 14:12-14—*money/possessions* . . . 409
Luke 15:11-32—*money/possessions* . . . 409
Luke 16:13, 19-31—*money/possessions* . . . 409
Luke 18:1-8—*prayer* . . . 231
Luke 18:17—*faith in children* . . . 221
Luke 18:18-24—*money/possessions* . . . 409

John 12:13—*Jesus' triumphal entry* . . . 243
John 14:9—*knowing the Father* . . . 221

Romans 1:26-27—*homosexuality* . . . 478
Romans 3:23—*sin nature* . . . 11
Romans 4:19-22—*God's promises* . . . 232

Romans 6:23—*sin* . . . 345
Romans 8:28—*God's help* . . . 241
Romans 9:13—*personhood in the womb* . . . 5
Romans 12:19—*judgment/vengeance*
. . . 238, 452

1 Corinthians 6:9-10—*homosexuality* . . .
478-479
1 Corinthians 7:5—*sex in marriage* . . . 276
1 Corinthians 7:12-15—*divorce* . . . 419
1 Corinthians 10:13—*temptation* . . . 343,
483
1 Corinthians 10:31—*glorifying God* . . . 338
1 Corinthians 13:5—*nature of love* . . . 428
1 Corinthians 13:11—*childhood/maturity*
. . . 313

2 Corinthians 4:4—*spiritual blindness* . . .
229
2 Corinthians 11:14—*Satan* . . . 239

Ephesians 1:4—*personhood in the womb*
. . . 5
Ephesians 1:16-17—*spiritual wisdom*
. . . 240
Ephesians 4:26—*anger* . . . 438
Ephesians 5:33—*marriage* . . . 373
Ephesians 6:1-4—*child discipline and
training* . . . 134

Philippians 3:13-14—*dealing with failure*
. . . 233
Philippians 4:6—*faith* . . . 236

Colossians 3:20-21—*child discipline and
training* . . . 134

1 Thessalonians 5:17—*prayer* . . . 231

1 Timothy 1:9-11—*homosexuality* . . . 479
1 Timothy 3:4-5—*child discipline and
training* . . . 134
1 Timothy 5:8—*money/family* . . . 410
1 Timothy 6:9—*wealth* . . . 341
1 Timothy 6:10—*money/possessions* . . . 409

2 Timothy 4:7—*keeping the faith* . . . 341

Hebrews 12:5-11—*child discipline and
training* . . . 134

James 1:27—*helping others* . . . 250

1 Peter 5:8—*Satan* . . . 318

2 Peter 2:7—*sin and culture* . . . 283
2 Peter 3:9—*God's patience* . . . 229

Jude 1:7—*homosexuality* . . . 479